HOUSING, FAMILY, AND SOCIETY

HOUSING, FAMILY, AND SOCIETY

Earl W. Morris
Mary Winter
Department of Family Environment
Iowa State University

JOHN WILEY AND SONS
New York
Santa Barbara
Chichester
Brisbane
Toronto

Library of Congress Cataloging in Publication Data:

Morris, Earl W
  Housing, family, and society.

  Includes bibliography and indexes.
  1. Housing—United States. I. Winter, Mary,
1940– joint author. II. Title

HD7293.M657   301.5′4′0973   77-24772
ISBN 0-471-61570-6

Printed in the United States of America

10 9 8 7 6 5 4 3 2 1

To our parents,

Walter and Thelma Morris
Leigh and Ruth Winter

who taught us to set high standards,
instilled in us the desire to attain them,
and fostered confidence in our
abilities to do so.

Preface

When we began to write this book we thought that we should write a book on housing in the United States that would integrate a social-scientific framework with the more traditional approaches to the study of housing. In the earliest stages of reviewing the work in the field we reflected on the great amount of change that had occurred since Abrams' (1946) book was published, for example. But it was not necessary to go back that far. The topic of human housing in the United States has been best characterized as being in extreme flux since we first became involved in the study of housing about 15 years ago.

We finally concluded that the emphasis should be on developing a useful framework for analysis rather than on the more customary programs and policies approach. Our conclusion was based on having personally experienced a historical period filled with (1) rapid demographic change, including both the lingering effects of the baby boom and the recent steep declines in the birth rate, (2) the change in the dominant migration patterns from an east to west to a north to south pattern, (3) the changed movement from the farms and small towns to the cities into a direct reversal of movement from the cities back to the small towns, and (4) the decreasing supply of cheap fossil-fuel energy and its potential for irrevocable alterations in our housing behavior.

What was needed, we concluded, was not a book that detailed any specifics. To us, teaching housing from such a book is like teaching physics from a book with chapters on "airplanes," "boilers," and "bridges." What does one do when the need arises to change to rockets, solar heating systems, and hover craft? Physicists write about thermodynamics, aerodynamics, and the like. Therefore, we became convinced that social scientists who wanted to study housing needed to take similar approaches in order to avoid rapid obsolescence of their knowledge. What we felt was lacking in any existing housing book was a sound framework within which it would be possible to analyze the impact of *any* public or private activity on the well-being of families.

Although housing problems are multifaceted and require multidisciplinary approaches for dealing with them, it seemed to us that a reasonable point of departure was the traditional social problems approach from the field of sociology. We coupled that idea with more modern social scientific approaches to the understanding of social processes such as family decision-making theories, systems analysis, consumption economics, and demographic analysis. It is now possible for the reader to analyze housing problems and housing programs in a way that transcends temporary conditions subject to rapid change.

When faced with such convincing evidence of the need for a means of analyzing such occurrences, we shifted our emphasis to developing a problem-oriented book that would present a means for understanding problems as they arose. Such an approach, we thought, would provide a framework for analyzing and evaluating potential solutions to any housing problem, including ones of which we are not yet aware.

Our experience with students in our classes has shown the usefulness of this framework. Almost any action, controversy, or proposal can be analyzed. Changing a residential street from two-way traffic to one-way traffic, the impact of a shopping center on a neighborhood, the controversy over the location of a public housing project have all been successfully assessed by undergraduate students studying their hometowns or other situations familiar to them. Students have analyzed a classic rural-urban clash over zoning in upstate New York, and the impact of the energy crisis. The framework remains the same: the specific details change with the analysis.

This book is primarily intended for undergraduate courses. It could be of value for graduate courses, however, if supplemented with substantial readings. It could be useful as a supplementary text in urban problems courses, in social problems courses, in planning courses, and in other courses that include some attention to social aspects of housing.

While it would be helpful if the users of this book were to have a basic background in sociology, social psychology, or economics we did not make that assumption. Therefore, a considerable portion of the book deals with the concepts of sociology and the other social sciences as they apply to the study of housing.

We have taken great care to define all difficult concepts used in the book, even those that are used in conventional ways. Definitions may be found at the end of the chapter in which the concept is used extensively. All terms and concepts defined appear in the index; boldface type indicates the page where the definition can be found.

The book does not leave the integration between the social science and the subject matter entirely up to the student or the professor. We do not simply present theories and related material on housing to be "learned." Instead, we work through the logic of the analyses found in the literature. We point out strengths and weaknesses of method, gaps in knowledge, and needs for further research.

We have taken great care with our references to the literature. Consequently, our bibliography is voluminous. It includes every work to which we make any direct references, and all works that served to inspire any of our ideas of which we were consciously aware. We did this because a number of themes we have written about run counter to conventional wisdom, both lay and professional. Therefore, we felt it was necessary not only to outline our arguments but to show as clearly as possible that they are not simple speculation and did not develop in a vacuum. Instead, they have been logically developed in the process of reflection, careful review of the literature, and our own empirical analyses. Most importantly, they grew out of research findings, research conducted by ourselves, our students, and others whose names appear in our bibliography.

We acknowledge many of our students, colleagues, and friends who played so large a part in the development and testing of the model presented in the book and of the book itself. Initial stages of development occurred at Cornell University. The graduate students, now professional colleagues, who played a part in that phase were Steven E. Andrachek, Peter M. Gladhart, Sherman Hanna, Suzanne Lindamood, Linda M. Nelson, Jeffrey Seaman, K. Kay Stewart, and Joseph L. Wysocki.

We also thank graduate students at Iowa State University who were interested enough in the framework to assist in further development and empirical tests. Included in that group are Marie Anderson, Lance P. Barrs, Ann F. Bresler, Carol A. Bross, Sue R. Crull, Diane M. Fiedler, Robert A. Findlay, Christine M. Harris, Linda M. Prentice, Kathleen P. Sampson, and Kathleen M. Yockey. We are indebted to Chris Harris for drawing many of the early versions of the figures in the text.

We also thank past and present colleagues for special assistance. Maryann Griffin and Abigail K. Patrick were among the first to offer encouragement in the development of the model. We are grateful to Mary S. Pickett for assistance with the section on housing needs of disabled persons. Special thanks go to Ivan F. Beutler for his assistance with the economic materials included in the book.

Early reviews of the manuscript by Joseph L. Wysocki, Betty Jo White, and James E. Montgomery were most helpful in preparation for the final manuscript. Careful reviews of that manuscript by Gary Coates, Peter M. Gladhart, and Joseph L. Wysocki were crucial to the refinement of the final product. Special thanks go to Sue R. Crull and Joseph L. Wysocki for their careful work in preparing the Teachers Resource Book that accompanies the text.

Finally we are indebted to John A. Pease for about 200 years worth of drinking coffee and talking about sociology at Western Michigan University and to Stanford M. Lembeck and Ruth H. Smith for about 200 years worth of lunches and talking about housing at The Pennsylvania State University.

Gratitude goes to the Iowa State University Library for excellent service but especially for the faculty study room we were allotted for several quarters. The original manuscript was reproduced by a computer text processing program called THESIS 3.5, written by personnel at the Iowa State University Computation Center. We are grateful to Tony Bible of the Center for his assistance when we encountered problems with the program.

And we never would have finished without the editing of Barbara E. Warner, the keypunching of Bernice C. Huguley, and the proofreading of Ruth G. Winter. A portion of the quality of the manuscript is a result of the fact that they had the same high standards that we did. Having said all of that, we admit that the errors that remain are ours and not theirs.

EARL W. MORRIS
MARY WINTER

Boone, Iowa
June, 1977

Contents

PART 3. RESPONSES TO RESIDENTIAL DEFICITS 145

List of Illustrations

List of Tables

Part 1
The Sociological Perspective on Housing

> Economics is all about how people make choices. Sociology is all about why they don't have any choices to make. James S. Duesenberry*

Part 1 presents the conceptual framework for the analysis of housing that constitutes the remainder of the book. The framework is the basis for the study of housing in the United States, although it could be used to study housing in other countries as well.

Chapter 1 presents a general orientation to the relevance of biological, psychological, social, and economic theory to the study of housing. That general orientation is an introduction to a method of studying the determinants and consequences of housing for the society and its members. After the general outline of the basic approach to housing is presented, the analysis is more narrowly focused on the development of the necessary sociological concepts.

Chapter 2 outlines the concepts necessary for understanding housing problems in terms of cultural norms, the criteria by which the family, the community, and the society evaluate housing. Chapter 3 presents a description of the American family and its development in relation to housing. Chapter 4 presents the systemic functional model of family housing adjustment that constitutes the basic model of *Housing, Family, and Society.*

* From "Comment" by James S. Dusenberry in Universities-National Bureau Committee for Economic Research, *Demographic and Economic Changes in Developed Countries* (Princeton: Princeton University Press, 1960, p. 233.)

Chapter 1
The Study of Housing

"Home is the place where, when you have to go there,
They have to take you in." Robert Frost*

This book is about the complex processes by which American families make decisions about their housing. The dwelling and its neighborhood are studied in terms of their potential to impinge upon the physical and mental health and upon the social and economic well-being of individuals, families, and communities. The ways in which the structure of American society determines how families are housed, the consequences of housing for families, and the decisions families make are included in the theory.

American housing is studied through the development of a theoretical sociological model of housing and the family. The type of theoretical model developed is a *systemic functional model.* This chapter presents the basic elements of the model and defines the ways in which the concepts of system and function can be useful in the study of housing.

A SOCIOLOGICAL PERSPECTIVE

The study of social problems has long been a focus of attention in sociological theory and research. Housing, as a social problem, had received relatively little attention from sociologists (Merton, 1948) until rather recently. The appropriateness of studying housing problems from the sociological perspective was pointed out by Wirth (1947) in his description of the sociology of housing:

> *This discipline [sociology] is concerned with what is true of man by virtue of the fact that he leads a group life. What sociologists must discover about housing, therefore, is all those aspects which are fac-*

> *tors in and products of man's involvement in social life. At first glance, this may seem to be virtually everything, for the politics and economics of housing, as well as art, architecture and law, business, financing and administration, designing and planning, are also factors in and products of social relations (p. 137).*

In this book housing is analyzed in terms of the sociological model of humans as beings who seek respect from both self and others. Thus, housing behavior is viewed as being motivated by a potential threat to status or a loss of respect from significant others. A family perceives that its housing is or threatens to fall below the level necessary in their society. The resulting discrepancy or potential discrepancy, which may involve one or many aspects of its housing, creates dissatisfaction that culminates in the motivation to change housing conditions.

Green (1953a) has shown the relevance of the Parsonian social systems point of view for housing. The main concern, according to Parsons (1951), is the analysis of the orientations of actors who are members of social organizations and are engaged in social interaction with other actors (Parsons, 1951, pp. 3–4). Thus, the internal biological and psychological makeup of the individual actors is assumed to be unimportant. The latter, of course, is an assumption made to permit social analysis, not an assertion that biological and psychological factors are of no consequence.

The sociological approach is appropriate here for several reasons. Most housing problems relate to conditions that arise from the social structure of American society. Such problems are defined as problems because of the normative structure of the society. Finally, such problems depend for solution upon collective social action. More complete knowledge of America as a social system and of housing as a product of that system can aid in achieving more benign effects upon physical, mental, social, and economic health.

The material presented in this book includes analysis of the structure of the American family as it relates to housing. Specifically, the ways in which housing is obtained by families and the extent to which housing hinders or facilitates family functioning as a subunit of society are examined. The extent to which housing meets the needs of families as social groups and of their members is explored. Also included is analysis of changing needs related to family development over the life cycle, of subgroups in the society who may or may not have unique housing norms, and of groups with special housing needs such as the elderly. We also examine the potential for conflict about housing within the family and among families within the society.

Not all of these topics will receive equal emphasis, but they represent most of the key topics that should be included in a social scientific analysis of housing. The most important questions will be considered extensively. How can the housing needs of the family group be met? Do subgroups have different subcultural housing norms? Do the elderly, the disabled, and others have special needs, and, if so, to what extent?

At least four levels of analysis are important here: the societal level, the community level, the family or household level, and the individual level. The levels are nested in that the components of families are individuals; the components of communities are individuals and families; the components of societies are individuals, families, and communities. Some attention is also paid to other types of organizations involved in housing, such as business, industry, and labor, that relate to families and their housing in other ways.

It should be clear from the title of this book that our main focus is on the family or household level. The other levels will be discussed when appropriate because they are the source of housing needs (Rodgers, 1962) and constraints upon the ability of families to adjust their housing to fit their needs.

The Evaluation of Housing Conditions

One of our themes is the delineation of the process by which housing and neighborhoods are judged in cultural terms. That is, how do they come to be thought of as good or bad? Families judge their own housing and that of others using certain culturally derived criteria known as *norms.* A family whose housing does not meet the norms experiences one or more *deficits.* The character of the dwelling and the neighborhood play a role in determining the response of others to a family. These responses, in turn, influence the family's response to itself (Gutman, 1970, pp. 124–25).

It is quite clear that others' responses to a family whose residence is an elegant mansion or a suburban dwelling are very different from responses to a family whose home is an apartment in a decaying tenement, or in a public housing project. Such differential community response is one of the determinants of the level of self-respect that characterizes families in various social classes. How does a family feel about itself when its housing is located in an area referred to by outsiders as a slum? How does a child feel about himself when "going home" means climbing stairs to an apartment that he knows others think of as second-class housing?

Once a type of housing or location becomes imbued with symbolic overtones (either postive or negative), its consequences for the resident family can be much greater than any direct effects of the physical object itself. Poor quality housing can affect the health of the family (Wilner, Walkley, Pinkerton, and Tayback, 1962; Britten and Altman, 1941; Wamben and Piland, 1973; Martin, 1967). Equally serious are the possible social and psychic effects that may arise from family reactions to living in socially undesirable housing. Research has shown that housing may affect behavior, attitudes, and even health as a result of its indirect social effects (Mitchell, 1971; Fanning, 1967).

Housing is shelter and protection. It provides the setting for many of the basic biological and social processes necessary to sustain life. It also symbolizes the status of the family to both the wider community and to the family itself. The motivation that prompts housing behavior is not simply the desire for shelter, but the desire for the right kind of shelter.

Housing Adjustment and Adaptation

The family is not passive in its interplay with its housing. Because it is aware of the responses of others to its housing, the family can make use of its economic, social, and psychic resources to obtain the kind of housing required by the norms. Such familial responses, termed *housing adjustment and adaptation,* are the family's efforts to redress the discrepancies between the housing it has and the housing it and others feel it should have, when such deficits appear.

The occurrence of deficits produces residential dissatisfaction. When the dissatisfaction becomes strong enough, the family may make routine adjustments. In this society routine adjustments might include finishing the basement for a recreation room or an additional bedroom, converting the sewing room to a bedroom, or moving to a different residence. The family may also make less routine housing-related adaptations. For example, they may limit family size or even send grandmother to a nursing home to obtain an extra bedroom. In the sociological model, pathology would include the severe disruption or even destruction of the family or household because there were no available modes of adjustment or adaptation. There is some evidence that the severe housing shortage in Western Europe after World War II did produce such socially pathological conditions (Grootenboer, 1962).

To date, the United States has not experienced shortages of housing in such extreme terms. There have been shortages for certain groups such as the low-income population or the elderly. Thus, social pathology that appears to be housing related may be the result of other factors, chiefly poverty.

When housing adjustment and adaptation do not work, conflict can result. For example, two groups seeking the *same* goals may come into conflict when success with meeting goals by one group is perceived as preventing the other group from meeting theirs. Such conflict may be represented by racial and ethnic discrimination in housing that results in segregation. Thus, for example, blacks and whites may seek the same housing goals and seek to use the same means to achieve them. Nevertheless, whites may perceive the situation in such a way that if blacks are able to meet their goals in the same neighborhoods as whites, then the whites feel as if they have not met their housing goals.

Two groups seeking *different* goals may also experience conflict when one group seeks to prevent the other from meeting their goals. This second situation involves a condition in which different housing goals, such as those of people desiring to live in mobile homes, cannot readily be met because zoning and other laws prevent or make difficult the meeting of such goals.

In this book, relatively less attention is paid to the first type of conflict than to the latter. Ethnic and racial intergroup conflict is a complex topic beyond the scope of this book. Conflicts over housing-related norms and values are covered, however.

ECONOMIC, PSYCHOLOGICAL, AND BIOLOGICAL MODELS

Virtually all the natural, physical, social, and psychological sciences have something valuable to offer in the quest for understanding housing and its relation to the total well-being of people. Not only the sciences, but ethical, aesthetic, and perhaps other approaches from the humanities are important as well. There are strikingly similar approaches applied in the various sciences, especially in dealing with problems at the interface between disciplines. Most of these approaches can be seen in terms of the basic model of the human being from which this analysis proceeds.

The economic model presents the individual as meeting needs that can be satisfied in the marketplace. The individual or household maximizes the fulfillment of those needs through a calculation of the relative costs of the available goods in relation to the budget constraint. Thus, in terms of housing, the individual or household obtains as much housing as resources will afford. Of course, housing has to fit in with the preference schedule that ranks housing relative to the other goods (Diesing, 1962; Ferguson, 1972).

The biological model presents the human organism as needing an external environment within which it can meet its physiological needs and maintain its internal organization within tolerable limits. The role of human housing is to provide shelter from destructive extremes in the environment. The biological model is not simply an equilibrium-seeking model. Humans need shelter not only to preserve, for example, body temperature within a certain range, but also to permit the healthy growth and development of the young.

The basic psychological model presents the human as being motivated toward the satisfaction of certain psychic and psychobiological needs that arise primarily from factors within the individual. Social psychology is similar except that it views the source of at least a portion of those psychic needs as arising in social interaction. The psychological question for housing, in overly simplified terms, is whether the current housing meets an individual's psychic needs. In psychological terms, then, housing should satisfy personality needs such as self-fulfillment, privacy, and the like.

FUNCTIONAL ANALYSIS

The basic approach of this book is to analyze the response of people to their environment in the social system framework that has been referred to as functional analysis. Functional analysis in sociology was developed as an analogy with the study of organisms in functional biology (Cannon, 1932) and the study of mechanical systems (Sorokin, 1928). Functional analysts view the social system as one that tends to maintain a state of equilibrium. That equilibrium, or *preferred pattern,* is preserved through self-regulating mechanisms.

The structural-functional mode of thinking has come to permeate all of the sciences, even the humanities (Parsons, 1975, p. 68; Merton, 1957, pp. 46–48). What is functional analysis?

> *First of all, certain functional requirements of the organism are established, requirements which must be satisfied if the organism is to survive, or to operate with some degree of effectiveness. Second, there is a concrete detailed description of the arrangements (structures and processes) through which these requirements are typically met in 'normal' cases. Third, if some of the typical mechanisms for meeting these requirements are destroyed, or are found to be functioning inadequately the observer is sensitized to the need for detecting compensating mechanisms (if any) which fulfill the necessary function. Fourth, and implicit in all that precedes, there is a detailed account of the structure for which the functional requirements hold, as well as a detailed account of the arrangements through which the function is fulfilled (Merton, 1957, p. 49).*

The theory of functional analysis is that the environment external to the organism or social system is different from the internal environment. The internal environment is more stable, at least in part because it is regulated by various control mechanisms (Parsons, 1975). The temperature of the environment may vary from hour to hour and day to day. The internal temperature of the organism remains much more constant (Adolph, 1968). When minor changes in environmental temperature occur, routine mechanisms respond to maintain internal temperature within an optimum range. Mechanisms are invoked that counteract heat loss, speed up heat loss, increase the rate of internal heat production, or reduce that heat production as required. When environmental conditions exceed the ability of routine mechanisms to maintain a sound temperature, emergency procedures must be invoked or heat prostration will occur.

The core idea in functional analysis is that there are limits set by the biological, psychic, and social nature of humans. The typical organism has a tolerance for extremes that cannot be exceeded without producing effects and consequences. The limits outline the range of conditions under which life is possible. When the limits are exceeded, a state of disequilibrium exists. The application of this idea in biological research was laid out explicitly by Cannon (1932) in his discussion of "thresholds of adequate supply" or "deficiency threshold" with reference to blood sugar levels (Cannon, 1932, p. 218). Adolph (1968) states it in terms of "set points":

> *One characteristic of a regulated activity is its usual rate or intensity. . . . Evidence that a set point exists is the fact that any departure of rate from the ordinary does not endure but the rate returns to its usual setting. A standard is evidently maintained to which the activity returns as soon as conditions permit (Adolph, 1968, p. 22).*

The equilibrium sought by the system is not necessarily the original equilibirum. A new equilibrium may be sought that harmonizes with new environmental conditions.

In the housing adjustment model, the limits are the cultural, community, and family norms that define appropriate housing conditions. When the limits are exceeded, when housing conditions do not meet the norms, disequilibrium, in the form of a normative deficit, occurs.

Equilibrium Maintenance

It is important to distinguish among the limits, the fact that they have been exceeded, the effects of this excess in the form of stress, and the consequences of the stress. The disequilibrium that occurs when a limit is exceeded is referred to as a deficit. (Deficits are discussed in detail later in this chapter.) The immediate effect of a condition that exceeds a limit of some kind (a deficit) is stress (Glass and Singer, 1972). If the stress is not quickly removed or otherwise treated, further consequences will follow. Figure 1 presents a causal diagram relating limits to stress and consequences.

The consequences are of three types: adjustment, adaptation, and pathology. Adjustments may be in the form of minor behavior changes, physiological changes, such as the formation of callous material on the skin in places subject to frictions, or changes in the location of habitat. Adaptation involves structural changes that are relatively permanent. For example, the development of the arm and torso muscles of persons confined to wheelchairs is a permanent structural change. Similarly, low-income families may change family structure in response to their poverty.

Pathology may be physiological in the form of illness, psychological in the form of mental illness, or social in the form of antisocial behavior or extremely low levels of social or economic well-being. Well-being may be defined in both absolute terms and in terms of relative well-being among subunits of the society or other social organization. One of the resultant forms of pathology is intergroup conflict. The distinctions among the three types of

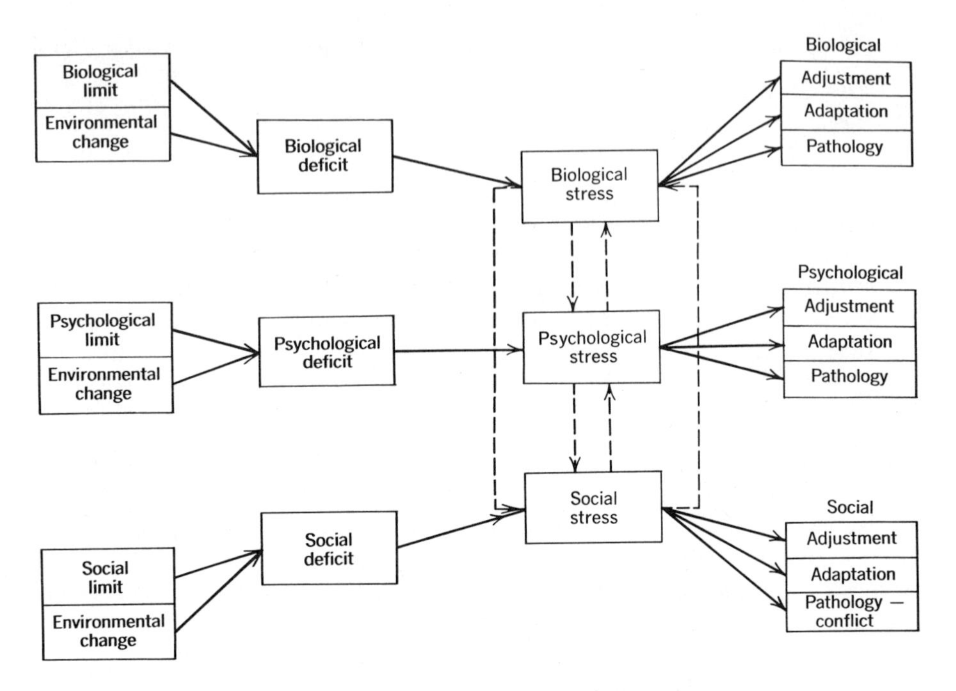

Figure 1 Causal model of deficit-induced stress.

consequences are not always clear-cut, for they represent conceptual ranges on a continuum, from minor adjustments to serious pathology and even death.

When some element or condition in the environment deviates from its set point, standard, or norm, a deficit results. The deficit may be biological, psychological, or social. If the deficit is great enough, it will trigger stress of some kind. The stress in turn may produce stresses at other levels. Biological stress may produce psychological stress (see dashed lines in Figure 1). The stress produced may result in (1) routine adjustment mechanisms, (2) adaptation through changes in the norms or standards or changes in the means used to meet the norms, or (3) pathology in the form of physical or mental ill health or severely decreased socioeconomic well-being.

When biological limits are exceeded, for example, if there is too little fresh air or too much radiation, the result will be stress that is biological in nature, and illness may occur. There may also be psychological and social as well as economic consequences. When psychological limits are exceeded, for example, when crowding produces psychological stress, mental illness may result. As indicated in Figure 1, stress in one aspect may produce consequences in other areas. An example of this point is the development of stomach ulcers as a result of psychological stress. The source of psychological stress may be that a household head is concerned about the fact that he or she is unable to provide the proper kind of housing for the family's children.

Adaptation can have consequences for several system levels:

> *... adaptation refers to a response or structural change in an organism brought about by disturbances to an internal or organism-environment equilibrium. Adaptive responses or changes have been subdivided into those that are relevant to evolution or survival of the species, and those that aid the individual organism to survive and function in his particular environment. Still another distinction is between adaptive responses that maintain internal equilibria, and those that maintain organism-environment relationships (Glass and Singer, 1972, p. 6).*

In addition to the routine adjustments and adaptation, two types of pathological consequences may result from stress: deterioration of mental or physical health and deterioration of social and economic well-being. The first type may, but does not necessarily, involve perception of the occurrence of stress and the concomitant consequences. The second type does involve conscious awareness.

Glass and Singer (1972) make a strong case for the belief that the consequences of most environmental stresses for humans are heavily weighted toward those that are mediated through conscious processes rather than direct physiological stimulation:

> *A great variety of environmental events are capable of producing a stress response, but it is also recognized that the induction of stress depends on the mediation of cognitive factors. As we go up the phylogenetic scale, stress reactions become less dependent on the direct impact of stimuli and more contingent on associated cues that signify the implications and consequences of these stimuli. For this reason, many investigators of human behavior prefer to speak of* psychological *stress, that is the threat or anticipation of future harm. (Glass and Singer, 1972, pp. 5–6).*

Because we have assumed individuals and families can only make decisions about those stresses that they are consciously experiencing, the attention in this book will be given to those aspects of housing that are perceived to be problematical, felt to be salient, and conceived of as having potential solutions.

This book does not dwell on biological factors in part because biological stresses related to the quality of American housing are relatively infrequent, those involving noise and the like notwithstanding. Such biological stress, although extremely important, tends to be correlated with poverty in this country. There may be unsuspected physiological effects of housing related to affluence. Examples include the potentially harmful effects of new technology in appliances, home furnishings, and paints. To concentrate much of our efforts on consequences of biological stress in addition to social and psychic stress would unduly broaden the investigation.

Biological conditions interest us only when the deficits produce social or psychological stress in addition to physiological stress. Our interest in psychological stress is limited to the cognitive aspects.

The Concept of Deficits

The concept of a limit exceeded by some aspect of the environment is too general and vague for in-depth analysis of the topic of housing. Therefore, the concept of a deficit is developed formally in the paragraphs that follow.

A deficit is defined as a deviation above or below a limit characteristic of a specific organism or social system in the relevant environment. A deficit, as the concept is used here, is based on a subtraction of a number representing a norm from a number representing the current, actual state the norm is used to evaluate. The purpose is to discover the magnitude and direction of the difference between the norm and the current state.

All of the usual rules of arithmetic apply to the measurement of deficits. A deficit is formally defined as:

$$a - b = c$$

where: a is the actual state
b is the norm or set point
c is the value of the deficit

There are three types of deficits. For each deficit there are three propositions which define the type. Any value other than zero indicates the current state of the system is in an "undesirable" range. Positive values indicate undesirable *surpluses* and negative values indicate undesirable deficits. Stated simply, the term deficit is used for both surpluses and deficits because the values of the variables other than zero represent undesirable or negatively evaluated ranges of some state.

A Type I deficit can take on both positive and negative values. In this case any departure from zero represents movement into an undesirable range. Therefore, both surpluses and shortages are undesirable.

An example of a Type I deficit might be the distance of a dwelling from the workplace. Being too close is undesirable because of noise, pollution, traffic, for instance. Being too far is also undesirable because of the time and cost of long-distance commuting.

TYPE I DEFICIT
If $a > b$, $c > 0$
If $a < b$, $c < 0$
If $a = b$, $c = 0$

A Type II deficit is one in which only surpluses are undesirable. Therefore there is no negative range. An example is the case of smog where excesses are undesirable but deficits are not—they do not exist. Another example would be the amount of odor in the air from a nearby glue factory. Any amount above the threshold of odor perceptible to humans is too much. Any amount below that is simply an imperceptible amount.

TYPE II DEFICIT

If $a > b, c > 0$
If $a < b, c = 0$
If $a = b, c = 0$

A Type III deficit only takes on negative values. This type of deficit would appear where a shortage of bedrooms was undesirable but having many bedrooms was desirable.

TYPE III DEFICIT

If $a > b, c = 0$
If $a < b, c < 0$
If $a = b, c = 0$

The concept of awareness of deficits as used here is very similar to that of feedback in systems terminology (Back, 1971, pp. 662–63; Buckley, 1967, p. 53). A deficit is a deviation from a preferred state. If the deficit produces adjustments that reduce the deficit, then, in systems terminology, such adjustment would have been the result of *negative* feedback. If, on the other hand, the deviation is magnified by the response (adaptation or pathology), *positive* feedback would have occurred. In the long run, responses that amplify a deficit cannot continue unabated (Back, 1971). Obviously, responses that continue will encounter diminishing returns in relation to the increases in the deficit prompting the response. Deficits and the responses produced are the core concepts for analysis of the goal-seeking nature of social organizations studied in systemic functional models.

SYSTEMIC FUNCTIONAL MODELS

A recently published outline of systemic functional models in sociology begins with a set of criteria for a theoretically sound model (Sztompka, 1974, pp. 3–32). First, the goal is the explanation of phenomena and processes. Why do Americans possess their particular types of housing? Why do they seek such housing? What separates successful from unsuccessful housing seekers?

Second, while explanation consists of the answers to special "why" questions, theory consists of interconnected explanations. Third, the construction of a theory depends upon the development of a conceptual model based on the portion of reality studied by the theory. In our case, the reality is families and their housing.

A conceptual model consists of a set of basic assumptions about the nature of reality and a set of ideas used to describe potential variations among elements of the topic of interest. If it is assumed that families are rational decision-making units, then the explanation of why they seek the type of housing they do could be very different from an explanation developed under the assumption that families are motivated primarily by religious zeal.

If a model does not allow for variation among families in terms of rationality-nonrationality, it may not be possible to explain the seemingly self-destructive consequences of nonrational behavior. If there is no provision for variation among families in terms of prestige in the local community, it may not be possible to explain the (nonrational?) sacrifices families make in order to have housing that impresses their neighbors.

Fourth, according to Sztompka, the set of sociological models referred to as functional models, when appropriately generalized, are a "well-detailed, precise, and promising conception for the construction of a theory of society" (Sztompka, 1974, p. 180). Fifth, there are a number of assumptions that must be made and concepts that must be defined in order to develop a theoretically sound systemic functional model. The assumptions made and the concepts used are presented in Part I.

Sixth, when properly developed, such a model is free of the defects most commonly attributed to functional analysis. The three defects are the teleological bias, the static bias, and the ahistoric bias (Sztompka, 1974, p. 137).

The teleological bias is one in which the outcome in a specific system is interpreted as if it were the cause of the process which brought it into being. The fact that, in functional models, social systems have been treated as if they had goals which were consciously sought, has mistakenly been thought to be defective. The argument is based on the fact that, in terms of systems, goals are future states and future states cannot cause current behavior. Obviously, it is not suggested that future states can cause anything in the present. It is, however, a prime assumption in the model that social organizations are goal-seeking systems. Further, a present state such as an unmet goal can, indeed, produce behavior that would result in a future state in which the goal is met.

The static bias, according to Sztompka (1974), involves the inability of a model to incorporate the concept of internal change. Such change occurs totally within the system, rather than in response to the environment. It is true that many functional analyses are based on the assumption that the structure and the processes going on in the subject social system are stable; yet it is not necessary to assume a static version of a functional model. Indeed, the present model includes the assumption that this form of change does, in fact, occur.

The ahistoric bias, related to the static bias, involves the inability of a model to encompass developmental change. Such change produces fundamental alterations in the nature of the system. That this form of change is capable of conceptualization within general functional models is shown by the widespread adoption of the developmental approach in the social sciences (Rodgers, 1962; Cannon, 1932; von Bertalanffy, 1933; Back, 1971; Hill and Hansen, 1960; Hill, 1971; Smelser, 1964). We must conclude that specific research and specific researchers may have been characterized by one or more of these biases, but that those biases are not inherent in systemic functional analysis.

Functional analysis has recently become less fashionable and its terminology—but not the basic approach—is undergoing renovation by terminology from so-called "modern systems theory" (Buckley, 1967). The shift to a new language may have facilitated a shift (which was probably already underway) from a preoccupation with equilibrium maintenance toward attention to change, development, conflict, and social pathology. Regardless of the terminology used, functional analysis is simply one of the forms of systems analysis. In this book, the older terminology will be used to avoid terms that inordinately complicate the presentation.

THE FRAMEWORK AND SOCIAL CHANGE

Back (1971) shows the relevance of functional analysis to the analysis of social change in a fashion similar to Adolph (1968) and many others for biology.

> *The biologist has distinguished mechanisms, some of which maintain equilibrium under changing conditions, some of which create change in the system, and some of which are indicators of breakdown of adaptation. Study of the essential characteristics of these processes can help the sociologist in understanding stability and change in social systems (Back, 1971, p. 661).*

Enormous change has been occurring in the rural-urban-suburban distribution of the American population and in the rates of population growth. The perceived relationship between the growth of cities and growth of the population, on the one hand, and the deterioration of the environment on the other also prompts change. In spite of such change, there is as yet no evidence to suggest that the place of housing in American society is significantly declining. The majority of American families view housing as an important manifestation of status and a source of satisfaction. Specific ways in which housing is obtained and the specific ways in which housing reflects on the status, prestige, and respect of families can be expected to continue in a state of flux.

A trilevel suburban house may have been very desirable in the early 1970s, especially if it had two or three bathrooms, air conditioning, a dishwasher, washer, dryer, and microwave oven. However, continued changes in the supply of energy and the attitude of Americans toward wastefulness and environmental deterioration could produce great changes. The amount of respect and gratification derived from having such a plethora of appliances using multiple kilowatt hours of electricity could decline significantly.

The value of the present framework for the analysis of housing conditions and problems lies in the fact that the effects of social, economic, and environmental change can be assessed. Such an assessment in terms of adjustment, adaptation, and pathology could promote housing policy that focuses on the prevention of serious problems rather than the cure of them after they become serious.

DEFINITIONS

Adaptation. A relatively permanent structural change in response to stress. Included are changes in norms or changes in the means used to meet the norms that appear when the stress of housing dissatisfaction is great.

Adjustment. Minor behavioral changes, physiological changes, or changes in location in response to stress; routine mechanisms within a system for dealing with stress.

Ahistoric bias. The inability of a model to encompass developmental change, thus leading the investigator to ignore, for instance, changes in the family related to the life cycle, or changes in the society due to rising affluence.

Assumption. A statement of relationship or definition, accepted as true for purposes of analysis. Assumptions are not tested. They are assumed to be true in order to test other relationships; to be contrasted with hypothesis.

Conceptual model. A set of basic assumptions about the nature of reality and a set of ideas used to describe potential variations among elements of the topic being studied.

Consequences of stress. Deterioration of mental or physical health and/or deterioration of social and economic well-being. Stress may result in routine adjustment by system mechanisms, adaptation, or pathology.

Cultural norms. Rules or standards, both formal and informal, for the conduct and life conditions of members of a particular society.

Deficit. A deficiency or imbalance created when a limit is exceeded by some aspect of the environment.

Developmental change. Change that occurs in a system as a result of biological or social maturation processes; the kind of change implied in the transition from childhood to adulthood and in the progression of families through the life cycle.

Disequilibrium. A departure from equilibrium; a state of a system in which one or more preferred states do not exist; a disturbance of the pattern of a system.

Equilibrium. The preferred state of a system that tends to be maintained by internal compensatory mechanisms when disturbed; the particular patterns in a system that tend to be preserved through self-regulatory mechanisms.

Functional analysis. A method of analysis based on the view of a social system as a self-regulating entity. The analysis typically is concerned with the system's structure and the system processes involved in the functioning of the system.

Limits. The range of biological, psychic, or social tolerance of a system that cannot be exceeded without producing adjustment, adaptation, or pathology.

Normative deficit. A deficit based on subtraction of a number representing a norm from a number representing the current, actual state; a gap between actual conditions and those prescribed by norms.

Pathology. Deviation from healthy, normal, efficient conditions in physiological, psychological, or social functioning—different from adjustment and adaptation in that the continued existence of the system as a system is in doubt.

Static bias. The inability of a model to incorporate the concept of internal change, change that occurs within the system rather than in response to the environment.

Stress. Internal tension created by deficits.

Systemic functional model. A conceptual model used as the basis of functional analysis. Included are basic assumptions defining a social system, its structure and basic processes, and the expected variations in them.

Teleological bias. A bias in conceptualizing a system in which outcomes are interpreted as causes of the processes that brought them into being. This bias reverses the traditional time-order assumption that an effect must not precede its cause.

Type I deficit. A deviation from the norm in either direction, positive (surplus) or negative (deficit), both of which are undesirable.

Type II deficit. A deviation from the norm in which only a surplus is undesirable.

Type III deficit. A deviation from the norm in which only a shortage is undesirable.

Chapter 2
Cultural Norms and the Evaluation of Housing

> 'Tis one thing to know what we ought to do, and another thing to execute it; and to bring up our practice to our philosophy: he that is naturally a coward is not to be made valiant by councell. Aesop's Fables

This chapter outlines the concepts that will be used to provide an understanding of the way in which families, communities, and the society evaluate housing and respond with behavior to adjust their housing when they are dissatisfied. The chapter defines and explicates housing norms which may be cultural, community, or family norms. The norms are the preferred states, goal states, or limits discussed in Chapter 1. Unmet norms (normative deficits) tend to produce adjustment behavior. Or, in the event that adjustment is not successful, they produce adaptation or pathology.

CULTURE AND SOCIETY

The terms "culture" and "society" are often used loosely and interchangeably. Therefore, there is a need to distinguish between them and indicate how they are used in this book. Culture, in its most elementary form, is the set of rules and standards for behavior, interaction, and living conditions. At all times the terms "culture" and "cultural" are used to refer to the system of rules, norms, standards, and values (the way things *ought* to be). These terms are never used here to refer to artifacts or products of culture. "Society" and "social" refer to the behavioral, interactional sphere, and the conditions of life (the way things *are*) of the members of the social-cultural system. Unfortunately, it is conventional to apply the term "society" to not only the behavioral, interactional life conditions system, but also to the whole that includes both cultural and social systems, a practice continued in this book. "Social" is reserved for reference to the societal sphere.

The number of households and the number of available dwelling units are *social* facts. The rule or standard that more than one family per dwelling unit is not acceptable is a *cultural* fact. A key process in the study of housing is to compare an element from the cultural system with one from the social system. More specifically, behavior or conditions (social), must be compared with norms (cultural) to ascertain the acceptability of the conditions.

CULTURAL NORMS AND SANCTIONS

A specific housing condition or set of conditions becomes a deficit when the condition has been subjectively defined as undesirable. The criteria used in making such subjective evaluations are *cultural norms.*

Cultural norms include the full range of rules that society promulgates in more or less formal ways to govern the way people live and behave. They are the standards by which the behavior exhibited or conditions experienced by the members of a culture are evaluated as "good" or "bad." Thus, the definitions of standard-substandard, adequate-inadequate, expensive-inexpensive, and well located-poorly located housing are expressed through cultural norms.

In addition to norms that define goals there are norms that prescribe the kinds of means that may be used to achieve the goals (Merton, 1957, p. 140–141). Means are of two kinds: resources that may be used to attain a goal, and behaviors that may be used to attain a goal. The resources may be of several kinds, economic, social, and psychological, as well as "natural."

The scarcity of means is a matter of cultural definition (Stanley, 1968). One may be said to be poor (i.e., lacking money resources) only when a cultural norm defining poverty can be referred to. An income of 3000 U.S. dollars may represent poverty in the context of American norms. It would represent near luxury in the context of Bolivian poverty norms.

One can imagine a set of norms in a particular society that would denote substandard housing. Housing at or above that standard would represent a cultural goal. Since money income is the prime resource (the means) in American society for obtaining housing, a cultural standard for income may exist that is something along the lines of "enough money to afford standard (or better) housing and sufficient food, clothing, etc."

Of course, there are norms having to do with the legitimate means of obtaining income. Thus, there are norms that prescribe the goal (housing) and norms that prescribe the means (money income) as well as norms that prescribe the means for obtaining money income (employment).

Many general and specific types of behavior are more or less socially acceptable means of obtaining or improving housing. A family may buy or rent housing, use their own time, energy, and skill to fix up a dwelling, or hire someone else to do the maintenance and repairs.

An important distinction must be made between norms and behavior, or between norms and actual conditions. Cultural norms are the rules for behavior. They state what behavior or conditions are prescribed or proscribed. They are *not* the behavior or conditions themselves. Thus, neither the average behavior of a group, nor the typical conditions under which they live are to be thought of as sound indicators of cultural norms. Behavior may deviate from the norms to the extent to which people cannot or will not conform.

Norms range from bodies of formal written laws such as those governing the operation of motor vehicles to informal rules governing the proper way, for example, to greet classmates at school. In housing, they vary from zoning ordinances that specify, among other things, the minimum distance a house must be set back from the street to very informal rules about having a quiet place in the home for school-age children to study.

The level of informality or formality is not necessarily indicative of the amount of importance the society attaches to the particular norm. Differences in formality arise chiefly from the way norms are expressed, which can be through written law, administrative regulation, or verbal communication. Cultural norms as applied in practice by American families often become formalized as a part of the law that regulates housing.

In addition, public agencies may develop rules of thumb to evaluate housing that are really shortcut ways of measuring cultural norms (crowding indexes, for example). Such measures often are quite useful, although they may be rather rough measures of reality.

Not all housing law, of course, is a faithful reflection of the cultural norms applied by families. Indeed, housing legislation at times may appear to be directly opposed to the cultural norms that are applied in daily life. Nevertheless, there is a strain toward consistency between informal and formal norms. Although there may be a tendency for societies to formalize those norms that seem most important to the maintenance of the society, the importance of the norm derives from its influence on daily life and not simply its means of expression:

> *A house can meet the legal standards set in a local code, pass a housing code inspection, and still be unfit for human habitation by the personal standards of most middle-class Americans (NCUP, 1968, p. 274).*

Norms for Families and Family Norms

Norms that apply to the behavior and conditions of families originate at three sources: the culture, the family itself, and the individuals within the family (Rodgers, 1964, p. 268). Of particular relevance to this analysis are cultural norms from the society and family norms from within the family (Lennard and Bernstein, 1969, p. 86; Tallman, 1970, p. 95).

For the purpose of this book, there are two broad classes of norms that are important: norms that govern housing behavior and conditions and norms for family functioning in the pursuit of housing that meets the norms. Thus there are four sets of norms that can be distinguished and are important to the study of housing: (1) cultural norms for housing, (2) cultural norms for family functioning, (3) family norms for housing, and (4) family norms for family functioning. Cultural and family norms for family functioning will be discussed in the next chapter. Norms for housing are discussed in Chapters 5, 6, and 7.

Socialization: Learning the Norms

Each member of the society more or less effectively learns the norms of the society of which he is a member. While acquisition of the norms occurs primarily in the younger years, it is nevertheless a lifelong process. According to Freedman (1968):

> *One of the fundamental principles of sociology is that when many members of a society face a recurrent problem with important social consequences they tend to develop a normative solution for it. This solution, a set of rules for behaviour in a particular situation, becomes part of the culture, and the society indoctrinates its members to conform by explicit or implicit rewards or punishments (p. 216).*

In general, the prime transmitters of the norms are the child's parents and older siblings. Next in importance may be teachers and other adults who represent the society: the clergy, for example. In addition, the mass media transmit norms to members of the society and appear to exert a homogenizing force on the society's norms (DeFleur and DeFleur, 1967, pp. 777–89).

Norms for many kinds of behavior are learned from peers. Norms for sexual behavior (Davis, 1948, p. 217), college aspirations (McDill and Coleman, 1963), and delinquent behavior (Cohen, 1955) all fall into this category. It would seem, however, that norms related to housing are primarily learned within the family rather than from peers.

An individual learns or internalizes the culture both by directly learning the norms and by indirect methods including discovering the kinds of behavior for which one is rewarded or punished and noting the behavior one observes in others (Chombart de Lauwe, 1966; Gillin and Gillin, 1948, p. 660; Tarde, 1903, p. 60; Parsons and Shils, 1954, p. 16). Thus, a social studies teacher may explain that home owners are the backbone of the society. The door of a *single-family suburban dwelling* may close dramatically on the television screen in a popular family series. Credit may be more difficult to obtain because one lives in a mobile home or because one rents rather than owns.

Sanctions

The rewards or punishments administered in support of norms are termed *sanctions.* Norms, along with the accompanying sanctions, are one of the means by which the members of the society are encouraged to behave in the "proper" way. Sanctions may be positive (rewards for conformance) or negative (punishments for deviation or nonconformance).

Sanctions may be imposed from within the family, or they may be imposed by others. Perhaps the most effective norms are those that are so well taught and widely accepted that individuals apply their own personal sanctions in the form of guilt feelings, loss of self-respect, or shame when a norm is violated.

Sanctions may be applied unfailingly or capriciously. The violation of the norm that prescribes that teenage children may not share their parents' bedroom is so unfailingly enforced in the United States that this behavior seldom occurs. Sanctions applied for living in a racially mixed neighborhood, for example, are more sporadically enforced. Often lending institutions will not grant home mortgages or home improvement loans in a "changing" neighborhood. At other times, they may be granted, depending upon other conditions, such as the social class level of the neighborhood.

Sanctions vary as to their severity. The negative sanctions for norm violation that are meted out may be severe, as in the withholding of credit, or very mild, as in the raising of eyebrows regarding one's choice of a neighborhood. Positive sanctions may vary in terms of their desirability. The rewards that come from living in a "good" neighborhood may include high-quality education, dependable municipal services and utilities, and social approval by one's colleagues and friends. The rewards that accrue from having a fireplace may be no more than feelings of contentment.

Permitted Deviation from Norms

For any cultural norm there is an ideal level of conformance and some range of permissible variation around the ideal. Behavior within that range may be deemed acceptable and might even be moderately rewarded or at least not punished. Outside that range, behavior would be negatively sanctioned. Such a range of permissible behavior or conditions may be depicted by a continuum, with the ideal range in the middle, permissible deviation near the middle, and the unacceptable range of behavior at either extreme (Figure 2).

An example of the range of conditions permitted might be shown by the number of bedrooms prescribed by sleeping space norms. There seems to be a cultural norm that states that the ideal is just enough bedrooms for each child to have his own (APHA, 1950, p. 39), plus one extra bedroom for guests. Having no guest room, representing permissible deviation, would not

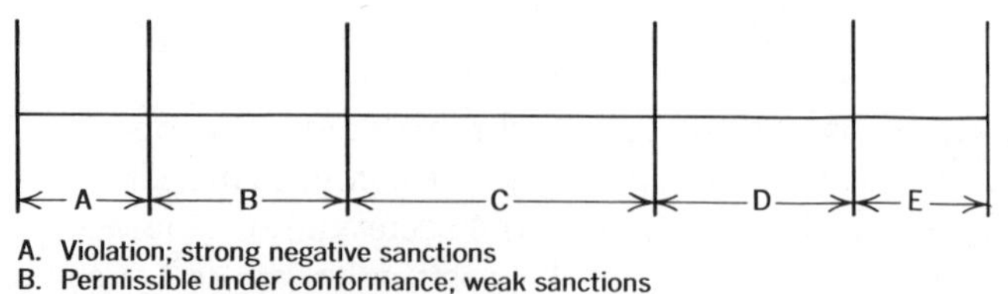

A. Violation; strong negative sanctions
B. Permissible under conformance; weak sanctions
C. Ideal range; strong positive sanctions
D. Permissible over conformance; weak sanctions
E. Violation; strong negative sanctions

Figure 2 Range of permissible deviation from cultural norms.

be severely sanctioned. As long as pairs of older children of opposite sexes do not have to share bedrooms, much range is permitted.

There can be too many or too few bedrooms, as prescribed by the norm. When a family has a large excess of bedrooms (beyond the number required by the norms), the sanctions are likely to be economic. An unusually large house would be expensive. When there are far too few, the sanctions applied would be quite severe and would come primarily from within the family.

Norms may differ greatly in terms of the range of permissible deviation. For some norms there is a relatively wide range. For others, very little variation is permitted. Permissible deviation in the norm for the number of bedrooms is the former type. The range in behavior permitted regarding who may share bedrooms is of the latter. Violation of some norms only induces negative sanctions for underconformance; and violation of some others only induces negative sanctions for overconformance. The difference has to do with the differences in the type of deficit involved, as discussed in Chapter 1.

Three sets of norms may enter into the analysis of a housing problem: those of the society (cultural norms), those of the community (community norms), and those of the family (family norms). A specific family may reject the cultural norm for home ownership and hold instead a norm that favors rental. That such a family has different ownership norms is demonstrated by reference to their standards and expectations and not to whether or not they *are* actually renters. A specific community or family may have norms that either correspond closely with or differ greatly from the cultural norms. Thus they may be conventional or unconventional in their orientation to housing.

When a family or a community has norms for its housing or for general functioning that differ from cultural norms, there is an explanation for the difference. The most probable explanation in the case of the family is that it and its members have experienced a different socialization process from most members of the society. That may occur by isolation, by membership in a subculture, and possibly by other means.

Communities made up primarily of families with norms that differ from the cultural norms may have unusual norms. Isolation of a community may have a similar effect on community norms as isolation of a family does on family norms. A community may consist primarily or solely of persons from a subculture with a variant version of the general culture. In any case, the development of unconventional norms can be expected to require a rather long process of socialization including multiple applications of negative and positive sanctions.

A particular attitude or affective orientation toward a behavior or condition may be classified on two dimensions (Figure 3). Given the perspective of a particular family, an attitude may be held by the family in question, the community, or by the society (1), or may involve "ideal" conditions or actual, current conditions (2). This distinction does not refer to the conceptual differentiation between actual conditions and ideal conditions. Rather, it refers to the distinction between norms that apply to a specific time, place, and situation, and norms that apply to improved or ideal circumstances. The former indicates how one should act in a given immediate situation. The latter indicates how one should act if one is, for example, rich, young, and strong, and therefore able to act "perfectly."

Family norms (*a*) are the family's standards with respect to itself. Thus, for example, the family may or may not share the standard of the community or the society in favor of home ownership. Community norms (*b*) are the rules prescribing proper conditions and behavior for a particular group of people in a particular geographic location. One example of a "community" with housing norms that are different from cultural norms is Manhattan Island, the only vertical community in the United States. The other four boroughs of New York City consist mainly of neighborhoods of single-family dwellings. Cultural norms (*c*) are the standards of the society for families and communities in that society.

Deviation from norms is often permitted in response to the extenuating circumstances of actual conditions. Thus a family preference (*d*) is the yard-

	(2) Conditions under which the norm applies	
(1) Source of the norm	Ideal	Actual
The family	(*a*) Family norm	(*d*) Family preference
The community	(*b*) Community norm	(*e*) Community preference
The society	(*c*) Cultural norm	(*f*) Generalized preference

Figure 3 Typology of norms and preferences of the family based on the holder of the norm or preference and the conditions under which it applies.

stick a family applies realistically to its housing, given all the limitations and opportunities relevant to the situation. Since a preference is a relaxed norm to be applied immediately, it is by definition that which makes permissible deviation (Figure 2, ranges B and D) permissible. Rodman (1963, 1966) has suggested the concept of "value stretch" to refer to a somewhat similar phenomenon. However, his interpretation of the theoretical meaning of stretched values implies actual alterations in norms or values.

The present use of "preference" as a temporary state of mind is similar to its use in consumption economics. A preference represents the quantity and quality of goods the consumer prefers to buy (under immediate conditions) relative to all other possible quantities and qualities of the good (see, for example, Ferguson, 1972, pp. 17–33).

An example may help to clarify the concepts. There is clearly a cultural norm that prescribes home ownership. A specific family may also have a norm in favor of home ownership. Given their limited income, however, the family may decide that the best thing to do is rent. Such a decision does not imply a change in family norms, but is simply a temporary relaxation due to circumstances.

The relaxation of cultural norms produces community preferences (*e*) and generalized preferences (*f*) that represent the standards of other families for the behavior of a given family in their actual (extenuating) circumstances. Negative sanctions tend not to be applied or are less severe under such circumstances.

It is important to distinguish preference development from the process by which family and community norms are developed. Preference development occurs very quickly and is temporary. Family norms and community norms are not altered in preference development. Preferences are produced by the constraints of circumstances. Family and community norms are produced by socialization. Only in the long run can preferences produce changes in family and community norms. If being forced to develop lower preferences over a period of time is experienced as the administration of negative sanctions, different norms might develop.

A deficit exists when there is a gap between the actual conditions and those prescribed by cultural, community, or family norms. The difference must be great enough to be noticed and the gap must be thought of as undesirable. Thus, a family has a housing problem whenever a housing condition the family feels is important deviates perceptibly from the cultural norms, the community norms, or the family norms. When evaluating their current dwelling, a family generally is aware of the community and cultural norms that govern housing conditions. Some families may also have established norms of their own in accord with the cultural norms. However, because of their life conditions—for example, having limited income—it may be that they are unable to conform. Their housing would be deviant from both family and cultural norms.

Family preferences, community preferences, and generalized preferences may permit the relaxation of norms in accord with the circumstances. If the circumstances change, the relaxation of the norms may no longer be permissible. In the example of the low-income family who rents, if in later years the family's income rises, the continued deviation from the family's norms may come to be felt as a problem since the extenuating circumstances no longer exist. As a result, actual or potential negative sanctions and/or potential positive sanctions may cause the family to seek housing that is in accord with the norms.

Aspirations and Expectations

Two future-oriented concepts derive from norms and preferences. Aspirations are desires (family norms) for some future time. The intervening period between the present and the point at which aspirations apply may or may not be filled with preparation. "God helps [fulfill the aspirations of] those who help themselves." Expectations are the realistic assessment of what future conditions will be. Aspirations are to expectations as family norms are to preferences. Norms and preferences are used by families to form their current housing choices. Aspirations and expectations are used to guide efforts to plan and organize the future.

Change in Norms

Housing norms must be assumed to be relatively fixed in order to permit study of their influence on behavior at a specific point in time. Norms nevertheless are subject to change over time. At one time in American history, having no indoor plumbing was not subject to sanctions. Today such conditions are unacceptable according to informal American housing norms. Often such conditions are subject to formal norms, through regulations of the local or state health department.

Norms may change in response to the chronic existence of problems as in the case of mobile homes. At one point, "trailer living" was considered to be second class. Today, mobile home living is becoming increasingly more acceptable. A chronic shortage of relatively inexpensive housing has recently encouraged many householders to turn to mobile homes. As a result the norms that led people to feel the mobile home was only for unstable gypsy-like people appear to have changed.

Norms may also change by prescribing increasingly higher standards as economic (Winnick, 1957, p. 6) and technological (Rossi, 1955, p. 156) conditions improve. Increasingly luxurious but relatively inexpensive bathroom fixtures have become widely available as a result of the development of new materials and improved technology. Almost all American dwellings (94.1% in 1970) have complete plumbing facilities. Bathroom norms presently prescribe not only that there be a full set of facilities but that they be quite elegant, as well.

Progressions in the norms that apply to an individual family as it passes through the family life cycle are thought of as a different type of change. The norm does not change, the family changes by moving to a later point in the cycle. Therefore, different norms apply to it. This type of change may be termed family developmental change. In contrast, the changes in norms that characterize society represent contextual or environmental change from the viewpoint of the family. The latter, of course, may represent developmental change of the society.

Some types of norms may change quickly indeed in the manner of the appearance and passing of fads. Generally, such rapidly changing norms involve decorative and style-related characteristics of housing. Thus, the tri-level suburban home for a time dominated single-family home construction. The focus of attention in this book will seldom turn to such fleeting aspects of the evaluation of housing. The point is not that fashions, styles, and fads are not deserving of attention. There has been a long history of serious analyses of fads and fashions (Tarde, 1903; Ross, 1908; Bogardus, 1924). Rather, the analysis in this book focuses on more stable standards for housing.

Subgroup Differences

Since norms are, by definition, group phenomena, a key question in the study of norms is the degree of agreement within the group about what the norms are. Thus consensus, group solidarity, and integration are key concepts. The manner in which the orientations of individuals toward the behavior and living conditions of others and themselves within the group are aggregated into an indication of group orientation is a complex and relatively unsolved problem for social science. If there is a minority within a group in disagreement with the overall group about appropriate behavior, integration of the group may be lowered.

Many subgroups exist within a society as complex as the United States. Each nuclear family represents one of the smallest of such subgroups. Subgroups may be based upon wider family and kinship ties, as well as ethnic, racial, or religious bonds.

To a degree, every group has its own culture. Specifically, it has developed some norms that apply to its members and to the behavior and conditions of the group itself but not to the society as a whole. Most such groups nevertheless are full-fledged members of the society and participate fully in its culture both as groups and as individuals. They may be said to be both culturally and socially integrated into American society.

There may be subgroups located within the boundaries of the society which clearly represent a different culture. The Hutterites are an example of such a consciously separate group that does not participate fully in the society. They not only have a different normative system, but they also do not engage in full interaction with other groups in the society. They are neither culturally nor socially integrated into the society and simply represent a separate culture.

Mexican-Americans, on the other hand, represent a third type of subgroup that maintains a contrasting culture (normative system) but nevertheless attempts to participate relatively fully in the behavioral, interactional system of the society. They are socially but not culturally integrated into American society and in the present frame of analysis will be referred to as a subculture. Groups that are both culturally and socially integrated are referred to as subgroups.

CULTURAL NORMS AS HOUSING NEEDS*

The housing literature is replete with discussions of family housing "needs" (Agan and Luchsinger, 1965; Duvall, 1967; Rossi, 1955; Foote, Abu-Lughod, Foley, and Winnick, 1960; Beyer, 1965). Seldom is the term "needs" explicitly defined, however. Sometimes the definition of *housing need* appears to arise from the biological characteristics of humans that imply a need for certain kinds of protection from weather, predators, and enemies.

Often an implicit cultural definition appears to be employed. It is said, for example, that families with preschool children "need" play space and space for the storage of children's toys (Johnson, 1952). That such prescriptions are derived from the culture becomes obvious when it is noted that the need for play space and equipment are very different in other cultures. The Siriono of the Bolivian jungle, for example, simply have no need for space in which to ride and store tricycles (Holmberg, 1956, p. 160). The play of the Siriono children consists primarily of imitations of adult behavior. Their toys are miniature versions of adult equipment: weapons for boys and domestic devices for girls.

The general sociological literature refers to three types of human needs. First are those that humans share with the animals exemplified by the needs for food and shelter. Second come those that are strictly human but are not culturally induced, such as the needs for respect, affection, and recognition. Third are those needs that are culturally induced by socialization (Etzioni, 1968).

The first class of needs must be met by a society to ensure the survival of its population. As will be shown below, such needs may be met either on the most primitive level or in a very sophisticated fashion.

* Much of this section originally appeared in E. W. Morris and M. Winter, "A Theory of Family Housing Adjustment" (*Journal of Marriage and the Family* 37), pp. 81–82. Copyright © 1975 by the National Council on Family Relations. Reprinted by permission.

The second class of needs would seem to be even more variable in the ways in which they may be filled. The failure of a society to provide for gratification of needs for respect, affection, and recognition would seem as a consequence to require high socialization costs and high personal costs for the society's members (Etzioni, 1968). The high costs involve the great effort it would require on the part of parents and teachers to produce subsequent generations with reduced needs for recognition and love.

In addition, the suppression of the self that would occur would be likely to produce pressures within the individual that could not be readily borne without mental aberrations. As a result, alienation, disenchantment, and other chronic pressures in the social system could be produced. Although it is difficult to measure, the extent to which societies meet the second class of needs should influence the level of satisfaction with the society and serve as an index of how well the society "works" (Etzioni, 1968). A discussion of the second class of needs is important in a book on housing because one of the ways Americans are able to fill their needs for respect and recognition is through their ability to obtain good housing.

The third class of needs, the culturally induced ones, include all the housing norms that are discussed in this book. Since the filling of the needs induced by socialization provides opportunity for achieving the second class of needs and since one of the needs in the first class is the need for shelter, all three types of needs are interrelated in the process of housing.

The concept of housing norms employed in the remainder of this book explicitly refers to the third class of human needs, those that are culturally induced. Such usage of the norm concept has had a long history in sociology (Tarde, 1903, p. 44; Parsons and Shils, 1954, pp. 9–10).

Certain minimum standards related to health must be maintained or human life cannot be sustained. Such standards are exceedingly low, however. Survival is possible in forms of housing that are very far below even the worst housing in the United States. The original Tierra del Fuegans, for example, lived in housing that was little more than a hollowed-out place in the ground with a makeshift skin windbreak (Cooper, 1946, pp. 110–11).

To emphasize the importance of culture in defining housing needs even where survival, health, and safety are concerned, a set of polar opposites of theoretically possible housing conditions can be posited. At one extreme, there are housing conditions under which no human being could survive for any lengthy period of time. A sealskin windbreak on an icefield in temperatures below −50 degrees Fahrenheit would represent this end of the continuum. At the other extreme are conditions where no aspect of the housing could have an adverse effect on survival. The two extremes would be characterized by a mortality rate of 100 percent due to housing conditions and a mortality rate of zero percent, respectively.

Any empirical set of housing conditions could be classified in terms of its effect on the death rate and would fall somewhere between the extremes. (It would, of course, be necessary to control for nonhousing factors and the length of time under consideration. Thus, all statements about mortality rates should be read as if they had a general "all-other-things-equal" qualification attached).

Numerous examples could be given to illustrate various positions along the continuum implied by the given housing conditions. No housing—as housing—exists at the end of the continuum characterized by 100 percent mortality. However, the housing of some primitive people would seem to be quite close to that extreme. Similarly, there is probably no housing that is at the opposite extreme. The single-family housing enjoyed by the upper-middle-income groups in the United States may approach that point more closely than most other forms of housing.

A specific society with a given level of social organization, technology, geographic environment, and availability of natural resources could achieve a rather broad range of housing conditions depending upon the place of housing in its overall hierarchy of values. A society may choose the level of housing conditions it will strive for. Inherent in that choice is a decision as to how much housing-related mortality will be accepted, for any specific set of housing conditions carries with it an effect on the mortality rate. In an indirect way the effect on the death rate is a matter of choice arrived at through the application of societal values and cultural norms.

Therefore, housing *needs* reasonably may be equated with *cultural norms* for housing. Housing needs do not derive from minimum shelter needs or minimum health and safety standards in any absolute sense. They do, however, derive from cultural standards against which actual housing conditions are judged.

UNFILLED HOUSING NEEDS

At any given time, some of a family's needs may be filled while others remain unfilled. The analysis of needs and the measurement of the existence of needs logically are separate from the question of whether the needs are currently filled.

A later chapter demonstrates a widespread cultural need for home ownership. All or most families who own their own homes may have an ownership need, but it has been filled. Many renting families may have an unfilled need for ownership. It does not follow that home owners have no need for ownership. Both types of families have the need, a point which is measured by reference to cultural norms (ownership norms) rather than social conditions (presence or absence of ownership).

The point seems obvious, but it has often been misunderstood by social scientists who have attempted to show differing needs on the part of various subgroups or particular types of families (Riemer, 1950 and 1951; Dean,

1953; Rainwater, 1966). It is incorrect to conclude that families who already have housing with particular characteristics no longer have needs for such characteristics. It is especially important not to conclude that groups of people have different needs based on the housing they typically live in.

CULTURAL NORMS AND CULTURAL VALUES

Those familiar with the housing literature may find the emphasis on cultural norms as the criteria for judging housing conditions to be in striking contrast to the use of values by many researchers (Cutler, 1947; Dean, 1953; Beyer, Mackesy, and Montgomery, 1955). Norms are more useful as criteria, however, because values are general guidelines for evaluation of goals (norms), rather than the goals themselves (Williams, 1970, p. 440). Values may assist in the understanding of general cultural patterns in society. They may be used only in unspecific ways to guide the judgment of housing conditions and behavior in terms of their appropriateness in the society.

One of the difficulties with the concept of values is the tendency to blur the distinction between values as societal phenomena and the manifestation of a particular value in a given family's life. Individuals and families may exhibit in their own value configurations a more or less faithful reflection of the society's values. But even in the case where a dominant societal value is also dominant for a given family, its implication for specific housing behavior may not be at all obvious.

For example, a society may be characterized by certain values, such as familism. The presence of familism should suggest, in general, that people would tend to feel that their housing should be arranged in ways congenial to family life. Familism, either as a societal value or as a family value orientation, may or may not lead a family to desire a family room as opposed to a formal living room in their dwelling. Familism could, as well, lead them to desire the formal living room because it would provide pleasure to the family to have an elegant place for entertaining.

Thus, diverse and opposite kinds of housing behavior may be implied by a single value orientation. In addition, many values may be expressed by a single residential choice (Smith, Kivlin, and Sinden, 1963, p. 51). Under differing conditions, very different responses may be implied by orientation to a given value. Hence a tool is needed that more nearly indicates what specific housing behavior or conditions are socially desirable in specific situations. Such a tool is the concept of the cultural norm.

MEASURING CULTURAL NORMS

The importance of norms is derived from the fact that people, in daily living, use them to control and predict the behavior of other members of the society. If there were no dependable connection between norms and behavior, both the family and the social scientist could simply ignore the norms. Obviously, they cannot. Careful measurement of the cultural norms is necessary in order for behavior to be accurately explained and predicted.

According to Williams (1970), cultural norms for a group are:

> *discovered in two main ways. Norms are inferred from* testimony; *that is, people either explicitly state the norm, or from their description of the approved and disapproved conduct for certain situations one can clearly infer implicit norms. Aside from testimony, cultural norms may be discovered by observing spontaneous behavior in real life situations, for example, the meting out of socially supported rewards and penalties . . . (p. 30).*

Labovitz and Hagedorn (1973) indicate, in addition, that norms may be measured indirectly by reference to postulated effects of hypothesized norms, by the use of written documents, and by inference from behavior (p. 292). They go on to point out the well-known tautological fallacy of inferring norms from behavior when testing the influence of norms on behavior.

While the average behavior or conditions of all families combined may be relatively near that prescribed by the cultural norms, cultural norms are not measured in that way. Conclusions about the existence of cultural norms may be based upon testimony regarding standards for behavior and the occurrence of sanctioning behavior but not the behavior being sanctioned.

For example, the fact that poor families have many children may not be used to show that they either desire many children or that their behavior has been influenced by a cultural norm in favor of large families. The occurrence of a high fertility pattern among low-income groups may be simply because of their lack of resources to achieve underlying desires for few children or to conform to norms prescribing small families.

The existence of family size norms must be inferred from sources other than childbearing behavior, especially when we are testing whether a norm is effective in governing behavior. That is, if cultural norms are to be used as independent variables to predict or explain behavior as a dependent variable, they must be separately defined and measured.

Louis Wirth (1947) clearly recognized the importance of the distinction between behavior and norms in his discussion of the study of housing:

> *One of the ways in which we can approach the subject of housing, therefore, is to attempt to discover the specific content of the value it constitutes for different individuals and groups in our society. This can obviously not be judged merely by the kind of housing that people have, for the kind of housing they have is clearly restricted*

> *by other factors than merely their ambitions and desires or the pictures they carry around in their heads of the housing they would like to have, or the kind of housing that is possible in our present state of technological advancement (p. 138).*

Wirth later illustrates his point with this example:

> *In this connection it is important not to mistake the actual state of affairs for the underlying attitudes of people. Just because people live in slums does not mean that they wish to live in them or that they hold housing in low esteem as a value. It may simply be that they are not able to help themselves (p. 138).*

Thus, the fact that the behavior of many families does not conform to a given cultural norm may not be used as evidence either that the norm does not apply to the nonconforming families or that the norm does not exist. By definition, cultural norms (if they are indeed cultural norms) apply to all families in the society who are both culturally and socially integrated. Norms for specific occasions or for specific types of families, of course, only apply on those occasions or to those families.

Failure to conform may occur in at least two ways. The example of home ownership may illustrate the point. Although there is a cultural norm prescribing home ownership in American society, many families do not own homes. Some nonowners may have family norms that favor rental. Other nonowners may simply be unable to achieve their family norm as well as the cultural norm prescribing ownership.

The first type of nonconformance is a case in which cultural norms and subgroup norms, in this case, those of a specific family, do not coincide. Thus some families may simply apply their own family norm, one that favors renting, and ignore the cultural norm for ownership. That many families violate a norm because they do not accept it as applicable to their family does not necessarily have implications for the question of whether or not the cultural norm exists.

The second type of nonconformance can be attributed to external forces that prevent conformance. The families who cannot, but would like to, own may be those who are too poor, have poor credit ratings, are discriminated against because of race or other characteristics, or who are otherwise prevented from owning a home.

The sound measurement of cultural norms requires reference to what people say are the norms and to the kinds of behavior that are rewarded and punished. Testimony about the norms may be obtained from three sources: "lay" members of the society, official representatives, and experts.

Member Testimony

The basic source of knowledge about the norms is what the people say. If there are, indeed, cultural norms regarding the matter in question, then most members of the society can be expected to be able to verbally report that fact. Asking a member of the society, for example, "How many bedrooms should the average family with four children have?," would elicit a normative response; the respondent ordinarily can be expected to answer with his idea of the cultural norm for the number of bedrooms needed by such a family (Morris, 1977). Instead of giving a specific number of bedrooms, however, the respondent may reply, "Well, it depends." Further questioning ("Depends upon what?") will elicit the specific rules to be applied: the rules that govern the allotment of bedrooms to family members on the basis of age and sex.

One source of testimony from members of the society, albeit an inefficient source (Zelditch, 1969, p. 17), is surveys of representative samples of the population. Respondents' answers to the question regarding the proper number of bedrooms for a family with four children could be tabulated. The average response would represent a rather valid measure of the bedroom norm. If the question were asked properly it might also elicit clues regarding the range of deviation permitted under various conditions. Such questions have only recently been included in housing surveys (Morris and Winter, 1976a; Winter and Morris, 1976; Morris and Winter, 1976b; Morris, 1976; Morris and Patrick, 1974).

Prior to the studies just mentioned, American housing norms had not been systematically investigated using survey research methods. Surveys had been undertaken regarding many aspects of housing. Such surveys have tended to include questions either to describe actual housing conditions or to elicit the respondents' desires, aspirations, preferences, or expectations regarding the kind of housing they would like to have. Since aspirations and expectations are desires and preferences about the future, they are not suitable substitutes for direct measures of cultural norms.

Desires are a reflection of the kind of housing a family feels it should have and, therefore, are expressions of family norms. While it may be true that the average of all family norms is very close to the cultural norm, cultural norms are not measured in that manner. In particular, family norms for a given family tend to differ from cultural norms if the family has had a long history of housing that did not meet cultural norms. Such responses are, in part, the *result* of the fact that their housing does not meet the norms. People in very poor housing tend to desire better housing than they have but housing that is somewhat below cultural norms. A family living under crowded conditions is likely to report they would like to have an amount of space that is somewhat higher than the current amount of space available. A similar family that is not crowded is also likely to want additional space.

Preferences, on the other hand, are family norms that have been relaxed because of extenuating circumstances at a specific instant at which the choice or decision must be made about whether or not to buy, rent, or improve a dwelling.

Official Testimony

Another source of testimony that may be used to assess norms is that of "official" representatives of the society. The congressional declaration that the American society should work toward the goal of "a decent home and suitable living environment for every American family" is the official statement of a cultural norm made by representatives of the society. That such a norm is so general as to render it impossible for use to assess the state of housing conditions for research purposes does not detract from its status as a norm.

Congress has stated some rather specific cultural norms by means of legislation, however. An example is the norm embodied in the 1968 Housing Act, which stated that the Secretary of the Department of Housing and Urban Development "shall not approve high-rise elevator projects for families with children unless . . . there is no practical alternative" (CBC, 1970, p. 252).

There is a fine line between official promulgation of norms (translation of informal norms into formal ones) and reports by official representatives as to what they feel are the norms. Both are cases of official testimony about norms. It is likely that the latter often precedes the former. For example, officials in the Department of Housing and Urban Development began to speak and act against high-rise housing for families with children well before legislation formally prohibiting the construction of high-rise housing for other than the elderly was passed by Congress.

Expert Testimony

The third source of testimony, "experts," may be inherently the most susceptible to error (Caplow, 1948, p. 730). It is sometimes difficult to determine if the expert is reflecting what he thinks the norms *ought* to be, or what the norms actually *are.* Testimony of the latter type is acceptable; testimony of the former type cannot be used as a means to measure the content of norms. Experts are traditionally considered objective but often they are not in areas such as housing that are so intimately interwoven with the very fabric of the culture.

There are self-styled housing experts who state, for example, that there is no longer a norm for the owned, single-family home. The norm has changed, they say, because the American population is so very mobile, and does not want to be tied to ownership of a single-family dwelling. And the experts who, of course, own their single-family dwellings, point to the behavior of the construction industry (building more than the usual number of apartments, for example) as evidence that the norm has changed. They may not take the trouble to examine either demographic data concerning the apartment residents, the market constraints preventing home ownership, or the family norms of the people living in the apartments. It would be preferable to attempt to directly measure changes in cultural norms rather than infer changes from construction trends.

Frequently the people consulted about housing by communities and various levels of government are people with highly cultivated aesthetic tastes who find it necessary to propound against the unsophisticated tastes of the masses. Most dangerous to heed are declarations by experts that the norms are wrong and should be changed, perhaps to fit their predilections. Such was Dean's (1945) approach to the norm for home ownership. Yet his scholarly volume, pointing out the risks of home ownership, did little to alter the cultural norm, whatever effect it might have had on government programs (Caplow, 1948).

Echoes of Dean are heard in the voices of experts who state that multifamily housing must become the norm, because America is running out of land or because suburban sprawl is ugly or expensive. Architects, builders, investors, and planning consultants who receive higher fees for longer and taller buildings may be experts in development and construction, but their obvious interest in multifamily housing precludes objectivity. it is likely that the 76 million people who live in suburbia (more than live in either central cities or in rural areas) find suburban sprawl much less ugly than a multifamily apartment building.

A recent government report (RERC, 1974) has shown that single-family suburban sprawl is somewhat more expensive in terms of capital costs and total amount of environmental pollution but possibly lower in psychological costs. The current debate in housing is much concerned with two questions. Can society afford the single-family dwelling and urban sprawl in economic terms? Can it afford the psychic costs of the alternatives? The "experts" have one opinion. The people have another.

Expert testimony about the cultural norms for housing can be useful if the expert is, indeed, able to act as an impartial observer of society. It may be of little value if he or she simply reports current housing behavior. Or, worse yet, if a personal view of what the cultural norms should be is being promoted.

Sanctioning Behavior

The second method for measuring housing norms is through the observation of sanctioning behavior. Which housing conditions are rewarded? Which call forth punishment? Such observations must record both the sanctions applied by other members of the society (including official agencies) and the sanctions applied from within the family. Sanctions *tend* to be applied by representatives of the group or organization that is the source of the norm. Society-wide norms *tend* to be enforced by individuals and agencies that represent the society. Community norms *tend* to be enforced by community representatives, and family-level norms by family members. However, community representatives may enforce cultural norms, and families may administer sanctions in the name of the society and the community.

The Federal Housing Administration's early version of *Minimum Property Standards for One and Two Living Units* (HUD, 1965) established minimum space requirements for eligibility for an FHA-insured mortgage. In effect, the standards "punished" small dwellings and "rewarded" larger ones by the withholding or granting of mortgage guarantees. The income tax laws reward home ownership (Slitor, 1968, p. 17).

At first glance, the origins of official sanctions may appear to be ambiguous in terms of which came first, norms or sanctions. Did the sanction originate first, thereby "creating" the norm? Or was there already a norm, so that, when laws were made the lawmakers simply expressed the norms of society? For example, is the income tax law partially responsible for the strength and existence of the home ownership norm? Or was there already such a norm before the income tax laws were passed? Are the HUD space standards, which have served to set limits on the sizes of millions of new housing units, an expression of an already existing cultural norm? Or have the standards created the conditions?

Lending institutions have long been criticized as "tastemakers," dictating housing standards according to hoped-for high resale values. Mortgages are not often granted for the purchase of homes made from very unusual materials or techniques, homes that are very small or very large, or homes in "changing" neighborhoods. In short, mortgages are not easy to obtain on homes that might be difficult to resell. Are lending institutions "dictating" norms or simply reflecting those that already exist? Clearly the answer lies somewhere between the two positions. Certain types of houses are poor mortgage risks because they are nonnormative. The reason they are nonnormative in part may be that they have not been favored by the practices of lending institutions. The norms influence the practices of lending institutions, and the practices of lending institutions, in turn, not only reinforce the norms, but also limit the production of unusual kinds of housing.

Similar arguments apply to the influence of the trade unions on building codes. Innovative building materials and techniques could be used if there were less stringent building codes. Building codes exist, not only to protect the consumer, but to protect the interests of the trade unions as well.

For many purposes, questions concerning the origin and promulgation of norms and sanctions are irrelevant once the norms and sanctions are in existence. The important questions to ask are, "If there were no building codes, and lending institutions were not preoccupied with resale values, and there were no minimum space standards, would American housing norms or conditions be significantly different? Would norms prescribing the proper amount of space, the quality, tenure, and structure type, and the quality of the neighborhood be any different?" The answer would seem to be "No," for norms and sanctions tend to emerge together. As a norm develops, the rewards and punishments enforcing it tend to accompany it.

A view that closely parallels the argument that norms are "created" by lending institutions, the federal government, the building trades, advertising, and so on, is that the American people really do not know what they want or need in housing because they have not experienced all types of housing arrangements. Such an argument may be countered by reference to Michelson's (1970) concept of "mental congruence," which:

> *exists if an individual thinks that particular spatial patterns will successfully accommodate his personal characteristics, values, and style of life. If a great number of people in a society believes that families can best be raised in suburban space, for example, then there is a state of mental congruence between "familism" and "suburbanism"; this relationship between a physical phenomenon and a social end is a social fact worth noting, even if the relationship is not empirically substantiated as necessary (p. 30).*

Thus, a family with children does not need to experience living on the seventh floor of a high-rise apartment building to know that they would not like it. Nor does an individual family have to rent to know that they would not like being tenants. Nor does a family need to experience living in a plastic house to know that they would rather live in conventionally built housing. Desiring the latter, however, may be due to the fact that plastic housing simply does not fit in with cultural norms or family desires. The family living in a plastic house would be likely to incur negative sanctions from their friends and associates. The family would reject it because it violated the norm rather than because a plastic house could be shown objectively to provide inadequate shelter and space for family living.

The source of norms and sanctions does not matter as much as their content, to whom they apply, who may administer sanctions, and the severity of the sanctions that may be applied. That there are many institutions working to perpetuate the norms is not seen as undesirable. That is the nature of norms. What matters is that norms exist, and, as such, they motivate behavior.

DEFINITIONS

Aberration. Deviation from the usual or the ordinary.

Aspirations. Desires or norms oriented toward the future.

Behavior. The overt action or reaction of a system; to be distinguished from such nonbehavioral concepts as attitudes, aspirations, norms, and housing conditions.

Community norms. Rules prescribing proper conditions and behavior for the people living in a particular community.

Cultural integration. Integration having to do with agreement and/or complementarity of norms within a system or between systems.

Cultural system. The whole that includes all the values and norms within a society; see culture.

Culture. The system of rules, norms, standards, and values for behavior, interaction, and living conditions; the way things "ought" to be.

Expectation. Realistic assessment of future conditions or behavior; not what would be desired for the future, but what is felt to be plausible in the future.

Expert testimony. Reports concerning what the cultural norms are by scholars, social critics, academics, and others with "credentials."

Family norms. A set of rules or ideals for behavior and conditions arising from within the family itself; the family's standards with respect to its own behavior and conditions; the way things "ought" to be as perceived by the family itself.

Formal norms. Written or clearly defined rules, regulations, or codes to which members of the system are required to conform. Laws, codes, and regulations are examples of formal norms.

Informal norms. Unwritten, generally accepted rules for behavior or conditions; to be contrasted with formal norms.

Member testimony. Reports by individuals within the society indicating the cultural norms of the society; what the "person on the street" reports.

Official testimony. Representation of norms by members of government legislative or regulative bodies or others appointed by the society to make or enforce norms; either official promulgation of norms or observations by officials as to what the norms really are.

Overconformance. Complying with norms in the extreme; having more than the norms prescribe.

Permitted deviation. The range of permissible variation around the ideal or norm. Negative sanctions are not administered for behavior that falls within the range of permitted deviation.

Preference. A relaxed norm; the norm applied by a social system to itself in light of actual conditions and extenuating circumstances. Preferences, by definition, make the permissible deviation permissible.

Sanctioning behavior. Actions that reward conformance to or punish deviation from the norms.

Sanctions. Rewards or punishments that reinforce the process of socialization and help maintain the social system's norms. Sanctions may be positive (rewards for conformance) or negative (punishments for deviation or nonconformance).

Social. Referring to the behavior and life conditions of members of a society; the way things are.

Social integration. The behavioral and interactional system of a subgroup is meshed with and congruent with that of the greater society or with other subgroups within that society.

Socialization. The process by which the society teaches its members to adopt the normative system already extant; the acquisition of the social system's rules for behavior and being, usually by the younger or newer members, especially children.

Society. The combination of both the social and cultural spheres; the total sociocultural system.

Subcultures. Smaller groups within a culture that are socially but not culturally integrated with the whole; subgroups that have norms and other rules that differ markedly from those of the society as a whole.

Subgroups. Smaller groups within the culture that are both culturally and socially integrated with the whole; groups distinguished from the whole by characteristics other than separate normative systems.

Tautological fallacy. Making an unsound conclusion by inferring norms *from* behavior when testing the influence of norms *on* behavior; the cause (norm) is erroneously inferred from the effect (behavior).

Underconformance. Actual conditions that are below the range of permissible deviation; having less than the norms prescribe.

Values. General guidelines for evaluation of goals (norms). Values are *not* the norms themselves; they are much more general, and serve to organize norms which in turn govern specific behaviors and conditions.

Chapter 3
The Family and Its Housing

> Its curious age and sex composition make it an inefficient work group, a poor planning committee, an unwieldy play group, and a group of uncertain congeniality. Its leadership is shared by two relatively inexperienced amateurs for most of their incumbency, new to the roles of spouse and parent. They must work with a succession of disciples having few skills and lacking in judgment under conditions which never seem to remain stable long enough to bring about a settled organization. Reuben Hill*

Housing behavior of families is the focus of the present analysis because in the United States the family bears the responsibility for obtaining housing for its members (Hill, 1971). The family makes the decisions about the allocation of money, time, and other resources to housing, food, clothing, etc. This chapter and the one that follows present the conceptual model of the family and the housing adjustment and adaptation processes. In this chapter, the family is defined and assumptions are made about the family as a social system, including a discussion of trends in the viability of the family as a social organization in the 1970s. The assumptions are explicated in terms of the systemic functional model, introduced in Chapter 1. These assumptions are based on the ways in which the structure of the American family and the processes that occur within it are conceptualized.

THE FAMILY AS A SOCIAL SYSTEM

The assumptions of the present model are typical in a systemic functional model of the family (Sztompka, 1974). The first four assumptions, plurality, wholeness, integration, and boundedness, are interrelated. The family is made up of individual members, their characteristics, and the interrela-

* From "Modern Systems Theory and the Family: A Confrontation" by Reuben Hill (*Social Science Information* 10), p. 14.

tionships among them (plurality). The aggregation of individual members and their interrelationships constitutes an entity that has properties not inherent in the individual members (wholeness).

All individual members of the family affect and are affected by all other members (integration). While all members are assumed to have direct influences on all other members, and to be directly influenced by all others, there may be indirect relationships as well. This assumption is more restrictive than the integration assumption for most other social organizations. The typical integration assumption only requires indirect relations among the elements as a minimum. The relationships within the family are closer than the relationships to elements outside the family (boundedness). Although elements of the family may have relationships with elements from other systems, the boundary of the family is clear and relatively unambiguous.

The next four assumptions, self-regulation, double-level regulation, rationality, and goal integration, are assumptions about how the family functions in pursuit of its goals, one of which is housing. The family's overall goal, or preferred state, is the global concept of family well-being. Mechanisms within the family keep it directed toward the maintenance of well-being (self-regulation). There are partial preferred states which, when met, contribute to the achievement of family well-being. One such partial preferred state is assumed to be housing that meets cultural and family norms. Thus, for present purposes, the family is seen to be concerned with goals at two levels (double-level regulation): the attainment of housing (one of the partial preferred states), and the relative contribution of that housing to its overall well-being (the global preferred state).

The family selects means with a view to their effectiveness in meeting goals at both levels (rationality). In addition, at least a portion of the goals of individual family members are such that, if met, they serve to meet goals of the family (goal integration). Thus, there is a self-conscious unit within the family that chooses relatively effective means to achieve global and partial goals of the family. The process of choosing goals tends to be effective and the search for well-being is successful in part because family and individual goals are integrated. Analyses of family managerial behavior (Gross, Crandall, and Knoll, 1973; Deacon and Firebaugh, 1975) have focused on the concept of a managerial subsystem to refer to the processes implied in this group of assumptions.

To analyze the housing behavior of families within the context of the community and the larger society, three additional assumptions are needed: plurality of subsystems, heterogeneity of subsystems, and boundary interchange. Families are subunits of larger social systems, communities, which in turn are part of an even larger system, the society (plurality of subsystems). Families may also be subsystems of subcultures, which cut across communities.

The subsystems (family, community, subculture) may differ greatly among themselves (heterogeneity of subsystems). One of the key analyses deals with the differences among families in family functioning and is presented later in this chapter. Another analysis covers differences and similarities among subgroups regarding housing norms (Chapter 15).

The well-being of families, including the achievement of normative housing conditions, depends on the welfare and activities of other parts of the community and the society (boundary interchange). Thus, community decisions made regarding housing conditions can both help and hinder individual families in their quest for housing. This assumption refers to the relative openness or closure of the family system, a topic which is discussed in detail later in this chapter.

Summarizing the basic assumptions, then, the family is seen as a system of interrelated elements which is directively organized and self-regulating. At least some of the purposes of individual family members, when accomplished, meet one or more of the needs or preferred states of the family as a whole. These may be partial or global preferred states.

As outlined in Chapter 2, the goals of the individual and the family are seen to have their source in the norms, learned in the process of socialization. These norms originate at the society, community, or family level, and, when appropriate, at the subcultural level. The norms are enforced through the administration of sanctions at one or more of the levels.

FAMILIES AND HOUSEHOLDS

In the same way that housing may be conceived of as an actual, empirical object as well as a set of norms that define what that object *should* be, the family may be conceived of as an empirical family or as a normative prescription of what the family should be. For the purposes of analyzing the process of family housing adjustment behavior, it is crucial that the analysis focus on empirical families. These are the units that engage in housing-related behavior. Family housing adjustment and adaptation behavior is performed by all families, not just families that meet the cultural norms for families. If the focus were not on actual families, one could be placed in the position of ignoring important housing problems by defining deviant families out of the analysis. Omitted would be those cases where normative housing deficits accompanied by severe constraints might force the breakup of the marital couple as a response to a housing deficit. This kind of case must be included in the analysis.

A distinction must be made between the study of traditional family social problems and the analysis of the problems of families. Traditional family social problems derive from the definition of the family (Ball, 1972,

p. 295). Such definitions of the family are normative in order that departures from the definition be denotable as problems: broken families, common law marriages, etc.

When the focus of study is the problems of families (their housing, for example), a definition of the family is needed that would define a family both with and without a housing problem. It is necessary to ensure that problem families are included within a working definition of the family (Weigert and Thomas, 1971, pp. 189–90).

Among the differences between the two orientations is the fact that one deals primarily with relations among family members (its internal functioning). The other orientation is concerned primarily with the relations of the family to other groups or institutions such as the community, the housing market, and the like. The two complement each other. It is important to know about the effectiveness of the internal family organization as it may block the family's relations with other families and other organizations and impede their ability to obtain housing.

The overall orientation to the family used in this book is based on the developmental approach (Hill and Hansen, 1960; Rodgers, 1962; Rodgers, 1964). This approach to the study of the family is drawn primarily from the structural-functional school of sociology. Thus, the nature of the family in a given society is seen in terms of its structure and the processes occurring within it as its functions are performed.

Family Structure

The use of the term "family" rather than "household" implies a structure including at least two related persons. The family as a kin group is similar to Reiss' (1965) conceptualization. Since the term family appears to imply something about actual or potential childbearing, the definition of the family used here, as a minimum, includes either a couple with an actual or potential childbearing record, or two generations related by direct descent, either actual or legal. Thus, a family may consist of a married couple, a couple living together, a mother and child, a father and a child, a grandmother and a grandchild, or a grandfather and a grandchild. The child in each case could be natural or adopted. (For a similar, although more open, view see Weigert and Thomas, 1972.)

The focus on families rather than households implies that housing-related behavior of individuals not in families is excluded from the analysis. To some degree, it is. There is a discussion of the housing norms of single individuals and childless couples (Chapters 5, 6, and 7), and their housing behavior (Chapters 8, 9, and 10). The housing needs and behavior of the elderly also are analyzed (Chapter 11). Nevertheless, the chief focus is primarily the family, its housing norms and deficits, and its subsequent behavior through the life cycle.

The reason for this focus and the exclusion of households that consist wholly of unrelated individuals is that family units tend to endure in time while other groupings are less likely to continue as a unit after the current residence becomes inappropriate. The housing adjustment behavior of the members of such households is likely to be conducted independently of one another to a greater extent than in families.

The U.S. Census Bureau defines a *household* in terms of "living arrangements." Living arrangements are either in *housing units* or in *group quarters.* The group of persons living in a housing unit is defined as the household. Group quarters are living arrangements with five or more persons unrelated to the head or with no designated head and six or more unrelated persons. Such living arrangements include hospitals, institutions, military barracks, dormitories, and the like (USBC, 1972b, pp. App5–6).

Since a household is defined as the people living in a housing unit, there may be households in housing units that consist of as many as four people unrelated to the head. The key is in the definition of housing unit, which is a dwelling place with either a separate kitchen or a separate entrance. Thus, the census definition of the household sidesteps the issue of whether the household represents a social organization for purposes other than current housing arrangements.

The members of the household are classified according to their relationship to the head. One person in each household is designated as head by the members of the household. If a woman is designated as head and her husband is living in the household, he is substituted as head of the household by Census Bureau procedures for ease of tabulation.

There are two types of household heads: (1) the head of a family who is designated as head and (2) a primary individual designated as head. The difference is that a head of a family is living with at least one related person in the household while a primary individual as head is living with nonrelated persons. Thus a household can include a group of unrelated individuals sharing the same dwelling.

The census definition of the *family* is: "two or more persons living in the same household who are related by blood, marriage, or adoption" (USBC, 1970, p. 101). Two or more nuclear families (husband, wife, and children, if any) would be counted as members of the primary family if any member of the second family is related to the head of the household. The extra nuclear families not related to the head would simply be counted as unrelated persons.

The household may be a meaningful unit for some analyses. But it is not, typically, the housing adjustment and adaptation unit. Families making housing decisions tend to make them as a unit. A decision to move by a family usually means that all members move together to the same new dwelling. Members of households who are not members of the same family may make separate housing decisions and move separately. Or they may move simultaneously to different dwellings. College roommates do not tend to make housing decisions as a unit, nor do young unmarried persons sharing an apartment.

There are, of course, groups of unrelated individuals who share a residence and whose housing behavior resembles that of families bound by kinship relations. Unmarried, like-sex, older adult friends may develop such strong ties that their household becomes a unit that persists in a time orientation greater than is implied in housing adjustment. Their housing behavior would be of interest, but there is little information available. Census materials cannot be utilizied for it is impossible to distinguish between *groups* of unrelated individuals and *families* of unrelated individuals. Such groups have not been the focus of other housing research, either. Thus their norms and behavior cannot be effectively analyzed.

Family Functions

Reiss (1965) concluded that the only universal function of the nuclear family was nurturant socialization: training the children to become members of the family and the society while filling the child's biological and psychological needs. The idea did not originate completely with Reiss. Elmer (1932) noted that for the family, socialization is the "most universal and far reaching function" (p. 5). It is not crucial to the present study that nurturant socialization be cross-nationally universal since only the United States is under consideration. It is important to the overall theory that nurturant socialization is performed primarily by the family in American society.

The present definition of the family requires that when there are children there be a real, fictive, or surrogate parent to perform the nurturant socialization functions including the teaching of cultural norms about family living and housing. Indeed, it would appear that the only effective means of passing the culture on from one generation to the next is to have a kin-based social structure that teaches the norms while providing love and warmth (nurturant socialization). The key *function* is nurturant socialization; the key *structure* is the family as previously defined.

In the United States, one of the functions of the family is to obtain housing that will, among other things, permit effective socialization. Thus the attainment of housing is one of the partial preferred states that contribute to family well-being, the global preferred state. Nurturant socialization is a process by which the criteria used in judging the presence-absence or quality of achieved states vis-à-vis preferred states are taught. Successful socialization perpetuates housing as a partial preferred state, for it is one of the means of ensuring the continuation of the norms and values that guide American families in solving their housing problems.

Obviously, families without children to socialize engage in housing behavior. Also, nonfamily households sometimes appear family-like in their housing behavior. In the long run, however, the cultural framework within which housing behavior occurs depends for its continuity on procreation and socialization.

The Developmental Definition of the Family

Concepts from the developmental approach that are applicable to the present analysis include the view of the family as a "semiclosed system of interacting personalities" (Rodgers, 1962, pp. 33–34). Burgess (1926) originated the concept of the family as a "unity of mutually interacting personalities." The notion of system, added later, generally denotes a bounded aggregate of subunits that may be characterized by a set of relations among themselves. The relationships that exist include the roles that are assigned each member (Rodgers, 1962). That the interacting members of the family are personalities implies that they are humans with needs and dispositions that have arisen partly out of their individual psychobiological development and partly out of the operation of the socialization processes in the family. Thus the family development concept of the family makes the assumptions of systemic functional analysis of pluralism, wholeness, integration, and boundedness by choosing certain values or ranges of values on the continua implied in each assumption.

Such a view of the family, of course, does not differentiate families from other bounded social organizations with interaction among the individual members (Zimmerman, 1947; Ball, 1972). It is necessary to couple that view of the family with (1) a statement of the types of members that must be included in a social group in order to meet the definition of a family: that they be related by blood, marriage, descent, or adoption, and (2) a statement of the key function(s) performed by the family: nurturant socialization.

There are a number of implications of the notion that the family is a semiclosed system that were elaborated by Parsons (1955). First, the family in American society virtually never is an independent microsociety but operates as a specialized subunit of the society (Parsons, 1955, p. 35). Second, parents act in their socializing roles both as members of the family and as members of various other societal units. Third, parents socialize children into familial roles and into roles in other groups (Parsons, 1955, p. 35).

That it is a semiclosed system implies there are inputs into the system from outside (boundary interchange). Those inputs are primarily in three forms. Cultural norms prescribe the appropriate behavior of the individual members of the family and the family as a unit. Sanctions for behavior are prescribed by the norms. Societal rewards (salary, for example) for other kinds of behavior produce resources that may or may not be used to conform to housing norms. That the family is partially closed implies that the family itself may also have its own set of norms that may not coincide with those of the culture. Not all families are equally closed, of course. In fact an important characteristic of families may be the degree to which they are influenced by external forces.

There are a number of points in the developmental approach as presented in the literature, however, that do not seem to be fruitfully applicable to the analysis of housing adjustment. The definition of the family most often discussed in this approach seems to be the normative rather than the empirical family. Such a practice is appropriate when the focus of analysis is the social problems of the family. There are family social problems to the extent that there are departures from the normative family. For example, the family life cycle is conventionally conceived of as beginning with a wedding (Rowe, 1966, p. 219). However, it is frequently the case that couples live together and engage in the same processes and functions as married couples. Childbearing by the married couple sometimes appears to be assumed, as evidenced by the relatively minor attention paid to the elaboration of life cycle stages for childless couples (Rowe, 1966, p. 213). In addition, the developmental approach, as practiced to date, generally has emphasized the study of the welfare and behavior of individual members of the family rather than of the family as a unit (Hill and Hansen, 1960; Rowe, 1966, p. 213).

INTEGRATION, PROBLEM SOLVING, AND HOUSING ADJUSTMENT

Differences in various aspects of family structure and processes explain why some families are able to engage successfully in housing adjustment behavior and others are not, even though they have similar incomes and family composition. Intrafamilial constraints that can affect the process are those concerned with the character of the family and its skills at decision making and problem solving. These are important since family housing adjustment is a problem-solving process that entails relatively complex decision making at several points. The constraints can impede or facilitate the family's attempts to maintain a balance between housing norms and their current housing. Some of the more important dimensions of family functioning and their relation to housing-related family responses are discussed in this section.

Family Integration

One of the most important concepts used to describe the character of the family is the degree of family integration. In general, family integration has to do with four factors. What is the extent of concordance among family norms for the various partial goals and the well-being goals? How much congruence is there between that set of goals and the family's norms and preferences for the means to accomplish those goals? To what extent is there agreement among family members about what the family's norms for goals and means are? How much concordance is there among individual goals and between individual goals and family goals? This set of four aspects of integration refer basically to the cognitive and evaluative aspects of integration. There is also an affective aspect of integration concerning whether the family members have strong emotional ties to one another and to the family as a unit.

Families with a high degree of integration along all four dimensions will be better able to successfully accomplish family housing adjustment (Hill, 1963). Time and energy will not have to be devoted to the task of integration, but can be directed primarily toward the achievement of normative housing.

Adaptability

Although adaptability as an attribute of a family's effectiveness as a functioning unit is not directly a part of integration, it has an important role to play in problem solving. When severe problems arise, adaptability may permit the maintenance of integration. In the absence of adaptability, highly integrated families fall apart. Angell's (1936) typological study of responses of families to the loss of income due to the depression made extensive use of the two concepts, "integration" and "adaptability." In general, higher levels of integration produced effective responses to the loss of income, as did higher levels of adaptability.

These two concepts would seem to relate to the present analysis at two very different points. Families who are more highly integrated would be likely to be able to successfully engage in family housing adjustment when the housing deficits are within a reasonable range of solution. When the deficits are great and constraints severe, more creative responses are called for and adaptable families may find it easier to employ unusual means to obtain housing or to alter their family norms. It appears, however, that extremely high levels of integration reduce adaptability. In addition, moderately high integration combined with an ability to adapt family norms in response to serious problems represents a kind of optimum level of organization for problem solving.

Specialization

Integration may require role specialization including cognitive and evaluative recognition of the legitimacy of the specialized roles. One of the early occurrences in groups that endure for any length of time is role specialization among the members (Bales and Slater, 1955, p. 259). While the focus of attention is the functioning of existing groups (families and communities) rather than the genesis of groups, specialization seems to happen in response to the occurrence of problems. Differentiation of skills and orientations is required when too many problems occur for the entire group to deal directly with all of them simultaneously (Bales and Slater, 1955, p. 300).

Problems faced by families can be divided into two classes, those involving instrumental behavior and orientations for solution and those requiring expressive behavior or orientations. According to Zelditch (1955), task or instrumentally oriented roles refer to:

> *the manipulation of the object-world in order to provide facilities for the achievement of goals defined within the system (p. 310).*

Similarly he defines expressive role behavior as:

> *laughing, playing, release of inhibited emotions, the expression of affection for each other, a warmth and a symbolization of common membership through supportive, accepting behavior (Zelditch, 1955, p. 310).*

With regard to instrumental and expressive role behavior, there tend to be two modes of specialization, specialization among persons and specialization over time. Some family members specialize in expressive and some instrumental behavior. In Western society the father and other males tend to be instrumentalists and the mother and other females expressionists. It is important to the smooth functioning of the family to have a clear-cut and stable pattern of specialization between expressive and instrumental matters. The members of the family should not be in doubt about who is responsible for warmth and love under given conditions or who is responsible for discipline or knowledge. The point is not that the mother should always be expressive and the father instrumental, but that family members should not have to expend great effort to decide who to turn to in a given situation (Zelditch, 1955, p. 12).

Time-wise specialization makes it possible for specialized persons to engage in the opposite kind of behavior. Sometimes the entire family plays. Sometimes they all engage in work. Sometimes fathers become lovers. Sometimes mothers become disciplinarians. Specialized persons must have the opportunity to engage in other behavior to maintain their specialized position. The instrumental person must be able to engage in expressive behavior within the family in order to receive enough love and affection to maintain his or her authority. The expressive person must have enough instrumental responsibility to maintain the right to be the prime expressivist in the family (Bales and Slater, 1955, p. 305).

Rewards that accrue for family housing adjustment are both instrumental (living in a good school district, receiving a job promotion) and expressive (achieving the respect of others, developing self-respect within the family). Such adjustment requires both kinds of behavior and orientation on the part of family members. Someone must be able to deal with the realities of brokers, mortgage bankers, and landlords, while a certain amount of expressive behavior is necessary to assure that the interests of all family members are considered. The family that has developed a degree of specialization with which it is comfortable will be better able to deal with a normative housing deficit.

Solidarity and Consensus

The extent to which the members identify with the family group and feel loyalty toward it and its goals may influence its effectiveness in housing decisions. A concept to describe relatively permanent states of agreement or commonality within the family is solidarity (Jansen, 1952). The prime function of the family is nurturant socialization. In that regard, the family must produce subsequent generations that know the family and cultural norms and feel those norms are legitimate and deserving of conformance:

> *Lasting changes in behavior require the construction and internalization of a common culture, and the new elements of the common culture have to acquire a certain reward value in themselves. The love attachment can provide an element of immediate reward, whereas the reward that might eventually come from an improved relation to the environment may come entirely too late to produce learning (Bales and Slater, 1955, p. 304).*

A concrete manifestation of solidarity is the family's ability to develop consensus about the existence and nature of a family housing problem and the appropriate behavior to use in attempting a solution. Consensus is similar to the concept of solidarity. However, solidarity is general while consensus is specific. Consensus by nature is issue-based in that there has to be something to have consensus about. Consensus is simply obtaining enough agreement to make a decision or solve a problem at a given point or interval in time.

Scheff (1967) points to the need to measure the degree of consensus. He indicates that consensus is of two types: (1) simple agreement and (2) common orientation or a cognitive aspect and an affective or evaluative aspect. Thus, the members of a family may agree that their family has a housing problem. They may or may not have a common feeling that something should be done about it. The development of consensus in a housing decision or any decision is complicated by the fact that not only does each member have his particular orientation to the situation, but also, each member has a perception of each of the other's orientations which may or may not be correct (Scheff, 1967). It is conceivable, for example, that family members might give one another the impression that they like the present housing in order not to appear to complain. In reality, though, all members of the family as individuals would like to move.

Conventionality

The conventionality concept (Morris, 1969) refers to the similarity of family norms to community and cultural norms. A society with a high level of integration would have a high percentage of conventional families. A more limited kind of conventionality would be the similarity of family norms to social class norms or norms of other subgroups of which the family is a member.

It seems obvious that families with unconventional family norms for housing would find it difficult to find housing that fits their norms. That would especially be true in old established communities where housing norms had been stable for many years. On the other hand, some groups of families, the poor, for example, might have compromised their family norms enough that rather poor quality housing might produce rather high levels of housing satisfaction. Their unconventionality might make housing easier to obtain, as a large amount of semideteriorated housing is available.

Decision-making and Problem-solving Skills

The past history of the family with regard to its experience with housing and its experience operating as a family makes a difference in the way in which the family deals with a normative housing deficit. To some degree, problem-solving skills are related to the family's level of integration, adaptability, degree of specialization, solidarity, and conventionality. An additional dimension seems to be related to the family's problem-solving history. Success in dealing with previous problems generally results in greater skill in solving later problems. Further, successful problem solving tends to raise expectations about future success and to raise the standards for judging the problem to be solved. Family norms rise as a function of previous success (Tallman, 1971, p. 336).

Laboratory experiments have pointed up the importance of the history of the family in problem solving. The development of a common culture within the problem-solving group is of major importance in these experiments (Bales and Slater, 1955). Since families endure much longer than laboratory experiments, their development of an internal family culture reaches very high levels (Bales and Slater, 1955). Such an internal family culture wields a great deal of influence on problem-solving behavior.

The growth of the common culture within a family is closely analogous to learning by individuals. The family culture consists of two areas of importance to the present analysis. The first is the family's housing norms. The second is family functioning norms for use in decision making and problem solving including housing adjustment situations. Successful family problem solving serves to teach and reinforce the family's norms for family functioning and for housing. Socialization of the young is fostered through their observation of the application of cultural and family norms in problem situations.

A great deal of research has shown that there are class differences in problem-solving ability. Such findings suggest that greater middle-class verbal ability and other skills account for the difference in ability to solve some kinds of problems (Straus, 1968; Deutsch, 1963; Geismar and LaSorte, 1964; Hess and Shipman, 1965). An important aspect of problem solving appears to be the amount of communication between husband and wife (Wilkening, 1954 and 1958; Blood and Wolfe, 1960; Hill, Stycos, and Back, 1959). Modes of communication and decision-making modes, of course, are subject to cultural norms and may vary among class levels and other social groupings (Wilkening, 1958, p. 187).

Working- and lower-class people apparently solve problems to some extent with nonverbal and motor skills instead of communication (Miller and Riessman, 1964; Kohn, 1963; Hurvitz, 1964; Rainwater, Coleman, and Handel, 1959; Straus, 1968). Tallman and Miller (1974, p. 15) indicate that because those studies were predominantly made on individuals solving problems the results may not apply to families. Groups have been shown to be superior to isolated individuals in solving some kinds of problems under some conditions (Kelley and Thibaut, 1969; Zajonc, 1965).

A striking finding of recent research shows that problem solving is most effective when the family functions in its problem solving in accord with the family authority norms of its class. In an experiment studying problem solving by families in contrived puzzle-like situations, Tallman and Miller (1974) found verbal ability to be unrelated to problem-solving success. Instead, problem-solving superiority among middle-class families was found to result primarily from the location of decision-making leadership and power. Thus, the differences among classes in some kinds of problems, at least, are not the result of greater ability to converse and exchange information about the problem to be solved.

Postulating differing leadership norms for middle- and working-class families, they hypothesize that families with leadership patterns in accord with class-specific norms would be superior problem solvers. They found that middle-class families with shared decision making were superior to middle-class families in which husband or wife usually made the decisions. Blue-collar families in which the husband made the decisions were superior to other blue-collar patterns.

Except in the case of husband-dominant families, middle-class families were superior to blue-collar families. Thus, blue-collar families appear to have norms favoring husband dominance while middle-class families tend toward shared decision making. Effective group problem solving by the family is related to having leadership patterns that are congruent with class norms.

The family's ability to achieve and implement decisions may not depend so much on the particular style (patriarchal or democratic for example) as on the fit of the family style with cultural norms and with the expectations of the various family members. Housing decisions are more likely than others to both deeply affect all family members and require their participation to produce satisfactory housing behavior. Under such conditions it is likely that middle-class families whose norms are likely to favor egalitarian decision making would be more effective in the solution of housing problems.

THE FAMILY AS A CHANGING INSTITUTION

In addition to dealing with potential change in the norms for housing, included in various places throughout the book, it is important to briefly examine changing norms for family functioning in a broad historical sense and relate them to changing norms for housing. The basic question is the extent to which the family as a basic societal institution is fading out. If, indeed, recent analyses are correct (Orleans and Wolfson, 1970; Cogswell, 1975), then an analysis of housing behavior that focuses on married couples, their children, and the traditional socialization process will be obsolete in only a few years.

Views of the Family as a Declining Institution

It is widely acknowledged that the family as an institution has been changing more or less continuously since at least as early as the beginning of the industrial revolution. The first social scientists to study the family concerned themselves with the change and evolution of family patterns. Apparently in response to the great amount of (then) recent change in social institutions and accumulating improvements in social scientific theory and methods, the latter half of the nineteenth century produced many works on the evolution and change of the family (Bachofen, 1861; Comte, 1875; Grosse, 1896; LePlay, 1855; MacLennan, 1886; Morgan, 1877; Spencer, 1896; Starcke, 1889; Westermarck, 1908).

The early researchers concerned themselves primarily with evolutionary schemes to explain the development of modern family institutions such as the conjugal family, from prehistoric patterns of matriarchal and patriarchal extended family systems. (See Goode, 1963, pp. 7–10 for a detailed discussion of the conjugal family as a type.) Their work was frequently organismic in that it attempted to explain the evolution of social institutions through biological analogies.

The evolutionary-organismic models proved to be difficult to substantiate empirically. The view of the family began to change to an emphasis on the structural and functional integration of family institutions with other societal units and with the society as a whole (Hobhouse, Wheeler, and Ginsberg, 1915; Grosse, 1896). The family was increasingly analyzed to ascertain whether its structure (e.g., extended or nuclear) and its functions were harmonious with the needs of the society. To a lesser extent, the society was examined to determine whether its structure and functioning served the needs of the family (Goode, 1963).

The early twentieth-century sociologists increasingly began to question the evolutionary, organismic, and strict functionalist theories. They began to focus their attention less on the family as an institution serving societal ends and more on the functions the family performs for the individual members. They noted the loss of functions that were primarily economic and social to other institutions. Zimmerman (1947) refers to this line of thinking as the negationist school and finds its roots in Spencer (1896), Starcke (1889), Westermarck (1908), MacLennan (1886) and Engels (1902). He describes the school as follows:

> *Negation and evolution in the theory of family sociology have held that progress, or the constant linear or stair-step movement toward human betterment, consisted in the dropping of family bonds and the perpetual creation of new types of families (Zimmerman 1947, p. 22).*

Currently, evolutionism has been discredited and ostensibly rejected. However, most family sociology continues in the negationist tradition which emphasizes the simplification of family structure and the loss of functions to other institutions. Indeed there has been a recent upsurge of alarmist predictions of the demise of the family.

The negationist school of family sociology includes two groups. One group sees the family as passive in the evolutionary process with economic and other institutions leading the way. The other consists of activists who see the family as causative and leading other institutions in societal progress. The passivists include the Marxists who grant primacy to economic and technological factors (Engels, 1902). The activists include Spencer (1896) and others. The family is seen by both groups to have changed from a unit performing multiple functions to a much narrower companionship and affection-oriented unit (Burgess and Locke, 1945; Elmer, 1932; Sorokin, 1941).

There are both logical and empirical flaws in the negationist school of thought. The logical flaw is that a unidirectional evolution away from family bonds and obligations toward individual freedom and gratification logically concludes with no family at all. The implication for housing of the negationist family evolution hypothesis would be that typical dwelling unit types needed in Western societies would go through several stages. One stage might have been characterized by large complex housing units possibly arranged in compounds to fit large extended families. The next stage might be as today: single-family detached housing to fit the needs of conjugal families with children and a large minority of smaller more compact units consisting of apartments and mobile homes. The final stage would be characterized by some kind of dormitory housing for that period when the family would have died out completely. While scholars seldom entertain the expectation that such a trend would actually culminate that way, Orleans and Wolfson (1970, p. 49) speculate along these lines.

Achieving an objective view of current trends in the American family is difficult. It is a challenge to separate temporary fads in the way opinion leaders speak and write about the family from the way the family really is. Very striking demographic changes have clearly taken place in recent years. Births have very rapidly moved from a low during the 1930s to a high during the 1940s and the 1950s to a lower level in the 1970s than during the depression. The changes in birth rates have produced large changes in the number of young adults about a generation later. (The mean length of a generation is about 25 years in the United States.) The very high proportion of the population in this age group makes whatever fad they are currently pursuing seem like a major social force.

The growing proportion of one-person households in the society might be thought of as a social trend consistent with the family negationist hypothesis. The same might be said of the rising divorce rate. The argument loses a great deal of its force when the rising *proportion* of young adults (who are likely candidates for single-person households just before marriage) is noted. Similarly, the very high rate of remarriage among divorced persons should be noted alongside the fact that marriages last longer now than in earlier years. Marriage breakup caused by the death of a spouse has declined because mortality rates have fallen. A rising divorce rate has substituted in part for the declining mortality rate.

An empirical flaw in this argument is that actual cultural change has been now in one direction, then in another. At times the family takes on new functions, even retaking lost ones. It then becomes stronger and more central in the society. At other times it loses functions and declines relative to other institutions. In addition, the empirical evidence shows that the family is at times active, and, at other times, passive, in the process of societal change. The evidence suggests, however, that more often than not it is passive (Ogburn, 1954). A more appropriate view, therefore, is of the family as an adjustment mechanism for changes in the society.

The Family as a Societal Adjustment Mechanism

An understanding of change in the institution of the family as a facet of overall cultural change is important for the present analysis. Such an understanding is needed because changes in norms that relate to housing would require a certain degree of change in the family or at least flexibility in order to permit change in housing norms. Perhaps more demanding is the requirement that the family change in response to changing technological, economic, and social conditions in order to conform to relatively unchanging housing norms.

A balanced view of the family in relation to the society has been taken recently by some theorists (Nye, 1974). They view the family as an institution that, when needed, becomes stronger and performs new functions or recedes and permits other institutions to take over its functions. It may lead the society in new directions by socializing the children in ways that help them face the problems of a changing society (Inkeles, 1955).

For example, Hill (1949) emphasized the role the family plays as a kind of counterwheel in social change:

> *For too long, American families have been called upon to take up the slack in a poorly integrated social order. For too long, the family has been ignored in social planning, and the strains are telling. The modern family lives in a greater state of tension because it is the great burden carrier of the social order, the bottleneck through which all troubles pass (p. 355).*

It is not at all clear that any important social problems would be solved by shifting such a burden from the family. The family bears a burden of caring for the individual because other roles the individual plays in society are burdensome. The individual is not being freed from family ties in the negationist sense but, instead, is ever more dependent upon the family precisely because the society needs or requires it to be so. The fact that the family performs that function can only be seen as valuable to the society and to individual family members.

Vincent (1966) analyzes the family as "an adaptive institution" that changes in response "externally to the demands of other social institutions and internally to the needs of its own members" (p. 29). Although he does not see the family as the main source or cause of social change, he does see it as permitting social change by its great adaptability. The family:

> *to a greater degree and more frequently than is true of other major institutions, facilitates social change by adapting its structure and*

activities to fit the changing needs of the society and other social institutions (Vincent, 1966, p. 29).

The family is able to provide such adaptability for two reasons. First, it has a strategic position in providing for the affectional-expressive needs of family members, especially in times of social change when affectional needs would seem to be great. Second, it has a prime position in socialization of family members, both child and adult, in order that the family members learn the attitudes and behavior needed for changed conditions. Thus, the family is sometimes cause and sometimes effect in the process of cultural change.

Individual families may change in various ways while the society manifests the aggregate effects of all families and may or may not exhibit a longer-range trend. Farber (1964) and Yost and Adamek (1974) focused on the culture-wide trend. Change during the lifetime of individual families may occur as the result of normal developmental processes in the absence of cultural change. Such changes have been the focus of much of the efforts of family sociologists, beginning with Loomis (1936) and culminating in the efforts of Reuben Hill and his associates (Hill, 1971; Rodgers, 1962; Rodgers, 1964; Hill and Hansen, 1960).

It can be concluded that the norms for family functioning have been changing. Many of the changes have occurred in response to societal needs arising from urbanization and industrialization. The change has been neither linear nor unidirectional but has reversed in direction from time to time.

The implication of this trend is that housing similar to that needed now will be needed in the future for some time. That is to say, housing norms are unlikely to change drastically. Self-contained units that may or may not be detached will be required to house a family largely organized in terms of the conjugal pair and their children, much as today. The institution of the family may change from time to time in the functions it typically performs for the society. Perhaps the specific functions it performs for the family members will change, too. It is not, however, expected to disappear or become unrecognizable.

The *need* for housing similar to that which exists now, therefore, is unlikely to disappear. If the patterns of the past hundred or more years may be taken as indicative of the patterns that will continue into the future it is most likely that the typical housing unit will be a single-family detached unit owned by the family that occupies it. That family will probably consist of husband and wife and one or two children. Some couples will be too old or too young to have children at home or will have chosen not to have children as some couples do now.

There is as yet no sound basis for expecting great increases in unusual family or household types such as communes or individuals living alone aside from demographic trends relating primarily to the rising and falling birth rates of the past 20 years. Higher density housing, smaller units, and changes in neighborhood patterns may become more or less prevalent to serve the needs of these groups as they rise and fall as a proportion of the population. However, the prediction that housing needs for given types of of families will change greatly is unlikely.

DEFINITIONS

Adaptability. Capability for creating responses or structural changes within the social system to resolve imbalances within the system or between the system and its environment.

Boundary interchange. The assumption that the well-being of families depends upon the welfare and activity of other parts of the community and the society.

Boundedness. The assumption that the relationships within the family are closer than the relationships to elements outside the family.

Consensus. Concrete, issue-based agreement among elements of a social system to a degree which makes possible decision making and problem solving at a given point in time.

Conventionality. Similarity between family norms and community and cultural norms.

Decision making. The cognitive process by which a family chooses specific adjustment or adaptive behavior.

Demographic changes. Increases or decreases in the total population and in the proportion of the population in various categories.

Double-level regulation. The mechanism by which the family attempts to direct itself to achieving both the global preferred state and partial preferred states, e.g., the attainment of suitable housing and overall well-being.

Egalitarian. Equality of power and influence in decision making and other family processes.

Empirical. Referring to concrete real world phenomena; to be contrasted with conceptual. Concepts are abstract representations in the human mind of empirical objects. Empirical is often used to refer to research; empirical research uses concrete data; conceptual or theoretical aspects of research involve the mental or verbal manipulation of ideas.

Expressive role. The behavior orientation that focuses on the affective domain, nurturing, and emotional outlet; the feeling domain as opposed to the cognitive, object-oriented one; to be contrasted with instrumental role.

Family. A semiclosed, mutually interacting system of personalities related by blood, marriage, descent, or adoption performing the function of nurturant socialization; two or more persons living in the same household who are related by blood, marriage, or adoption.

Family development. A conceptual framework that approaches the family as a semiclosed system of interacting personalities organized to perform the function of nurturant socialization for the young. This framework specifies life cycle stages through which the family may pass; thus it deals with developmental change.

Family function. A function performed by the family in furtherance of its attempts to improve family well-being; e.g., the performance of nurturant socialization of the young in order that they know and respect the family's norms.

Family integration. The concordance or congruence within a family (1) among family norms for the various partial goals and well-being goals; (2) between this set of goals and the family's norms and preferences for the means to accomplish these goals; (3) among family members concerning family norms for goals and means; and (4) among individual goals and between individual goals and family goals.

Family life cycle. A conceptualization of the stages of family life in terms of (1) changing age and sex composition of the family and (2) changing goals and norms that accompany these changes.

Family structure. The arrangement or pattern of organization that defines the interrelationships within the family. Structure includes both composition and norms for the relationships among the members, such as decision-making patterns.

Global preferred state. The overall family goal of the attainment of family well-being.

Goal integration. The assumption that the goals of individual family members, if met, serve to meet the goals of the family. See cultural integration.

Group quarters. Living arrangements with five or more persons unrelated to the head or with no designated head and six or more unrelated persons. Group quarters include living arrangements such as hospitals, military barracks, dormitories, and the like.

Heterogeneity of subsystems. The assumption that the family, as one of a group of subsystems within a larger system, differs from the other subsystems in the nature of the elements, the relationships between the elements, and the preferred states involved.

Household. A group of related or unrelated people sharing the same housing unit; excludes groups living in dormitories and the like.

Housing unit. A dwelling with either a separate kitchen or a separate entrance.

Instrumental role. The behavior orientation that involves maintenance of partial preferred states requiring contact with external systems, including work, the economy, and, in general, task-oriented matters; to be contrasted with expressive role.

Integration. An assumption that individual members of the family have direct influences on other members. When applied to most other social organizations this assumption posits direct or indirect influence by members on each other.

Intrafamilial constraints. Restrictions having their sources within the family. These include such factors as poor allocation of roles within the family, ineffective role performance of individual members, and ineffective overall performance of the family as a unit.

Matriarchal. Of or pertaining to dominance by a female, especially in the family; to be contrasted with patriarchial.

Negationist school. An approach to understanding the family based on the view that families have changed and will continue to change from a unit performing many functions to a simpler, companionship and affection-oriented unit.

Nurturant socialization. Filling children's biological and psychological needs while teaching them to become members of the family and the society.

Partial preferred state. One of the many goals that contribute to family well-being. Housing that meets cultural and family norms is a partial preferred state.

Patriarchal. Family system of or pertaining to the male, especially the dominant male in terms of, for example, inheritance, residence, family authority, and land ownership; to be contrasted with matriarchal.

Plurality. The assumption that the family is made up of individual elements or members, their characteristics, and the interrelationships between them.

Plurality of subsystems. The assumption that the family is one of many subunits of larger social systems, including communities and societies.

Problem solving. The process by which a family identifies a situation or circumstance that requires action, gathers information about the situation, evaluates selected alternative actions, takes action, and evaluates the consequences.

Rationality. The assumption that the family selects its means consciously to achieve its goals.

Role. A set of norms that prescribe the appropriate behavior for a given set of situations or relationships; e.g., the father role or the mother role.

Role specialization. Differentiation of skills and orientations that occurs when too many problems occur for an entire group to deal with them simultaneously. Even mildly complex groups develop specialized roles.

Self-regulation. The assumption that mechanisms exist within the family system that keep it directed toward the maintenance of well-being by controlling the partial preferred states that contribute to well-being.

Solidarity. Relatively permanent states of agreement or commonality; the extent to which members identity with the social system and feel loyalty toward it and its goals; a general sense of identity, rather than an issue-based one.

Time-wise specialization. The mechanism that allows instrumentally or expressively oriented specialists within the family to engage in behavior opposite to that of their usual mode. At one time a mother may be primarily playing an expressive role; at other times she may be required to play an instrumental role.

Wholeness. The assumption that the aggregation of individual family members and their interrelationships constitutes an entity that has properties not inherent in the individual members.

Chapter 4
Housing Adjustment and Adaptation

And this was part of the family song too. It was all part. Sometimes it rose to an aching chord that caught in the throat, saying this is safety, this is warmth, this is the *Whole.* John Steinbeck*

A full understanding of housing adjustment behavior requires a complex analysis. Assessment of the influence of the society (cultural norms), the influence of the family's own orientation (family norms), and the current state of the family's housing are essential elements of such an analysis. So are the external barriers to or constraints on adjustment behavior and the family's internal organization and functioning. This chapter presents a detailed theoretical framework for the analysis of the housing-related responses of families taking account of all those factors.

HOUSING AS AN ADJUSTMENT PROCESS

Family housing behavior has long been conceptualized in terms of adjustment and maladjustment. In an early series of papers in the *American Sociological Review,* Svend Riemer (1943, 1945, 1947) developed the idea of "maladjustment to the family home." Riemer stated:

> *In our material, maladjustment to the family home is most strikingly related to crowding. . . . Next in importance is the influence of the market value of the home. . . . Naturally, improvements in the satisfaction with the family home are to be expected as its financial value increases. It is noteworthy, on the contrary, that a process of accomodation seems to take place at all financial levels (Riemer, 1945, p. 645).*

* From *The Pearl* by John Steinbeck (New York: Viking, 1968), p. 6.

Rossi's (1955) study of residential mobility represented a major theoretical advance in the study of housing behavior. He organized his interpretation around the concept of the family life cycle and viewed housing needs as directly related to family composition:

> *What are the needs which must be met by housing? Housing needs are determined primarily by the composition of the household. Families change as they go through a life cycle of growth and decline. . . . Housing needs change rapidly in [the] early years as space requirements quickly grow and as the family at the same time becomes more sensitive to the social and physical environment provided by the location of its dwelling (p. 178).*

Rossi's reference to sensitivity to the social and physical environment hints at the view that housing needs are the norms for housing. He neither explores the idea in depth nor tests the hypothesis that cultural norms are behind the housing behavior of his sample. The idea is, at most, implicit in his study.

Most research specifically related to residential mobility as a housing adjustment process and to other behavior related to housing adjustment has followed Rossi's lead and has viewed changing family composition as directly responsible for changes in housing needs (see e.g., Speare, 1970; Chevan, 1971; Long, 1972).

A theoretical paper (Sabagh, Van Arsdol, and Butler, 1969) building on Rossi's approach foreshadowed but did not fully develop the perspective used in this book:

> *The actuation of mobility by family life cycle changes depends on . . . the way in which changes in family structure are evaluated and related to housing needs (Sabagh, Van Arsdol, and Butler, 1969, p. 90).*

They make reference to ideals, aspirations, expectations, and family norms in connection with residential mobility behavior. Those concepts may correspond rather closely to our usage of family norms, cultural norms, family preferences, and generalized preferences.

Goodman (1974) discussed housing adjustment in terms of disequilibria. These disequilibria are induced by changes in family factors such as income and family composition or changes in the place of work within the local labor market that increase the time and money spent commuting. He referred to such disequilibria as "housing stress." Some of his measures of disequilibria are similar to the normative deficits (space, expenditures) discussed in this book. Like others before him, however, he focused on life cycle and family composition changes themselves, rather than on the specific disequilibria and corresponding stresses associated with such changes.

On theoretical grounds it seems preferable to base the idea of changing needs on the progression of norms that govern a family's behavior as the composition and other factors change. Thus, as composition and size of the family change over time, the norms that apply to them would be different in different life cycle stages (Rodgers, 1962). The norms, of course, represent changing needs for housing as the family changes.

A model that explicitly defined housing needs as the progression of norms through the life cycle and included the range of cultural norms governing the family's relation to its housing was first presented by Morris and Winter (1975). That paper, an earlier version of the present model, emphasized behavioral responses (residential mobility, residential alterations and additions, and structural family adaptation) with little attention to the possibility that families may also change their norms rather than their housing conditions.

By the time the first model was developed, there had been a great deal of research on residential mobility as a housing adjustment mechanism. A considerably smaller amount of research had been completed regarding residential alterations and additions. However, there existed almost no recent research on structural family adaptation as a response to normative housing deficits.

The earlier model provided the basis for further research on residential mobility (Morris, Crull, and Winter, 1976; Morris, 1976; Morris, 1977; Bresler, 1975; Barrs, 1975), residential alterations and additions (Bross, 1975; Yockey, 1976a; Harris, 1976b), and housing satisfaction (Yockey, 1976a; Yockey, 1976b; Harris, 1976a; Harris, 1976b; Morris, 1976; Crull, 1976a; Morris, et al., 1976). Further work based on this model also examined the existence, content, and strength of space, tenure, structure type, quality, and expenditure norms (Morris et al., 1976; Morris and Winter, 1976a; Winter and Morris, 1976; Yockey, 1976a; Morris, 1976; Morris and Winter, 1976b; Crull, 1976a; Crull, 1976b). Those research results and theoretical developments in the social sciences (e.g., Sztompka, 1974; Deacon and Firebaugh, 1975) have led to the development of the model presented in this chapter.

THE MODEL OF FAMILY HOUSING BEHAVIOR

The present methodological view of the sources of influence on the occurrence of housing adjustment behavior coincides roughly with the "configurational" framework of Acock and DeFleur (1972). They suggest there are three sets of variables necessary for effective prediction of behavior. There is (1) weak predictability to be obtained from variables that measure "social influence" (cultural norms), (2) weak predictability to be obtained from "attitude influence" variables (family norms), and (3) strong predictability in "interaction influence" (current conditions and the extrafamilial constraints on changing those conditions). A forth set of variables (not mentioned by Acock and DeFleur but necessary to the analysis) concerns the internal functioning of the family or the intrafamilial constraints, which could be expected to be intermediate in their strength of influence.

Family housing behavior can be understood fully only if the whole configuration of influences is taken into account not only at a specific instant in time but also at significant times in the past. Cultural norms can be expected to have an influence on housing behavior, as would family norms. Their influence, as measured by empirical correlations, would appear to be relatively small (but not therefore unimportant) because norms include a range of permissible deviation and are influenced by factors such as family income, the availability of suitable housing, and race and sex discrimination.

It is necessary, therefore, to take account of current conditions of housing, the constraints on behavior, and the family's mode of operation and effectiveness in problem solving, as well as the family's history with regard to all four sets of influences. In general, the influence or empirical correlations of situational variables with housing behavior would be stronger than for cultural norms or family norms. The additional variables are needed to take account of the differences between cultural norms and family norms as well as the translation of norms into preferences, as discussed in Chapter 2.

The four types of variables in conjunction comprise both a theoretically and an empirically sounder analysis than the use of any single set of variables. No study thus far has analyzed all four sets of variables. Therefore the disparate findings of various studies that relate more or less directly to the main theory must be pieced together.

Families periodically evaluate their housing to test whether it is, for example, as roomy, luxurious, or well furnished as their needs require. The relative weighting of cultural norms and family norms varies from family to family. Some families may feel cultural norms are equally as important as those of their own family. Thus, when "calculating" the deviation of their housing, they may weight the two sets of norms equally. Other families may be less influenced by others and may give more influence to their own family's norms. The weighting, of course, is merely academic if the family's norms coincide exactly with the cultural norms.

There may be strong pressures that push families to give at least some weight to cultural norms even if their family norms are very unusual. Sanctions of various kinds may be imposed on such families that would tend to encourage them to adopt behavior and family norms that are more similar to those of the culture. In general, families of higher social status are better able to endure the negative sanctions that accompany unconventional behavior. Low-income families are more likely to need to develop an ability to accept negative sanctions. Their housing is likely to be further from cultural norms than is the case for higher-income families.

The family is seen to be engaged in a dynamic process of evaluation of its housing in terms of both sets of norms. Obviously, families are not in a perpetual meeting in which they evaluate their housing. Most of the time spent as a group is concerned with other matters. In addition, family activity and the family related behavior of the individual members are intermittent so that family behavior is a kind of rhythmic coming together (for family purposes) and separation (for performance of nonfamilial roles) (Parsons, 1955, p. 39).

Housing adjustment tends to occur whenever the family has a *normative deficit* that causes a significant reduction in *housing satisfaction,* discussed in detail in Chapter 8. When the deficit is both perceived by the family and involves a salient housing condition, the deficit reduces housing satisfaction.

The use of general housing satisfaction as the adjustment criterion rather than satisfaction with specific aspects of the dwelling is justifiable. Families appear to make their important housing decisions on the basis of an assessment of the overall dwelling. Moderate dissatisfaction with one specific item may be overcome by high satisfaction with some other item. Thus the average satisfaction would be moderate.

In general, a family's housing tends to lag behind its needs. The unfilled needs (deficits) serve as a source of motivation for adjustment behavior to bring needs and housing into closer accord. Of course, it is possible for a family to anticipate changing housing needs and engage in anticipatory adjustment behavior. Obviously, the family is not simply a reactor responding to cultural and situational pressures when they arise. Families often plan ahead to avoid potential situations of crowding (Morris, 1977) or otherwise nonnormative housing.

Families are self-regulating, rational systems. They process information and attitudes for the purposes of planning their future housing-related behavior. Taking into account their current housing, the current level of satisfaction, and their aspirations for the future, along with their reasonable expectations, the family may act at least somewhat rationally to achieve their housing norms.

Constraints on Adjustment Behavior

When there is a reduction in housing satisfaction, overcoming the normative deficit that produced the dissatisfaction depends upon overcoming any constraints that impinge on the family's ability to engage in adjustment behavior. There are three kinds of constraints. The first involves intrafamilial strengths and weaknesses when confronted with problems. The second includes economic, social, and political barriers. Third are the attractive features of the present dwelling and its location.

Intrafamilial constraints have to do with such factors as the allocation of roles within the family, the effectiveness of the role performance of the individual members, and the effectiveness of the overall performance of the family as a unit. Family systems vary greatly along such dimensions (heterogeneity of subsystems). Thus, as is discussed in Chapter 3, families may be more or less successful in overcoming normative housing deficits.

The *extrafamilial constraints,* discussed in Chapters 12 and 13, involve such apparent family characteristics as income, social class status, race, and sex of the household head. A family's income is based on the rewards the society grants them for performing their functions in the occupational and investment worlds. Social status is based on the prestige and respect the society grants them for performance of various functions. Their race is relevant to the extent that the society values one race more highly than others and therefore grants more or less ready access to various rewards of the society. Sex of the household head is relevant to the extent that the society applies negative sanctions to households headed by females. One example of such sanctions is limited access to credit.

A somewhat different class of constraint includes the supply of housing and the supply of mortgage money relative to the demand for such. Thus, the extrafamilial constraints are factors that, in the short run at least, are beyond the direct control of the family.

The *attractive features of the dwelling* with which the family is highly satisfied may operate to deter adjustment. Some undesirable features may not be severe enough to overcome other desirable ones. For example, the desire to move from a rented to an owned home may be mitigated by the proximity of relatives and friends, an unusually good school district, or a very large yard.

Responses to Normative Deficits

The dissatisfaction produced by a discrepancy between the family's housing and the cultural, community, or family norms motivates four types of responses. The responses that may be made to perceived, salient discrepancies are: residential mobility, residential alterations or additions, normative family adaptation, and structural family adaptation. The first two represent housing adjustment behavior; the second two are adaptive responses.

Residential mobility, discussed at length in Chapter 9, refers to changing residence within the same labor and housing markets. The motivation for such short-distance moves is primarily housing-related. Migration, on the other hand, is a longer distance move, primarily motivated by nonhousing factors such as climate preference or economic opportunity. Housing adjustment may take place during such a move (obtaining a dwelling with an extra bedroom, for instance), but it is not the primary reason for the move.

Residential alterations and additions, discussed in Chapter 10, refer to the various activities that families can do to bring their current residence into line with their needs. Adding a room or a patio, partitioning and finishing one end of the basement for a teenager's bedroom, converting the sewing room to a nursery for the expected baby, and finishing the attic for bedroom space are all forms of residential alterations and additions. So are placing the baby's crib in the dining area in a one bedroom apartment, remodeling the kitchen or bathroom, and knocking out a wall between a small living room and a small old-fashioned parlor to make a larger area. The list is almost endless, and activities range from very minor changes that involve no cost (changing the use of a room by changing its furnishings) to very large, expensive changes (adding a complete two story wing).

Unlike residential mobility, there seem to be two sources of motivation for residential alterations and additions. Some families make changes because they are dissatisfied with their dwelling and want to raise their level of satisfaction. Other families make changes because they are already satisfied, do not want to even consider moving, and want to continue to make improvements, perhaps in response to rising family norms over time.

Normative family adaptation may also be used to relieve the stress of dissatisfaction caused by housing deficits. A family can alter its family norms for housing, either making them more demanding, or less so. Reducing norms may remove a deficit and the corresponding stress. Such reductions in norms may be a temporary relaxation, or may be relatively permanent changes in the norms. The latter generally is a "when-all-else-fails" response, but may be taken so that the stress caused by nonnormative housing would not lead to more serious family problems.

Normative adaptation can also involve raising the standards, thereby creating dissatisfaction in the absence of changes in family structure or housing conditions. This response most typically would accompany rising affluence either for a single family or for the whole society.

Changing the norms is a far more serious adaptation than it might seem at first glance, for the family is essentially creating a new set of rules to guide their behavior. The range and implication of such changes are explicated in Chapter 14.

Structural family adaptation includes two forms of adaptation: compositional adaptation and organizational adaptation. Such adaptations are far more fundamental than the routine adjustments implied by moving or making alterations in a current residence. They are probably somewhat more fundamental than normative adaptation, we well.

Compositional adaptation refers to actions a family may take to alter its composition or maintain it at a given level to fit the current or expected housing; this is detailed in Chapter 14. Within compositional adaptation, there are two classes of actions: those having to do with childbearing and the launching of children and those that concern the addition or subtraction of other members from the household.

Families with just barely enough space might postpone the birth of an additional child to avoid overcrowding. Families could also anticipate childbearing by purchasing a large dwelling, intending to "fill it with children." An unusually large house might even subconsciously encourage childbearing.

Compositional adaptation might not be thought of as housing behavior. Suggesting that "it is time" for a twenty-year-old son to "get his own place" would perhaps not be thought of as a means to obtain an extra bedroom. Taking foster children into a family when the family residence is a large dwelling would be labeled almost anything but housing behavior. Nevertheless such actions clearly can be viewed as responses to dimly perceived pressures of crowding or excess space.

The implications of organizational adaptation may be of even deeper and more fundamental importance than those of compositional adaptation. This form of adaptation involves alterations in the power and dominance relations among family members, in the modes of interaction that are used in decision making, in the techniques of information gathering, and in other similar organizational factors. Because the family is what it is, reorganization is a difficult, emotion-laden process. Thus, normative adaptation typically would be considered first, then compositional adaptation, and finally organizational adaptation.

Behavioral Propensities and Constraints

A propensity to engage in residential mobility or alteration appears to develop in stages. The progression is from deficit to dissatisfaction, to a desire to reduce the deficit by means of a specific behavior, to an expectation that the behavior can be accomplished, and finally to the occurrence of the behavior itself. At each stage constraints operate to prevent some families from proceeding to the next stage.

Not all families with a housing deficit become dissatisfied, apparently because psychological constraints prevent perception of the deficit or limit the development of salience. Not all dissatisfied families develop a desire to either move or alter their housing. The constraints here are likely to be either psychological, in the form of an inability to translate dissatisfaction into a desire to act, or social, in the form of influences from other families encouraging them to remain as they are.

Not all families who desire to move or to make residential alterations expect to be able to do so. The constraints at this point tend to be a mixture of social constraints and anticipated economic and political barriers. Finally, not all families who expect to move actually do so, either because they have changed their minds or because market and other economic factors prevent them from acting. Thus, as the propensity to behave moves closer to the actual behavior, the constraints move from psychological, primarily intra-familial constraints to social, economic, and political extrafamilial constraints.

THE FLOW OF ADJUSTMENT AND ADAPTATION

Figure 4 presents the model of family housing adjustment and adaptation in the form of a flow diagram that depicts the processes as they occur in the family, conceived as a system. The rectangles represent *conditions* or states that are true by definition. The diamonds represent *decisions,* and the circles are *processes*. Flow through the diagram begins in the upper left corner with Condition A and proceeds in the directions indicated by the arrows depending upon the outcomes of the decisions. The subscript 0's in Condition A indicate the housing conditions, norms, and deficits at an initial time point. The subscript 1's in Conditions I, J, and K indicate the housing conditions, norms, and deficits at a later point in time. The subscripts a, b, and c on the deficits in I, J, and K indicate these are alternative outcomes.

The goal of the family as it works its way through the housing adjustment process is to maintain the overall normative housing deficit either at zero or an effective zero. The family seeks one of the partial preferred states of a self-regulating system by maintaining good housing in the sense that the departure from zero deficit is either unperceived or perceived but not salient. It is assumed that by maintaining perceived, salient deficits at or near zero overall well-being is, if not maximized, at least is not reduced.

There are four means by which an effectively nonzero deficit can be reduced. First, the housing conditions (Processes D and E) can be altered. Second, the family norms (Process F) can be changed. Third, the family situation can be changed so that different norms apply (Process H). Fourth, and last, the intrafamily organizational constraints on decision making (Process G) can be reduced. Thus, the outcomes of the process may be changed actual housing conditions as a result of mobility or alterations (Condition I), altered family norms (Condition J), different norms applying as a result of compositional adaptation (Condition K), or changes in family organizational structure (e.g., husband-wife power relations) that reduce intrafamily constraints. Any of those outcomes becomes a part of the equation that determines a new housing deficit and the process begins again. Only a single attribute of the current dwelling unit (e.g., ownership) is considered in a given pass through the system. Other attributes of the housing unit may be considered at the same time, but they are treated in the system as constraints. For example, the dwelling may not be owned by the family, but

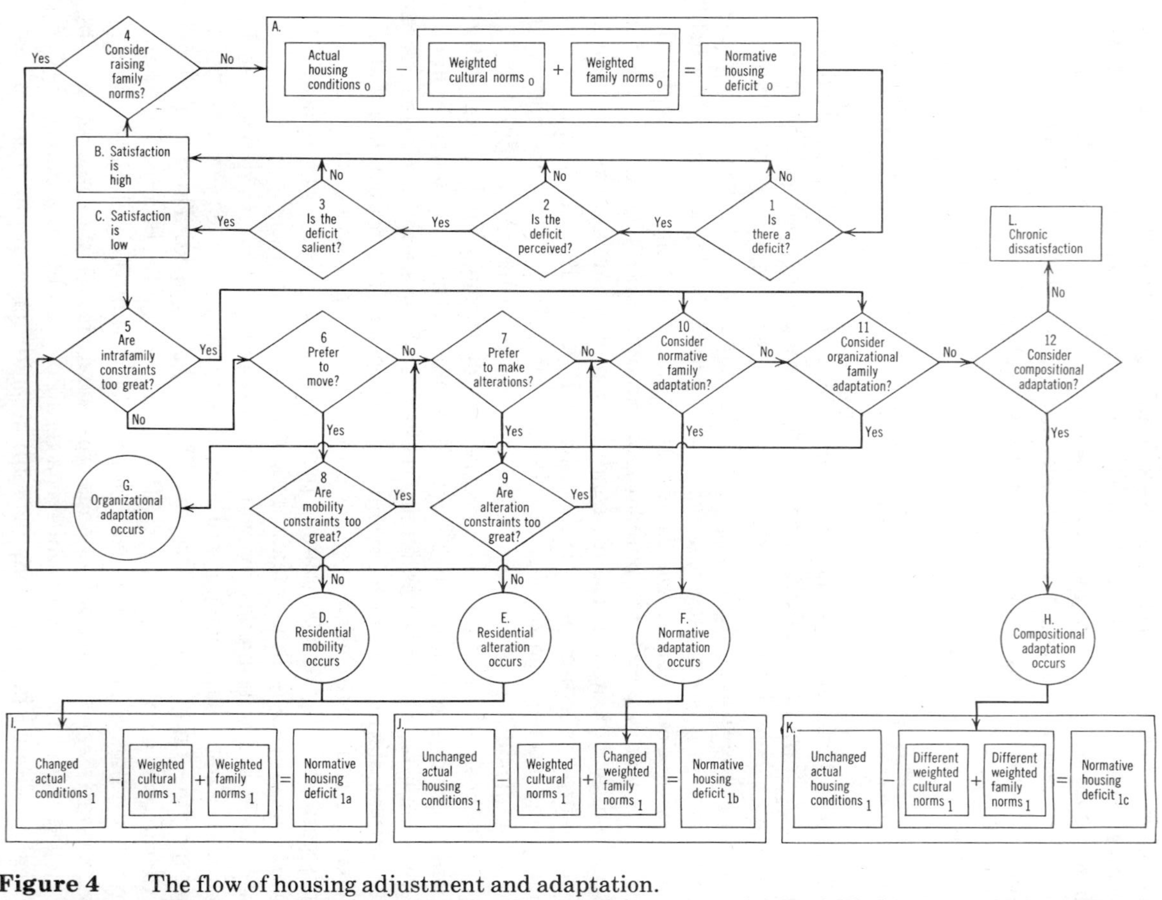

Figure 4 The flow of housing adjustment and adaptation.
Adapted from Figure 1, A Theory of Family Housing Adjustment, by Earl W. Morris and Mary Winter (*Journal of Marriage and the Family* 37), p. 85. Copyright © 1975 by the National Council on Family Relations. Reprinted by permission.

it is roomy and located in a good school district. There would be a normative tenure deficit pushing the family to move. The desirable location of the dwelling and its size operate as constraints impelling the family to relax tenure norms to retain the location and the space.

For a given attribute of the dwelling unit, the behavior and decision making of the family engaged in family housing adjustment and adaptation are viewed as occurring somewhat as follows (see Figure 4):

Condition A Periodic housing evaluation occurs during the daily life of the family. The evaluation of housing conditions, of course, is more important at some times than at others. The relative importance of housing conditions depends upon changes in the family's situation and the contribution of housing to the family's overall well-being. The changing importance of housing relative to, for example, food can also affect the ability to quickly perceive housing deficits and the level at which they become salient.

Decision 1 As long as there is no deficit from cultural norms (including those of the community) and family norms, any specific evaluation at this point in time would simply verify there was no deficit. This step does not necessarily enter the family's consciousness.

Decision 2 At this point the family is either aware or unaware of a deficit. The family proceeds to the next decision point if they perceive a deficit. Otherwise the family continues with an existing but unperceived deficit. Satisfaction remains high.

Decision 3 If the perceived deficit is not salient, that is, if it is not important to the family, satisfaction remains high.

Condition B If there is no deficit, if the deficit is not perceived, or if the deficit is not salient, then Condition B is true. Satisfaction with the particular aspect of the dwelling is high. Therefore, Decision 4 must be made.

Decision 4

At this point the family considers whether their norms might be too low. Perhaps there has been a rise in family income. If the answer is "no" they simply return to the beginning and wait for the next housing evaluation. If they decide to raise norms, they do so at Process F which then leads them to a new deficit evaluation at Condition J.

Condition C

If the results of Decisions 2 and 3 are positive then Condition C exists. A perceived, salient deficit reduces satisfaction. The degree of satisfaction-dissatisfaction depends, in part, upon the magnitude of the deficit (as perceived) and the degree of salience.

Decision 5

At Decision 5, the question is whether the family is able to, for example, develop a consensus as to the preferred means for reducing the deficit. The kind of constraints that operate here are intrafamily variables, including the level of solidarity, consensus about housing, dominance relations and the like. If the constraints are not too great, the family proceeds to the housing adjustment decisions at 6 and 7. If the constraints are too great they proceed to Decisions 10, 11, or 12 to consider reducing their norms to raise their satisfaction or to consider structural family adaptation.

Decisions 6 and 7

The family must choose between the two types of housing adjustment behavior as behavior preferences. For most families, the typical order would be as diagrammed, indicating moving as the first preference. If moving were subject to insuperable constraints (Decision 8), residential alteration would be entertained in its turn. Finally, if neither moving nor altering the dwelling were possible (Decision 9) then structural adaptation or normative adaptation (Decisions 10, 11, and 12) would be considered.

Individual families and groups or classes of families may place the alternatives in the opposite order. Farm families, for example, would be much less likely to consider residential mobility first, unless there were nonhousing factors to be considered, as well. Owners as a class would be more likely than renters to prefer residential alteration to residential mobility. If mobility is preferred and the constraints permit, then Process D occurs which in turn leads to a new housing evaluation at Condition I. If alteration is preferred and the constraints permit, alteration occurs at Process E which also produces Condition I.

Decisions 8 and 9

Carrying out a specific behavior depends on overcoming the constraints on that behavior at Decisions 8 and 9.

If the family prefers to move they must be able to find a new dwelling that will correct the deficit and not create other deficits. The new dwelling must be for rent or for sale at a price they can afford. If such conditions cannot be met, they must step back and test residential alteration against the constraints on that type of behavior.

The constraints that operate at this stage may be grouped as economic, political, or social in nature. The standard market constraints impinge most clearly upon residential mobility. The supply of available dwellings, the supply of mortgage money, and the interest rate are examples.

There are other constraints that are basically political in the sense of wielding of power by, for, or against various types of families. Racial discrimination, for example, is a political constraint. Even if a family prefers to move, a dwelling is available in their price range, and they can obtain a mortgage at an acceptable interest rate, they may not be able to buy because of their race.

Another type of constraint would be the desirable characteristics of the present dwelling and neighborhood. For example, the family may desire to remain in the current neighborhood because relatives and friends are living there.

Giving them up in order to achieve a reduction in, say, a space deficit may be too high a price to pay.

Constraints, both those at Decision 5 and at 8 and 9, represent judgments that giving up alternative values (housing-related and nonhousing-related values as well as monetary and nonmonetary values) is too "costly." The nondeficit aspects of the current dwelling and the neighborhood can thus be seen as constraints since they may represent something to be given up in order to reduce the deficit under consideration.

Processes D and E

Finally, if the constraints can be overcome, the adjustment behavior occurs and a new state of housing conditions is achieved (Condition I). The process begins again, as new conditions are related to the cultural norms, community norms, and family norms to test for the existence of a new housing deficit.

Decision 10

If, at any point, the intrafamilial, economic, political, or social constraints are insuperable the family may have to temporarily relax or permanently alter its norms to avoid the stress of dissatisfaction.

Process F

Norms are altered through normative family adaptation. The process begins again at Condition J.

Decisions 11 and 12

If neither mobility nor alteration is feasible and normative adaptation has been rejected, then changes in family structure may be required. Changes in composition could change the situation enough that less demanding norms would apply. Alternatively, changes in organization could lift intrafamily constraints. In case of crowding, the household size could be reduced, for example.

Process H

Compositional adaptation occurs, and different norms now apply, leading to a new evaluation at Condition K.

Process G An alternative form of structural family adaptation is to change the family organization patterns: role specialization, the degree of integration, etc. If organizational adaptation occurs, its effect is felt at Decision 5, for the intrafamilial constraints are reduced.

Conditions I, J, and K Conditions I, J, and K indicate that the evaluation process begins again, either with different housing conditions (I), changed family norms (J), or different norms that apply (K).

Condition L If everything else fails, even changing family norms, the result is chronic dissatisfaction. This may be one of the key sources of cultural change. If there is a critical mass of chronically dissatisfied people (urban blacks in the late 1960s, for example) great pressure for changes in cultural norms, in the allocation of resources, and in other conditions may be demanded.

CONCLUSION

A perceived, salient gap between actual housing conditions and those required by the norms produces a normative housing deficit for a family. The family feels pressure (potential or actual sanctions) from within the family or from outside the family to overcome the deficit. On the basis of a process of weighing alternatives they choose residential mobility or residential alteration as means to remove the deficit. If such behavioral responses cannot be accomplished, the family adapts either their family structure or their family housing norms.

The utility of the model of housing adjustment as presented here seems most likely to lie in its value, first, as a guide to research, and second, as a means of teaching the implications of various housing actions. For example, Angell (1976) used the model to estimate the number of Minnesota families making various housing decisions as a program planning tool for Cooperative Extension housing programs. He expanded the decision-making portion of the model somewhat to include decisions about whether to buy an existing new house or to have one built and whether to have an owner-built home or have someone else build it. He also included choices of types of ownership (conventional ownership, condominium or cooperative ownership, and a number of others). He has shown that the model has application as a teaching device and as an aid in policy making by families and communities.

The model of family housing behavior developed in Part I is necessarily simplified as any model must be. Even the most sophisticated model airplane cannot perform as readily as the real thing! The model surely makes family housing behavior appear more consciously pursued than it is. Families are self-regulating, but at least part of such regulation occurs subconsciously and not in the orderly rational fashion depicted.

Nevertheless, the model is a close approximation of reality, and can provide the basis for the refinement and testing of detailed hypotheses. Such testing should in turn lead to further refinement or the model. The implications of such research could result in the development of housing policy that fosters family housing adjustment and adaptation. Most housing policy seems to simply respond to the state of the economy, or to the preconceptions of architects, builders, designers, planners, and social critics. The present model permits policy making to take full cognizance of family desires for housing, with attention to social and cultural forces that shape such desires.

DEFINITIONS

Alterations and additions. Family activities that bring a current residence into line with family needs. Activities may range from minor changes (converting a sewing room to a nursery) to major ones (adding a new two story wing); one of the housing adjustment behaviors.

Compositional adaptation. Actions a family may take to change its composition or maintain it at a given level to fit current or expected housing; one form of structural family adaptation. Postponing the birth of additional children because of space deficits or purchasing a larger house in anticipation of offspring are compositional adaptations.

Constraints. Factors that restrict a family's ability to engage in housing adjustment behavior. Constraints may involve intrafamilial strengths and weaknesses in problem solving, economic, social, and political barriers, and attractive features of the current dwelling.

Extrafamilial constraints. Factors external to the family that influence the family's ability to adjust their housing behavior. Included are family characteristics such as race, sex of the household head, social class, and income, as well as the supply of housing and mortgage money relative to the demand for both.

Housing adjustment. A process that may occur when a family experiences a normative housing deficit that causes a significant reduction in housing satisfaction. Housing adjustment takes place through residential mobility and residential alterations and additions.

Housing satisfaction. A state of the level of contentment with current housing conditions. Low levels of satisfaction are experienced as stress. The term may refer to the entire continuum of satisfaction from very dissatisfied to very satisfied. Thus, the level of satisfaction is inferred in addition to the idea of a state of being satisfied.

Hypothesis. A statement of a temporary assumption about a causal relationship between an independent variable (a cause) and a dependent variable (an effect). The assumption is temporary until empirical data refute or support the assumption.

Migration. Intercommunity, intermetropolitan, or long-distance moving, usually for purposes other than housing adjustment.

Normative family adaptation. Alteration of family norms to make them either more or less demanding. Reduction of the norms may remove a deficit and the corresponding stress. Raising the norms may create dissatisfaction in the absence of changing housing conditions, a response often found under conditions of rising affluence.

Organizational adaptation. Alterations in power and dominance relations among family members, in modes of interaction that are used in decision making, in techniques of information gathering, and in other similar organizational factors; one form of structural family adaptation.

Residential mobility. Moving to a different dwelling within the local area (within a single labor market or housing market); usually involves adjustment of actual housing conditions to better meet housing needs; one of the housing adjustment behaviors.

Salience. The level of importance placed on perceived housing deficits by the family.

Structural family adaptation. Alteration of the family structure (compositional adaptation) or organization (organizational adaptation); generally a more fundamental change than either moving and alterations in the current dwelling or normative adaptation.

Part 2
American Housing Norms

We cannot see anything until we are possessed with the idea of it, take it into our heads,—and then we can hardly see anything else. Henry David Thoreau

Earlier chapters have outlined the concepts involved in a sociocultural orientation to the study of housing. At this point it seems necessary only to underline the conviction that housing norms are important components of the conscious thought processes of American families. Therefore, the discussion that follows outlines the

fairly well-defined consumer norms [that] indicate what a "decent" and "average" household should expect from the society (Greer, 1966, p. 519).

Some cultural norms and family norms for housing in the United States have been unusually durable and very widely accepted. The purpose of Part 2 is to elaborate several of those norms and discuss differences among norms that apply as the family progresses through the life cycle. Whether or to what extent housing needs are different for childless couples, single individuals, and single-parent families will also be discussed. Norms for space (Chapter 5), tenure and structure type (Chapter 6), and quality, expenditures, and neighborhood (Chapter 7) will be emphasized.

NORMS AND THE DEFINITION OF HOUSING

A separate dwelling for each family in the United States is a deeply embedded cultural norm (APHA, 1950, p. 7). One of the classic indicators of housing shortages has been the amount of "doubling up," having more than one nuclear family per housing unit (Beyer, 1965, p. 133). Housing policy in the United States, indeed in all of Western society, has maintained as a goal the provision of a dwelling for every family (Mogey, 1964, p. 524).

The norms discussed in Chapters 5 to 7 are of two types: definitional norms (those that define those characteristics required for a structure to be acceptable as housing) and specification norms (those that prescribe the detail and elaboration of the dwelling unit above the minimum housing level). The emphasis will be placed on the specification norms that constitute the cultural definitions of *adequate* housing, and, as such, do not merely specify *minimum* standards for housing (Rapkin, 1955, p. 138).

Minimum standards are based on cultural norms and should not be ignored, but overwhelmingly the housing in the United States meets or surpasses those minimum standards. Structures that do not meet minimum standards are seen by most people as something other than housing. Words such as "shacks," "hovels," and so on, are applied to such structures. Thus, in the United States, a housing unit is, at least, a weather-tight group of interconnected rooms with complete kitchen facilities and a complete bathroom for the exclusive use of the residents of the unit.

That there are minimum standards which must be met before the structure is thought of as "housing" is not an original idea. The census definition of a dwelling unit is based on certain minimum attributes to distinguish housing from structures or units that are not housing. Occupants of a space termed a "housing unit" must be able to live and eat separately from other people and must have either direct access to that unit or have complete kitchen facilities for their exclusive use (USBC, 1970, p. 113).

The distinction between the definitions used by the Census Bureau in 1960 and 1970 provides evidence of changes in the definition of housing:

> *The 1960 concept of kitchen facilities was a* kitchen *or* cooking equipment. *A kitchen was a room used primarily for cooking and meal preparation; cooking equipment was defined as a range or stove, whether or not regularly used, or other equipment such as a hotplate regularly used to prepare meals. The 1970 concept of kitchen facilities is* complete kitchen facilities, *defined as including a sink with piped water, a range or cook stove (excluding portable cooking equipment), and a refrigerator (excluding ice boxes). These facilities must be located in the same building as the living quarters but need not be all in the same room (p. 114).*

Thus in ten years one of the definitions of a housing unit has undergone a drastic change, from a room with cooking equipment, which could have been merely a hot plate, to a kitchen complete with running water, a refrigerator, and a range. And it is likely that the definition of a housing unit will be altered again for the 1980 Census, as well, to reflect changes in minimum standards that will occur during the 1970s.

There are two types of housing problems just as there are two types of housing norms. Substandard structures, when used as housing, represent the severest housing problems. Evidence of the recognition of this type of problem includes the fact that the 1968 estimates of the number of units of housing required included all substandard units in the need (PCUH, 1968, p. 40; NCUP, 1968, p. 70). The second type of housing problem is based on variations of housing from specification norms. Thus, as noted in earlier chapters, *housing* may not be enough when norms prescribe the "right" kind of housing.

Some families live in units that do not meet the minimum definition of housing, as is obvious in assessments of housing conditions (PCUH, 1968; NCUP, 1968; SCNHN, 1971). A family living in housing that lacks a kitchen or bathroom or is in very poor repair has serious housing problems. Certainly one of the first goals of any housing program should be to raise all housing to at least the minimum standard.

Simply to alleviate the substandard housing conditions through the provision of a new "housing project" with a complete bathroom and kitchen, however, without regard for the full range of cultural norms for housing, may solve the problem of inadequate housing while substituting a new set of problems. The stigma associated with living in public housing, for example, will not be erased until such housing is built in accord with important cultural norms rather than simply to satisfy minimum standards.

Chapter 5
Space Norms

> It would have been foolish to stand upon our dignity in a place where there was hardly room to stand upon our feet. Mark Twain

Space norms prescribe the amount of space a family should have and are dependent upon family size and composition. Most attempts to measure space norms at least take into account family size. Obviously, a suitable amount of space for three people could be too small for a five-member household. Quite different amounts of space might be prescribed for two different four-person households, depending upon the age, sex, and relationships among the household members.

Space in a dwelling may be expressed in terms of the number of square feet in the dwelling. Or it may be specified by individual rooms, the number of rooms, or the number of bedrooms or other specific rooms. Measures of crowding (a deficit of space) have been developed by establishing a relation between a measure of space and the occupants of the space. Thus, the number of square feet per person, persons per room, or persons per sleeping room have been used to measure crowding. Such measures seem not to be directly relevant culturally. Families neither evaluate their housing, nor are they motivated to engage in family housing adjustment behavior on the basis of either the ratio between the number of square feet in the dwelling and the number of persons in the household or the number of persons divided by the number of rooms.

A preferred method of relating the occupants to the amount of space would be to take account not simply of the number of persons but also the age, sex, and family role of each person. Several such measures have been developed that obtain indications of the need for space in relation to the available space.

MEASURES BASED ON SQUARE FEET

The American Public Health Association (APHA, 1950; 1971) and the U.S. Department of Housing and Urban Development (HUD, 1965; 1966;

1971) have been the officials and/or experts whose use of a specific number of square feet for minimum space requirements has been felt nationwide. Other groups have also established minimum space standards that are dependent upon the number of square feet (NCUP, 1968, pp. 273–80) but have not been influential.

The Committee on the Hygiene of Housing of the American Public Health Association (1950) published a set of recommended space standards for one- to six-member families. The APHA outlined ten activities that are generally performed within the dwelling unit:

> *sleeping and dressing; personal cleanliness and sanitation; food preparation and preservation; serving food and dining; family recreation and self-improvement; extra-familial association; housekeeping activities; care of infants or the sick; circulation between various areas of the dwelling; operation of utilities (p. 17).*

The APHA then analyzed each activity to delineate the space required for the furniture and equipment needed for each activity, the space to use the equipment while performing the activity, and the storage space needed (APHA, 1950, pp. 18–19).

The recommendations were given in terms of space for activities and not the sizes of rooms, for it was recognized that equipment, storage, and/or space for a single activity might be provided in different rooms and that more than one activity might occur in a single room. The APHA also recognized that there is not necessarily an arithmetic relationship between the number of people and the amount of space needed. Thus, the difference between, for example, the amount of space needed for food preparation by a two-member family and that needed by a three-member family may not be the same as the difference between food preparation spaces needed by three- and four-member families.

The space requirements for sleeping and dressing include space for a single bed, chair, bed table, and both a storage chest and closet, as well as sufficient space to make the bed, pull out the drawers of the storage chest, open the closet door, and sit on the chair (p. 19). It is perhaps obvious that the size of a single bed is culturally specific. So are the use of closets and chests for clothes storage and the necessity for both a bed table and chair.

Similarly, the space needed for family recreation and self-improvement included space for a sofa, chairs, end tables, radio-phonograph (a television set was not included, for the recommendations were published in 1950), a stand or shelf for plants, and "unclassified" space. Storage space for books, magazines, records, and games, and the space needed to use the furniture and storage units were also specified (pp. 26–27).

The APHA space standards were presented as the amounts of space

TABLE 1 Optimum floor space required for basic household activities according to the number of persons in the household

Household Activity	Number of Persons					
	1	2	3	4	5	6
Sleeping and dressing	74	148	222	296	370	444
Personal cleanliness and sanitation	35	35	35	35	70	70
Food preparation and preservation	8	76	97	97	118	118
Food service and dining	53	70	91	105	119	141
Recreation and self-improvement	125	164	221	286	357	383
Extra-familial association	17	17	34	34	51	51
Housekeeping	48	91	110	127	146	149
Care of the infant or the ill	—	124	124	124	124	124
Circulation	20	20	35	35	45	45
Operation of utilities	—	20	20	20	20	20
Total floor space recommended	400	750	1000	1150	1400	1550

Source. American Public Health Association, Committee on the Hygiene of Housing, *Planning the Home for Occupancy* (Chicago: Public Administration Service, 1950), p. 36. Reprinted by permission.

needed for each activity calculated separately for various household sizes (Table 1). Adding the individual space allowances and rounding to the nearest 50 square feet, the recommended number of square feet according to family size is: 400 square feet for one person, 750 for two persons, 1000 for three persons, 1150 for four persons, 1400 for five persons, and 1550 for six persons.

Although the APHA standards are relatively old, they may still be applicable today. With the exception of the advent of television, family activities and furniture sizes have not changed a great deal in the last 25 years. If the standards were to be recompiled, space requirements would probably only be somewhat higher.

The *optimum* standards recommended by APHA in 1950 are much higher than the 1971 *minimums* in their *Recommended Housing Maintenance and Occupancy Ordinance.* The latter document, a revision of an earlier publication (APHA, 1952), was prepared as a model housing code for adoption by local communities. The code specifies the *minimum* standards permitted for the level of maintenance and facilities provided, as well as space standards for occupancy for all dwelling units within the community.

The standards are those that are thought to be necessary to "insure that the quality of housing is adequate for protection of public health, safety and general welfare" (p. 73). A housing code, when adopted, is effectively a formal specification of space norms and can be legally enforced. Although other organizations have developed model codes, the prototype for most housing codes adopted by local communities is the model code recommended by the American Public Health Association.

The space standards recommended for adoption in the 1971 version are given in terms of habitable space, defined as

> *excluding bathrooms, water closet compartments, laundries, furnace rooms, pantries, kitchenettes and utility rooms of less than fifty (50) square feet of floor space, foyers, or communicating corridors, stairways, closets, storage spaces, and workshops, hobby and recreation areas in unheated or uninsulated parts of structure below ground level or in attics (APHA, 1971, p. 76).*

Thus, the amount of habitable space specified is less than the total space in the dwelling unit. Therefore, the amount of space recommended as minimum would be somewhat smaller than the amount recommended as optimum (APHA, 1950), simply because the minimum includes only habitable space. Nevertheless, the minimum standards are still well below the optimum standards. The amount of space recommended by the model ordinance is 150 square feet for one person, 250 square feet for two persons, 350 for three persons, 450 for four persons, 550 for five persons, and 650 for six persons (p. 98).

The difference between the optimum amount of space, based on household activities (APHA, 1950, p. 36), and the minimum amount of habitable space required by the model housing code is a clear example of the range of permissible deviation from the standards or norms (Figure 2, Chapter 2). The standard for optimum amount of space represents an attempt by APHA to express the ideal range prescribed by the norm. The minimum standard, on the other hand, denotes the limit of underconformance permitted.

Aside from the general rationale of standards for public health, safety, and well-being, there is no stated basis for the minimum floor areas specified in the model code. Contrary to the standards recommended as optimum, based on careful analyses of culturally prescribed household activities, the figures recommended as minimum standards seem to be arbitrary. While it could be argued that habitable space that is 15 by 10 feet is, indeed, a very small amount of space, even for one person, and that making the case for an even smaller amount of space would be difficult, why not argue for a larger amount, say 20 feet by 10 feet? Such an argument only points up the arbitrariness of the standards. Nevertheless, the standards expressed in the APHA model housing code have been adopted into law by thousands of communities across the country (NCUP, 1968, p. 276).

The suggested optimum space norms were expressed in total square feet of space in the dwelling unit. The suggested minimum standards were expressed in total square feet of habitable space. Yet a third method of expressing space standards in terms of the number of square feet is by stating a minimum number of square feet per room. This method was used by the U.S. Department of Housing and Urban Development for almost 30 years as a part of the criteria for judging the acceptability of a dwelling for a Federal Housing Administration (FHA) insured mortgage. Recent HUD standards (HUD, 1973a and 1973b) are based on furnishability of the room.

Standards expressed in square feet per room were included in minimum standards for one and two living units (HUD, 1965) and multifamily housing (HUD, 1971), both designed to meet the needs of moderate- and middle-income families. Standards for low-cost housing (HUD, 1966), designed expressly for low-income families, also were expressed in square feet per room. Each publication established minimum standards for separate rooms and for combined rooms (kitchen-dining area, living room-dining room, and so on). Some of the space standards for separate rooms for single-family and two-family houses, dwelling units in multifamily structures, and dwelling units constructed for low-income families are presented in Table 2. Similar comparisons could, of course, be made for the combined rooms.

An interesting aspect of the standards emerges when comparisons are made. Even though all three publications specified that the objective of the space standards was to provide each unit with sufficient space and facilities essential for family activities, there was a difference between the amount of space prescribed for low-income housing and that established for middle-income housing. While the difference was slight, the fact that there was a difference emphasizes the arbitrary nature of the minimum standards. Unless it can be argued that low-income families perform their activities in less space than middle-income families or that their activities are quite different and require less space, the reasoning behind such a change in standards is obscure. A recent study (Yockey, 1976b) suggests that such conclusions are not true.

As in the recommended housing ordinance (APHA, 1971) previously discussed, there was no rationale presented for the standards established. If indeed the standards were based on objective "housing need" criteria, then it is not at all clear why low-income families need less space than middle-income families.

Comparison of the three standards for number of square feet of space in the dwelling according to the number of persons in the household is somewhat inappropriate because the definitions of the space measured are slightly different. If it can be assumed that a five-member household needs a

TABLE 2 Minimum room sizes permitted for separate rooms according to HUD standards for one- and two-family houses, apartments in multifamily structures, and low cost housing

	Minimum Area (Square Feet)		
Type of Living Unit and Type of Room	1- and 2-Family Housing	Multifamily Housing	Low Cost Housing
Living unit with 1 bedroom:			
Living room	160	160	140
Dining room	80	100	80
Kitchen	60	60	50
Total bedrooms	120	120	110
Living unit with 2 bedrooms:			
Living room	160	160	140
Dining room	80	100	80
Kitchen	60	60	50
Total bedrooms	200	200	180
Minimum bedroom	80	80	70
Living unit with 3 bedrooms:			
Living room	170	170	150
Dining room	95	110	90
Kitchen	70	70	60
Total bedrooms	280	280	250
Minimum bedroom	80	80	70
Living unit with 4 bedrooms:			
Living room	180	180	160
Dining room	110	120	100
Kitchen	80	80	70
Total bedrooms	380	380	320
Minimum bedroom	80	80	70

Sources. U.S. Department of Housing and Urban Development, *Minimum Property Standards for One and Two Living Units* (Washington: U.S. Government Printing Office, 1965), p. 32; U.S. Department of Housing and Urban Development, *Minimum Property Standards for Multifamily Housing* (Washington: U.S. Government Printing Office, 1971), p. 70; U.S. Department of Housing and Urban Development, *Minimum Property Standards for Low Cost Housing* (Washington: U.S. Government Printing Office, 1966), p. 9.

three-bedroom unit, then the spaces in the individual rooms in the HUD standards can be summed to give an approximate size that is roughly comparable to the amount of habitable space in the APHA recommended housing code. Table 3 presents a comparison between the APHA optimum, APHA minimum, and HUD standards for five persons or a three-bedroom dwelling unit.

If the assumptions made in calculating the HUD figures are reasonably valid, then it can be seen that the HUD standards for middle-income housing fall between the minimum recommendation and the optimum recommendation. The standards for low-income housing are exactly at the minimum.

TABLE 3 Comparison between the optimum and minimum space standards for five-member households

Type of Standard	Source	Square Feet
Optimum amount of space in dwelling	APHA, 1950	1400
Minimum amount of habitable space in dwelling	APHA, 1971	550
Minimum amount of space in separate rooms, multifamily housing	HUD, 1971	630
Minimum amount of space in separate rooms, one and two family housing	HUD, 1965	615
Minimum amount of space in separate rooms, low income housing	HUD, 1966	550

Sources. American Public Health Association, Committee on the Hygiene of Housing, *Planning the Home for Occupancy* (Chicago: Public Administration Service, 1950), p. 36; American Public Health Association, *Housing: Basic Health Principles and Recommended Ordinance* (Washington: Author, 1971), p. 98; U.S. Department of Housing and Urban Development, *Minimum Property Standards for Multifamily Housing* (Washington: U.S. Government Printing Office, 1971), p. 70: U.S. Department of Housing and Urban Development, *Minimum Property Standards for One and Two Living Units* (Washington: U.S. Government Printing Office, 1965), p. 32; U.S. Department of Housing and Urban Development, *Minimum Property Standards for Low Cost Housing* (Washington: U.S. Government Printing Office, 1966), p. 9.

The crucial point to note concerning the HUD standards is that they were indeed official and were accompanied by formal sanctions administered by the federal government. In order to qualify for an FHA-insured mortgage, or for public housing funds, the dwelling units had to meet the space standards. Other standards for construction, siting, etc., also applied. If the space included in the rooms was lower than the minimums expressed, the dwelling would not qualify for an FHA-insured mortgage. By the same token, if the space included in the individual rooms was far in excess of that prescribed by HUD, it was also likely that an insured mortgage would not be approved. In the case of excess space, the total cost of the dwelling probably would exceed the maximum allowed by HUD.

Because of the nature of the building industry and the housing market, the HUD standards became virtual descriptions of new dwellings insured by FHA mortgages, rather than the minimum standards they were purported to be. Most FHA-insured dwellings just barely met the criteria, even though exceeding the minimum standards was permitted as long as the cost was not excessive. Standards were systematically promulgated through the administration of rewards and punishments. In essence, these minimums dictated the size of millions of dwelling units. The extent to which HUD standards differed from cultural norms is, of course, not clear.

The recent HUD space standards (1973a and 1973b) require that rooms be of sufficient size to accommodate specific furnishings and circulation around those furnishings. Such standards, a better reflection of space norms, were not used until the mid-seventies, more than 25 years after the inception of the FHA mortgage insurance program. HUD recognized that builders find it more convenient to check a floor plan for the number of square feet in each room than for whether a table, six chairs, and a buffet can be comfortably arranged in the dining room. Therefore, minimum square footage for separate and combined rooms is also given. The most recent HUD space standards are identical to the old ones, except that larger areas are required for eating in all sizes of dwelling units.

The most important change is that the Department of Housing and Urban Development no longer distinguishes between housing for low-income families and that designed for moderate- and middle-income families, in terms of space requirements. The new standards apply to one- and two-family dwellings and to multifamily housing units for all income groupings.

Space norms expressed as a number of square feet are not particularly relevant as direct motivation for family housing adjustment behavior, since people react more to the number of rooms of various types with a kind of minimum room size standard in the back of the head. Nevertheless, such measures have been widely used by government agencies, financial institutions, and local officials and have contributed to an increase in the amount of space available in American housing.

THE PERSONS-PER-ROOM RATIO

A second way to measure space norms is to establish a standard based on the persons-per-room ratio. This figure is calculated by dividing the number of persons in the household by the number of rooms (excluding bathrooms) in the unit. It has become accepted practice to term housing units with more than 1.0 persons per room as "overcrowded" and those with more than 1.5 persons per room as "severely overcrowded." The APHA (1971) model housing code recommends that the maximum permissible persons-per-room ratio is 2.0 (p. 98). The range of deviation permitted around the ideal persons-per-room ratio seems to have been promulgated by official bodies or experts rather than by families judging their housing space and that of others.

The United States Bureau of the Census (1970) has long used the persons-per-room measure to describe occupancy patterns. The components of the measure, the number of persons in the household, and the number of rooms, are routinely collected in the census. The ratio is easily calculated. The establishment of a standard (1.01) permits an approximate comparison between actual conditions and normative conditions. Thus, city planners can analyze census tracts in which there is a high degree of crowding by, for example, comparing the average persons-per-room ratios of the census tracts in the city with the standards.

Dividing the number of household members by the number of habitable rooms results in a crude measure of whether or not the family has enough space to perform required activities. Even as a gross measure of space norms, however, the persons-per-room ratio has obvious faults, as pointed out by Louis Winnick (1957). He used this measure as a dependent variable in an analysis of census data, even though he recognized that the measure assumes that all spaces are alike in size and utility, and that all persons are alike in their use of space. Winnick's criticisms of the measure are simply another way of saying that the persons-per-room ratio is not culturally relevant. There is no means of accounting for either the type, quality, or size of the rooms or the age and sex of the household members.

A variation on the persons-per-room ratio is the persons-per-sleeping-room measure, as used by the American Public Health Association (1945) in developing *An Appraisal Method for Measuring the Quality of Housing.* Wilner et al. (1962) assessed the housing quality of their sample with this measure. As in the persons-per-room ratio, a standard has been established. In this case it is two persons per sleeping room. A higher ratio is considered to represent crowding.

Families do tend to think in terms of the allotment of bedroom space with a clear tendency against having more than two persons in a sleeping room. The persons-per-sleeping-room ratio, however, is not the same as persons per bedroom. The latter ratio implies a cultural definition of bedroom, a room not used for any other primary purpose. Sleeping rooms, on the other hand, may include a room the primary function of which is as a living room, for example. The obvious flaw in both measures, however, is that neither sleeping rooms nor bedrooms are allotted to family members *solely* on the basis of the number of people per room. Who may and who may not share bedrooms, according to cultural norms is more important in such decisions.

BEDROOM NEED AND BEDROOM DEFICIT

Bedroom need, a measure of the number of bedrooms a family needs for its specific members to avoid violating the cultural norms for bedroom sharing, is the primary way that American families assess their housing space needs (Morris, 1972b). Bedroom need is the crucial space measure because there is less variation in the number of other rooms in a dwelling than in the number of bedrooms. There is need for a place for food preparation, a place to eat, and a common area for living, regardless of the number of bedrooms in the dwelling. Although there may be some variation in nonbedroom space, or in what Winnick (1957, p. 17) has termed *overhead space,* it is the space enclosed as "bedrooms" which must vary most nearly in accordance with family size and composition.

Obviously, as a family increases in size, there must be somewhat more space for eating, living, and food preparation. But the needed increase in the number of spaces or the amount of space is not nearly as great as the needed increase in bedroom space. The APHA standards (Table 1) and the HUD standards (Table 2) reflect this position. The increase in the needed amount of space according to the number of persons in the household (Table 1) or according to the number of bedrooms in the dwelling unit (Table 2) is due almost totally to an increase in needed space for sleeping and dressing or bedroom space. Little increase is contributed by space needed for other activities or other rooms.

The preferred measure of bedroom need is a norm-based function of the family's size and composition. Bedroom-need norms are an expression of the number of bedrooms needed to meet the cultural norms that prescribe which family members should have separate bedrooms and which may share bedrooms. To determine bedroom need, then, the cultural rules concerning bedroom sharing must be known.

Several different attempts to develop operational measures of the need for bedroom space have yielded similar results. In addition to measures of the number of square feet of space needed according to family size (Table 1), the American Public Health Association (1950) discussed the division of space into rooms and thereby began to approximate more closely the idea of cultural norms rather than technical measures of the sizes of furniture and the human body. The criteria used are clearly normative and include

> *consideration of privacy to insure rest during sleep; sex separation to maintain standards customary in our society; and age separation to eliminate friction which may result if persons of greatly different age share the same bedroom (p. 39).*

According to the APHA standards, "single sleeping rooms are desirable, if economic limitations permit, for all individuals other than husband and wife" (p. 39). If bedrooms must be shared, however, then the following rules should apply:

> *1) not more than two persons may sleep in the same room;*
> *2) the two persons may be:*
> *a) husband and wife;*
> *b) two persons of same sex, but not excessive age difference;*
> *c) two children of opposite sex, both less than 6 years of age;*
> *d) a child less than 8 years of age and a person of opposite sex, not less than 18 years of age (sic) (p. 40).*

Recently researchers have used the need for bedrooms as an alternative to the number of persons in the housing unit and to provide a normative measure against which to relate the actual number of bedrooms. Greenfield and Lewis (1969) developed and tested an overcrowding index by comparing their index to the traditional persons-per-room index. Their index was designed to take into account both the HUD policies and the values of the society which consider "the needs of privacy by teenagers and single adults" (p. 284). The rules for bedroom sharing in their index were:

> *(a) A married couple may share a room; (b) No more than two children of the same sex may share a room past the age of twelve; (c) No more than two children of the opposite sex may share a room past the age of three; (d) All others must have individual sleeping chambers (p. 284).*

Researchers at the University of Michigan (Duncan and Newman, 1975; Goodman, 1974) devised a measure of required rooms for a family based on family composition. They allowed:

> *. . . a base of two rooms (exclusive of bathrooms) . . . for head and wife or single head. One additional room was allocated for each single person age 18 and above, one room for a married couple other than head and wife, and one room for every two children of the same sex under 18. Children under age 10 were paired regardless of sex if this reduced the room requirement (Duncan and Newman, 1975, p. 287).*

Their measure allowed only one nonbedroom space rather than the two allocated by Greenfield and Lewis. The other guidelines are quite similar, however. Empirical tests of their measure indicated that the variable derived by subtracting the needed rooms calculated from the number of rooms in the residence was an effective predictor of mobility expectations, actual mobility, and the fulfillment of mobility expectations (Duncan and Newman, 1975; Goodman, 1974).

Morris (1972b) and Gladhart (1973) developed a normative measure of bedroom need and used it to predict family housing adjustment behavior. Their measure was designed to reflect rather strongly-held incest taboos as well as less strongly-held convictions about the proper environment for the psychosocial development of children (Morris, 1977).

According to their index, no more than two people may share a bedroom and a bedroom is needed for:

> 1. *The parental couple (or single parent);*
> 2. *Each child aged 18 or over;*
> 3. *Each pair of same sex children, at least one between the ages of 9 and 17, whose ages differ by 4 years or less;*
> 4. *Each pair of children of any sex, both under age 9, whose ages do not differ by more than 4 years;*
> 5. *Each additional adult or couple (Morris 1972b, p. 5; Gladhart 1973, p. 30).*

From Table 4, it can be seen that there are obvious commonalities among the four measures, which clearly represent the broad outlines of the cultural norms for bedroom sharing. No more than two persons are allowed per bedroom. No other individuals should share the parental bedroom, other than husband and wife. Children of the opposite sex who are past an age well below puberty should not share bedrooms. Older teenagers and single adults should have their own rooms. Children of quite different ages should not share bedrooms.

The APHA, Greenfield and Lewis, University of Michigan, and Morris-Gladhart measures of the need for space represent attempts to index culture-

TABLE 4 Comparison of the criteria employed for bedroom assignment in four measures of bedroom need

	Measure developed by:			
Provision	APHA	Greenfield and Lewis	Morris and Gladhart	University of Michigan
Maximum of two persons per bedroom	yes	yes	yes	yes
Privacy for married couples or a single head	yes	yes	yes	yes
Maximum age for opposite-sex sharing	yes	yes	yes	yes
Privacy for young adults	no	yes	yes	yes
Proximity in age for same-sex sharing	yes	no	yes	no

Sources. American Public Health Association, Committee on the Hygiene of Housing, *Planning the Home for Occupancy* (Chicago: Public Administration Service, 1950), p. 40; R. J. Greenfield and J. F. Lewis, 1969, "An Alternative to a Density Function Definition of Overcrowding" (*Land Economics* 45), p. 284; E. W. Morris, "Departure from a Normatively Prescribed State as an Independent Variable: An Analysis of Housing Space Norms" (Ithaca, N.Y.: Department of Consumer Economics and Public Policy, Cornell University, 1972), p. 5; P. M. Gladhart, *Family Housing Adjustment and the Theory of Residential Mobility: A Temporal Analysis of Family Residential Histories* (Ithaca, N.Y.: Cornell University dissertation, 1973) p. 30; G. J. Duncan and S. Newman, "People as Planners: The Fulfillment of Residential Mobility Expectations," in *Five Thousand Families—Patterns of Economic Progress,* Vol. 3 (Ann Arbor: Institute for Social Research, University of Michigan, 1975), p. 287.

wide norms for space. A test of the applicability of the need for bedrooms has been conducted (Morris, 1976). The sample was drawn from a small city of about 30,000 population in the northwest part of Iowa.

Each respondent was asked how many bedrooms are needed by the average American family with the same sex and age composition as their own family. The results indicate that relative to this measure, the Morris-Gladhart index of bedroom need slightly underestimates the need as reported by the respondents. With the Morris-Gladhart index no allowance was made for a need for a guest bedroom while a sizable proportion of the respondents apparently felt there was such a need. Another reason that the measure underestimated the norm may be that some families feel that teenagers well before the age of 18 should have their own room rather than sharing with a same-sex sibling.

In addition, families were asked how many bedrooms their own family needed "right now." The responses were similar but more varied than the responses to the average family question. However, the correlation between the two measures was very high (Yockey, 1976b).

For most families the need for bedrooms changes throughout the life cycle. At any given point, however, a bedroom need and corresponding bedroom deficit (the number of bedrooms it has minus the number of bedrooms needed) can be calculated. The bedroom deficit has been shown to be a significant predictor of housing satisfaction, mobility desires, mobility expectations, family adaptation behavior, and residential alteration behavior (Morris, 1972a and 1972b; Gladhart, 1973; Bross, 1975; Morris et al, 1976; Morris, 1976; Morris, 1977; Bresler, 1975; Yockey, 1976a; Yockey, 1976b).

SPACE NORMS OVER THE LIFE CYCLE

Families with Children

Because the space norms that apply to families depend on the age, sex, and role of each family member, there are many changes that occur in the norms that apply as families with children progress through the life cycle. Prior to the birth of their first child, the couple should have a residence that is separate from either set of parents and from others, as well. The dwelling should have a sleeping room and two other spaces, one for food preparation and one for living, with an eating area that is part of either of those two. Thus, a young couple might have one bedroom, a living-dining room and a kitchen, or a kitchen-dining room and a living room. Because their income is not as high as it will be later in the life cycle, young families often find that a small apartment or a mobile home (Lindamood, 1974) provides sufficient space.

Children should have a sleeping space that is separate from that of the parents. Permitted deviation is that very young children may share the parental bedroom. But the child should have his or her own room well before the age of five. Thus the birth of the first child causes an abrupt change in housing needs. A larger dwelling, one with at least two bedrooms, is required. Families with one or more children living in a one-bedroom dwelling experience a normative deficit.

The birth of the second child, and all other subsequent children, may or may not cause an immediate change in the norms that apply. The spacing between the children is the critical factor here. If the children are close together in age, regardless of their sex, they may share the same bedroom when they are young. If there are more than four years between the first and second child, then the birth of the second child causes changes in the space needed. Another bedroom would be required.

Space norms that apply are subject to change as children approach prepuberty. At this stage, the sexes of the children determine who may properly share bedrooms. Hence the family that needed two bedrooms, one for the parents and one for the two children, a boy, four, and a girl, two, will feel a deficit sometime before the boy's ninth birthday. Even families with children of the same sex feel that additional bedroom space is needed as the oldest child becomes a teenager.

When the oldest child leaves home, the space needs may or may not change, depending on whether the move out of the parental home is viewed as permanent or temporary. A child in college, working in another city, or in military service often has a room reserved, at least temporarily, unless there is a great deal of pressure for the space, as there may be in large families. When a child marries or moves to his or her own dwelling, such a move is usually considered relatively permanent, and the room is converted to other uses.

When all the children have left the parental residence, the use of space may not be greatly altered. The couple still has many possessions and needs a place to put them, and they very likely want to have sufficient space to permit visits by children and grandchildren. Only when the couple can no longer maintain the amount of space are they likely to feel they have a positive deficit in terms of space.

There are also changes in the need for nonbedroom space over the family life cycle. As children approach adolescence, many families think teenagers should have space for entertaining their friends in a manner that will not totally disrupt the lives of other family members. A large living-dining room combination could accommodate many activities at once. A large bedroom could provide adequate space for each child. A family room or recreation room that is separate from the living room could serve the needs. Another alternative could be a bedroom-living room combination for the parents.

Around these broad outlines, some variation is permitted. Overconformance may be represented by a bedroom for each family member, except husband and wife, plus an extra bedroom for guests, and three or four additional rooms: kitchen, dining room, living room, perhaps a family room. Permitted underconformance may include having three children (of the same sex above an age threshold that is below puberty) in a bedroom, same-sex bedroom sharing with a rather wide difference in ages, or same-sex young adults sharing bedrooms, rather than having their own rooms. The variations permitted clearly are greater at some stages of the life cycle than at others, and separation of the sexes in bedrooms must not be violated for children past puberty.

Single-Parent Families

The norms that apply to single-parent families over the stages of the family life cycle are identical to those that apply to families in which both parents are present. More variation is permitted, however. Single-parent families are likely to face greater constraints and thus have a more difficult time achieving the amount of space prescribed by the norms. It is the constraints (and not differences in housing needs) that explain the fact that the median number of rooms in the dwelling for both owners and renters in families with the same number of children under 18 is consistently higher when the household head is male than it is for female-headed households. The only exception occurs in the case of the household head under 25 years of age (USBC, 1973f, pp. 7–11).

The overwhelming majority of single-parent families, almost 80 percent in 1970, are headed by a female, rather than a male (USBC, 1973g, p. 278). Such families are likely to have far lower incomes than families in which both husband and wife are present (USBC, 1973g, p. 873). Until October 1975, when the Equal Credit Opportunity Act took effect, lending institutions discriminated against such families. Female household heads had a much more difficult time obtaining a mortgage than male household heads. Hence, they were prohibited from purchasing sufficient space.

Single Individuals and Childless Couples

Norms that apply to single individuals and childless couples are not nearly as specific as those that apply to families with children, nor do they change as rapidly as the individual or couple progress through the "life cycle." A young single individual should have a sleeping area, living area, and cooking space which may be combined into one single space, as in an efficiency apartment. Young single individuals may share a dwelling with one or more other people of approximately the same age. Space needs for a childless couple are similar to those prescribed for a couple before the birth of their first child.

In spite of the fact that there is not a clear progression through a "family life cycle" that is related to the birth and maturation of children, there are standards that prescribe an increasing amount of space for single individuals and childless couples as they grow older. Single individuals are expected to have their own dwelling, rather than share a dwelling. Two bedrooms are prescribed for an older single individual. Two or three bedrooms are expected for an older, but not elderly, childless couple.

Sanctions for violating such space norms are not very severe. A childless couple with only one bedroom will not be severely sanctioned, nor will the single individual who rents a room or shares a dwelling. The "proper environment for children," of primary concern to society, is not an issue in these cases. Therefore the society and the community are not as specific regarding how single persons and childless couples should live.

CONCLUSION

There can be little doubt that the number of bedrooms needed, based on age and sex composition, is the way that the majority of American families define their space needs. It is important, therefore, that housing researchers and housing policy makers utilize similar measures when defining crowding and space needs. Measures of persons per room, persons per sleeping room, and square feet of space needed should probably be abandoned in favor of measures of bedroom need and bedroom deficit if culturally-relevant evaluation of residential crowding is required.

DEFINITIONS

Bedroom deficit. In general, the number of bedrooms a family has minus the number needed; specifically, having too few or too many bedrooms.

Bedroom need. A measure of the number of bedrooms needed by a family to avoid violation of the cultural norms for bedroom sharing; an assessment of housing space needs based on the family's size and composition.

Crowding. Deficit of space; variously measured by such concepts as square feet per person, persons per room, persons per sleeping room, and bedroom deficit.

Definitional norms. Housing standards (norms) that define those characteristics without which a structure would not be called a dwelling unit.

Minimum standards. Similar to definitional norms. In the United States, minimum standards are met by dwellings with, at least, interconnected weather-tight rooms with complete kitchen facilities and a complete bathroom for the exclusive use of the residents of the unit.

Persons-per-room ratio. Calculated by dividing the number of persons in the household by the number of rooms (excluding bathrooms) in the unit. "Overcrowded" housing is generally considered as that having more than 1.0 persons per room.

Persons-per-sleeping-room ratio. A variation on the persons-per-room ratio. More than two persons per sleeping room is considered overcrowded.

Promulgate. To put publicly into operation; to make known by open declaration.

Space deficit. An excess or shortage of space or living area. A positive space deficit occurs when a family has more space than the norms prescribe. A negative space deficit occurs when a family is crowded in comparison with normative standards.

Specification norms. Standards (goals) that define and prescribe the detail and elaboration of the dwelling unit above the minimum housing level and above definitional norms. These norms are the cultural definitions of *adequate* housing.

Chapter 6
Norms for Tenure and Structure Type

> You shall live in square gray houses, in a barren land and beside those square gray houses you shall starve.
> Prophecy of Drinks Water, a Dakota holy man, before the coming of the white man*

Cultural norms for tenure and structure type are so closely bound together that they are discussed together in this chapter. It seems quite clear that cultural norms prescribe ownership of a single-family dwelling for most families throughout the stages of the family life cycle. Foote et al. (1960, p. 224) pointed out that norms prescribing tenure and structure type may be partially a function of norms for space. Dwellings with large numbers of rooms and ample yard space tend to be available for purchase but seldom for rent. Small, compact dwelling units are more often found in multiple-unit dwellings, which are more often available for rent than for ownership.

The tendency, noted in 1960, for rented quarters to be smaller than owner-occupied dwellings was still prominent in 1970 (Table 5). The typical owner-occupied dwelling has five or six rooms while the typical renter-occupied dwelling has only three or four rooms. Similarly, the numbers of rooms in single-family dwellings are larger than in multiple-family dwellings (Table 6). Yet an explanation of ownership of single-family dwellings based solely on space norms that are more easily met in owner-occupied detached dwellings is not totally satisfactory. Tenure and structure type norms exist independently of space norms and must be taken into account.

A recent study (Michelson, Belgue, and Stewart, 1973) found that preferences for tenure and structure type were more important reasons for moving from apartments to houses than were space-related reasons. The norms for tenure and structure type are closely allied to one another, as will be discussed. But they can be shown also to operate independently from one another, as well as independently from space norms.

* From a display at the Lower Sioux Agency and Interpretive Center, Minnesota State Historical Society, Morton, Minnesota.

TABLE 5 Percentage of dwellings that contain a specific number of rooms by tenure of the dwelling unit, all year-around dwelling units, 1970

	Percentage of:		
Number of Rooms	All Dwellings	Owner-Occupied Dwellings	Renter-Occupied Dwellings
1	1.8	0.2	4.0
2	3.5	0.7	7.5
3	11.0	3.2	22.8
4	20.8	14.7	30.1
5	25.1	28.6	20.0
6	20.1	26.9	10.1
7	9.5	13.7	3.3
8	4.9	7.1	1.4
9+	3.3	4.9	0.8
	100.0	100.0	100.0
Median Number of Rooms	5.0	5.6	4.0

Source. U.S. Bureau of the Census, Census of Housing 1970, *Vol. 1. Housing Characteristics for States, Cities and Counties.* Part 1, U.S. Summary (Washington: U.S. Government Printing Office, 1972), p. 282.

TABLE 6 Median number of rooms by the number of units in the structure for owner- and renter-occupied dwellings

	Median Rooms	
Number of Units in the Structure	Owner-occupied Units	Renter-occupied Units
1 unit	5.7	4.8
2 units	5.1	4.2
3–4 units	4.8	3.8
5–9 units	4.4	3.6
10–19 units	4.1	3.4
20 units and over	3.9	3.2

Source. United States Bureau of the Census, Census of Housing: 1970, *Subject Reports,* Final Report HC(7)-3, Space Utilization of the Housing Inventory (Washington: U.S. Government Printing Office, 1973), p. 6; p. 9.

TENURE NORMS

Strong norms in favor of home ownership have existed since the founding of the United States. Indeed, there is reason to believe that home ownership as an ideal goes far back into the prehistory of Western society. Part of the impetus for immigration to the United States was suppressed desire for ownership of land on the part of European peasants (Jennings, 1938). Presidents Coolidge, Hoover, and Roosevelt, as quoted by Dean (1945), all felt that home ownership is the "backbone" of the economic and social system of the United States.

Even those who have warned against presumed risks of home ownership for families or the society have acknowledged its existence as a cultural norm. In his discussion of housing problems that followed the depression and World War II, Charles Abrams (1946) said:

> *Home ownership is America's tradition. American poets have sung its praises. Our chief executives have proclaimed it as a vital link in democracy. Any Congressman can deliver a homily on the subject without a minute's preparation and often does (p. 36).*

Dean, who argued against home ownership on economic grounds, refers to home ownership as an "institution" (1951, p. 59): a "value built deeply into the culture" (1945, p. 2). Caplow (1948) questioned the wisdom of home ownership but clearly demonstrated the existence of home ownership norms in a metropolitan area. Green (1953b) demonstrated the existence of home ownership norms among farmers.

It seems quite clear that Dean, Abrams, and the others were correct, because the norm for ownership has been sanctioned by the income tax laws and government-insured mortgages, as well as lending institutions and creditors who extend credit more readily to owners than to renters (Cohen and Hanson, 1972, p. 266). In addition, landlord-tenant law and custom in the United States have traditionally favored the landlord and placed the tenant in a relatively powerless position (Rose, 1973, pp. 1–12; Quinn and Phillips, 1972; Patrick and Griswold, 1973). Thus, the negative aspects of renting give additional credence to the ownership norm as negative sanctions for those not in conformance.

The income tax laws are more favorable to home owners than to renters because of two provisions. First, home owners are permitted to deduct their mortgage interest payments and their property tax payments from their taxable income. Second, the home owner is not required to report the rental value of his home, referred to as *net imputed rent,* as taxable income (Slitor, 1968; Goode, 1960; Aaron, 1972; White and White, 1965; Kindahl, 1960). In addition, capital gains tax on the return from the sale of the dwelling is deferred if another residence of equal or greater value is purchased within a specified length of time after the sale of the first residence.

In effect, the tax benefits amount to both a reduction in the price of housing for the owner, and favored treatment for the family who has chosen to invest their money in the dwelling they occupy rather than in other assets (Aaron, 1972, pp. 53–55). Because of the down payment required, the relatively higher monthly costs of ownership versus renting, and their inability to obtain a mortgage, low-income families are more likely to be renters than owners. Thus the tax laws not only promote home ownership, but also amount to subsidies for upper- and middle-income families.

There are tax benefits for owners of rental property, as well. The most important benefits permit the investor to deduct from taxable income an amount for depreciation that is greater than the "true" rate of depreciation (Aaron, 1972, p. 66). The entire cost of the building including the portion financed by the mortgage can be depreciated even when the equity in the building is very small (Slitor, 1968, p. 13). Whether or not the housing consumer reaps the benefits of the tax laws encouraging investment in rental housing depends upon how much of the savings the owner passes on to the tenants. The relationship between the tax laws and reduced housing expenses is not as direct for the renter as it is for the home owner.

There is little question that the federal mortgage insurance programs, administered through the Veteran's Administration (VA) and the Federal Housing Administration (FHA) have promoted home ownership for millions of families. Many of these would not have been eligible for conventional mortgages. Neither the FHA nor the VA lend money to prospective buyers. Instead, they insure lenders against loss. Lending institutions have been able to accept low down payments and extend long terms, thus lowering the monthly payments and easing the initial purchase expenses. With VA- or FHA-insured mortgages, a family with a moderate income could spend 25 percent of it on housing, the rule of thumb often applied by lending institutions, and still be home owners. The effect, however, is to increase the total amount of interest paid by the time the mortgage is paid off (NCUP, 1968, pp. 94–107). The FHA and VA programs have enabled millions of families to "buy homes sooner than they otherwise could have and to pay more than they otherwise could have afforded" (Aaron, 1972, p. 89). The effects of Farmers' Home Administration programs have been similar to those of FHA and VA, although the programs differ in their details.

In the long run, the home owner's financial position is likely to be better than the renter's because of the tax advantage, the "forced savings" that accrue as equity increases, and the fact that the value of the house has a good chance of keeping pace with inflation, unlike many other investments. One study (Shelton, 1968) estimated that ownership is less expensive if the home is occupied three-and-a-half years or longer, but not if the home is owned less than three-and-a-half years. Such analyses, of course, relate to the conditions that prevailed at the time and do not represent permanent generalizations.

The decision to own or rent is closely related to family income. A recent longitudinal panel study (Roistacher, 1974a) shows that the rate of switching from rental tenure to home ownership rises with increases in income. Switching from ownership to rental is associated with declines in income. That pattern lends indirect support to home ownership norms, in that income serves as a constraint which, when relieved, permits families to become owners.

In their study of housing market discrimination, Kain and Quigley (1972) found that, when other important socioeconomic variables were controlled in a statistical analysis, black households were less likely to be home owners than white households. The differential rate of ownership was attributed to market discrimination. The result was exclusion of many blacks from the investment opportunity that has been the prime means of accumulating wealth for low- and moderate-income families since World War II (Kain and Quigley, 1972, p. 273). The home ownership rate among blacks rose faster than among whites between 1960 and 1970. Yet the percentage of blacks who are home owners (42.0 in 1970) is still far lower than that of whites (65.4) (USBC, 1975b, p. 717).

The impetus for home ownership is clearly not based solely on economic benefits, however, or home ownership would vary with the market conditions much more closely than it does (Coons and Glaze, 1963). Potential home owners would establish their "demand price" (the price at or below which they would buy) and would then need to know the "supply price" (the price at or above which sellers would sell) for housing. The decision for or against home purchase would be based on the comparison between the demand price and the supply price. The family would decide to own when the demand price was higher and to rent when the supply price was the higher of the two (Coons and Glaze, 1963, p. 13).

The steady rise in the number and rates of home owners, (Table 7), supports the premise that the decision to own rather than rent is not made on purely economic grounds. The number of home owners has experienced a vast increase, but so has the population. It is the rate of home ownership that gives an indication of the strength of the norms.

From 1890 to 1930 the rate of home ownership stayed about the same. There was a slight drop between 1930 and 1940, the result of the depression. From 1940 to 1960 the rates of home ownership increased a great deal, largely as a result of the availability of FHA- and VA-insured loans. The home ownership rate increased only one percent between 1960 and 1970, although the actual number of home owners increased greatly.

The lessening in the rate of increase between 1960 and 1970 may have been a response to the demographic conditions that existed in 1970. By then, the baby boom babies born shortly after World War II were in their early

TABLE 7 Number and percentage of owner-occupied dwelling units, 1890–1974

Year	Number (000's)	Percentage
1890	6,066	47.8
1900	7,205	46.7
1910	9,084	45.9
1920	10,867	45.6
1930	14,002	47.8
1940	15,196	43.6
1950	23,560	55.0
1960	32.797	61.9
1970	39,885	62.9
1974	45,785	64.6

Sources. U.S. Bureau of the Census, *The Statistical History of the United States from Colonial Times to Present* (Stanford, Conn.: Fairfield, 1965), p. 395; U.S. Bureau of the Census, *Statistical Abstract of the United States* (Washington: U.S. Government Printing Office, 1961), p. 761; U.S. Bureau of the Census, Census of Housing 1970, *Vol. 1, Housing Characteristics for States, Cities and Counties,* Part 1, U.S. Summary (Washington: U.S. Government Printing Office, 1972), p. 16; U.S. Bureau of the Census, *Current Housing Reports,* "Advance Report H-150-74, Annual Housing Survey 1974, Part B, Indicators of Housing and Neighborhood Quality for the United States and Regions" (Washington: U.S. Government Printing Office, 1976), p. 1.

twenties and were candidates for establishing their first residence, likely a rented dwelling. Barring economic disaster, it is probable that by 1980 the home ownership rate will increase greatly again, reflecting the fact that the same individuals who contributed to the decline in the increase between 1960 and 1970 will be the new home owners of 1980. Such a trend can already be seen from the 1974 rate, although it is based on a smaller sample of the population than are the decennial census data.

The decision to own is founded primarily on noneconomic factors, as reported by several studies (Coons and Glaze, 1963; The Urge to Own, 1937; Branch, 1942; Rosow, 1948). Such reasons seem to be positive reactions to the ability to conform to the cultural norm for ownership. Rosow (1948) reported emotional goals such as psychic security, family security and ego satisfaction, living pattern goals, and status and prestige goals. All those reasons are ranked higher than financial goals. During the recent inflationary period, it is possible that, if the study were to be repeated, financial goals would have been more prominent. One of the best protections against inflation has been home ownership. The typical house value has had a good chance of keeping pace with or staying ahead of the rate of inflation.

SINGLE-FAMILY DWELLINGS

The historical tendency in the peasant populations of Western society for families to live in separate free-standing dwellings is so common and so much a part of Western culture that one is led to think of multifamily urban dwellings as cultural aberrations. Peasant societies, either Western or non-Western, that typically live in multifamily dwellings are uncommon enough that they seem striking. The single-family dwelling is so common in rural areas today around the world that the idea of rural multifamily dwellings would evoke laughter in most parts of the world.

There is no doubt that today in the United States there is

> *a penchant for the white cottage-picket fence-chintz curtains ideal . . . (Rosow, 1948, p. 154).*

The specific content of that ideal may not be enduring. The picket fence may give way to redwood. The chintz curtains may be replaced by antique satin draperies. The cottage may become the three-bedroom split-level. But the basic idea that each family should have its own separate structure with a certain amount of exterior space and relatively clear-cut boundaries has characterized American housing attitudes since the beginning. There is, of course, a considerable minority of other dwelling types in existence. Duplexes, row houses, garden apartments, and high-rise structures are the obvious ones.

The norm prescribing a single-family dwelling is relaxed for single individuals and families in which there are no children in the household. At this point in history, even though there have been recent construction trends in multifamily dwellings, along with a proliferation of variations on the row house (the townhouse, the low-rise, the fourplex, etc.), it seems premature to forecast the end of the single-family detached dwelling. Such a prediction would be questionable, chiefly because the norm is so strong for families with children that it spills over to families without children.

One recent study (Gladhart, 1973) measured the "need for a single-family dwelling" to assess the appropriateness of alternatives to the single-family dwelling for certain families. Assuming that "family role patterns reflect age composition" and that "babies and teenagers are more demanding of housing than children of other ages" (p. 10), he developed a scale measuring the need for a single-family house based upon the relative complexity of the children's age distribution. Based on an analysis of differential rates of residential mobility, he concluded that

> *the dominant feature of the tenure-type combination is the structure type. Owning a duplex is most similar to owning a conventional home. To occupy a single-family home as a renter or free renter is the next best thing to owning it if your family needs one (p. 45).*

While the single-family house is "the norm in North America" (Michelson, 1970, p. 100), the norm for structure type is almost inextricably bound to the norm for ownership. Slitor (1968, p. 36) noted the relation between tenure and structure type in his discussion of the influence of the income tax laws on housing conditions. One of the results of those positive sanctions applied for ownership has been the proliferation of single-family houses.

Being a home owner in American society means largely to own a single-family conventionally-constructed dwelling. There have not only been few alternatives available, but also, those that have existed have been thought of as inferior. While ownership in other forms of housing is increasing, to date it has not accounted for a significant proportion of the dwellings available for owner-occupancy. Cooperative and condominium forms of ownership, which permit owner-occupancy of a unit within a multiunit complex, are relatively recent pheonomena offering alternatives to the potential home purchaser. Condominium and cooperative forms of ownership account for 0.9 percent of all owner-occupied units and 0.6 percent of all occupied units (USBC, 1972b, p. 16). It was not until the 1970 Census that cooperative and condominium forms of ownership were even tabulated. Prior to 1970 they were included in the owner-occupied category (USBC, 1970, p. 116).

Another alternative to owner-occupancy of the conventional home—the mobile home—was not separately tabulated until the 1960 Census, and number of mobile homes rose dramatically between 1960 and 1970, from 0.8 million (1.3 percent) in 1960 to 2.1 million (3.1 percent) of all occupied units in 1970 (USBC, 1972b, p. S-19).

There are some exceptions to the usual pattern of predominance of the single-family detached dwelling. Philadelphia, Washington, and Baltimore, along with some other smaller cities in that area, are thought of as row-house cities where single-family *attached* dwellings are much more common than in other cities. The distinction between the row house and the single-family detached dwelling is not whether it is a single-family dwelling but whether it has any of its sidewalls attached to those of other units. Although the external appearance of a row house might be very similar to a single-story apartment building the social difference is great. Therefore, even if the norms of the area include the row house in the norm for the single-family owner-occupied home, it is still a single-family dwelling that is prescribed.

According to the 1970 Census (USBC, 1972b, pp. 320–22), there are more single-family attached dwellings (row houses) than single-family detached dwellings in six cities: Philadelphia, Washington, Baltimore, Allentown, Trenton, and Camden. The preponderance of row houses occurs only in those cities. While substantial numbers of attached dwellings possibly exist in other cities, it is probable that in the absence of an established row house tradition, those attached dwellings are frequently classified as multiunit structures. It is very likely, for example, that side-by-side duplexes that would be properly labeled attached dwellings when they have a complete wall separating the two halves would simply be labeled two-unit dwellings.

Another city that can be seen to have different community norms for structure type is New York City, where the number of multifamily structures is more than double that of single-family structures (USBC, 1972b, p. 312). The actual housing conditions in New York clearly brand it as a multiunit housing city. That does not necessarily indicate that norms for single-family dwellings do not apply to New Yorkers. It may be the case that the size, density, land cost, and other unique features of New York act as constraints that prevent utilization of single-family dwellings on a large scale. The preferences of New Yorkers differ from those of people in other cities. That their norms differ is not so obvious.

New York, like all other major cities in the country, has experienced a very substantial outward movement to its suburban areas, nearly all of which are predominantly single-family housing areas. The magnitude of the out-migration from the city to the suburbs may be a better indication of the strength New Yorkers' norms for structure type than the proportion of the city housing stock that is made up of multifamily housing.

If the tenure and structure type norms were to be ranked according to importance, it is likely that the norm for ownership is the more important of the two. As ownership of conventionally-constructed single-family dwellings has become increasingly more expensive, family behavior indicates a preference for compromising the norms for structure type rather than the ownership norm. Instead of renting an apartment for about the same price (Woods and Morris, 1971), very large numbers of families are choosing to own a mobile home. The motivation is probably because it is available for ownership, even though it is not the conventional single-family structure (Morris, 1971; Morris and Woods, 1971).

The increase in cooperatives and condominiums may also be indicative of the relative importance of ownership versus structure type. Faced with the increasingly high costs of single-family dwellings, the structure type norms are compromised first by the cooperative and condominium purchasers.

DISAGREEMENT REGARDING NORMS FOR TENURE AND STRUCTURE TYPE

Contrary to space norms, about which experts, official representatives, and the members of the society appear to agree, there is some disagreement about the current situation and whether or not there have been changes in single-family ownership patterns. The percentage of home owners, while still becoming larger, increased at a declining rate until 1970 (Table 6). Since then, the rate of increase appears to have begun to climb again. Apartment construction and mobile home production had boomed in the last decade, while construction of single-family houses had declined as a percentage of all current construction. Such trends could have occurred in response to changing economic conditions that called for relaxation of norms, to a change in the demographic composition of the demand for housing, or to changing norms.

Economic Factors

A recent government report (RERC, 1974) indicates that the single-family dwelling may soon prove economically infeasible for American communities. If that becomes the case, families will be forced to lower their norms or to suffer chronic dissatisfaction. The report estimates that the total investment costs of the "high density planned community," is 44 percent lower than the costs of a community consisting of single-family homes. The high-density, planned community consisted of:

> *. . . 40 percent high rise apartments, 30 percent walkup apartments, 20 percent townhouses and 10 percent clustered single family homes. All of the dwelling units are clustered together in contiguous neighborhoods . . . (RERC, 1974, p. 2).*

Operation and maintenance costs and environmental costs (measured by the energy needed for heating, and the amount of air and storm water pollution) are also likely to be lower.

It is significant that the analysis focused on costs to the community and included little reference to costs to the individual families in terms of possible lowered satisfaction caused by high-density housing. News Correspondent David Brinkley felt such considerations to be paramount; he commented on the NBC Nightly News:

> *A new government report says the American dream of the private single-family house is too expensive and inefficient. Far more effi-*

cient, it says, are apartments and houses clustered together, or attached in rows, because they're cheapter to build and maintain.

Three Federal agencies dealing with energy, housing and environment sponsored the study, and quickly said it did not mean the end of the single-family house, but it did point that way. In fact, the building of separate houses has already fallen drastically because the average single-family house is now too expensive for the average single family.

While this is one element in what is called the American dream, it is older than that. The Old Testament speaks of every man sitting under his own vine and fig tree, and in the 3,000 years since then, in every country, that has been the human ideal, and the U.S. has come closer than any to making it a reality for the greatest number.

Those who made this study with computer and slide rule no doubt have all the numbers right, but the same figures certainly would show that the most efficient system would be to put people into cotton uniforms and herd them all into barracks. That would save even more energy and money.

Americans are now importuned to work harder and produce more. But it does seem basic to human nature that people will work no more than the absolute minimum unless they can expect, in return for their work, to get something they want. If the kind of housing most people work for and aspire to is too expensive and inefficient, perhaps it's time for a government study on how to improve it, rather than to get rid of it (David Brinkley's Journal, NBC Nightly News, October 21, 1974. Reprinted by permission).

Demographic Factors

At this point, however, it seems that demographic trends are playing the largest part in the explanation of the construction figures (Table 8). The peak years for apartment construction are related to the percentage of the population between the ages of 20 and 29 and to the fluctuation in the number of marriages. Rented apartments are within the range of permissible deviation for young childless couples. Baird (1964) forecast an apartment boom in the late sixties and early seventies, which subsequently occurred, to accommodate new family formation by the baby boom babies. In addition, there has been a striking increase in the production of mobile homes in response to the rising numbers of young childless couples who were not ready or able to purchase a conventional single-family dwelling. The most recent figures available indicate a downward trend in the number of marriages and in mobile home and multiunit production.

It was obvious in the early 1970s that typical housing choice behavior had changed since 1960, for the number and proportion of apartment

TABLE 8 The relationship between family formation and the production of apartments and mobile homes, 1959–1975

Year	Percentage Multi-family* Units	Percentage Mobile Homes	Percentage of the Population 20–29	Number of Marriages (000's)	Marriage Rate/1000
1959	14.6	7.2	11.9	1494	8.5
1960	16.9	7.3	12.1	1523	8.5
1961	22.4	6.2	12.2	1548	8.5
1962	27.3	7.3	12.2	1577	8.5
1963	31.4	8.4	12.3	1654	8.8
1964	30.1	10.9	12.5	1725	9.0
1965	28.2	12.5	12.7	1800	9.3
1966	26.6	15.4	12.8	1857	9.5
1967	27.5	15.4	13.4	1927	9.7
1968	31.7	17.1	13.9	2069	10.3
1969	33.5	21.6	14.3	2146	10.6
1970	32.4	21.5	15.1	2179	10.7
1971	33.6	19.2	15.5	2196	10.6
1972	33.7	19.5	15.9	2269	11.0
1973	33.0	21.6	16.1	2284	10.9
1974	25.3	19.6	16.5	2232	10.6
1975	17.5	15.5	16.8	2174	10.2

* Units not in one- and two-family dwellings.

Sources. U.S. Bureau of the Census, *Statistical Abstracts of the United States* (Washington: U.S. Government Printing Office) 1960, p. 24; 1961, p. 28; 1962, p. 28; 1963, p. 28; 1964, p. 24, p. 755; 1966, p. 8; 1967, p. 10; 1968, p. 10; 1969, p. 10; 1970, p. 10; U.S. Bureau of the Census, Current Population Reports, *Population Estimates and Projections,* Series P-25 (Washington: U.S. Government Printing Office) No. 511, January 1974; No. 614, November 1975; U.S. Department of Health, Education and Welfare, Vital Statistics of the United States, Vol. III, *Marriages and Divorces* (Washington: U.S. Government Printing Office) 1969, pp. 1–5; 1972, pp. 1–5; U.S. Department of Health, Education and Welfare, *Monthly Vital Statistics Report* (Washington: U.S. Government Printing Office) Vol. 22, No. 12, December 1973; Vol. 24, No. 5, July 1975; U.S. Bureau of the Census, Construction Reports, *Housing Starts,* Series C-20 (Washington: U.S. Government Printing Office) January 1967; January 1974; March 1976.

dwellers and mobile home owners had risen considerably. Whether or not the need for the single-family owner-occupied house has changed is not as obvious. One way to assess whether or not there has been a shift is to survey the apartment and mobile home residents to discover if such forms of tenure and structure type coincide with their family norms. If this is the case, it may indicate a potential for change. If a rising proportion of individual families have norms for structure type that favor apartment living, it might foreshadow a shift in cultural norms. On the other hand, the young families may simply be responding to their as yet limited resources and accepting a compromise. The fact that marriage rates and the construction of apartments and mobile homes slowed down together is significant.

Changing Norms

There is evidence that the norms are not changing drastically. A study in the middle sixties (Lansing, Mueller, and Barth, 1964) found an overwhelming desire for the single-family dwelling among their sample. Even families living in multifamily structures indicated a desire for a single-family dwelling (pp. 46–49).

Michelson (1967) sought to estimate the number of "Potential Candidates for the Designers' Paradise" from a nationwide sample. He assessed the percentage of people who

1. want to trade a single-family dwelling for a dwelling in a multiunit complex;
2. want less private open space than they currently possess;
3. would rather live in the central city than the suburbs; and
4. prefer mass transit facilities to the private automobile.

He found that an exceedingly small percent of the sample (less than 6 percent) preferred any one of the options. Also, not a single respondent fit all of the categories.

Those who wanted to move to a multifamily dwelling tended to be single or married with no children at home. Families with children present did not want to live in multifamily housing. Families who wanted a smaller amount of open space were those who were married with no children present.

A more recent study (Hinshaw and Allott, 1972) of the housing aspirations of college students from a variety of income and ethnic groups in New York City found that:

The desire for single-family home ownership is ubiquitous and not in the process of radically changing (p. 107).

There is some slight indication that the norms may be changing, however. A recent study related *norms* for home ownership and single-family dwellings ("the best form of ownership and structure type for the average American family") to *family preferences* ("the best form of tenure and structure type for your family right now") (Winter and Morris, 1976). The overwhelming majority (over 90 percent) of all respondents felt that ownership of a single-family dwelling was the norm for American families.

Controlling for income and age and education of the head of the household revealed that there is a slight decline in the percentage expressing both norms and family preferences for single-family ownership among the young (under 40), those with the most education (beyond high school), and those with the highest incomes (over $15,000). Those groupings were somewhat less likely to report the single-family ownership norms, even though their income and education were more likely to permit the achievement of such conditions. Since it is young people with a greater amount of education who would be likely to change their norms first, such studies need to be continued to keep abreast of possible cultural changes.

TENURE AND STRUCTURE-TYPE DEFICITS

A normative deficit in either tenure or structure type is characterized by a residence that does not meet either cultural or family norms for tenure or structure type. From a cultural standpoint, normative structure deficits are Type I deficits. Either "too much" or "too little" single-family housing represents a deficit situation. Families living in a single-family dwelling when their composition does not dictate the need for one could be said to have a *positive* structure-type deficit. Those families living in a multifamily unit for whom the norms prescribe a single-family structure would be characterized by a *negative* structure deficit. Family structure-type deficits would follow a similar pattern.

Because cultural norms prescribe ownership, cultural tenure deficits are Type III deficits, for only negative deficits are undesirable. Family tenure deficits are Type I deficits, however. To rent when the norms prescribe ownership is to experience a negative tenure deficit. On the other hand, ownership when family norms prescribe rental is evidence of a positive tenure deficit.

The importance of single-family dwellings and home ownership vis-à-vis each other depends upon the specific conditions. Nevertheless, it is apparent that deficits in which a needed single-family dwelling is absent or needed home ownership is absent are both important determinants of dissatisfaction (Morris et al., 1976). Those findings validate the normative deficit status of those conditions. On the other hand, hypothesized deficits involving the presence of unneeded home ownership or single-family dwellings do not relate to dissatisfaction (Morris et al., 1976).

An urban study in Iowa (Morris, 1976) tested the relations between tenure and structure-type deficits that were culturally defined, were defined by the family, and were a combination of cultural and family deficits. In that study, almost a third of the respondents had a negative cultural tenure deficit (they were renters). Of those respondents, two-thirds also reported a negative family tenure deficit (they would rather be owners). No one reported a positive family tenure deficit. Thus there is a close correspondence between family and cultural tenure deficits.

Structure-type deficits present quite another picture, however. Two-fifths of the respondents had a cultural positive structure deficit (they lived in a single-family dwelling but did not need one), while only 3.5 percent reported a positive family deficit. Negative structure deficits had the reverse relationships. Ten percent of the sample indicated a negative family deficit (they lived in an apartment and would rather have a single-family dwelling), while only 4.2 percent of the sample had a negative cultural deficit.

The explanation for the lack of correspondence between cultural and family structure-type deficits is that most of the families in the study indicated that a single-family dwelling would be best for their family. Thus single individuals, childless couples, and couples with no children still living at home lived in a single-family dwelling and preferred that structure type for their household. Similarly, childless couples living in apartments wanted to move to a single-family dwelling, perhaps in anticipation of childbearing. While they did not yet need such a structure in cultural terms, it was their family preference.

The conclusion is that cultural and family deficits for tenure and structure type are rather closely aligned. The differences between the two are caused by the fact that only the absence of a single-family dwelling tends to produce dissatisfaction. Its presence, when not needed according to family composition, is not deemed undesirable.

NORMS FOR TENURE AND STRUCTURE TYPE OVER THE LIFE CYCLE

Cultural norms clearly prescribe ownership of a single-family dwelling for families with children, whether there are one or two parents present. Of the two norms, it is the norm for structure type that appears to be the stronger for families with children. It is preferable to rent a single-family structure if there are children than to own a unit in a cooperative or condominium.

More deviation is permitted when the children are younger than when they are teenagers. Thus apartment living is permitted when families have young children, as is a mobile home residence. Very few families with school-age children live in mobile homes (Lindamood, 1974; USBC, 1973e, pp. 8–10). Similarly, few families with school-age children select cooperatives or condominiums (USBC, 1973b, pp. 1–3).

When a new family is formed, their first residence is likely to be a rented apartment or an owner-occupied mobile home. If they live in an apartment, they are likely to become dissatisfied with their structure type before the birth of their first child. If they are unable to move to a single-family residence, the dissatisfaction will become stronger with the birth of a second child, or as the first child approaches school age. Families living in a mobile home probably do not experience a structure-type deficit until just before the oldest child enters school.

After the last child has left home, the couple no longer needs (in cultural terms) a single-family dwelling. The couple is not likely to experience positive tenure and structure-type deficits based on family norms until the dwelling proves too large or expensive to maintain. Only then is the household likely to report a desire to move to a rented dwelling, a unit in a multiunit dwelling, or a mobile home.

A tenure deficit is strongly related to income. It is permissible for young families whose income is relatively low, compared to what it will be later in the life cycle, to rent. When a family has school-age children, rental tenure is a strong indication to the community that the family has some sort of financial problem. Otherwise, the community asks, why would they rent? Tenure norms are relaxed somewhat for single-parent families, because of the constraints. The lower incomes and sex discrimination faced by female-headed households have made owner-occupancy difficult to attain (Morris and Winter, 1976b). Two-thirds of the male-headed households in which there are two or more persons own their dwellings. Less than half of the two-person female-headed households are home owners (USBC, 1973c, pp. 1 and 10).

Cultural norms are not as strict for childless couples or single individuals as they are for families with children. A single-family structure is not needed. Also, rental tenure is not as subject to negative sanctions for such households. Of the two norms, it seems that the ownership norm is stronger for single individuals and childess couples than is the norm for the single-family dwelling. The strength of the ownership norm is undoubtedly related to the positive sanctions available in the form of income tax deductions. Thus single individuals and childless couples are likely to have a negative family-level tenure deficit before they feel a negative family-level structure deficit. Hence condominiums, cooperatives, and mobile homes are normative structure types for such households (USBC, 1973e, pp. 8–10; USBC, 1973b, pp. 1–3).

CONCLUSION

The almost inescapable conclusion of this chapter is that perhaps the single most important aspect of housing in the United States, aside from pure questions of shelter, is single-family home ownership. It seems doubtful that rapid or extensive changes have occurred in norms for ownership and structure type. In fact, the evidence that exists suggests that the apparent trends are primarily due to cost and demographic factors. Housing policy that ignores these cultural norms seems inadvisable. Hinshaw and Allott (1972) put it succinctly:

> *This society is therefore faced with the choice of either providing access to this type of housing or of mounting a massive attack on "the American Dream" that is propagated in all forms of media and reinforced by cultural norms involving measures of status and self-worth as well as by traditional antiurban attitudes (p. 107).*

DEFINITIONS

Apartment. A set of rooms rented as a unit, usually in a multiple-unit building.

Baby boom. The large increase in the birth rate following World War II that lasted from about 1946 to 1957.

Capital gains tax. Tax on the "profit" gained from the appreciation or rise in value of assets including real estate. Such appreciation becomes profit (a capital gain) only when the property is sold.

Condominium ownership. Individual purchase of a dwelling in a multiunit dwelling in which common areas (hallways, elevators, grounds) are held in undivided common ownership. Individuals retain title to their own apartments and experience somewhat more autonomy than cooperative owners in that they are responsible for their own taxes, mortgage payments, and so on. Votes in business of the multiunit complex are distributed proportionately to the amount of property held.

Conventional construction. Building a home piece by piece on the site, as opposed to factory production of mobile homes, modules, or components.

Conventional ownership. Traditional form of home ownership termed "fee simple" in legal terminology. This form of ownership permits the greatest amount of freedom in use of the home and the most permanent occupancy.

Cooperative ownership. Purchase of stock in a housing cooperative by a tenant. Usually the shareholder occupies (leases) one dwelling in a multiunit structure. Management fees or assessments may be charged. The corporation makes collective decisions concerning policy, maintenance, etc. The tenant-owners each have one vote in corporate decisions.

Debt retirement. Monthly payment on the principal plus the interest of a mortgage loan.

Depreciation. A decrease in value due to wear and tear, decay, decline in price, etc.; assumed decline in value according to age of a building for purposes of income tax calculation.

Down payment. A portion of the sales price paid immediately by the buyer in purchasing a dwelling. The remainder of the sales price is usually paid by obtaining a mortgage loan either from the seller, a lending institution, or an individual. A larger down payment appreciably reduces monthly debt retirement payments and lowers interest totals.

Duplex. A two-unit dwelling with at least a partial common wall; usually side-by-side dwellings; also includes upper and lower floor apartments with separate entrances.

Equity. The difference between the market value and the amount owed on a piece of property; that return which the owner could obtain by selling at current market price and paying off the mortgage.

FHA-insured mortgage. A mortgage guaranteed by the Federal Housing Administration to protect the lending instutition against loss in the event of default by the borrower.

Garden apartments. A dwelling in a multiunit structure with relatively easy access to common open space.

High-rise. A multistory building of apartments or housing units usually with six or more floors, thus requiring an elevator.

Imputed net rent. Net rent (total rent minus expenses) is the amount of income that would be received if a home owner rented his home to another family. Assuming the home owner family is a landlord renting to themselves, there is income from imputed net rent on which a landlord would pay income taxes but a home owner does not.

Mobile home. Factory-built home capable of being moved on its own set of attached wheels; usually comes equipped by the manufacturer with appliances and furnishings.

Mortgage. A conveyance of property to a creditor as security for the repayment of the loan; borrowing money against the value of a house.

Mortgage interest. The cost of borrowing the principal in a mortgage loan.

Multiple family dwelling. Multiunit housing, including duplexes, apartment buildings, garden apartments, and high-rise residential structures.

Ownership. See conventional ownership.

Property tax. Fee levied by governmental units, including school boards, townships, counties, and municipalities, against the value of real property; used in support of schools, police departments, fire departments, recreational facilities, and other community services. Property taxes are local taxes paid by each property owner based on assessed value (some percentage of the market value, as determined by the local tax assessor) and the tax rate set by the municipality.

Rental. Tenure situation in which periodic payments are made to a landlord in exchange for the right to live in a dwelling.

Row house. Single-family attached dwellings with a least one common sidewall; common in Philadelphia, Baltimore, and smaller cities in that area.

Single-family dwelling. A house or housing unit which is structurally an entity of itself; a nonmultifamily structure; a detached house; a separate structure with a certain amount of exterior space and relatively clear cut boundaries; also includes *attached* single-family dwellings such as row houses, townhouses, and side-by-side duplexes.

Structure type. Categorization of dwelling types; mobile home, single-family detached dwelling, row house, townhouse, duplex, apartment, highrise, garden apartment, etc.

Structure-type deficit. Living in a structure that does not meet the norms; a positive structure-type deficit involves living in a structure type greater than needed, as in a family living in a single-family house when their composition does not indicate the need for one; negative structure-type deficit is living in a dwelling of an inferior structure type in relation to norms, as in a family living in an apartment when they need a single-family structure.

Tenure. The mode of holding or possessing housing. Ownership and rental are common tenure types. Ownership may be divided into conventional ownership, condominum ownership, and cooperative ownership. In addition, a form of rental tenure may involve payment of no rent as in the case of a family permitted to occupy a dwelling at no cost. There are also "salary in kind" arrangements as in parsonages provided for ministers and "tenant" houses for farm laborers as a part of their pay.

Tenure deficit. Actual tenure different from the norms; a positive tenure deficit would be experienced by a family who owns its own home but could (according to norms) gets by with rental; a negative tenure deficit would be experienced by a family who rents but for whom the norms prescribe ownership.

VA-insured mortgage. The Veterans' Administration guarantees to repay the lender a portion of the mortgage loan in case of failure to pay; much like FHA mortgage insurance.

Chapter 7
Quality, Expenditure, and Neighborhood Norms

On Forty-first Street
near Eighth Avenue
a frame house wobbles.

If houses went on crutches
this house would be
one of the cripples. Carl Sandburg*

The content of space, tenure, and structure-type norms appears to be relatively independent of income and social status. Income enters primarily as a facilitator for or a constraint on the achievement of those housing norms. The situation is somewhat different for quality, expenditure, and neighborhood norms. The content or specific prescriptions of these norms are much more closely related to income and social status. Some families voluntarily choose housing with deficits in ownership, structure type, and space. It appears they do so by developing preferences for conditions below the norms due to the influence of constraints such as limited income. Such preference shifts do not seem to arise from changes in family norms.

The situation with quality, expenditure, and neighborhood norms is different. It appears that voluntary deficits are accepted through changes in family norms. The changes in family norms seem to arise from the family's current position in the family life cycle and the family economic cycle.

Quality norms prescribe that housing should be of a quality level congruent with the family's social status. Expenditure norms prescribe that the family expenditure level be related to income or their "ability to pay." In the most general terms, neighborhood norms require that the family live in a neighborhood appropriate to their social and economic status. Some basic definitional norms contribute to neighborhood evaluation such as safety and a good school district for families with children. Beyond those factors, the

* From "Neighbors," in *Smoke and Steel* by Carl Sandburg (New York: Harcourt, Brace and World, 1920), lines 1–6. Reprinted by permission of Harcourt Brace Jovanovich.

informal specification norms for the neighborhood require that the neighborhood population not be greatly above or below the family's own status. In general, family norms appear to require that neighbors be relatively similar.

The purpose of this chapter is to specify, as far as possible, the content of norms for housing quality, expenditure, and neighborhood. Research in these areas is, however, relatively limited.

QUALITY NORMS

The most conceptually difficult of the six areas of housing norms is quality. The measurement of the desirability or quality of a dwelling unit involves the subjective reactions of people to attributes of a dwelling unit. Thus the definition and measurement of housing quality requires knowledge of the objective attributes that contribute to quality through the subjective reactions of families to those attributes.

A family may react subjectively to the presence of air conditioning in a dwelling unit. But the presence of the air conditioning system is not a subjective condition. Air conditioning either is or is not present. It also has the capacity to cool an ascertainable number of cubic feet of air per hour. There are a great many attributes of dwelling units that individual families may react to, and it is impossible to enumerate them all. Nevertheless, the most important ones to most families can be readily discovered.

The housing norms discussed in Chapters 5 and 6 and later in this chapter are all a part of the desirability equation. Most families are willing to pay extra for a dwelling unit if they can own it rather than rent it. They are willing to pay extra for a residence if it is detached from other units and if it has the correct amount of space (not necessarily a great amount of space). They are also willing to pay more for a dwelling if it is in the right location. All of those factors add to the desirability of the residence. Other things equal, they add to its market value. Obviously, uniform reactions are not totally pervasive among the American population because of differences in family norms.

To some degree the extent to which people react positively to attributes of the dwelling can be measured by how much they are willing to pay for a particular combination of such attributes. The price people are willing to pay for a particular type of dwelling unit is a reflection of how highly they value the combination of attributes they perceive in that type of dwelling. The combination of those attributes and their value to the family represents a kind of desirability equation that has an impact on market value through the demand side of the market. The impact on market value through the supply side of the market occurs as the desirability equations of families are translated into the floor plans, landscaping, and other actual features of dwellings. These attributes then become part of the supply of housing. At any particular point in time the interaction of supply and demand results in market value.

If there is a single desirability or quality norm it is one that is judged relative to the family's ability to afford housing with luxury attributes. Thus, families should have the quality they can afford but should not endanger their ability to maintain their rent or mortgage payments. The quality norm may be approximated by the luxury of the housing available relative to the percentage of income that the average family feels properly should be devoted to housing.

The desirability equation is based in a general way on the views of consumer behavior and demand for consumer goods of Lancaster (1971), Rosen (1974), and others. Consumer demand is based on the extent to which goods fill needs or wants of the consumer. Potential home buyers or renters consider the amount of satisfaction they expect to receive from a potential dwelling. Their assessment of potential satisfaction is based on the characteristics it possesses compared with other actual or potential dwellings. The family, of course, may be more or less correct in their assessment of future satisfaction.

Prices of a specific product are seen as a sum of the implicit prices of the attributes possessed by the product. An implicit price is the estimated price paid for a given attribute. There is one total price paid for any particular object, but that price theoretically could be broken down into the amount paid for each of the attributes possessed by the object. In the sale of automobiles the implicit prices are made explicit. The dealer adds to the total price of the automobile an amount for each additional characteristic included on the vehicle. He obtains the correct amount from a table provided by the manufacturer.

Obviously not all attributes of any object can be relevant to consumer decision making. Some writers distinguish between attributes and characteristics. Attributes are the objective properties possessed by or inherent in an object. Characteristics are those attributes that enter into consumer preference development and consumer decision making (Lancaster, 1971). Characteristics are assumed to be objectively measurable, that is, they are a subset of the total set of attributes. Consumers differ in terms of how highly they value given characteristics but agree about what the characteristics are.

A class of products, such as dwelling units, can be described by a table with types of dwellings across the top (Table 9). Down the side of the table are listed the characteristics possessed by each type of dwelling. Zeros in the table indicate total absence of the characteristic. Ones indicate the simple presence of the characteristic or the presence of one unit of the characteristic. Larger numbers indicate the number of units of a characteristic present.

A dwelling type is the set of all dwellings with the same set of characteristics. One possible type of dwelling (A) is an owner-occupied, single-family, three-bedroom, two-bathroom, split-level dwelling with carpeting on

TABLE 9 Hypothesized dwelling types

	Types of Dwellings				
Characteristic	A	B	C	D	E
For owner occupation	1	1	1	0	0
For renter occupation	0	0	0	1	1
Single-family	1	1	0	1	1
Multifamily	0	0	1	0	0
Mobile home	0	1	0	0	1
Bedrooms	3	2	2	3	2
Bathrooms	2	1	1	2	1
.	.	.	.	.	.
.	.	.	.	.	.
.	.	.	.	.	.
Split level	1	0	0	1	0
Carpet throughout	1	1	1	0	0

all floors. It might have some additional characteristics, as well. Another possible type (B) is an owner-occupied, single-family mobile home with two bedrooms, bath, and carpet on all floors.

The implicit price per unit of each characteristic is used as a weight to calculate the total price. Summing the quantities of each characteristic, multiplied by the implicit price of one unit of each characteristic, would produce the total price of the dwelling. Thus, in addition to the table of characteristics, there is also a table of implicit prices for each characteristic.

In actuality, housing prices are not derived in this manner. Rather they are the sum of the costs to the producer of including that combination of characteristics, in combination with the buyer's willingness to pay. Adding the profit and return on the investment produces the price in terms of its direct determinants. The consumer's willingness to buy the product with the given combination of characteristics (and thereby, indirectly, the producer's willingness to produce it) depends upon how highly the consumer values that combination of characteristics, each of which has some implicit price.

The source of the consumer's willingness to pay for the given type of dwelling is the perception of the extent to which important needs will be filled by such a purchase. In terms of the present approach, the sources of those perceptions are primarily in the cultural and family norms for housing. Rather than attach implicit prices as weights to the values in the characteristic matrix, the present modification of Lancaster's model attaches importance or salience weights to each characteristic. The weighted sums for the various dwelling types are measures of quality as conceptualized in the present approach. Quality in housing therefore is defined as the possession of highly valued combinations of characteristics given the cultural and family norms of the potential consumers.

Housing quality represents a combination of characteristics and the importance of the characteristics to the family. There is a related combination of those characteristics with prices families would be *willing* to pay if they had to. Further, there is an actual market with combinations of prices and characteristics that actually *must* be paid in order to make a purchase. Actual market prices reflect quality indirectly through the prices people would be willing to pay. Often the actual prices are below the prices many, even most, families would be willing to pay. Their willingness to pay higher prices results in part from the pressure of cultural norms. The lower actual prices result from the interaction of supply and demand.

It is an important assumption in this analysis of quality that families are able to make rather fine distinctions among dwellings and their characteristics. This point is simply another way of stating Lancasters's assumption that consumers agree about the objective attributes that have become characteristics. Social scientists who have studied housing are by no means unanimous in their acceptance of that point. Riemer (1951) felt that consumers are not able to evaluate dwellings effectively, especially the "unsophisticated consumer." Dean (1951) thought that consumers have "only vaguely formulated objectives" when they make housing decisions. Any realtor, however, can attest to the subtle differences between ostensibly similar dwellings that a potential home-buyer can distinguish. Granting that, it is obvious that social scientists should be able to measure the desirability of dwellings by reference to the cues that families use.

THE MEASUREMENT OF HOUSING QUALITY

Empirical measures of housing quality tend to be makeshift substitutes for the kind of matrix shown in Table 9. They are substitutes for knowing in detail the characteristics that are valued by consumers. It is assumed that a family rationally allocates its money for housing, consistent with their perception of the contribution of housing to their overall well-being. A family is most likely to choose housing with the combination of characteristics that uses all their housing money and gives the maximum satisfaction for that amount of money. Therefore, one of the most direct indexes of the desirability of a dwelling unit is its market value.

A problem with market value as a measure of quality is that it is community-specific, even neighborhood-specific. The desirable features (those that will increase the market value in that community) are dependent upon the norms and market factors (both supply and demand) that exist in a particular community. Thus, a dwelling that has a market value of $80,000 in a suburb of Chicago might have a market value of half that in a small community several hundred miles from an urban area. Each might represent the highest market value for the given community, with the difference in absolute value related to differences in market conditions. Similarly, different communities might rate the same housing features differently, based on, for example, ethnic differences. A brick veneer might be highly valued in one community, and a wooded lot in another, etc.

Market value (or rental price) is perhaps the best single-indicator measure of quality that (implicitly) combines all elements that contribute to quality. Its use as a quality measure may have to be limited to comparisons within a local market and among units within the same tenure, structure type, and size classifications. The three-bedroom, single-family house for sale with the highest market value in the community would be considered to have the highest quality. Comparisons between communities may be misleading, however.

A means of dealing with the disadvantage of market value as a measure of quality (due to the effects of supply and demand) would be to base a measure of quality directly on the characteristics of housing that produce satisfaction. Ideally it would utilize the characteristics matrix combined with cultural norms and importance weights. The measures of housing quality discussed below have only partially met the ideal.

Evidence that tenure, structure type, neighborhood, and space are important elements of housing quality can be found in measures that have attempted to represent housing quality with a single index (Survey Research Center, 1972; Kain and Quigley, 1970; USBC, 1969c). Those measures have, unwisely, included characteristics of the occupants as well as characteristics of the dwelling. Characteristics of the family in relation to their dwelling and neighborhood are important for ascertaining the presence of quality *deficits*. The objective measurement of quality, however, must not include such characteristics, since the quality, as measured, would change if a different family moved in. That is obviously silly.

Other measures have sought to index that portion of quality that is separate from tenure, neighborhood, structure type, and space. Early efforts to measure housing quality in that fashion conceptualized quality totally or partially as the minimum standards for health and safety (APHA, 1945; APHA, 1952; APHA, 1971; Twichell, 1948; Twichell, 1953; Morris, Woods, and Jacobson, 1972; USBC, 1967). Later efforts (Harris, 1976a; Harris, 1976b) to index quality aspects separate from tenure, structure type, space, and neighborhood added the presence of features and amenities far beyond such minimum standards.

One of the most comprehensive measures of housing quality was developed by the American Public Health Association (APHA, 1945; Twichell, 1948) for the primary purpose of helping communities delineate where to apply official remedies for poor quality housing, such as urban redevelopment and rehabilitation. This method involved a complex system of data collection in the field and the assignment of penalty scores in the survey office (APHA, 1946). Although it is relatively valid and reliable, the APHA system proved expensive to administer. It included measures of the adequacy of the space available for the occupants, as well as the structural characteristics and basic facilities.

The U.S. Bureau of the Census applied a series of evolving measures of the state of repair and structural quality of housing in the 1940, 1950, and 1960 Census enumerations. The 1940 Census used a twofold classification, "not needing major repairs" and "needing major repairs." It was not quite a measure of quality, however, A tarpaper shack could be classified as "not needing major repairs" but would not at all be thought of as high-quality housing. The 1950 Census categories "dilapidated" and "not dilapidated" were an improvement on the measurement of the state of repair, but the dichotomous classification led to dissatisfaction.

Census users, particularly those who needed structural condition data for decisions regarding which dwellings could be rehabilitated, indicated a desire for a third category between the two used in the 1950 Census, Such a three-way classification was developed for 1960: "sound," "deteriorating," and "dilapidated." The "dilapidated" category was the same as that used in 1950. The "not dilipidated" category of the 1950 Census was divided into two classes: "sound" and "deteriorating." (USBC, 1967, p. 1).

The 1960 Census enumerators were provided with written instructions and were trained with visual techniques as well (USBC, 1967, pp. 55–63). In spite of the directions and training, however, the Bureau of the Census concluded that the 1960 Census statistics

> *are unreliable. Our best estimate is that if another group of enumerators had been sent back to score the housing units of the United States, only about one-third of the units rated as dilapidated or deteriorating by either group of enumerators would have been rated the same by both groups of enumerators (USBC, 1967, p. 5).*

As a result of that study there was no direct attempt to measure structural housing quality in the 1970 Census. Due to the demand for such data, a substitute was developed that took advantage of the correlation between structural condition and the presence of certain equipment, facilities, and other characteristics. The variables used were lack of central or built-in heating, persons per room, a one-family structure, the education of the head of the household, and house value or rent (USBC, 1969c). This measure not only includes a space deficit measure but one of the components is simply a characteristic of the occupants. Education of the head may be correlated with low or high housing quality, but it certainly is not a direct measure of housing quality in any sense.

Kain and Quigley (1970) assumed that housing quality for both rental and owner-occupied dwellings was best measured by the market value of the unit. Their analysis estimated the factors that contributed to market value. For both types of tenure, it was found that measures of the physical condition of both the neighborhood and the dwelling, the amount of nonresidential land usage in the neighborhood, the age of the structure, and the number of rooms in the dwelling contributed to the market value. A measure of neighborhood prestige, the median years of school completed by adults in the census tract, was also related to market value.

Other factors related to the value for rental dwellings were structure type and the number of bathrooms, utilities, and appliances included in the rent. The market value of owner-occupied dwellings was also related to the floor space of the first floor and the size of the lot. All owner-occupied dwellings were single-family structures, so structure type was not used to predict value for owner-occupied dwellings.

Researchers at the University of Michigan (Survey Research Center, 1972, p. 362) developed a single index to measure housing and neighborhood quality. Their index accounted for many of the features that Kain and Quigley found to be related to market value of the dwelling. The Michigan index lends support to the idea that housing quality is dependent on normative housing conditions and on the existence of neighborhood, tenure, structure type, and space norms.

In the Michigan index, the household received one point for each of the following elements: ownership, a single-family dwelling, a suburban location, a neighborhood of single-family dwellings, having two or more rooms above the minimum number needed according to family composition, a value per room of $2000 or more, and the presence of the very basic amenities of running water, an indoor toilet, and not needing major repairs. As in other indexes of quality, characteristics of the occupants were included. The inclusion of the crowding measure means that household composition was included as part of the quality of the dwelling. Such inclusion is not appropriate when the dwelling is being assessed.

Morris et al. (1972) identified three dimensions of quality:

1. Structural quality, which refers primarily to durability of the shell;
2. Service quality, which is concerned with the kinds of equipment, facilities, and conveniences the dwelling provides; and
3. The state of maintenance and caretaking.

Their measure of quality consisted of 26 items that measured the three areas identified. Most items were housing characteristics that could be accurately and objectively detected by relatively untrained observers. The presence or absence of a characteristic was the prime basis for the assignment of scores to the various items. The resulting item scores were summed to provide a measure of housing quality. Their measure of quality was developed and tested in Puerto Rico. Hence it was sensitive to variations in housing at much lower levels than the vast majority of housing in the United States.

Harris (1976b) used the same technique as Morris et al. to develop an index of housing quality. In addition to basic physical condition of the dwelling and lot, she included the presence of full and half bathrooms, insulation and storm windows, air conditioning, and various amenities, including a freezer, dishwasher, washer and dryer, and fireplace. Her index of housing quality was thus sensitive to differences in quality found in the United States. The measure developed was highly reliable and was significantly related to housing satisfaction and the propensity to make residential alterations and additions (Harris, 1976b).

Harris was also the only researcher to attempt a definition of norms that specify dwellings above the very minimum levels of maintenance and repair. She treated the "mean existing level of quality for the scale developed . . . as a criterion until a measurement of the socially relevant norm is developed" (Harris, 1976a, p. 7).

A socially relevant norm for quality does exist, even though it is not as specific in content as would be desired. That norm is the relationship of quality to the socioeconomic status of the family. Possession of high-quality housing is one of the ways that families and households demonstrate their status within the society. The most culturally sound measurement of quality would include all characteristics of housing (attributes that families value). A matrix similar to that in Table 9 would be constructed and related to questions from a survey of families on the importance of each characteristic. The matrix could possibly be related to over all housing satisfaction.

Such an analysis should produce findings very similar to a market value analysis in the economic tradition. The analysis would be similar if market value is, indeed, an effective reflector of the satisfaction families expect to receive, and if, in turn, expected satisfaction is related closely to ultimately received satisfaction. The significance of this point is that market value should be a reflection of quality when quality is soundly measured. Sound measurement requires attention to the cultural sources of the subjective reactions of families to housing characteristics.

EXPENDITURE NORMS

Like quality norms, expenditure norms prescribe that a family behave differently depending upon its socioeconomic status. Several rules of thumb have traditionally been applied by lending institutions, realtors, and others to test how much a family should or should not spend on housing:

> *. . . no more than two or two and a half times his annual income . . . . one month's house expenses should not exceed one week's pay, or between 20 and 25 percent of his monthly income. . . . One week's pay should equal 1 percent of the price of the house. . . . (Beyer, 1965, p. 260).*

Rising taxes, utility costs, and interests rates in recent years have made those rules of thumb less appropriate. Yet it is surprising how often such rules are quoted. Such guidelines serve to denote maximum expenditures that help guarantee the financial soundness of the family and the landlord or the lending institution. The rules of thumb have grown out of the long-term relationship between the cost of housing and other consumer goods and the distribution of income.

In reality, the application of such rules is a shortcut way to measure housing expenditure deficits in much the same way that persons-per-room ratios are used to measure space deficits. A family spending more than 25 percent of its income would have a positive deficit. This is the aspect of expenditure norms that prescribe maximums on financial grounds. Norms also operate that set minimum expenditures. A family spending less than 25 percent would have a negative deficit (Crull, 1976a). These minimums are primarily related to status manifestation. "Anyone who is rich should live in rich housing."

At best, estimates of expenditure deficits are even more approximate than square-feet-per-person measures of crowding. The concept of percentage of income is not the way American families think about expenditures. Preliminary evidence of this conclusion is the declining percentage of income actually spent on housing as income rises.

A recent study (Crull, 1976a) tested for the existence of cultural and family norms for housing expenditures. That study also included an examination of the relationship between cultural and family norms for expenditures. Then the amount the family actually spent was related to norms according to income and tenure (Crull, 1976b). Over 70 percent of the sample reported cultural norms for housing expenditures ("percentage of income that the average American family should spend on housing") that were between 20 and 30 percent of family income. Slightly less than 70 percent of the sample reported family norms for housing expenditures ("percentage of income that your family should spend") that were in the same range.

Over 90 percent of that same sample indicated that they felt the owned single-family dwelling was the cultural norm (Winter and Morris, 1976). Almost 90 percent reported similar family norms. Thus there was less agreement regarding expenditure norms than tenure and structure-type norms. A few respondents even reported expenditure norms for the average family and for their own family in the range of 75 percent of family income. Such patently unrealistic replies may indicate further that norms for expenditures as applied by families are not conceived directly in terms of percentages.

When actual housing expenditures were compared with reported income, only about one-fourth of the sample spent between 20 and 30 percent of their income on housing. Over half the sample spent less than 20 percent of their income on housing. About one-fourth reported spending more than 30 percent on housing. As could be expected those spending less than 20 percent were concentrated in the upper-income brackets (over $10,000 annually). Those spending more than 30 percent of their income on housing expenses were primarily in the lowest income category (under $5,000) (Crull, 1976b). Most low-income home owners were elderly and had their house completely paid for. Very few low-income families were making mortgage payments. All of the low-income families with mortgages were spending more than 30 percent of their income on housing. Only three-fourths of the low-income renters were spending more than 30 percent. Thus, overspending is one of the means used to obtain ownership and single-family dwellings.

Roistacher (1974a) found similar relations between income, tenure, and percent spent on housing. In her analysis, those spending more than 25 percent on housing were primarily low-income families, elderly families, young renters, female-headed households, and single-person households.

The analyses by Crull (1976b) and Roistacher (1974a) emphasize the fact that rules of thumb are merely shortcut means to measure deficits, rather than the way families measure deficits. Had this not been the case, there would have been a much closer agreement between the norms and actual conditions. When deciding how much they should spend on housing, families do not think in terms of a flat percentage of their income. Rather, they think in terms of recent increases (or decreases) in income, their expectations of future income changes, the cost of a potential new residence in comparison to that of their present residence, and their current level of satisfaction.

Thus, analyses using complaints regarding housing costs (Rossi, 1955, p. 141) and a ratio of actual housing expenditures to expected housing expenditures based on family income (Goodman, 1974) found that neither variable was a particularly good predictor of residential mobility.

One explanation for such findings is that moving frequently results from or is accompanied by rising income. Most families experience rising income during early life cycle stages. Prior to moving they spend less than they can afford on housing. Later when income declines, most families have attained home ownership and have a paid-off mortgage. Therefore, falling income seldom produces residential mobility, unless the decline is great. Thus it is the increase in income (or even an expected increase in income, as noted by Smith et al., 1963) that prompts mobility.

As could be expected, then, the single best predictor of the amount spent on housing is family income (Roistacher, 1974a). As income increases, the amount spent on housing also increases, but at a decreasing rate. Housing expenditures are relatively inelastic. An increase in income does not lead to a proportionate increase in housing expenditures (Roistacher, 1974a). The elasticities are slightly higher among middle-income families than among very low-income families, probably because of the immediate need for other goods among low-income families.

In spite of the inelasticities of housing expenditures, a change in income was one of the best predictors of a change in the amount spent on housing (Roistacher, 1974a). Other variables that predicted change in housing expenditures were average income over a five-year period and changes in family size.

Thus families with a change in income that was not sudden, but rather represented a five-year trend, and whose family size had changed, creating normative space or quality deficits, changed their housing expenditures. The researcher concluded:

> *Our model reinforces what demand theory suggests: that changes in income and changes in family size are both powerful determinants of the change in housing expenditure and the change in real housing consumption (Roistacher, 1974a, p. 38).*

It must be remembered that the behavior of families compared in a cross-sectional analysis is not necessarily an indicator that a cultural norm is present. In a dynamic analysis, however, one of the soundest interpretations of the actual rises in housing expenditures that follow actual rises in income is that rising income either releases constraints on already existing family norms or raises family norms for space, tenure, structure type, quality, and location. Thus the family who has no deficits, but has experienced a rise in income, may engage in normative adaptation and raise its norms. Such adaptation was hypothesized in Chapter 4, in the model of family housing adjustment and adaptation.

NORMS FOR QUALITY AND EXPENDITURE OVER THE LIFE CYCLE

The relationship between the family life cycle and norms for housing quality and for housing expenditures is relatively strong and curvilinear. As the family progresses through stages of the family life cycle, higher quality and more expensive housing is prescribed until retirement.

The relationship is strong, but not because of changes in housing needs that occur as a result of changes in the family. Rather, socioeconomic status generally rises steadily with age. The principal wage earners approach their peak earnings between the ages of 50 and 60, barring an economic disaster such as loss of a job, and so on. Hence the quality and expenditure standards, related to socioeconomic status, specify that increasing amounts of money should be spent on housing and that housing should be of higher and higher quality.

Figure 5 shows the relationship between ideal quality norms, minimum or basic quality norms, and expenditure norms in relation to family income. The exact shape and relative levels of these curves are not known, but the research tends to indicate the general relationships shown in the figure. Quality norms are above expenditure norms but by a decreasing margin as income rises. Minimum quality norms have a much flatter curve as income rises and are well below both expenditure and ideal quality norms.

At retirement, expenditure norms may be lowered, as the family experiences a socially expected decrease in income. Standards for quality are probably not altered, because the family's social status does not change. The family may be capable of maintaining the level of quality for a time at least, because they are likely to own their home outright. Thus their expenditures would be lower (only maintenance, utilities, and property taxes), but the quality would remain the same.

The norms for quality and expenditures are relatively independent of the presence of children, the sex of the household head, and even marital status. Childless couples, female-headed households, and single individuals all seek housing quality and housing expenditures that are congruent with socioeconomic status. The achievement of high-quality housing for which a family or an individual spends according to income is an important manifestation of status in the United States for practically everyone.

Some families have developed family norms that are quite different

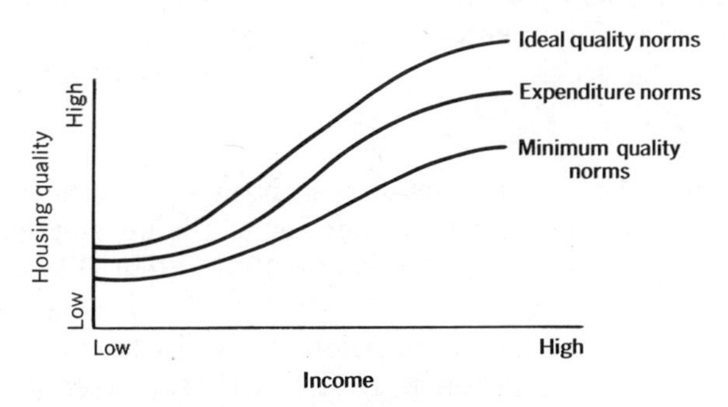

Figure 5 Ideal quality norms, minimum quality norms, and expenditure norms by income.

from those discussed. They may temporarily specify the least expensive shelter possible so that family income can be used for other purposes. They may deliberately seek poor quality housing, partly because of a rejection of social status indicators. Such instances, although often highly publicized, are relatively rare. Most individuals and families seek housing quality and housing expenditures that are in accord with their socioeconomic status.

NEIGHBORHOOD NORMS

The location of the dwelling unit and the nature of its immediate area are prime determinants of the family's ability to accomplish nonhousing goals. For example, the quality of the children's education, and thus their prospects for future social and economic security, is partially determined by the location of the dwelling unit.

Foote et al. (1960) identified three aspects of the location of the dwelling that potentially could be considered by families. First is location as site, which refers to the relation of the housing unit to work, shopping, schools, recreation facilities, and the locations of the homes of friends and relatives. Second is location as physical environment, referring to the individual aspects of the physical environment (the density, light, air, and condition of the other dwellings surrounding the housing unit), the quality of the community facilities (schools, libraries, and stores), and the quality of the municipal services and utilities (fire and police protection, garbage collection, water, and sewer). Third is the location as social environment, referring to the characteristics of the people in the area (Foote et al. 1960, pp. 180–81).

The distinction between the physical and the social environment is not clear cut, however. The quality of the schools in the neighborhood contributes to the social environment of the neighborhood. By the same token, the characteristics of the people in the neighborhood cannot be totally separated from the quality of the playgrounds, stores, the police and fire protection, street maintenance, and garbage collection.

Site Norms

Planners describe in some detail the optimum locations of community facilities and employment centers in relation to the housing unit and neighborhood (APHA, 1960; ULI, 1960; Perry, 1939; Stein, 1966). Yet there is little support for the view that the location *per se* is of great importance (Potakey, 1974, p. 56; Hinshaw and Allott, 1972; Foote et al. 1960, pp. 181–84; Beyer, 1955; Lansing and Barth, 1964, pp. 17–19; Greenbie, 1969, p. 363; Butler and Kaiser, 1971; Goodman, 1974). An automobile appears to be a necessity rather than a luxury. Thus, ready access to community facilities and places of employment is easy to attain. The importance of location could be greatly altered if automobile transport becomes expensive. Social, technological, political, and economic developments with respect to the allocation of petroleum, shifts to mass transport, and the like could create such a situation.

Most locational variables (location *per se* rather than the character of the location) appear to be relatively unimportant in housing choice. Probably the least important of the location variables is the relation of the housing unit to the place of employment. Ordinarily, people only require that it be within commuting distance. It is quite clear that the quality of the physical and social environment is more important in the choice of a dwelling unit. Families are choosing to live in the suburbs, even though it may mean costly (in terms of time and money) commuting from home to work.

The Physical And Social Environment

Of great importance among neighborhood norms is that the area be primarily, if not exclusively, residential (APHA, 1960; ULI, 1960; Perry, 1939; Stein, 1966). Commercial and industrial land uses should not be mixed with residential land uses. Often the ideal range of the norm prescribing an exclusively residential area is extended to prescribe an area that is composed totally of detached single-family dwellings, with multifamily dwellings and mobile homes excluded as well.

The norm seems to persist in spite of efforts on the part of planners and local, state, and federal agencies to promote development of a different sort. Being advocated are developments consisting of a variety of structure types clustered around public open space. While their efforts have been great, American families still appear to prefer a neighborhood of single-family dwellings, each with its own patch of private grass, flowers, or flagstone. In fact, an analysis of residential satisfaction (Lansing, Marans, and Zehner, 1970) found higher levels of neighborhood satisfaction among families living in lower-density developments.

Within the residential area, there should be at least adequate, if not high-quality municipal services. A community water supply, sanitary sewer system, refuse collection and disposal system, and adequate community housekeeping and maintenance services are required (APHA, 1971, pp. 38–55). There should be a minimum of safety and health hazards, including those related to traffic, the presence of odors, pollutants, noise, and vibration. There should be adequate police and fire protection, and access to community facilities including parks, playgrounds, schools, and shopping (APHA, 1960, pp. 1–11; 54–62; Lansing et al., 1970).

All housing units in the United States are within *some* school district. There is virtually no housing unit that is not in an area that could call forth police and fire protection of some form. Of more importance is the *quality* of the physical and social environment. American neighborhood norms specify that the housing unit be located in a *good* school district (Lansing et al., 1970). Because school districts are by and large relatively limited in area, it matters little where the school is located relative to the dwelling as long as it is in the district and of high quality.

While racial issues are, of course, very important in the controversy over school busing to attain integration, so are normative neighborhood deficits for both black and white families. Families who carefully and deliberately selected a *good* school district and paid extra to obtain a home there suddenly find that their children no longer attend that school. The school they are required to attend may be of lower quality than their former school. Even if the new school is objectively acceptable, it may not be perceived to be so. In the case of real or perceived differences in school quality, the family now has a school quality deficit, which they had taken pains to avoid.

Much of the conflict over school busing to achieve integration can be traced to the fact that some norms are relatively similar among all races and ethnic groups. Black families, as well as white families, place high value on a good education for their children. The neighborhood deficits of black families in the form of low-quality inner-city schools, resulted in protests, and finally the court-ordered busing programs. While recognizing the importance of social justice, it is not difficult to see that families with deficits in terms of school quality are likely to attempt to overcome them.

Safety means more than just freedom from traffic hazards. It means freedom from crime, as well. Evidence of the importance of the norms for safety and good schools is found in a recent study of the environmental preferences of college students (Hinshaw and Allott, 1972). Neighborhood safety and a good school were the two most important features specified by the respondents.

Finally, there also seems to be a norm that prescribes homogeneity in the socioeconomic characteristics of the residents of the neighborhood. The neighborhood should be relatively homogeneous regarding social class, age, race, and sometimes ethnic group. It should not differ greatly from the age, class, race, and ethnic background of the family. Planners have long advocated heterogeneity in the neighborhood (Bauer, 1951; Hallman, 1959; RERC, 1974; Jacobs, 1961) and have rejected homogeneity as undemocratic (Isaacs, 1948, 1949). Yet it is clear that cultural norms as practiced in daily life rather than public expression of liberal philosophy, prescribe homogeneity.

According to Gans, (1961):

> *a person's beliefs and actions are shaped in part by his age, income, occupation, and the like. These characteristics can, therefore, be used as clues to understanding the pattern of social relationships.*

> Life-cycle stage *(which summarizes such characteristics as age of adults, marital status, and age of children)* and class *(especially income and education) are probably the two most significant characteristics. Education is especially important, because it affects occupational choice, child-rearing patterns, leisure-time preferences, and taste level.* Race *is also an important criterion, primarily because it is a highly visible—although not necessarily accurate—symbol of class position (Gans, 1961, p. 137).*

Perceiving that people are similar to oneself and perceiving that they are friendly has been shown to be related to neighborhood satisfaction (Lansing et al., 1970). *Actual* homogeneity in the neighborhood in terms of age, education, income, and race was not related to the perception of similarity or friendliness. The latter findings, a surprise to the researchers, need further study to ascertain what factors lead to perceived homeogeneity. Further research may find that homogeneity *per se* is not as strong a factor in neighborhood norms as it is thought to be.

Hinshaw and Allott (1972), as well as others, have suggested that there may be a norm that prescribes suburban or noncentral city location. It seems likely however, that the preference for suburbia is a manifestation of the fact that only in a suburban area can a family find housing that meets all the most common housing norms: space, tenure, structure type, quality, and neighborhood (Foote et al., 1960, pp. 185–89; Lansing and Barth, 1964, pp. 21–22; Greenbie, 1969, pp. 363–64). Thus, as noted by some authors (Ktsanes and Reissman, 1959–1960; Jaco and Belknap, 1953), suburban areas simply represent new housing situations that express the durable norms and values of American families. Such norms have become increasingly difficult to achieve in central cities.

NEIGHBORHOOD NORMS OVER THE LIFE CYCLE

For all households, there are certain minimum standards for facilities and amenities in the neighborhood. Beyond those minimums (freedom from health and safety hazards, adequate community utilities and services), the content of neighborhood norms varies with the stage of the family life cycle.

For families with children, good schools and easy access to recreational facilities are clearly prescribed. Perceived homogeneity is far more important for families with children because the children will be interacting with other children from the neighborhood at school and play. Regardless of the fairness of the attitude, families generally feel that the "right" kind of playmates, and, later, dating partners, are important to the development of their children (Foote et al., 1960, p. 102).

Hence the couple who, at marriage, selected an inner-city apartment, to be near the center-city activities, very often moves to the suburbs shortly after the birth of their first child. Such a move may be prompted by space, tenure, and structure-type deficits, but neighborhood considerations are also important. Private play space that can be supervised from the kitchen window, the proximity of playmates, and the prospects for high-quality education all relate to such a move.

As children mature, an increasingly higher-quality neighborhood is needed, one that expresses the status of the family. Such standards are related as much to the increase in family income as they are to the stage of the family life cycle. Schools are still extremely important, as are facilities for teenagers. The latter may be difficult to achieve in the suburbs, however (Lansing et al., 1970).

As with other important housing needs, neighborhood standards for single-parent families may be relaxed somewhat because of the presence of constraints. Nevertheless, quality schools are still important, as well as access to recreation facilities. Homogeneity may assume less importance, so that the social needs of the single parent, as well as those of the children, may be satisfied in the same neighborhood.

Childless couples and single individuals may have quite different neighborhood norms. Although there have been no studies of their neighborhood norms *per se,* a study of different residential environments (Lansing et al., 1970) found that inner-city neighborhoods had a much higher proportion of single individuals and childless couples than did suburban communities. When the socialization and development of children are not important, accessibility to places of employment, cultural facilities, and downtown shopping, as well as hetereogeneity, may predominate. At least such conditions for single individuals and childless couples are not severely sanctioned.

CONCLUSION

Quality, expenditure, and neighborhood norms are not as clear and unequivocal as those for space, tenure, and structure type. Still, their content can be ascertained. Families with children need a neighborhood of single-family dwellings, so that each family has private open space. Good schools are a requirement, and have led to a great deal of strife and controversy in the past few years. The source of the controversy seems to be that the norms of black families are identical to those of white families.

Beyond such specifications, neighborhood norms are similar to those for quality and expenditures. Such norms all specify that, for families, childless couples, and single individuals, housing and neighborhood quality and housing expenditures should be consistent with the socioeconomic status of the family.

The norms for quality, expenditures, and neighborhoods have been treated in this chapter somewhat differently from other norms. The difference is that quality, expenditure, and neighborhood norms relate to class and income through variations in family norms rather than through variations in preferences. These three sets of norms may have ideal ranges that most people strive for. Family norms often differ according to social and economic status. Quality, expenditure, and neighborhood norms appear to be "contingent norms." The specific content of their prescriptions slides upward or downward depending upon socioeconomic developments experienced by the family.

DEFINITIONS

Attributes. Objective properties of a dwelling that exist, regardless of whether they are perceived; to be contrasted with characteristics.

Characteristics. The subset of the attributes possessed by housing or other goods that enter into consumer preference development and consumer decision making. Consumers may differ in terms of how highly they value given characteristics but agree about what the characteristics are.

Commercial land use. Use or allocation of properties for shopping, businesses, and other commercial enterprises.

Cross-sectional analysis. An investigation of a sample or population showing a typical selection of characteristic parts, relationships, etc., *at a given time;* to be contrasted with longitudinal analysis. Most survey research data are cross-sectional in nature.

Curvilinear relationship. A relationship in which the independent variable produces different degrees of change in the dependent variable at different values of the independent variable. A change from an income (independent) of $3000 to one of $4000 may produce an increase in housing expenditures (dependent) of $500, while an increase from $7000 to $10,000 may produce an increase in housing expenditures of only $250.

Elasticity. Relative responsiveness to change. Income eleasticity of housing expenditures refers to the readiness to increase housing expenditures in response to an increase in income.

Expenditure deficit. Deviation of actual housing expenditures from norms for housing expenditures. A family spending more than about 25 percent of its income on housing has a positive expenditure deficit. A family spending less than about 25 percent of its income on housing has a negative expenditure deficit.

Housing expenditures. All dwelling-related costs incurred by the occupants of a particular housing unit including rent, mortgage payment on principal and interest, taxes, property insurance, utilities, maintenance and repair, etc.

Housing quality. Characteristics of dwelling units that contribute to desirability through the subjective reactions of families to those characteristics; the desirability of a given residence as perceived by the observer, the occupant family, the potential owners, or others.

Implicit price. The assumed or estimated cost; the price that a particular characteristic (e.g., the amount of insulation measured in inches in the attic) is worth, although the actual cost is simply some unknown proportion of the total price of this dwelling.

Market value. The current value of a housing unit on the open market; what a house would sell for.

Neighborhood deficit. A surplus or shortage of any neighborhood feature when compared with the cultural or family norms for that feature. Poor quality neighborhood schools are a form of neighborhood deficit.

Quality deficit. Deviation of the quality of a family's dwelling unit from norms for housing quality; a shortage or surplus of actual (perceived) quality from the norms.

Residential land use. Use of real property for private dwelling rather than industrial or commercial structures.

Utilities. Services available to the public including water, gas, electricity, sanitary sewers, and the like.

Part 3

Responses to Residential Deficits

There is nothing either bad or good but thinking made it so. William Shakespeare*

Housing adjustment behavior occurs in response to low levels of housing or neighborhood satisfaction. The level of satisfaction results primarily from the presence of housing or neighborhood deficits. The deficits exist because housing does not meet cultural, community, or family norms. Deficits may also arise because current housing does not meet the special needs of individuals who are elderly or disabled. Part 3 examines the causes of residential dissatisfaction and the housing adjustments that result from that dissatisfaction.

The network of influences examined in this section can be presented in a causal diagram (Blalock, 1964, pp. 61–94), in which the arrows represent hypothesized influences or causal relationships (Figure 6). Thus the arrows from propensity to adjust housing to residential mobility and residential alteration represent a hypothesis that the propensity to adjust housing is a cause of subsequent housing adjustment behavior.

The propensity to adjust housing, in turn, is most immediately related to the level of satisfaction with the current dwelling and neighborhood. Satisfaction, in its turn, in related to housing deficits: if the dwelling were to have more negative than positive features, the level of satisfaction would be low.

Housing deficits are seen to be caused by the background characteristics, which represent resources and constraints. Having a shortage of space, for example, may result from limited income. Having an excess of bedrooms may result from being in a late stage of the family life cycle. Needing special facilities may result from age or disability.

The causal diagram presented in Figure 6 and the chapters in this section are concerned with *voluntary housing* adjustment behavior. Involuntary behavior—being evicted, for example—would have a different pattern of causal influences (Roistacher, 1974b) and is not discussed in any detail in this book. A housing change may also be caused by an event not necessarily

* *Hamlet,* Act 2, Scene 2.

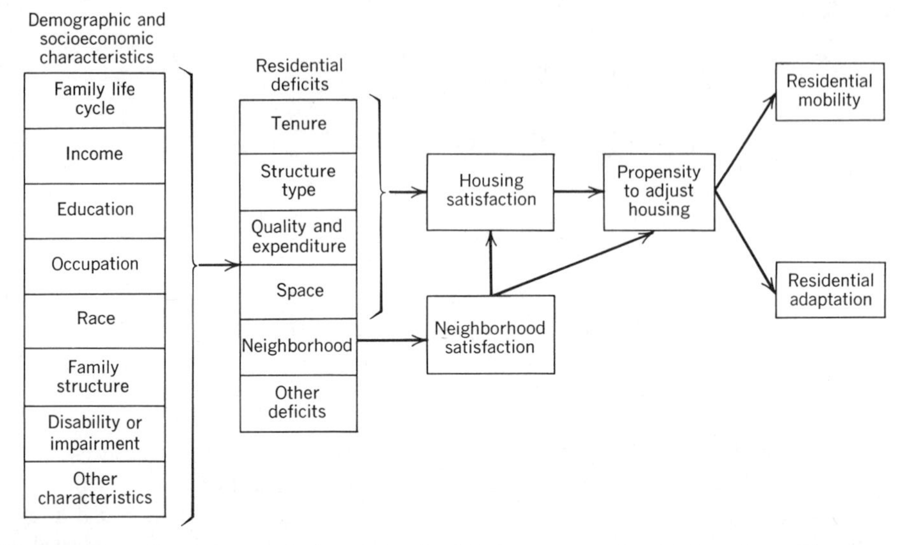

Figure 6 Causal model of hypothesized influences on family housing adjustment behavior.

related to housing satisfaction—a job transfer, for example. The family who moves involuntarily or for nonhousing reasons may be able to reduce the number of its housing deficits. Nevertheless, the impetus for such a move has little to do with housing adjustment.

The importance of satisfaction (Chapter 8) in the development of a propensity to engage in specific housing adjustment behavior has only recently been the focus of research. Much of that research has been conducted in the fields of business administration and marketing. In many cases, findings have only limited applicability to a durable investment such as housing (Morris, Winter, and Beutler, 1975).

The research on residential mobility is voluminous (see Chapter 9). One of the reasons for the amount of research is that, in addition to fertility and mortality, population movements have been one of the three key focuses of demography. Mobility research has been well supported because of interest in population problems on the part of private foundations and the government. An additional factor is the great visibility of the suburban movement and the rural-urban migration in the recent history of the United States. Residential mobility, particularly in the form of city-to-suburb moves, has resulted in striking changes in the residential patterns of the United States, obvious even to casual observers.

Research on residential alterations and additions (Chapter 10) has been limited to examination of remodeling and maintenance behavior. Not until recently has there been much research on residential alteration as an alternate form of housing adjustment behavior. Some types of alterations, such as converting a room from one use to another, have not been studied at all.

Physical changes that accompany the aging process and those associated with various disabilities have long been the focus of research. The view of the housing needs of the elderly and the disabled in terms of deficits that are analogous with normative deficits is quite new. Housing deficits (based on the special needs, as opposed to normative needs) of the elderly and the disabled, along with related satisfaction, and subsequent adjustment behavior, are presented in Chapter 11.

Chapter 8
Residential Dissatisfaction

> "Were they not satisfied where they were?" asked the little prince. "No one is ever satisfied where he is," said the switchman. Antoine de Saint-Exupéry*

A reduced level of residential satisfaction is a stress caused by housing that deviates from cultural, family, or community norms. When the level of stress exceeds the limits the family is willing to tolerate, the propensity to engage in housing adjustment behavior develops. In the absence of constraints, some sort of adjustment behavior is likely to take place. The purpose of this chapter is to explore the process by which residential dissatisfaction develops and the specific factors that cause dissatisfaction to arise.

A family's level of satisfaction or dissatisfaction with their housing is viewed here in four different ways. The first is in terms of the causes of satisfaction. What types of families are most likely to be satisfied or dissatisfied? What are the features of a dwelling that produce satisfaction or dissatisfaction? What is the relationship of deficits to satisfaction? The second way of viewing satisfaction is to focus on its consequences, as developed in Chapters 9, 10, and 11.

The third view is to focus on the intervening role of the stress experienced by families who have deficits and on the subsequent effect on behavioral propensities and actual behavior. What is the probability of the emergence of a behavior that would fill the unmet needs that produce the dissatisfaction? This method of viewing satisfaction is depicted in Figure 6 in the introduction to Part 3. The more complex relations implied in the third view, of course, relate to the total pattern of relationships to and from satisfaction. They thus constitute the focus of all of Part 3. The fourth view is the microscopic analysis of the process of becoming dissatisfied or satisfied. Only the first and fourth ways of viewing satisfaction are discussed in this chapter.

This chapter consists of three main sections. First there is a discussion of the dissatisfaction process. Next comes a discussion of the measurement of

* From *The Little Prince* by Antoine de Saint-Exupéry (New York: Harcourt, Brace and World, 1943), p. 73. Reprinted by permission of Harcourt Brace Jovanovich.

satisfaction. Finally, there is a review of research on the influences producing dissatisfaction.

THE DISSATISFACTION PROCESS

The analysis of the process of becoming either dissatisfied or satisfied requires a slight shift of focus from systemic functional analysis. It is necessary to concentrate more on the interactions that occur among the members of the family as they engage in housing adjustment. The framework for this kind of analysis is referred to as the interactional approach (Shaneveldt, 1966). The interactional approach (perhaps best thought of as a special instance of functional analysis) permits focusing on the process of interaction among the personalities who constitute a specific family system. This viewpoint fits well with the integration assumption made in Chapter 3 that the elements of a system influence one another and that all elements influence all other elements.

Interactional analysis of the family focuses on the nature and directions of those influences. Within the interactional approach the family is viewed as "a unity of interacting personalities each with a history in a given cultural milieu" (Dollard, 1935, p. 110). That definition of the family is totally consistent with the one used in this book. It places emphasis, however, on the point that the elements of the family system are personalities who interact.

In terms of dissatisfaction with housing, it can be seen that some amount of interaction among family members is necessary before the family "knows" if it is dissatisfied. One Sunday afternoon the wife casually mentions that three children in one bedroom really is not quite right now that they are getting a little older. Perhaps the children chime in with remarks about each having their own room or about how much more sloppy Anne is than Mary or Sue. A pang of guilt strikes the father. He has recently learned that several of his co-workers who are in a similar family life cycle stage have bought homes in a new subdivision. It is already too late to turn back. The family is dissatisfied.

The interactional viewpoint conceives of the family and the interaction process as much more fluid than other approaches do. A key concept is the "definition of the situation" (Thomas and Znaniecki, 1927). The concept is used to emphasize the idea that the events occurring at a given moment in time within a given family are important in terms of the symbolic meaning of the events to the family members:

> *The situation is the set of values and attitudes with which the individual or group has to deal in a process or activity and with regard to which this activity is planned and its results appreciated (Thomas and Znaniecki, 1927, p. 28).*

The discussion from Thomas and Znaniecki can be applied to housing satisfaction-dissatisfaction within the housing adjustment process. *The set of values and attitudes* refers to the cultural, community, and family norms. *The process or activity* refers to housing adjustment. *Its results appreciated,* of course, refers to the development of satisfaction-dissatisfaction. The definition of the situation is important in that the aforementioned family conversation may have been a dreaming session. On the other hand, it may have been perceived by all as a serious discussion aimed at deciding if they were dissatisfied enough to really do something about it. The question of whether all members of the family defined the situation similarly is also important. The father, for instance, may have taken none of the discussion seriously and, indeed, may have simply dismissed it as idle conversation.

The interactional approach permits an emphasis on socialization and the development of norms. A portion of any interaction process is the exchange of information about what values, norms, and attitudes are appropriate to the particular situation. Children learn most of their version of housing norms during family interaction related to housing adjustment. In particular, they learn about the kinds of compromises made in preference development. They also learn about the amount of tolerance the family sees as appropriate under unsatisfactory housing conditions.

The housing adjustment process includes family interactions that develop and solidify the family's housing norms and develop the preferences necessary to reconcile norms and constraints. The wife and children may decide to bring up the bedroom crowding problem again in hopes of getting family consensus on the problem. Once the norms and preferences are relatively well agreed upon, the evaluation of the current housing can occur. The amount of satisfaction-dissatisfaction can then be assessed.

Obviously, the conclusion about the degree of satisfaction is a matter for group interaction. It is necessary to assess the degree of family consensus about the matter. The specific means by which families achieve consensus about the level of satisfaction depends upon family structure and organization. The relative power of the father, mother, and children is important. In highly father-dominated families, family satisfaction may be achieved when the father is satisfied. In egalitarian families it is more complex and requires an assessment of individual family members' feelings.

The specific process (ignoring, for the moment, variability in family consensus) of satisfaction development involves three steps. First is the comparison of current housing with the norms. Next there is the assessment of constraints that might prevent change if there are deficits present. Third is the development of preferences for possible improved housing. If there are deficits present and there are no constraints that would prevent implementation of preferences, satisfaction would be low.

The process is dynamic, as well. After housing adjustment has occurred, the outcome is evaluated to ascertain whether the new housing situation has brought housing more closely into alignment with norms, preferences, and constraints. If it has, satisfaction can be expected to rise.

Preliminary research by the present authors has shown that satisfaction with current housing is less related to the *presence* of specific features than it is to *improvements* or *increases* in those features. People who have recently acquired an automatic washer have higher levels of satisfaction than people who were never without one. Dissatisfaction is produced by the *appearance,* not just the existence, of deficits. Satisfaction is produced by the *removal* of deficits rather than by their absence. Apparently, once a given deficit is removed, satisfaction rises in response. Then the dissatisfaction development mechanism can focus on the next most important deficit.

The effects of satisfaction, normative housing deficits, and the household characteristics are more complex than it would appear at first glance. For example, a low income may mean that a family has housing with many normative deficits. Therefore, they should have a relatively low level of satisfaction and a correspondingly high propensity to make housing adjustments. One would be led to believe that low-income families would have higher rates of housing adjustment than middle- and upper-income families.

There is a tendency, however, for low-income families to be satisfied with housing that has more deficits than middle-income families would tolerate. Low income acts as a constraint in that poor families cannot obtain nondeficit housing. In addition, it acts to lower expectations and thereby reduces the effect of income-caused deficits on satisfaction. The latter partially or completely offsets the potential need for more frequent housing adjustment by lower-income families. Thus, the propensity to adjust housing is reduced by the tendency for low-income families to be satisfied with less than optimum housing conditions.

At least two threads run through the satisfaction literature (Day, 1976; Miller, 1976). The first includes studies that concentrate on satisfaction as a result of a gap between the characteristics of the dwelling (in the case of housing) and the family's expectations about the dwelling. The second includes studies that concentrate on gaps between the characteristics of the dwelling and an idealized version of the dwelling.

The first relates, in the present model, to the question of whether the housing adjustment process results in housing that fulfills *preferences*. The second involves the question of whether the process results in the fulfillment of *norms*. The differences between the effects of preference deficits and normative deficits depends upon a number of factors. A deficit in terms of norms that does not represent simultaneously a deficit from preferences may have little enduring effect upon dissatisfaction. If expectations arising from preferences are quite low (which would be the case when constraints have forced preferences downward) dissatisfaction probably would be very mild. However, if the housing achieved in the adjustment process meets neither the norms nor the preferences, dissatisfaction would be high.

There are two types of consequences that may be produced by the occurrence of dissatisfaction (Day, 1976). The first is the type of response implied in dissonance theory (Festinger, 1957). The family either further lowers its expectations (reduces the level of preferences) or alters the perception of the deficit in order to reduce the dissonance. For moderate levels of deficits, the first type of response seems to be typical (Day, 1976; Miller, 1976).

For more severe deficits, the second type is more likely to occur. Rather than reducing dissatisfaction by altering expectations or perceptions, a moderate increase in a deficit beyond a certain threshold produces a great increase in dissatisfaction. The basic idea of dissonance clearly applies in both cases. In the latter case, however, greater effort is required to produce a reduction in dissatisfaction (Miller, 1976). It becomes necessary to improve the current housing or exchange it. Failing that, the norms themselves must be changed.

THE MEASUREMENT OF SATISFACTION

The general measurement of satisfaction, like self-regulation, can be based on two levels. Satisfaction with the global preferred state (overall life satisfaction) can be assessed either directly or by a summation or other weighted combination of satisfactions with the various partial preferred states. Within the global level and each partial level, well-being can be assessed either objectively or subjectively. Objective measurements are in terms of the actual levels of well-being achieved. Satisfaction with the levels achieved is the subjective measurement. Both are equally important, for it is the subjective reaction to the achieved states that serve as motivation to improve well-being.

Thus the measurement of subjective well-being is based on reported satisfaction. Objective measurement of well-being is based on measures of the existence of unmet needs. The concept of unmet needs is based on deviations of actual conditions from norms and therefore is represented by normative deficits. It is not obvious that subjective well-being, as manifested in reported satisfaction, is strongly related to objective well-being. It is an appropriate topic of empirical testing whether households with few normative deficits overwhelmingly can be expected to report high satisfaction. At the least, there are likely to be psychological variations in the tolerance for, and perception of, the existence of deficits which would produce variations in satisfaction.

The theoretically most probable cause of reported satisfaction is a measure of the extent to which unfilled needs exist. Consumers' needs can be defined in terms of cultural norms applied to judge various aspects of the life style or level of living. That statement implies that a consumer "needs" what others in the society, and the various subgroups of which the consumer is a member, think the consumer ought to have in order to be respectable. Reported satisfaction is expected to be low when an important need is not met or a number of lesser needs are not met.

A number of studies have attempted to assess the subjective reactions of people to their objective conditions. None of the studies has been particularly well designed for that purpose, however. Speare's (1974) analysis of residential mobility included residential satisfaction as an intervening variable in a causal model predicting propensity to move, and actual mobility. Speare's satisfaction measure was based on six items of housing and neighborhood satisfaction: satisfaction with the size of the house, with the yard, with the age of the house, with the immediate neighborhood, with the section of town, and with the distance from work. Unfortunately, the construction of Speare's index was based on correlations with the dependent variables. Hence the final index obviously could be expected to be strongly related to the propensity to move, and mobility.

Satisfaction indexes may be self-weighting in that the respondent considers the salient attributes of the matter in question, weights them in his or her mind, and reports an overall satisfaction level. On the other hand, weighting may be done externally by asking the respondent to report satisfaction about each of the attributes and also to report the importance of each attribute. The satisfaction scale, then, would use the importance responses to weight the satisfaction responses.

Perhaps the most satisfactory method of measuring satisfaction that has been applied in the empirical analysis of housing was the one used by Yockey (1976a), Harris (1976b), and Morris (1976). Yockey developed a scale of satisfaction with space-oriented characteristics of the dwelling. Harris (1976b) developed a scale based on quality-oriented (as opposed to quantity-oriented) characteristics. Morris (1976) developed on overall measure of satisfaction including quality, quantity, ownership, and structure-type satisfactions. All three of these studies used a set of paired items in which a question about satisfaction with a characteristic of the dwelling was paired with a question on the respondent's assessment of the importance of that characteristic to the family.

The scales were developed by weighting the satisfaction responses by the importance responses. A high level of satisfaction with a very important item received a higher score than a high level of satisfaction with an unimportant item. In Morris' (1976) scale, responses of "very satisfied" combined with "very important" received scores of 11. Responses of "very dissatisfied" with "very important" received scores of 0. Similar but not identical coding procedures were used in Yockey (1976a) and Harris (1976b).

All three studies conducted extensive reliability testing and less exhaustive validity testing. Reliability was found to be very high. Two tests of validity indicated that housing satisfaction in the weighted scales was valid. The scales had significant correlations with an independent overall measure of housing satisfaction. They also exhibited the theoretically predicted correlations with other variables almost without exception.

These tests, however, have not produced scales with absolute zero points, in that the point in the continuum where "satisfaction" switches to "dissatisfaction" has not been located. It is not at all clear that such a point exists. Nevertheless, some authors have searched for it (Speare, 1974; Maddox and Leavitt, 1976). It may not be important to locate such a point. It seems more important to know the relative differences in satisfaction between groups of respondents than to know exactly how far into the "satisfied" or "dissatisfied" range a particular respondent or group of respondents are.

Butler et al. (1969) pointed out the widespread tendency on the part of housing practitioners to reject measures of satisfaction on the ground that most people report satisfaction even when outside observers would expect high levels of dissatisfaction. Among those practitioners it was felt:

> *. . . people do not consciously recognize the features or combinations of features that elicit positive or negative feelings, and therefore direct questions about dwelling or neighborhood preferences are not true reflections of satisfactions or dissatisfactions (Butler et al., 1969, p. 19).*

Without specifically questioning the correctness of such a position, Butler et al. continued with their analysis of direct questions on satisfaction with a large number of characteristics of the dwelling and with the overall dwelling.

It seems reasonable to assume that consumers are able to report their feelings of satisfaction relatively accurately, with the possible exception of their ability to express extreme dissatisfaction to an interviewer. Such response bias would amount to a shifting of the subjective threshold or zero point of each question downward when expressing satisfaction-dissatisfaction verbally. The shift would be relatively unimportant if all respondents shifted the same amount. Obviously, that is unlikely. For example, Yockey (1976b) found that feelings of apathy or powerlessness may begin to deal with the problem of response shifts. People who are apathetic and feel powerless may have a reduced sensitivity to deficits and therefore a reduced tendency to *be* dissatisfied. However, they also would have a much reduced tendency to *report* their dissatisfaction.

It is unquestionably true that survey respondents in the United States by and large respond in the "satisfied" range of most satisfaction-dissatisfaction questions. Obviously a portion of that pattern must arise from the "true" level of satisfaction. Many of them must indeed be satisfied. "Unwarranted" satisfaction (satisfaction with a patently undesirable situation) may be attributed to three factors. Those factors are low salience, idiosyncratic standards, and reporting error, including random and systematic error.

The first seems obvious. A respondent would be less likely to report dissatisfaction with the presence or absence of a nonsalient attribute. The second amounts to a special case of "true" satisfaction. Some people with peculiar tastes may be highly satisfied with what seems to others a very unsatisfactory situation. Such would be households with family norms that differ greatly from the cultural norms.

The third breaks down into random error, control of which is left to the probabilistic aspects of statistical inference, and systematic error, which conceivably can be corrected. If this type of error is related to education, for example, it could be corrected by including education in the analysis. Systematic error in reported satisfaction seems most likely to arise from the operation of perceived constraints that produce a tendency to lower preferences below cultural and household norms, a point developed further in Chapter 15. Thus low income in the forms of a budget constraint may induce severe compromises of norms, which in turn, would reduce the dissatisfaction response.

THE CAUSES OF DISSATISFACTION

The hypothesized relationships between the characteristics of the family, normative residential deficits, and residential satisfaction are shown in Figure 7. The figure, a part of the causal model presented in the introduction to Part 3, depicts satisfaction as resulting from the housing and neighborhood deficits. Neighborhood satisfaction is also seen as having an independent

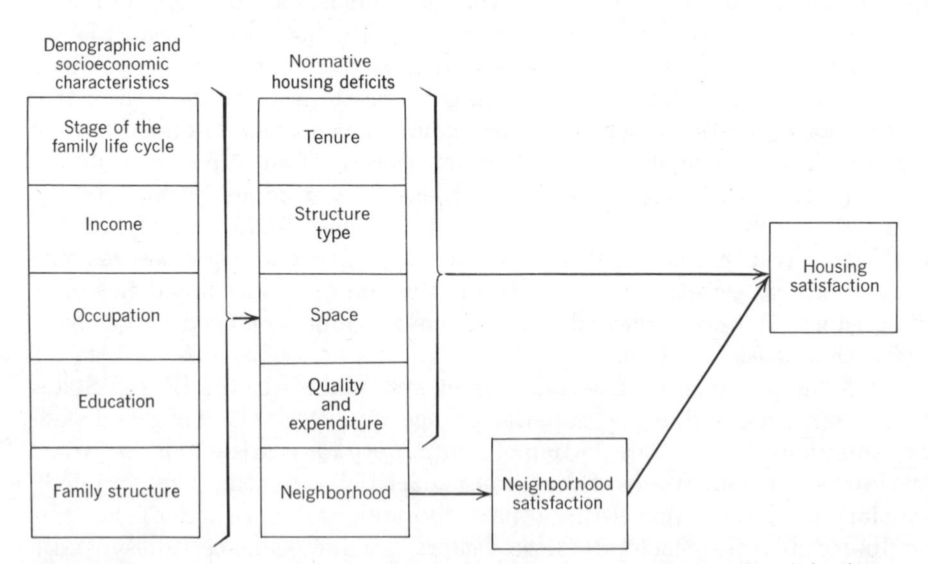

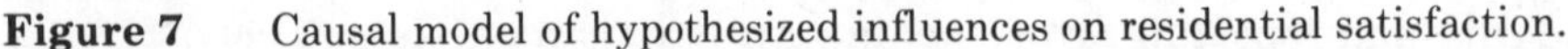
Figure 7 Causal model of hypothesized influences on residential satisfaction.

influence on housing satisfaction. This section of the chapter tests, as far as possible, that model. Tests are limited by the research available, however.

Until recently the analysis of housing satisfaction has been heavily concentrated on satisfaction as a consequence of the characteristics of the family or the dwelling. There was a considerable interest in the features of a dwelling that families viewed as desirable. Caplow (1948) found satisfaction unrelated to level of education in any consistent way. Peterson, Phillips, and Stevenson (1951) reported that housing satisfaction was higher among families in higher "land classes" (dairy and poultry farming) than among families in lower land classes (general and subsistence farming). Caplow (1948) found the level of satisfaction to be related to the age of the dwelling, to the size of the dwelling, and to being too close to the central city. He also found renters to be consistently more dissatisfied than owners on all the aspects of their housing about which he questioned them. The difference between owners and renters was due mainly to the lack of ownership rather than to specific differences in the dwellings themselves.

Recent studies, however, have shown that normative deficits explain most of the relationships between housing and household characteristics and satisfaction. The apparent influence of most housing and household characteristics that have been shown to be associated with satisfaction are eliminated when deficits are introduced. The pattern appears to hold for culturally defined deficits, deficits that are defined by the family, and for deficits that are a combination of cultural and family definitions.

Morris et al. (1976) have shown that the influences on satisfaction are confined to housing deficits when included in a multivariate analysis. None of the demographic and socioeconomic variables had an independent effect on satisfaction when normative housing deficits were included in the analysis. A limitation of the study was that the measures of satisfaction were single-item measures of overall housing and neighborhood satisfaction. Presumably, overall satisfaction would include the respondent's assessment of importance, but the weighting would be internal and implicit, rather than external and explicit. For the purposes of assessing the determinants of satisfaction, the study was limited because the set of deficit variables was a mixture of family deficit measures and cultural deficit measures. Thus, comparisons could not be made between the relative strength of cultural deficits, family deficits, or some combination of the two as predictors of satisfaction.

Morris (1976) analyzed the influences of housing deficits and household characteristics on housing satisfaction. Cultural deficits in space, tenure, and structure type contributed an increment to the explantation of satisfaction greater than the joint contribution of five household characteristics. When deficits based on family norms were used, the same pattern appeared, as well as when combined cultural and family deficits were used. Only age and income had statistically significant relationships to satisfaction when combined with the deficit variables. The older the household head and the higher the income, the greater the satisfaction. Among the deficits, the greatest contribution to satisfaction was bedroom deficit followed by tenure deficit. Least influential were deficits in type of structure. Thus, satisfaction is strongly related to having sufficient bedrooms for the composition of the family, being an owner, and, indeed, being an owner of a single-family dwelling.

The findings of Morris (1976) contrast somewhat with those of Morris et al. (1976) where it was found that none of the background variables had significant effects on satisfaction. A portion of the difference is due to the inclusion of different variables in the two studies, and, in particular, to the inclusion of neighborhood satisfaction in Morris et al. (1976). Another important difference was the use of a weighted satisfaction scale with multiple component items by Morris (1976). The other study used a single-item measure of satisfaction.

Yockey (1976a) used a measure of satisfaction with two aspects of housing (space and neighborhood) to predict the propensity to engage in residential alterations. Her preliminary space satisfaction measure was a summation of the satisfaction with the number of rooms, number of bedrooms, size of bedrooms, size of the lot, and sufficiency of housing space available. The neighborhood satisfaction scale was a summation of satisfaction with neighbors and neighborhood people, neighborhood children, conditions of other housing, nearness to community services, schools, parks and recreation, and traffic safety (pp. 26–27). Both scales scored high on reliability tests.

As expected, the only predictor of space satisfaction was family bedroom deficit. The families who had fewer bedrooms than they needed were more likely to be dissatisfied with the space in the dwelling. All other socioeconomic and demographic characteristics were not significant.

Harris (1976b) has shown that variation in housing quality relates positively to housing quality satisfaction which, in turn, is related negatively to the desire to make alterations or additions to the current dwelling. She tested alternative housing quality satisfaction measures in two different models for predicting the propensity to make residential alterations. Both satisfaction scales contained the same individual satisfaction components. One of the scales included subjective importance weights for each of the components, however, while the other did not. Included in each scale were satisfaction with the floor plan, physical condition, comfort, style, image of the house, number of bathrooms, cooking facilities, ease of cleaning, landscaping, and ease of lot care. As predicted, housing quality was strongly correlated with the satisfaction scale. The scale, of course, was intended to measure satisfaction with the presence of quality. The actual correlation with quality is a measure of the validity of the satisfaction scale.

Characteristics of the household did enter her model, however. Satisfaction was positively related to age and negatively related to the number of children. Income was not a predictor of satisfaction, however. Including a measure of quality (not a quality deficit) absorbed the influence that income would have had. The findings regarding age, which support those of other studies, appear to be explained by the mixture of improved housing as age increases and a rising tendency to be more tolerant of housing deficits; her model did not include neighborhood satisfaction. The fact that housing satisfaction is lower among large families may be the result of two related factors. First, there was no measure of crowding in the analysis. Second, larger families probably have had to give up a certain amount of quality in order to obtain larger amounts of space.

In an analysis of satisfaction among home owners, Bross (1975) found that, in addition to deficits, length of ownership, recent mobility, and income were related to housing satisfaction. Neighborhood satisfaction had by far the strongest relationship to housing satisfaction, however. Length of residence may be a function of age, of course. Income may have a direct effect on satisfaction because of its relationship to quality norms and quality deficits. Housing quality was not assessed in her study.

Neighborhood deficits and the absence of neighborhood deficits have been shown to be related to neighborhood satisfaction in the same way that housing deficits are related to housing satisfaction. Lansing et al. (1970) studied satisfaction with ten different communities, ranging from suburban to central city, and from highly planned developments to more typical, less planned suburban developments. Residents in the more highly planned neighborhoods reported higher levels of overall neighborhood satisfaction. The reasons for reacting favorably were the accessibility to community facilities and to other areas, the friendliness of the neighbors, good schools, and neighborhood safety. Dissatisfaction with specific neighborhoods as a place for children under 12 was associated with poor quality schools and lack of safety.

Satisfaction with the immediate neighborhood was related to factors associated with density (Lansing et al., 1970). Less satisfied people were those who heard their neighbors often, indicated a high noise level in the neighborhood, had no privacy in their yard, had inadequate outdoor play space, and neither knew nor interacted with their neighbors. Other factors related to neighborhood satisfaction were home value, liking the neighbors, living in a well-maintained neighborhood, and wanting to spend more time with neighbors. Finally, respondents were more satisfied if their dwelling cost more than the neighborhood average, but their income was less than the neighborhood average. Satisfaction was also related to living in a more expensive neighborhood with residents of a higher socioeconomic status than in the rest of the community (Lansing et al., 1970).

Studies among both blacks and whites that have related neighborhood satisfaction to the presence of serious deficits, in the form of urban violence, lack of safety, high crime rates, and poor quality schools report findings similar to each other. Nathanson (1974), Kasl and Harberg (1972), and Droettboom, McAllister, Kaiser, and Butler (1971) found that the perception of deficits resulted in a low degree of neighborhood satisfaction.

It is quite important to note that all the studies of satisfaction reviewed involve the correlation of satisfaction with the presence of characteristics of the dwelling or neighborhood, not improvements or increases in those characteristics. Thus, all of these studies can be expected to understate the dynamic relationship between satisfaction and improvements that occurs during housing adjustment.

DURATION OF RESIDENCE AND SATISFACTION

A variable that has often been used by researchers as a predictor of the propensity to move and of actual mobility is duration of residence. This variable, derived from the "axiom of cumulative inertia," has been found to be negatively related to residential mobility (Myers, McGinnis, and Masnick, 1967; Speare, 1974; Morrison, 1967). There has to date, however, been no satisfactory explanation for duration of residence *per se* to be related to residential mobility.

Morrison (1967) viewed duration of residence as an index of increasing integration into the local area. Speare (1974) suggests that the relationship occurs because satisfaction increases over time with an increase in the number of friendships in the area and with familiarity with commercial and community facilities. He found that duration of residence was related to mobility but not to the propensity to move. Those findings may suggest that constraints on mobility rise with duration of residence, but the propensity to move remains constant over time.

McAllister, Butler, and Kaiser (1973) found that the amount of local visiting was high immediately after a family had moved to an area. It subsequently dropped but then rose slowly with rising duration of residence. Such findings offer moderate support for Morrison's assumption over the longer time span but not for very short durations of residence.

An alternative explanation in light of findings regarding housing and neighborhood satisfaction is that the relationship found between duration of residence and mobility is, in part, an artifact of cross-sectional analysis. The direction of causation appears to be the reverse of that hypothesized by Speare (1974), Morrison (1967), and Myers et al. (1967). Duration of residence *per se* does not appear to influence satisfaction. Rather, high levels of satisfaction produce long duration of residence. Dissatisfied families are likely to move quickly and satisfied families to remain. Very short durations of residence in a dwelling should be accompanied by high satisfaction as recent movers typically would have experienced a reduction of housing deficits.

Morris et al. (1976) and Bross (1975) found a direct relationship between recent mobility and housing satisfaction. Lansing et al. (1970) had similar results for neighborhood satisfaction. After the immediate euphoria, which is captured in a variable that measures recent mobility, the dynamic relationship as compared with the cross-sectional relationship between length of residence in a dwelling and satisfaction should be positive. Satisfaction is properly viewed as the cause, and duration of residence, as the effect.

Barrs (1975) provided a partial test of this hypothesis by showing that duration of residence was not a predictor of satisfaction or the desire to move. Over 40 percent of the variation in duration of residence was the result of the duration of the marriage, the sex of the head of the household, income, and other variables. Therefore, a new duration of residence variable was created that controlled for such factors. The new variable was not found to be related to neighborhood satisfaction, housing satisfaction, or the desire to move.

A CAUSAL MODEL OF RESIDENTIAL SATISFACTION

The tested relationships between household characteristics, housing and neighborhood deficits, and residential satisfaction are shown in Figure 8. Conclusions are very tentative, however, because the network of relationships as an entirety has not yet been tested.

Only age and income are shown to have independent influences on satisfaction. The apparent effects of age may be due to neighborhood satisfaction that produces long durations of residence. Very long durations of residence, of course, are only possible among older people. Thus a spurious relationship to age appears. The influence of income may be due to its relationship with quality. For the moment, they are assumed to have effects that are independent of deficits.

Tenure, structure type, space, quality, and neighborhood deficits have been shown to produce lower levels of housing and neighborhood satisfaction. Neighborhood satisfaction, in turn, is the strongest influence on housing satisfaction.

Recognition of the role of residential satisfaction in housing adjustment and adaptation has been relatively recent. Hence conclusions regarding stages in the development of dissatisfaction and relationships to family

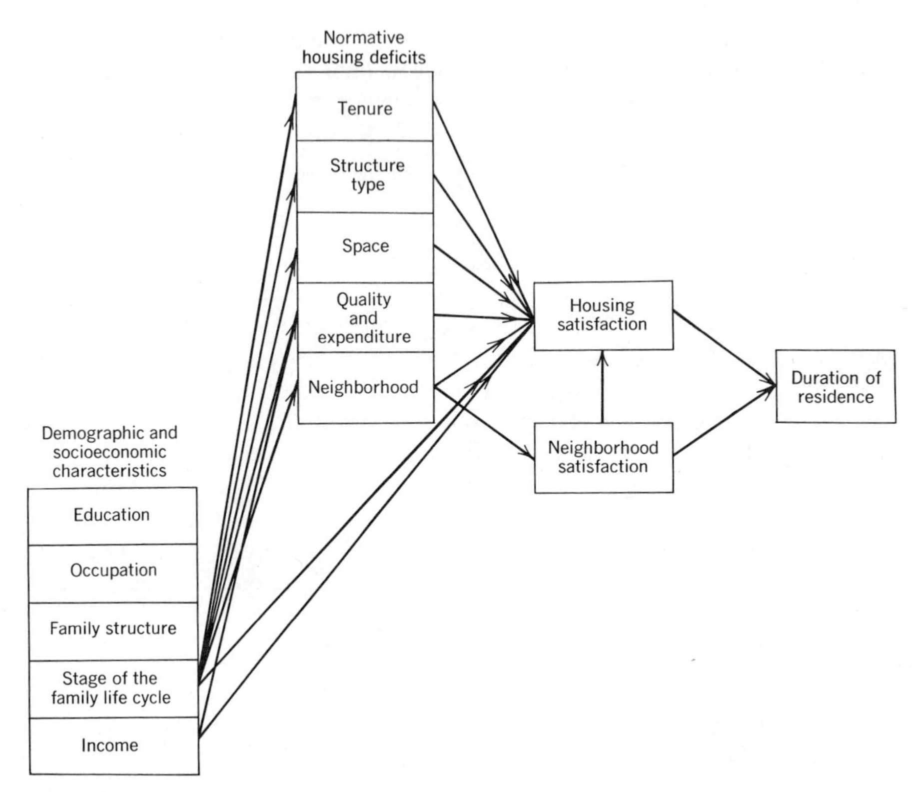

Figure 8 Causal model of satisfaction with hypotheses substantiated in the research literature.

characteristics and normative deficits require further research. In particular, studies are needed to further refine the measurement of housing and neighborhood satisfaction.

DEFINITIONS

Budget constraint. The effect of having a limited amount of money to spend for housing, food, etc.

Causal model. A representation of reality that hypothesizes a causal relationship between two or more variables.

Correlation. The strength of association between two variables; an estimate of the strength of a causal relationship between an independent and a dependent variable.

Dependent variable. That which is caused: the effect or consequence of an independent variable; a hypothetical or theoretical conception of a factor or variable in a causal model; to be contrasted with independent variable.

Independent variable. The cause or determinant of a dependent variable; a hypothetical or theoretical conception of the role of a factor or variable in a causal model; to be contrasted with dependent variable.

Interactional approach. A framework for studying the family system that focuses on the process of interaction among the members of the family. Emphasis is on the family members as interacting personalities. Another key element in this approach is the emphasis on the symbolic meaning of words and events to the members; the definition they attach to a situation.

Intervening variable. Hypothetical or theoretical conception of a variable viewed as an effect of an independent variable and a cause of a dependent variable.

Multivariate analysis. Analysis of a dependent variable in terms of several independent variables; an attempt to discover the multiple causes of a variable.

Negative relationship. A relationship in which the dependent variable increases when the independent variable decreases; to be contrasted with positive relationship. For example, there is a negative relationship between mobility and age; as age of the household head increases, the likelihood that the household will move decreases.

Neighborhood satisfaction. Contentment with a neighborhood based on the relative absence of perceived neighborhood deficits and low salience of the deficits that exist. See housing satisfaction.

Objective well-being. Measured in terms of actual levels of well-being achieved and the relative absence of unmet needs as detected by an impartial observer; to be contrasted with subjective well-being.

Positive relationship. A relationship in which the dependent variable increases when the independent variable increases; to be contrasted with negative relationship. For example, there is a positive relationship between satisfaction and the length of residence; as satisfaction increases, length of residence increases.

Predictor. An independent variable with a strong effect on the dependent variable; a variable, knowledge of which provides information about another. For example, the income of a family is a good predictor of housing expenditures. Hence if family income is known, a relatively accurate estimate of the family's housing expenditures can be made.

Propensity to adjust. Inclination or tendency to make a change in one's housing in response to deficits.

Random error. Error in the measurement of a variable that results from chance factors such as a slip of the tongue by a respondent or a slip of the pencil by an interviewer or data analyst; to be contrasted with systematic error.

Reliability. The degree to which repeated measurements of a given concept using maximally similar measurement techniques produce similar results; to be contrasted with validity.

Response bias. Directional shifts in data due to the characteristics of the population being studied; a reduced or increased tendency on the part of respondents to perceive or report a status or condition; one form of systematic error.

Significant relationship A statistically significant relationship between two variables, which, tests show, is so strong that it is not attributable to chance.

Spurious relationship. A relationship between two variables, which, upon further analysis, turns out to exist because the two variables are the effects of a common cause with only an incidental correlation between them.

Subjective well-being. A psychological feeling of being well off; to be contrasted with objective well-being.

Systematic error. A type of error that, once its cause is known, can be corrected; to be contrasted with random error. For example, if having a low income produces a reluctance to report dissatisfaction to an interviewer, it would be possible to correct the data to reflect the downward bias due to low income.

Validity. The degree to which repeated measurements of a given concept using maximally different techniques of measurement produce similar results; in general, the degree to which a variable measures what it is supposed to measure; to be contrasted with reliability.

Weighted scale. A measuring instrument composed of multiple items and a set of weights used to achieve a combined scale superior to a simple addition of the individual item scores. A total scale score is computed by weighting each item response according to its importance.

Chapter 9
Residential Mobility

Then move your family westward;
good health you will enjoy,
And rise to wealth and honor
in the State of Illinoy   American folk song

Much research has been done on residential mobility since Peter Rossi's (1955) classic study, *Why Families Move.* Research has been focused on the determinants of residential mobility, stated reasons for moving, characteristics of the origin and/or the destination of the movers, or combinations of the three aspects.

Some researchers have viewed residential mobility as an adjustment process. Rossi (1955) noted that residential mobility is:

> *the process by which families adjust their housing to the housing needs that are generated by shifts in family composition that accompany life cycle changes (p. 9).*

Following Rossi's lead, Chevan (1971) also characterized mobility as:

> *the mechanism whereby the composition of the family at different stages of the family life cycle is matched to the housing needs implied by that composition (p. 451).*

The interpretations by Foote et al. (1960, pp. 97–118; pp. 155–58), Smith et al. (1963, pp. 23–24), Gutheim (1948), Duncan and Newman (1975), Goodman (1974), and Roistacher (1974b) also present the view that mobility is an adjustment process in which families adjust to changing housing needs. The purpose of this chapter is to review research regarding residential mobility in light of the housing adjustment model.

RESIDENTIAL MOBILITY VERSUS MIGRATION

Residential mobility refers to changing residence within a given local area. Thus, mobility occurs within a single labor market and within a single housing market. Migration, on the other hand, involves moving from one labor market to another, and from one housing market to another. Residential mobility generally is referred to as a local move, an intracommunity move, or an intrametropolitan move. Migration is termed intercommunity, intermetropolitan, or long distance moving (Foote et al., 1960, pp. 158–59; Bogue, 1959; Simmons, 1968).

Approximately 20 percent of the population moves at least once each year. Two-thirds or more of all movers can be characterized as residentially mobile, while the remainder are migrants (Foote et al., 1960, p. 159; Simmons, 1968, p. 622; USBC, 1974; Roistacher, 1974b, p. 55; Duncan and Newman, 1975, p. 281). The primary impetus for migration is related to economic factors, such as a job transfer or the prospects for a new job. The primary reasons for residential mobility are housing-related factors (USBC, 1966c).

When a family moves for job-related reasons, housing adjustment may occur. The family may change from renting to owning or may move into a house with more bedrooms. Nevertheless, the primary reason for the move is related to employment:

> *. . . a family first chooses the area it is going to work in and then maximizes housing consumption within that area (Roistacher, 1974b, p. 63).*

Thus it is mobility and not migration that is the focus of this chapter.

While easily distinguished conceptually, the classification of given moves as "residential mobility" or "migration" has caused certain analytical problems. The U.S. Bureau of the Census in the *Current Population Reports* series, (between 1949 and 1974) classifies as migrants those individuals who live in a different county from the one they did one year before the date of the enumeration. That distinction is also used by Whitney and Grigg (1958), Long (1972), and Roistacher (1974b).

Defining residential mobility as moves within county boundaries may underestimate the amount of residential mobility and overestimate the amount of migration. Within most metropolitan areas, a family may move across county lines and still be within the same labor and housing market. In border areas, a family can move across state lines and still be making a "local move."

Consequently some researchers have defined mobility to include all moves within a given standard metropolitan statistical area (Van Arsdol, Sabagh, and Butler, 1968; Butler, Van Arsdol, and Sabagh, 1970; Goodman, 1974). Also defined as mobility are moves within the same city or town (Smith et al., 1963; McAllister, Kaiser, and Butler, 1971), within the same small state (Speare, 1970), or within a given general area even though state boundaries might be crossed (Chevan, 1971; Gladhart, 1973). Such classifications require judgments on the part of the researchers regarding what constitutes a local move. Those judgments provide a more theoretically meaningful data base than the simple county line distinction.

ACTUAL MOBILITY VERSUS POTENTIAL MOBILITY

Most studies of residential mobility have investigated either *actual mobility* behavior or *mobility potential*. Actual mobility refers to whether or not a move occurred. Potential mobility refers to desires, plans, inclinations, or expectations about mobility. Taken together as a class of phenomena the latter are referred to as mobility potential or the propensity to move. There have been studies of retrospective mobility, measuring "the number of previous moves, duration of residence, and residence status at past points in time" (Van Arsdol et al., 1968, p. 250). Studies of subsequent mobility, which "portray the behavior of a population or sample after initial contact" (Van Arsdol et al., 1968, p. 251) have also been completed. Examples of retrospective studies of mobility are Smith et al. (1963), Long (1972), and Whitney and Grigg (1958). Rossi (1955), McAllister et al. (1971), Butler et al. (1970), Roistacher (1974b), Roistacher (1975), Duncan and Newman (1975), and Goodman (1974), on the other hand, have studied factors related to subsequent mobility.

An additional variation has to do with the use of family histories, a method that makes it possible to reconstruct the sequences of residential mobility, the births of children, and other changes in the family. Previous mobility may be analyzed as if it were subsequent mobility since moves made during a given year, say 1965, may be analyzed by relating them to the characteristics of the family prior to or at the beginning of 1965 (Speare, 1970; Chevan, 1971; Gladhart, 1973; Morris, 1977).

Several studies of the propensity to move have been performed using a variety of measures of the concept. Leslie and Richardson (1961), Lansing and Barth (1964), Lansing, Mueller, and Barth (1964), Greenbie (1969), Butler, Sabagh, and Van Arsdol (1964), and Morris et al. (1976) are examples of such studies. The propensity to move or mobility potential is the most important causal factor associated with actual mobility (Duncan and Newman, 1975; Roistacher, 1974b; Roistacher, 1975). Yet the two are conceptually and empirically distinct. The early literature, however, has tended to be somewhat vague on this point.

The distinction between mobility and mobility potential must be emphasized for two reasons. First, intrafamilial and extrafamilial constraints may preclude family housing adjustment behavior. Extrafamilial factors often constrain actual mobility. A family might indicate that they would like to move, plan to move, or would choose to move, and thus have a high propensity to move. When faced with carrying out the actual behavior, however, social, economic, and political constraints may be impossible to overcome. Thus they may be unable to move (Varady, 1974; Duncan and Newman, 1975; Roistacher, 1975; Droettboom et al., 1971).

The second reason for noting the distinction between studies of potential mobility and actual mobility (either retrospective or subsequent) is that the measurement of potential mobility is somewhat less accurate than the measurement of actual mobility. Actual mobility is indicated by whether or not a family moved to a different residence. There is seldom any question regarding whether they should be classified as "movers" or "nonmovers." Studies of actual mobility are more readily compared with one another because there has been more uniformity of measurement.

Categorizing a family as "potentially mobile" or "potentially nonmobile," on the other hand, may be based on a variety of questions. "Do you think there is any chance you people will move in the next twelve months? Would you say you definitely will move, you probably will or are you uncertain?" (Lansing and Barth, 1964, p. 15); "Do you expect to move within the next year?" (Barrs, 1975); "Would you like to stay here or move to a new dwelling?" (Morris et al., 1976); "If there were no housing shortage, would you like to stay here or would you like to move from this place? Are you very anxious to stay here (move out) or doesn't it matter too much to you?" (Rossi, 1955, p. 67); "Do you plan to move from this place within the next year? If you had your choice, would you stay here or move?" (Van Arsdol et al., 1968, p. 254); "Do you think you might move in the next couple of years?" (Duncan and Newman, 1975, p. 280).

Responses to such questions may be scaled (Lansing and Barth, 1964), categorized (Rossi, 1955), or treated as indicators of differing dimensions of potential mobility (Van Arsdol et al., 1968). Nevertheless, in spite of sophisticated statistical treatment, the slight differences in questions mean that the phenomenon being measured in different studies may be somewhat different.

It seems, however, that the actualization of mobility evolves in stages. The stages go from desires to expectations to definite plans to eventual mobility. At each stage constraints apply which reduce the percentage of those who attain the next stage (Duncan and Newman, 1975; Morris et al., 1976). Thus research regarding both mobility and potential mobility is reviewed in the rest of this chapter.

CAUSAL MODELS OF MOBILITY

Results from studies of mobility or the propensity to move are used to test the causal model shown in Figure 9. Some of the hypotheses that are represented by the arrows are impossible to test from published research results. In many cases, the causal influences hypothesized may not yet have been studied.

Similar causal models of mobility have been developed and tested by Pickvance (1973), Pickvance (1974), Speare (1974), Morris et al. (1976), and Morris (1976). Pickvance viewed tenure, rather than tenure deficit, as an intervening variable between household characteristics and mobility. Speare used satisfaction as an intervening variable between characteristics of the household and the dwelling and mobility.

Morris et al. (1976) tested the prediction of the propensity to move, rather than actual mobility. Morris (1976) also used propensity to move. His key focus, however, was to ascertain differences among space, tenure, and structure-type deficits as defined in three different ways, by the culture, by the family, and by both. He found that the combined deficits were slightly better predictors of satisfaction and mobility potential. The differences were not significant, however.

The following dimensions of residential mobility are examined:

1. Demographic and socioeconomic determinants of mobility (background characteristics).

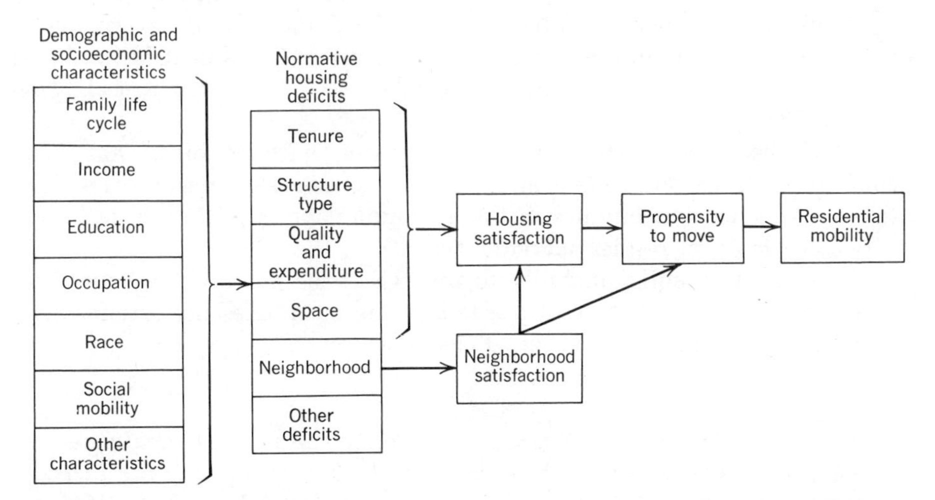

Figure 9 Causal model of hypothesized influences on residential mobility as a housing adjustment behavior.

2. Normative influences on mobility (normative housing deficits).

3. The influence of levels of housing and neighborhood satisfaction on mobility.

Thus the hypotheses presented in Figure 9 will be discussed in order, from left to right.

DEMOGRAPHIC AND SOCIOECONOMIC CHARACTERISTICS

Stage of the Family Life Cycle

Virtually all studies of residential mobility have used some measure of the stage of the family life cycle as a predictor or control. The age of the head of the household has been used (Leslie and Richardson, 1961; Van Arsdol et al., 1968; Rossi, 1955; Butler and Kaiser, 1971; Butler et al., 1964; Lansing et al., 1964; Lansing and Barth, 1964; Speare, 1970; Long, 1972; Okraku, 1971; Butler et al., 1970; Speare, 1974; Roistacher, 1974b; Roistacher, 1975; Goodman, 1974; Duncan and Newman, 1975). Also used have been duration of the marriage (Gladhart, 1973; Chevan, 1971; Morris et al., 1976), or an index of life cycle stage based on the ages of the children (Gladhart, 1971; Smith et al., 1963; Speare, 1970; Okraku, 1971; Sabagh et al., 1969; Goodman, 1974; Duncan and Newman, 1975). Some studies have included the number of people in the household (Rossi, 1955; Okraku, 1971; Smith et al., 1963; Butler and Kaiser, 1971; Roistacher, 1975) or number of children (Long, 1972).

That the family life cycle is associated with mobility has been demonstrated time and time again. Younger households, unusually small or large households, and families in the expanding stages of the life cycle are likely candidates for residential mobility.

To relate residential mobility to the age of the head of the household, size of the family, and stage of the family life cycle does not satisfactorily *explain* the phenomenon, however. It is similar to:

> *noting that being aged 18 is a good predictor of college attendance. The important thing is not being aged 18, but rather it is the fact that most families expect their children to go to college and college starts only after 12 or more preliminary years of schooling (Morris, 1972b, p. 2).*

Thus, the coincidence of family life cycle stages and residential mobility occurs because families in some stages of the family life cycle are more likely to live in deficit housing. Their housing is less likely to conform to housing space norms, neighborhood norms, tenure and structure-type norms, expenditure norms, or other housing norms. Stage of the family life cycle is a good *predictor* of residential mobility. It plays a role in *explanation* of residential mobility only when other factors such as the balance between family composition and the family's housing are considered.

The history of the family, including its residential history, begins with marriage. The first moves that occur are those associated with family formation. Thus each member of the couple moves to their common dwelling, often directly from their parents' homes. The high rates of individual mobility for persons between the ages of 20 and 24 (USBC, 1974) reflect family formation mobility. Studies of family mobility often do not include the changes in residence associated with new family formation as family residential mobility (Chevan, 1971; Goodman, 1974).

Probably the best discussion of the relationships among housing needs, residential mobility, and the family life cycle is found in *Housing Choices and Housing Constraints* (Foote et al., 1960, pp. 100–18). The authors divided the family life cycle into six stages: newly married, child-bearing, child-rearing, child-launching, post-child, and widowed individual. They then characterized the housing needs and family behavior at each stage. They noted three stages at which mobility is likely to be motivated by a discrepancy between the amount of space a family has and the amount normatively prescribed. The first stage is the child-bearing stage when mobility is prompted by an increase in household size and accomplished before the oldest child is in school. The child-launching stage, when the oldest child approaches or is in the early teenage years may also produce space deficits. Finally, mobility may occur during the post-child period when the couple finds itself with too much space.

It could also be expected that the amount of mobility would be highest at the first point and lower at each subsequent point. At the first stage, mobility is not only prompted by lack of space, but by tenure, structure type, and neighborhood deficits as well. The combination of all these discrepancies should lead to higher mobility rates among younger families.

When the presence of teenagers or near-teenagers exerts pressure on the amount of space, the family may already own a single-family dwelling in a suburban neighborhood. Consequently, the impetus to move because of space deficits may not be sufficient to overcome neighborhood ties. Mobility may be lower because of the tendency for families who own their dwelling to alter it. Thus they may either add rooms or convert rooms into bedrooms in order to provide a separate bedroom for each teenager. During the post-child stage the couple is least likely to move because a surplus of space is not as strong a motivation as a lack of space.

Only a few studies, however, have examined in detail the phenomena associated with stages of the family life cycle. Goodman (1974) found that a *change* in life cycle stage was related to mobility. Thus:

> *. . . households experiencing a life cycle change have a higher average probability of moving than households remaining in the same stage (p. 81).*

Families may also move in anticipation of a life cycle change, of course.

In his analysis of family histories Chevan (1971) found a strong relationship between the birth of one or more children and the rate of residential mobility. He noted the decline in mobility over the duration of the marriage and with the birth of subsequent children. He interpreted his findings in the following manner:

> *Housing adjustments of an earlier period may retard future moves as additional children are accomodated in existing space. It is the first child who puts the greatest strain on available space because this child ushers in household furniture and appliances unnecessary in the childless home. The evaluation of schools, neighborhood and dwelling unit introduces a locational factor that may have had lower priority for the childless couple and this may lead to a move (Chevan, 1971, p. 455).*

Long (1972) analyzed the mobility data from the U.S. Bureau of the Census Current Population Surveys for 1968, 1969, and 1970. He found that, for all ages of the head of the household, families with children only under 6 years of age had consistently higher mobility rates than (1) families with children both under 6 and between the ages of 6 and 17, and (2) families with children between the ages of 6 and 17 only. He concluded that:

> *School-age children appear without doubt to represent "ties" to a community, but the direction of causality may run in either of two directions: families may choose to stay in a community because "it is a good place to raise children"; or a married couple may find a community a good place to stay once they have children of school age and are developing friendships in the community built around the children (Long, 1972, p. 382).*

The studies relating residential mobility to family growth, a previous move, and the age of the children lend support to the hypothesis that mobility is influenced by cultural norms for space, as well as those for tenure, structure type, and neighborhood. The initial move is likely to be precipitated by the birth of the first child. That move may take place either before or shortly after the child is born. The exact timing depends on the family's actual housing conditions and its ability to overcome constraints.

Whether or not a family moves again prior to the oldest child's entry into school probably depends upon whether or not the family was able to achieve the normatively prescribed housing conditions with the first move. If they attained ownership of a single-family dwelling in a suburban neighborhood within a good school district, containing enough space for the number of children anticipated, they are unlikely to move. It is clear, however, that most families want to be relatively settled around the time the oldest child enters school.

The family may move again as the children approach the teenage years. The likelihood of such a move depends upon whether or not their earlier moves successfully anticipated future needs. Moves during this stage may also be prompted by rising income. Higher quality and expenditure norms accompany such increases.

The findings of a study of families who moved from one owner-occupied home to another within the same area (Smith et al., 1963) support the hypothesis that an increase in the ages of the children is related to a space deficit. Because their sample was limited to families who moved from one owned single-family dwelling to another, the researchers eliminated families whose moves were related to tenure and structure type deficits. Thus the importance of ages of children in prompting mobility was highlighted. Their analysis showed that the chief reason for mobility was lack of space associated with the space needs of maturing children. The need for more space was most clearly felt by the preschool families and the grade-school families. It was not felt as strongly by the teenage families who had presumably made earlier housing adjustments.

Household Size. A variable related to family life cycle, household size, has also been shown to be related to mobility potential. Larger families are likely to be more mobile than smaller families (Rossi, 1955; Sabagh et al., 1969; Butler and Kaiser, 1971; Okraku, 1971). Long (1972) and Roistacher (1975) reported a curvilinear relationship between household size and mobility, however. Long found a positive relationship to mobility for families with more than three children and a negative relationship for families with fewer than three children. Roistacher found a similar pattern using family size rather than number of children.

A better analysis, however, might be based on *changes* in household size. Roistacher (1974b) and Goodman (1974) found that *changes* in family size were likely to cause mobility. Families with a decline in family size were as likely to move as families who had experienced an increase in family size. The more extreme the change, the greater the probability of moving (Goodman, 1974).

Single-parent Families, Childless Couples. The need for space is a prime motivation for the mobility of intact families (husband, wife, and their children). It could be expected that single-parent families with minor children would exhibit similar patterns of mobility. A separate bedroom is needed for a single parent as well as for two parents. The growth of the children would provide the same impetus for mobility in single-parent families as that found in two-parent families. The constraints might be somewhat different, however.

Few researchers have concentrated on families that are not composed of husband, wife, and children. Studies that have included other household configurations have yielded somewhat contradictory results. Female-headed households have been shown to have higher mobility rates than intact families with the same number and ages of children (Long, 1972; Goodman, 1974). Researchers have also found a greater desire to move among female-headed households than among male-headed households, and the same rates of potential mobility, regardless of sex of the household head (Morris et al., 1976; Butler et al., 1964; Rossi, 1955). Such results may have occurred because the definitions of "other" households have not been consistent. Another explanation is that some have studied actual mobility while others have studied propensity to move.

There is no clear hypothesis for childless couples, however. It could be argued that, since there are no dramatic changes in space norms experienced by families without children, such households would be less mobile. On the other hand, since they would not face as severe economic and social constraints as families with children (hesitation to change school districts; the children's attachment to neighborhood friends), they might be more mobile.

Childless couples were reported to be less likely to move by Rossi (1955) than their counterparts with children, but he did not control for the age of the head. Other studies, however, found higher mobility rates among childless couples than among families with children (Long, 1972; Goodman, 1974; Chevan, 1971).

Thus, although the evidence is somewhat limited, it seems that single-parent households respond to essentially the same pressures as families composed of husband, wife, and minor children. Childless couples exhibit relatively higher mobility rates than families with children. The mobility of childless couples declines with an increase in the age of the head as does the mobility of families with children.

There seems to be little doubt that the residential mobility that is related to the family life cycle is often motivated by space deficits. Families in the child-bearing and child-launching stages are most apt to experience space discrepancies. Hence they are the most likely to move. In addition, families in the early years are more likely to be renters, to live in apartments rather than single-family homes, and to live in a neighborhood that is not necessarily desirable for childrearing. All of the latter are conditions that depart from cultural norms for families.

The probability of moving is related to the effectiveness of previous housing adjustment behavior. If a family was able to secure an owner-occupied house in a good school district with sufficient rooms to meet the cultural norms that would appear at later stages of the family life cycle, they would be unlikely to move. If they were able to successfully engage in residential alteration, the family would be less likely to move. Evidence from studies that have included single-parent households and childless couples only underscores the relations between normative deficits associated with particular stages of the family life cycle and residential mobility.

Socioeconomic Status

According to the theory of family housing adjustment, housing needs are broadly based on cultural norms. American families, regardless of socioeconomic status, should feel similar normative pressures. The ability to overcome constraints, particularly extrafamilial constraints, may vary with socioeconomic status, however.

Butler et al. (1970) used a socioeconomic index composed of education, occupation, and income to classify their sample into low, low-middle, high-middle, and high socioeconomic classes. They found that:

> *while there are major differences in mobility within age levels by [socioeconomic status], the differences are not as large as one would hypothesize . . . (p. 14).*

The U.S. Bureau of the Census *Current Population Reports,* compiled annually, provide comprehensive comparisons of individual (as opposed to family) mobility. The mobility status of the population according to age, income, education, and occupation is reported each year.

The most recent report (USBC, 1974) that covers mobility between March 1970 and March 1974 shows that mobility rates vary according to occupation group. The highest mobility is found among skilled and semiskilled blue collar workers. While the amount of education is positively associated with intercounty migration rates, it is not related to mobility rates (USBC, 1974). Duncan and Newman (1975) found similar results with regard to education.

The *Current Population Reports* had found consistent differences in annual mobility rates according to income. Prior to 1974, individuals with less than $7000 annual income had higher mobility rates than those with more than $7000 annual income (USBC, 1971). Between 1970 and 1974, however, the pattern was not the same. Those with incomes below $7000 had slightly lower rates than those with incomes above $7000 (USBC, 1974). The lowest rates were among the lowest- and highest-income groups.

Other analyses of the relationship between income and mobility have also had mixed results. Lansing et al. (1964) found that income made no difference in moving *plans* (p. 9). Goodman (1974) found little relationship between family income and mobility. When he related a ratio of net income to needs, based on family composition, findings indicated that poor families were more likely to move than nonpoor families. Further controls, however, indicated that the poor families tended to move because they were likely to be renters or to have less space than required by the norms. Both, of course, are deficit conditions.

Perhaps the best explanation of the relationship between mobility and income is offered by Roistacher (1974b). Using longitudinal data, she related income *changes* to mobility. Her findings indicated that extreme changes in income, either decreases or increases, are associated with higher rates of mobility. Thus:

> *. . . mobility is a means by which families adjust housing consumption to fit altered economic status (p. 50).*

Income is seen to have primarily indirect influences on mobility and propensity to move via the normative housing deficits. An increase in income has a direct effect by making moving to a better house possible.

Race

Race is a significant predictor of residential mobility. Black families tend to engage in local moves more often than white families. The difference has consistently appeared in the annual *Current Population Reports* (see, for example, USBC, 1974), although blacks make relatively fewer long distance moves than whites.

Straits' (1968) study of black mobility in Chicago showed higher rates of residential mobility among blacks than among whites. The higher rates were attributed to a greater incidence of undesirable dwelling characteristics among blacks than among whites. Factors leading to moves among blacks included greater crowding, a higher likelihood of a rent increase, and a higher probability of eviction. Thus, Straits speculates that the influence of race (one of the background factors) operates on residential mobility through its influence on normative housing deficits (undesirable dwelling characteristics).

Recent studies (McAllister et al., 1971; Goodman, 1974) that compared the mobility rates of blacks and whites, with controls for socioeconomic, demographic, and attitudinal factors, yielded similar results. In both studies, black mobility rates were consistently higher than those of white families. Controls for tenure and crowding revealed that higher rates of black mobility could be attributed to the different rates of ownership and crowding between blacks and whites.

Race does not seem to affect mobility rates directly. Deficit tenure status, space deficits, and other normative housing deficits that are more prevalent among blacks do influence mobility differentials between the two racial categories. More blacks live in housing that does not meet cultural norms. Such conditions, likely to be caused by poverty and discrimination, produce higher rates of mobility.

Social Mobility

Research regarding the relation between social mobility and residential mobility has yielded contradictory results. Examination of the research methods, particularly regarding the measurement of social mobility, indicates support for the hypothesis that social mobility and residential mobility are not closely related.

One of the first to note the possibility of a relationship between vertical social mobility and residential mobility was Peter Rossi (1955):

> *Families moving up the "occupational" ladder are particularly sensitive to the social aspects of location and use residential mobility to bring their residences into line with their prestige needs. In the findings of this study, some of the households who were strongly dissatisfied with their housing's social environment were expressing the way in which their home no longer fitted in with their social aspirations (p. 179).*

This statement was only speculation by Rossi about the meaning of his findings. He did not include a measure of social mobility in his study.

Studies (Whitney and Grigg, 1958; Leslie and Richardson, 1961) that have supported Rossi's hypothesis have suffered from severe methodological problems. The reasons for moving, as measured by Whitney and Grigg, are imprecise. Upward mobility was poorly measured by Leslie and Richardson.

Recent research has cast doubts on the findings that social mobility or social mobility commitment are related to residential mobility. In their study of mobility potential, Butler et al. (1964) found that, when other independent variables (age of household head, family type, and housing and neighborhood satisfaction) were held constant, "social mobility commitment for the most part, did not differentiate movers from nonmovers" (p. 151).

The relation between social mobility and actual residential mobility was studied by Butler et al. (1970). They used panel data collected at two different points in time. They were thus able to classify their sample, based on a socioeconomic index of occupational changes, into stationary, upwardly mobile, downwardly mobile, and fluctuating patterns of social mobility. They found that the desire to move and plans to move were highest for the upwardly mobile group. Actual mobility did not follow the same pattern, however. Thus, people who are upwardly mobile are more likely to desire to move than those who are not upwardly mobile. That their actual mobility rates do not differ perhaps indicates the need to achieve a higher socioeconomic status with its increased economic rewards before residential mobility is possible.

NORMATIVE INFLUENCES ON MOBILITY

The basic causes of normative housing deficits are seen to be household characteristics (Figure 9). Household characteristics differ, of course, in terms of the strength of their influence on the various normative housing deficits. The stage of the family life cycle, for example, is likely to have more influence than the level of education on the presence or absence of space deficits. Income may have a greater influence on quality deficits than on home ownership. The effects of the background factors on residential mobility are primarily indirect. They operate to create normative housing deficits. Such deficits, in turn, may produce low satisfaction levels, a high propensity to move, and, ultimately, residential mobility.

The contribution of space, tenure, and structure-type deficits to the prediction of satisfaction and propensity to move was tested by Morris (1976). Cultural deficits, family deficits, and variables that represented having both a cultural and a family deficit were used in three different models. In all of the models, the additions of housing deficits to socioeconomic and demographic characteristics added a significant increment to the prediction of satisfaction and mobility.

Reviewed in this section are studies with three types of evidence regarding the influence of normative deficits. Studies of residential mobility in which normative housing deficits have been used as independent variables are the most important. Also reviewed are studies in which normative housing deficits were included in lists of stated reasons for moving or were represented by comparisons between the previous and the present dwelling.

The review shows that families who engage in residential mobility are those who have too little space (primarily bedroom space), are renters, and live in a structure that is not a single-family house. It also appears that they live in poorer-quality housing relative to their income, spend an unusually high or unusually low proportion of their income on housing, and live in older, heterogeneous central-city neighborhoods.

Stated reasons for residential mobility should relate to the most pressing housing deficits that the respondent retrospectively reports. Thus, it can be expected that families who were crowded in the previous dwelling would list lack of space as the primary reason for moving. Previous apartment renters should report the desire for ownership of a single-family dwelling as the primary reason for moving. Families who lived in poor quality housing or a less desirable neighborhood would tend to cite a desire for housing or neighborhood improvement as the primary reason for moving.

Finally, it could be expected that a comparison of the important characteristics of the previous dwelling to those of the present dwelling would show that residential mobility served to reduce normative housing deficits. Families who moved from rented to owned housing, for example, could be seen as having reduced a tenure deficit.

Researchers have discussed the comparison between the present and previous residence in terms of "push-pull" factors. They have emphasized that negative aspects of the original dwelling "push" families toward moving, while attractive features of the destination dwelling "pull" families to that residence (Straits, 1968; Rossi, 1955; Sabagh et al., 1969). Attempting to delineate the relative importance of various "push" and "pull" factors seems fruitless, however. What is important is not the isolated objective characteristics of the origin or the destination dwelling. Rather, the difference between the two in the relevant features would seem to be a better indication of the normative housing deficits that served to motivate the move.

Space Deficits

The reason most often stated for residential mobility is the need for more space (Rossi, 1955; Smith et al., 1963; Gans, 1967; Michelson et al., 1973; Ross, 1962). In light of this finding, it is interesting that measures of the need for space, lack of space, or crowding have rarely been used as independent variables in the study of residential mobility. When used, however, they have proven effective predictors of both actual and potential mobility.

Controlling for the effects of duration of the marriage, tenure and structure type, as well as the need for a single-family dwelling, Gladhart (1973) found that bedroom deficit was a significant predictor of residential mobility. The greater the shortage of bedrooms, the higher the probability of moving.

Morris et al. (1976) introduced housing satisfaction as an intervening variable between bedroom deficit and the propensity to move. They found that bedroom deficit was not directly related to the propensity to move. Rather, the relationship was indirect, operating through the reduction in satisfaction, lowered in part by a shortage of bedrooms. Those findings were replicated by Morris (1976) with culturally-defined bedroom deficits, family-defined bedroom deficits, and a combination of family and cultural deficits. In all instances, space deficits were related to satisfaction but not to the propensity to move.

Using different measures of space deficits with the same data, researchers at the University of Michigan had different results. Goodman (1974) calculated the required number of rooms needed by a family, based on family composition. A variable created by subtracting the required number of rooms from the actual number of rooms was a good predictor of mobility. That variable was also a good predictor of planning to move for housing-related reasons. In addition, families with a space deficit were far more likely to fulfill their expectations and actually move than families without space deficits (Duncan and Newman, 1975). The persons-per-room ratio, on the other hand, was a much weaker predictor of mobility (Roistacher, 1974b). The findings of the three studies indicate the need for appropriate, rather than convenient, measures of normative deficits.

Lansing and Barth (1964) divided their sample into two categories, "crowded" and "uncrowded," based on the relationship between the number of rooms in the dwelling and the number of people in the family. Their analysis indicated that respondents in the "crowded" category were more likely to expect to move than families who were not crowded.

The incidence of complaints regarding space varies with the amount of space available, lending credence to space complaints as a measure of a space deficit. Rossi (1955) found that:

> *For a given family size, the smaller the dwelling unit, the more likely the household is to cite space complaints as a primary reason why it left its former home. Similarly for a given dwelling size, the smaller the household the less likely the family is to cite space complaints as having had an impact on its moving decision (p. 143).*

The incidence of space as a stated reason for mobility varies with stage of the family life cycle. Smith et al. (1963) found that grade-school families were more likely to experience space pressures than either preschool or teenage families. All three groups were more likely to state the need for more space as a reason for moving than all-adult families. Michelson et al. (1973) found that space-related reasons were of primary importance for families moving from house to house or from houses to apartments. Such reasons assumed less importance for families moving from apartments to houses. Space was not the *prime* reason for moving from apartments because the families' reasons had to do with ownership and structure type.

Tenure Deficit

The relationships between tenure deficits and residential mobility are clear. Renters are more likely to desire to move than owners (Okraku, 1971; Rossi, 1955; Lansing et al., 1964; Roistacher, 1975; Duncan and Newman, 1975; Nathanson, 1974). They exhibit higher mobility rates (Speare, 1970; Butler and Kaiser, 1971; Gladhart, 1971; Goodman, 1974; Roistacher, 1974b; Roistacher, 1975; Duncan and Newman, 1975). Tenure deficit is only in one direction, that of renters who prefer to own. Very few owners indicate a desire to rent (Rossi, 1955).

There are complementary explanations for such findings. First, renters deviate from the cultural norm of owner-occupancy and hence are likely to move to achieve ownership (Zimmer, 1973). Second, renters as a class would be less likely than home owners to engage in residential alterations to meet other housing norms (space and quality, for example). Hence mobility would be the typical adjustment behavior open to them.

Finally, renters may be more likely to move than owners because their position is less secure. First, they have little investment in the home, not only in economic terms, but in social terms as well (Speare, 1970). Second, landlord-tenant law favors the landlord over the tenant, as noted in Chapter 6. Hence renters, particularly low-income renters, are more likely to be forced to move than home owners.

Recent studies (Morris et al., 1976; Morris, 1976) found a direct relationship between tenure deficit and desire to move. Morris et al. found that households experiencing a positive tenure deficit (owning the dwelling when they wanted to rent) wanted to move. So did families who had a negative tenure deficit (renting when they wanted to own). In addition, families with a negative tenure deficit had reduced housing satisfaction. Those with a positive deficit did not. The authors interpreted their findings as indicative of two factors. First, there is a lack of strong sanctions for overconformance to housing norms. Second, desire to move arises from other deficits and is not necessarily related to the normative housing deficits analyzed. Households with a positive deficit were usually elderly families who might wish to move to a better climate, to a more supportive environment, or to be near children.

Morris (1976) found that so few families had positive family tenure deficits that he dropped the variable from the analysis. He analyzed the impact of cultural negative tenure deficits, negative family tenure deficits, and combined negative cultural and family tenure deficits. All three types of tenure deficit were found to be related to satisfaction and the propensity to move.

Findings from studies of stated reasons for mobility and comparisons between present and former residences indicate the importance of a normative tenure deficit in motivating mobility. The motivation occurs either because of a desire for ownership, the lack of alternative behaviors, or the insecurity of rental tenure.

A recent study (Zimmer, 1973) of retrospective mobility examined the family's move to the present residence. In all cases, the percentage of families who owned their present dwelling was at least double that in the former residence, indicating that:

> *there is a widespread desire to be a homeowner and this factor alone accounts for much of the movement within the metropolitan area (p. 348).*

Zimmer's conclusion is supported by Michelson et al. (1973). They found that, among families moving to houses from apartments, the dominant reasons were preferences for the tenure and structure type of the new residence. It can perhaps be assumed that the tenure desired was ownership, although it was not explicitly stated. Similarly, Gans (1967) found the desire for ownership of a free-standing dwelling to be an important reason for moving to suburban Levittown, New Jersey.

Rossi (1955) found a difference between owners and renters in the type of housing complaint that motivated mobility. Renters gave as reasons for mobility things that they could not alter. On this list were cost of the dwelling and the amount of space it contained. Owners were not as likely to indicate dissatisfaction with such factors.

The findings of McAllister et al. (1971) regarding differential mobility among blacks and whites support the hypothesis that renters are more often forced to move than owners. After finding that the high rates of black mobility could be directly attributed to a higher proportion of renters among the black sample, the researchers compared stated reasons for moving. They found that far more blacks than whites (21 percent versus 5.9 percent) indicated that they were forced to move, not that they wanted to move. In addition, involuntary mobility was the reason most often given by blacks, and least often stated by whites. It seems safe to assume that most involuntary moves were moves by renters.

Structure-Type Deficit

As noted in Chapter 6, tenure is a reasonably good proxy for structure type. There are few owners who live in multifamily units, and renter-occupancy of a single-family house is less prevalent than owner-occupancy of such dwellings. Hence it is likely that the relationship between structure type and mobility would be similar to that between tenure status and mobility. Structure type would be dichotomized into two classes, single-family conventional structures and all other structure types.

Only four studies have included deviation from structure type norms as a predictor of mobility or potential mobility, however. Lansing and Barth (1964) found that families who lived in housing that differed from their preferred form of housing were more likely to desire to move than other families. Included in their study as "deviant" were families who lived in apartments and wanted to live in houses and vice versa. The latter group comprised only 3 percent of the sample, however (Lansing et al. 1964, p. 47). Thus, families experiencing a structure-type deviation were predominantly apartment dwellers who wanted a single-family house.

Gladhart (1973) combined tenure and structure type into nine categories of various tenure-structure type combinations. He used the need for a single-family dwelling (Chapter 6) as an independent variable. He hypothesized that, as the need for a single-family dwelling increased, families in owner-occupied single-family dwellings would be less likely to move. Families in other classes of tenure-structure type combinations would be more likely to move. His findings largely supported the hypothesis.

Using Gladhart's measure for the need for a single-family dwelling, Morris et al. (1976) analyzed the effects on housing satisfaction and the propensity to move for both positive structure deficit (having a single-family dwelling when it is not needed) and negative structure deficit (needing a single-family dwelling and not having one). The findings regarding the two variables were similar to those reported regarding positive and negative tenure deficits. Households with a positive structure deficit wanted to move but were not dissatisfied with their housing. Those who had a negative structure deficit had reduced housing satisfaction and a desire to move. Morris (1976) replicated the results with positive and negative cultural, family, and combined structure-type deficits. There were slight differences in each model, however.

Because of the close correspondence between tenure and structure type, the findings regarding tenure deficits and structure type deficits seem to reflect the same phenomenon. Young families with both negative tenure and structure deficits are dissatisfied with their housing and want to move. Older household heads, principally widows, are not necessarily dissatisfied but may want to move for reasons unrelated to normative deficits.

The importance of a structure-type deficit in prompting residential mobility is supported by the findings of Michelson et al. (1973) and Gans (1967) who studied stated reasons for moving. In the former study, structure-type preference was an important reason given by respondents moving from apartments to houses. In the latter study the majority of the respondents moved to a suburb from the Philadelphia metropolitan area. The desire for a free-standing house was a prominent reason given for moving.

There is little question that tenure and structure type, as motivating forces for mobility, are interrelated (Zimmer, 1973). Residential alteration cannot overcome a structure-type deficit just as it cannot overcome a tenure deficit. Hence mobility is the only behavioral option open to apartment dwellers seeking to correct such deficits.

Quality and Expenditure Deficits

Evidence regarding the role of housing quality and expenditure deficits in motivating residential mobility is quite limited. Nevertheless, the hypothesis that lower quality, inexpensive housing can be a causal factor in the decision to move is supported. A move is likely to occur, particularly if the family has experienced an increase in income. In the absence of a rise in income, it is likely that a quality deficit alone would not be sufficient to motivate mobility (Foote et al., 1960, p. 142).

Roistacher (1974b) used the state of repair of the dwelling unit to predict mobility. Her findings indicate that the rate of mobility is higher for families living in poorer-quality housing. However, she found that there was only a slight improvement in dwelling unit condition as the result of the move. Butler et al. (1969) reported that those who plan to move are likely to live in poor-quality housing. Sabagh et al. (1969) speculate that housing unit deterioration, in effect, a reduction in housing quality, would motivate families to move. Their interpretation has not been supported in completed research.

Two studies of residential mobility related moving to value of the dwelling. Gladhart (1971) used market value of housing services received per room as a proxy for quality of the housing services received and found:

> *a prime motive for moving among occupants of low-priced housing is the desire to increase the value of services received. As the price of housing rises, the importance of quality as an incentive to mobility diminishes, beyond a certain level, increased quality (increased rent or value per room) is a deterrent to mobility (p. 12).*

In a sample of families who had moved from one owner-occupied dwelling to another, Smith et al. (1963) found that the majority of their respondents purchased homes that were valued at between two and three times their annual income. Those who were outside this range were in two classes. They were either high-income families whose dwelling cost less than twice their annual income, or low-income families either with sufficient equity in their previous house to afford a new, high-cost dwelling or with the assurance of a large increase in income. The researchers also found that, when the value of both the previous and the current residence were measured in constant dollars, the majority of the families purchased new homes that were between \$3000 and \$10,000 higher in price than the previous residence.

Expenditure deficits have been poor predictors of residential mobility (Goodman, 1974). Families spending more than 25 percent of their income on housing were no more likely to move than families spending less than 25 percent of their income on housing.

Using the same data, however, Roistacher (1974a) found that an increase in income was the best predictor of an increase in housing expenditures. Further, an increase in income was a good predictor of mobility (Roistacher, 1974b), and a higher income was a good predictor of changing from renting to owning (Roistacher, 1974a). Relating these three findings tends to support the hypothesis that a rise in income causes actual expenditures to be inconsistent with income. Hence the family moves to higher-quality, more expensive housing and switches from rental to ownership.

Analysis of the relationships between income, quality deficits, expenditure deficits, and mobility has suffered from a variety of problems. First, indexes of housing quality that measure more than very basic amenities are just now being developed. The application of the market value of the dwelling as a proxy for quality has also not been used consistently. Another problem has been the weak conceptualization of the relations between income and expenditures (see Chapter 12). It seems, however, that families who move either achieve improvements in housing quality or maintain the level of quality enjoyed in the previous dwelling. Further, they are responding to increases or decreases in income that cause their expenditures to be inconsistent with their income. Moreover, their housing quality may have become inconsistent with their social status.

Neighborhood Deficits

Neighborhood factors that have been shown to be related to mobility potential are density, heterogeneity, quality, and location (central city versus suburb). Also related to mobility potential are the presence of severe deficits, such as high crime rates and poor quality schools. Although the evidence is somewhat limited, neighborhood deficits have been shown to be factors motivating residential mobility.

Lansing et al. (1964) found that families in high-density housing areas were more likely to plan to move within the next five years than families in low- or medium-density housing areas. Rossi (1955) reported greater potential mobility in areas with heterogeneous populations than in areas with homogeneous populations. Butler et al. (1969) reported that families planning to move are more likely to live in the central city and in poorer quality neighborhoods.

Studies by Nathanson (1974), Droettboom et al. (1971), Varady (1974), and Kasl and Harberg (1972) all showed that neighborhood deficits are related to the desire to move. Droettboom et al. found that the perception of the seriousness of crime and violence in the neighborhood was strongly related to overall neighborhood dissatisfaction and the desire to move. Such perceptions were poor predictors of actual mobility, however. The majority of the people who wanted to move did not. Among movers, the major portion went to another residence in the same neighborhood. The authors concluded that constraints, in the form of low income and racial discrimination, prevented actual mobility.

Kasl and Harberg (1972) found that the perception of the neighborhood as unsafe, as well as the perception of poor quality schools, was strongly related to neighborhood dissatisfaction and the desire to move. Nathanson (1974) reported similar findings among an all-black sample.

On the other hand, Varady (1974) found that white families are likely to plan to move from a neighborhood which is undergoing racial change. Major factors that influenced plans to move were age, tenure, and the ages of the children. Nevertheless, with those factors controlled, there was a difference in moving plans according to the racial composition of the neighborhood.

Thus the presence of perceived and actual neighborhood deficits can be seen to have an important influence on satisfaction and the desire to move. They are not as strongly related to actual mobility, however.

There is little doubt that families are moving to the suburbs (Taeuber and Taeuber, 1964; Hodge and Hauser, 1968). There is also little doubt that their reasons are to improve their housing and neighborhood conditions, rather than to seek employment opportunities (Schnore, 1965, p. 165). There is conflicting evidence, however, regarding which is more important, the housing characteristics or the neighborhood characteristics.

Gans (1967), Smith et al. (1963), Rossi (1955), and Greenbie (1969) report house-related reasons as more important than the desire for a better neighborhood. Bell (1958) reported reasons that were about equally divided between those that were house-related and those that were related to the quality of the neighborhood. What is clear is that families are seeking housing and neighborhood conditions that they feel only can be found in the suburbs.

Bell's (1958) study of families who moved to suburbia found that the most important reasons for moving there were related to a desire for the "suburban life style." The emphasis was on the proper environment for raising children and on the activities available in suburban areas. Bell's findings were supported by Gans (1967), who found that families choosing suburbia were drawn there because of the opportunities for themselves and their children. Suburban living *per se* did not "cause" their life style. Rather, they were attracted there because their chosen life style was available in that setting. That is, they felt there were fewer neighborhood and housing deficits in suburban living.

HOUSING AND NEIGHBORHOOD SATISFACTION

The hypotheses shown in Figure 9 imply that the key determinant of the propensity to move and, in turn, actual mobility, is dissatisfaction with the dwelling. In addition, neighborhood satisfaction affects housing satisfaction and mobility. On the face of it, it would seem obvious that people would not tend to consider moving unless they were dissatisfied with one or more aspects of the dwelling or its location. The main determinants of the level of satisfaction, of course, are the normative deficits.

The influence of overall satisfaction on the propensity to move was analyzed in a nationwide sample survey (Butler et al., 1969). Respondents who were dissatisfied with their housing, their neighborhood, and with specific features of the dwelling were more likely to plan to move than families who were satisfied. Nathanson (1974), Droettboom et al. (1971), and Kasl and Harberg (1972) have shown the impact of neighborhood dissatisfaction on the desire to move.

A recent study (Speare, 1974), employing a more complex analysis, presented a "satisfaction model of residential mobility." Satisfaction was veiwed as an intervening variable between housing and household characteristics and the consideration of moving. Speare's measure of satisfaction was a sum of six individual satisfaction items.

Speare then used satisfaction as an intervening variable between selected household and housing characteristics. The characteristics were age of the head, education of the head, duration of residence, tenure, income, crowding, an index of the presence of friends in the area, and type of area (urban or suburban). He found that crowding, age of head, duration of residence, tenure, and the index of neighborhood friendships all were related to the propensity to move through satisfaction. Only duration of residence and tenure were directly related to wanting to move or actual mobility. He concluded that satisfaction is appropriately viewed as an explanatory variable for the desire to move.

Another study (Morris et al., 1976) treated housing and neighborhood satisfaction as intervening variables between normative housing deficits and the desire to move. Neighborhood satisfaction was related to housing satisfaction and desire to move. Housing and neighborhood satisfaction were the most important predictors of the desire to move. Only two characteristics of the family, duration of the marriage and sex of the head, were directly related to the propensity to move.

Housing and neighborhood satisfaction have only recently become the subject of mobility research. While further research is needed, it does seem safe to conclude that the chief cause of the propensity to move is a decline in housing and neighborhood satisfaction.

A CAUSAL MODEL OF RESIDENTIAL MOBILITY

Based on the foregoing review of the literature, a causal model of residential mobility can be constructed (Figure 10). The arrows represent causal relationships supported in the published research. Some potential relationships that exist empirically may have been omitted because they have not yet been tested. For example, education may exert some indirect influence on mobility, but the relationships are not yet obvious in the literature.

The most important immediate cause of residential mobility is the propensity to move, a disposition favoring a change of residence. Direct arrows have been drawn from income and sex of the household head to residential mobility. An increase in income may act directly to produce residential mobility by reducing some of the constraints on moving to better housing.

Propensity to move is primarily related to a reduction in housing satisfaction and neighborhood satisfaction. It is also influenced directly by some of the household characteristics and the normative deficits. Tenure deficit and structure-type deficit are directly related to the propensity to move as well as to housing satisfaction. Therefore, they are both indirectly and

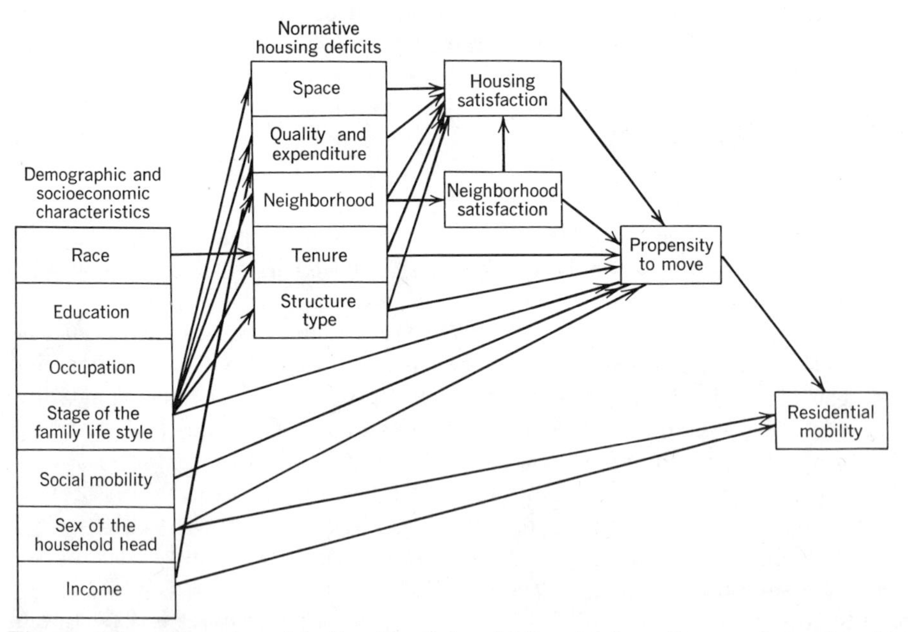

Figure 10 Causal model of residential mobility with hypotheses substantiated in the research literature.

directly related to the propensity to move. Female-headed households have a higher propensity to move than male-headed households. Families who are upwardly mobile socially also have a higher propensity to move than other families.

The major cause of a reduction in housing satisfaction is the combined influence of the normative housing deficits and a reduction in neighborhood satisfaction. Neighborhood satisfaction is directly affected by neighborhood deficits. Normative deficits in turn are influenced by the characteristics of the household. Stage of the family life cycle is by far the most important and is related to all of the normative deficits. Causal analyses by Speare (1974) and Morris et al. (1976) have found that stage of the family life cycle has a direct effect on the propensity to move as well. Race has been found to be related to tenure deficits, as blacks are more likely to be renters than whites. The effect of income on quality deficit is clear and direct. Quality is expensive. The influence of income on the other deficits has not been found by the researchers.

While much is known about the network of influences on residential mobility, there are many hypotheses yet to be tested. There are probably other household characteristics that influence residential mobility, as well as other deficits that have not been taken into account. Nevertheless, the model gives a clear picture of the relationships among characteristics of the household, normative deficits, and satisfaction that influence the propensity to move and residential mobility behavior.

DEFINITIONS

Controls. Several analytical techniques used to clarify the relationship between a dependent and an independent variable. For example, the influence of crowding on reported satisfaction may be stronger for middle and upper-class families than for lower-class households. Social class is the control variable in this example.

Direct relationship. In a direct relationship, a variable influences another variable directly without the intervening influence of other variables; the influence may be either positive or negative; to be contrasted with indirect relationship. For example, decreases in household size have a direct effect on the occurrence of residential alterations.

Family formation. The act of forming a separate household; may occur through (1) the marriage of two people living in their parents' homes followed by setting up a separate residence; (2) divorce in which the two divorced people each establish separate households; or (3) departure by an individual from the parental home or a group quarters residence to set up a separate residence.

Indirect relationship. In an indirect relationship, a given variable influences another variable only through a third (intervening) variable; to be contrasted with direct relationship. For example, family life cycle stage has an effect on housing satisfaction only due to its influence on the presence or absence of housing deficits. In this case, the housing deficits are intervening variables between life cycle stage and satisfaction.

Longitudinal analysis. Analysis of data gathered at a series of time points from the same individuals or individuals sampled from the same population; to be contrasted with cross-sectional analysis. Only in longitudinal analysis is it possible to analyze the effects of *changes* in an independent variable on changes in a dependent variable.

Panel study, panel data. One type of longitudinal study using data collected at two or more points in time by interviewing the same respondents each time.

Retrospective mobility. A measure of mobility based on the respondent's present recollection of previous moves.

Social mobility. Movement either up or down the socioeconomic scale. One instance of social mobility is moving up or down the occupation ladder.

Subsequent mobility. Mobility measured through a longitudinal study in which information on the independent variables assumed to influence residential mobility are gathered at one time point and then subsequent mobility assessed by a later follow-up contact to ascertain whether a move has occurred.

Chapter 10
Residential Alterations and Additions

I was foolish about windows.
The house was an old one and the windows
were small.
I asked a carpenter to come and open the
walls and put in bigger windows. . . .
One neighbor said, "If you keep on you'll be
able to see everything there is." Carl Sandburg*

Residential alterations and additions consist of two main phenomena: increases in the amount of space or number of rooms in the dwelling, and improvements in the quality of the dwelling. Regular repairs and maintenance are not categorized as residential alterations and additions. The recurrent shortages of mortgage money and the inflation of housing prices have begun to force many home-owning families to consider remodeling or making additions to their current dwellings, rather than buying a different house. In addition, many families are still paying off mortgages assumed in the early 1960s with interest rates of 5 or 6 percent. Many are understandably hesitant to buy a more expensive dwelling with a larger mortgage and an interest rate of 8 to 9 percent.

The purpose of this chapter is to outline the findings of the research on residential alterations and additions in light of the model of housing adjustment behavior. The extent to which residential alterations are alternatives to mobility is also explored. However, research on the topic is very sparse.

Residential alterations are more limited in applicability than residential mobility. They are only useful for overcoming space and quality deficits. Little or nothing can be done to the present dwelling to overcome tenure, structure-type, or neighborhood deficits. Occasionally a renting family may purchase their current dwelling and thus overcome a tenure deficit. Yet the vast majority of home purchases involve residential mobility. Mobile home

* From "Foolish about Windows" in *Good Morning, America* by Carl Sandburg (New York: Harcourt, Brace and World, 1928), lines 1–5 and lines 12–13. Reprinted by permission of Harcourt Brace Jovanovich.

dwellers may overcome neighborhood deficits by moving their home to a new park. Mobile homes are a relatively small proportion of all dwellings, however, and moving mobile homes to other parks is very infrequent.

Residential alterations and additions are primarily done by owners of single-family dwellings. Owners in condominiums and cooperatives are typically limited in the changes they may make in their apartments and are less likely to practice residential alteration. Especially unlikely are additions.

Renters very seldom invest money in a dwelling owned by someone else. The crucial factor may not be ownership *per se.* Rather it is security in the continuity of tenure. Some renters who have been long-term tenants in the same residence or in the same neighborhood engage in residential alteration to a significant degree (Winter, 1976).

THE MEASUREMENT OF ALTERATIONS AND ADDITIONS

The study of residential alterations and additions as housing adjustment behavior is plagued by conceptual and measurement problems. The problems in measuring potential mobility, as discussed in Chapter 9, are trivial in comparison. There are two primary difficulties. The first is making the distinction between improvements and regular maintenance. The second problem is the common practice of assessing alterations by collecting information on the expenditures rather than counting the occurrence of specific activities.

Maintenance versus Improvements

To analyze the impact of demographic and socioeconomic characteristics, normative housing deficits, and satisfaction on residential alterations and additions, one must be able to distinguish between alterations and maintenance. Residential alterations and additions are typically undertaken to correct normative housing deficits in space or quality. Included in this classification are such things as remodeling, finishing the basement, putting in a new bath or kitchen, or building an addition.

Most routine maintenance activities are not considered housing adjustment behavior. Included in this class are exterior painting, repairing or replacing storm windows, roof repairs, and repair or replacement of any of the major systems: heating, plumbing, or electrical. Such activities are undertaken to maintain the quality of the dwelling rather than improve it. Some replacements, of course, represent improvements as well. If the replacement is larger, of higher quality, more dependable, etc., a portion of the cost will be due to the improvement factor.

One form of housing adjustment behavior, however, might be the *omission* of expenditures for maintenance and repairs. If the expense of a dwelling unit, especially a large dwelling unit or one in an extremely desirable location is too great given a reduction in income, omission of maintenance and repairs can ease the burden. This form of housing adjustment behavior, a response to a positive expenditure deficit, is likely to occur in times of unemployment or upon retirement.

Conceptual differences between maintenance activities and adjustment activities are relatively clear. In practice, however, there is a great deal of overlap. For example, the U.S. Bureau of the Census conducts quarterly surveys of property owners regarding expenditures for residential alterations and repairs. The Census Bureau carefully makes a conceptual distinction between maintenance and improvements. The distinction lies along the same lines as the one made above. Yet under the heading of construction improvements are included major replacements: complete furnace or boiler, water heater, entire roof, all siding, all water pipes, sink or laundry tub, to name a few (USBC 1976c). It is, of course, true that such replacements are costly and add to the value of the house. Yet it is difficult not to conceive of the replacement of a furnace as a major *maintenance* activity.

On the other hand, when is painting a maintenance activity and when is it an improvement? Distinguishing between maintenance and improvements can be difficult unless the reasons for the activity are known.

If the purpose of the research is to ascertain factors associated with upkeep and improvement as investment decisions (Winger, 1973), then it is important to know all activities. Even routine maintenance can be viewed as an investment activity, in that the quality of the dwelling, and hence the owner's equity, is maintained or improved.

Research designed to assess factors associated with using family labor versus hiring the work done (Shonrock, 1975; Meeks and Firebaugh, 1974) should also examine all maintenance and improvement activities. While adding to the literature on maintenance and improvement activities, the applicability of the findings of such studies to housing adjustment behavior is relatively limited.

Unfortunately, most of the literature on alterations and additions suffers from failure to separate the two phenomena. Meeks and Firebaugh (1974) sought to distinguish between improvement behavior and maintenance behavior. They used Census Bureau classifications, and so have major replacements included with improvements.

Yockey (1976a) used the number of different kinds of activities completed during the preceding five years. Included in this category were both maintenance and improvement activities. Yockey (1976a), Harris (1976b), and Winter (1976) studied the propensity to perform residential alterations and additions, as measured by a question regarding plans to make changes, alterations, and additions. The types of activities included by the respondent, however, were both maintenance and improvement activities.

Needham (1973) categorized plans to alleviate housing problems into two classes: plans for structural improvements and plans to add rooms or buy a new home. Thus the latter category lumped additions and mobility together. The categories used by Bross (1975) are perhaps the closest to appropriate categories for studying housing adjustment behavior. She used alteration and improvement activities, which included all work done. She also analyzed a subset of those activities which included additions, remodeling, and redecorating. Her classification still needs to be refined, however, Not all improvement activities were captured in the subset.

An important criterion in the social rather than the technical meaning of maintenance and improvements has to do with whether the activity is dwelling-oriented or household-oriented. In the dwelling orientation, all activities that maintain or restore the dwelling to its original condition are termed maintenance. Improvements are any changes that increase the size or quality of the dwelling beyond its original size and quality. Taking the household orientation, improvements include any activities that increase the size or quality of the dwelling beyond its condition when purchased by that household. Maintenance includes activities that maintain or restore the dwelling to its condition at the time of the purchase.

Thus, there are two possible ways to deal with the distinction between maintenance and improvements in future research. One is to classify activities according to the family's reasons for undertaking them. Meeks and Firebaugh (1974) used this method and were able to distinguish between activities that needed to be done because the dwelling was deteriorating and those that were done simply because the family wanted to improve the dwelling.

A second method is to classify activities based on what happens to the dwelling rather than on the reasons that the family gives for undertaking the activities. A family who buys an older home with the idea of "fixing it up" may undertake activities that are, in their eyes, major improvements. For the house, they are maintenance activities. The family was able to purchase the home for less because maintenance was not up to date. In a way, they bought the obligation to catch up on maintenance. From the point of view of the house they are regular maintenance activities that were not performed earlier. If this method were used to distinguish between improvements and maintenance, then improvements or enlargements of the house only would include responses to normative housing deficits, rather than desires to return the house to its original quality.

The Value of Alterations and Additions

Maintenance and improvement activities are most commonly measured by obtaining information regarding the type and number of activities done, and the cost of the various activities (Bross, 1975; USBC, 1976c; Yockey, 1976a; Meeks and Firebaugh, 1974; Shonrock, 1975; Winger, 1973; Beyer,

1952; Cowles, Dickson, and Wood, 1947). Minimum criterion amounts have often been set before the activity is included as an alteration or addition (Beyer, 1952; Bross, 1975). At other times the focus has been solely the amount of money spent (USBC, 1976a; Winger, 1973) with no minimum set.

Using the amount spent on the addition or alteration poses two problems. First, there is the difficulty of equating the expenditures of families who hire the work done and those who do it themselves. What is missing, of course, is the value of the home owner's labor. Thus a family may spend relatively little money on improvements and maintenance. Yet the true cost may be far higher. The value added to the dwelling may be the same for two different dwellings. The dollar cost, however, may be vastly different.

A related problem is that focusing on money spent or activities that cost money eliminates many minor activities that are inexpensive, even free, but are housing adjustment activities. The most common of such activities is the conversion of a room from one purpose to another by changing its furnishings. Changing a guest room to a bedroom for regular use by a family member, converting a bedroom vacated by a young adult child who has left home to a sewing room or den, and making the sewing room into the baby's bedroom are examples that come to mind. There are few studies completed to date that have examined this phenomenon.

A class exercise used by the authors when teaching undergraduate housing courses has tapped some of these activities. The students were asked to trace the housing adjustments and family changes that occurred since marriage to families with at least one child over age 18. Most of the students, as could be expected, traced the history of their parents.

The most common conversion that occurred, according to a group of students from New York City, was the use of dining rooms or dining alcoves in one-bedroom apartments as nurseries. "When I was born, my parents put my crib in the dining room" was typical.

Similar adjustments were noted by Winter (1966) in her study of the play activities of preschool children in apartments and single-family houses. One family, a graduate student and his wife with three preschool children, a boy and two girls, maintained sex separation in the children's sleeping rooms in a two-bedroom apartment by using the sofa in the living room as the parents' sleeping space. Another couple with three children in a one-bedroom apartment also slept in the living room. Further, the living room was divided into two areas, a living space and a playroom.

The families analyzed in the student assignments and those in Winter's study were predominantly young renters who expected to move in the near future. Hence their residential alteration, although relatively effective, was viewed as a temporary solution rather than a permanent state of housing conditions. Therefore the situation could be more readily accepted. No studies known to the present authors have been done of these or other room conversions, however.

A CAUSAL MODEL OF RESIDENTIAL ALTERATIONS

Figure 11 presents the hypothesized causal model for residential alterations and additions which will be tested in this section of the chapter. Only space and quality deficits appear in the model. The other portions of the model are similar to those for residential mobility. Few of the research studies available use the same measure of residential alterations and additions. Thus the conclusions about the relationships among the variables in this model are more tentatively made than in the mobility model.

Stage of the Family Life Cycle

Most studies of residential alterations have included measures of the family life cycle stage. The most typical measure has been age of the household head (Needham, 1973; Winger, 1973; Shonrock, 1975; Yockey, 1976a; Harris, 1976b; Winter, 1976; Meeks and Firebaugh, 1974) or age of the wife (Joslin, 1959). A set of family life cycle categories has also been used (Cowles et al., 1947). The findings relating the family life cycle to making housing alterations and additions are not as consistent as would be desired. Shonrock (1975), Harris (1976b), and Winter (1976) found that alterations and additions declined with age. There was little difference in planning to make improvements according to age of the household head in Needham's (1973) sample of low-income families. Joslin (1959) found that the type of improvement desired varied with age of the wife, but that no relationship existed between wife's age and improvements completed. Meeks and Firebaugh (1974) found a positive relationship between age and maintenance activities. A negative relationship existed between age and improvements.

Some of the studies (Winger, 1973; Yockey, 1976a; Cowles et al., 1947) have found a curvilinear relationship between age and alteration activities.

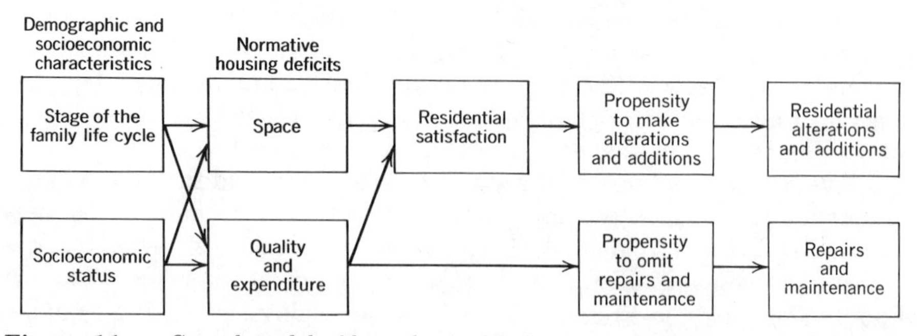

Figure 11 Causal model of hypothesized influences on residential alteration as a housing adjustment behavior.

Those findings show increases in residential alterations with increasing age, up to a point somewhere between the ages of 50 and 65. After that age, families are not as apt to make changes and improvements in their dwelling. The curvilinear relationship helps explain the apparent lack of relationship in other studies.

The pattern that emerges is residential mobility early in the life cycle, as the family seeks housing that meets space, tenure, structure-type, and neighborhood norms. Once a family has achieved a dwelling that meets the norms, they are likely to make alterations to that residence. Such improvements are especially likely to occur in later stages of the family life cycle, often when the youngest child is in high school. The improvements are usually completed before retirement, however.

This trend, of course, is related to income (Cowles et al., 1947). Rising income results in quality deficits because it produces rising quality norms. It also facilitates alterations and additions to overcome such deficits. The family often is basically satisfied and does not want to move.

Studies that have separated additions to obtain more space from alterations associated with quality improvements have noted that younger families are more likely to desire additions (Needham, 1973; Winter, 1976). Those studies probably explain the findings of Harris (1976b) and Bross (1975). Harris found that the number of children under 18 years of age was positively related to planning residential alterations. Bross found that both increases and decreases in household size were related to the amount of money spent for additions, remodeling, and redecoration. Families with children plan additions to achieve more space. Older families use alterations to improve space rather than increase it.

Socioeconomic Status

Like the findings of the family life cycle, the relationships between socioeconomic status and alterations are somewhat mixed. Winger (1973) found that expenditures on maintenance and upkeep were positively related to income. Income was positively related to past improvements (Yockey, 1976a) but not to plans for further alterations. Income was positively related to improvements but not to maintenance (Beyer, 1952). Needman (1973) found no relationship between income and plans for structural improvements. She found a positive relationship between income and plans to add a room or buy a new dwelling. Cowles et al. (1947) noted that the amount spent on alterations increased with income. Bross (1975), however, found no relationship between income and the amount spent on either additions and renovations or alterations and improvements. Similar findings were reported by Meeks and Firebaugh (1974).

Shonrock (1975) noted a curvilinear relationship between socioeconomic status and alterations. Middle-class families were more likely to indicate a higher number of improvement activities than either upper- or lower-class groups. Yockey (1976a) found the reverse between education and planning alterations and additions. Families in which the head had a low or high level of education were more likely to be planning alterations or additions than families headed by an individual with a moderate amount of education.

Clearly one of the factors producing the inconsistent findings is variation in measurement. Simply to say that different measures are responsible is not quite sufficient, however, for the relationship seems to be somewhat more complex. Yockey (1976a) and Bross (1975) offer clues to its understanding.

Bross used a variety of housing and household characteristics, the amount spent on past improvement activities, and housing satisfaction to predict expected mobility. While the amount spent on alterations was not a significant predictor of expecting to move, families headed by an individual with higher occupational status were more likely to expect to move. Bross concluded:

> *The unexpected appearance of occupational status as an important predictor of expected mobility when the residential [alteration] variables are included in the predictive equation, in addition to the strong negative relationship between length of ownership and additions and renovations leads to the interpretation that there may be a portion of households who have been in their home a short time, who expect to move due to job transfers, who are making residential [alterations] not only to increase their own enjoyment while they are living in the home, but also to increase the salability of their dwelling unit (Bross, 1975, pp. 84–85).*

Yockey (1976a) used two separate equations to predict planning future alterations, one for those expecting to move, and one for those not expecting to move. For those not planning to move, planned alterations were more frequent among households with an employed head. For those planning to move, planned alterations were more frequent among owners and among households headed by an individual with either a low or a high educational level. Yockey concluded:

> *. . . mobility may be resulting from the inability of past alterations to satisfy the needs and preferences of the household, or it may be from non-housing related reasons and therefore, alterations are undertaken for the purposes of resale (Yockey, 1976a, p. 60).*

Thus a tentative pattern of relationships between socioeconomic status and alterations begins to emerge. Middle-income families tend to perform maintenance and improvement activities to overcome deficits and to maintain the value of the property. Upper-income families engage in maintenance and some improvements, but tend to move to overcome deficits. (Even when someone else is hired to do the improvements, there is still a certain amount of mess involved.) Lower-income owners, on the other hand, tend to postpone improvements and maintenance until they expect to move. Then the activities are performed, not to overcome deficits, but to improve the resale value.

Normative Deficits

Normative deficits have rearely been used in analyses of residential alterations or the propensity to make alterations. It could be expected that those with normative space deficits and normative quality deficits would be likely to make alterations and additions to overcome such deficits. Research findings offer very tentative support for those conclusions.

Harris (1976b) found that a variety of factors were good predictors of achieved housing quality. among them were family life cycle stage, socioeconomic status, tenure, and structure type. When those variables, along with housing quality, were included in a model to predict future residential alterations, however, the level of quality achieved was not a significant predictor of desired residential alterations and additions.

Yockey (1976a) had similar results when using space deficit to predict planning to make alterations and additions. Bross (1975), however, found that bedroom deficit had a curvilinear relationship to the amount spent for alterations and improvements, and additions and renovations. Families with about the right amount of space, according to their family composition, were least apt to spend money on residential alterations. Those with positive or negative deficits were apt to engage in residential alterations and additions. Her findings are undoubtedly related to the curvilinear relationship between age and alterations. Younger families tend to remodel or make additions to get more space. Older families tend to remodel to create more usable space, or to add comfort to an otherwise satisfactory dwelling.

Although it has not been rigorously tested, families with positive expenditure deficits (spending more on housing than expenditures norms would require) may forego maintenance and repair activities. Performance of those activities is not viewed as a housing adjustment technique but omission of them is. The hypothetical relationship is shown in Figure 11 as a hypothesis, but does not appear in Figure 12 because it has not been well documented. The indication is that when income has recently declined housing satisfaction would remain high. In order to remain in the currently satisfactory dwelling, expenditures are reduced by omission of repairs and maintenance. Therefore, there is a direct arrow to propensity to make repairs and do maintenance but not through satisfaction.

The conclusions are very tentative, but suggest that there is a relationship between normative space and quality deficits and alterations. The relationships are not as strong as those of age and income to alterations, however.

Residential Satisfaction

Residential satisfaction is hypothesized to be the immediate cause of the propensity to engage in residential alterations. Research using satisfaction with the dwelling or the neighborhood or both has shown only weak relationships, however. Harris (1976b) found that satisfaction with housing quality, weighted for saliency of the characteristics included in the scale, was a significant but weak predictor of housing satisfaction. Yockey (1976a) found no relationship between space satisfaction and planning to make alterations and additions.

The reason for the weak or absent relationship between satisfaction and planning future alterations may be the curvilinear relationship between satisfaction and alterations. As in residential mobility, people who are dissatisfied with their dwelling tend to make home improvements. Such alterations are undertaken partly to overcome deficits and partly to improve the resale value so they can move. People who are highly satisfied with their dwelling and neighborhood may love the dwelling so much that they want to continue improving it.

Using only satisfaction with space and neighborhood, Yockey (1976a) developed a typology of satisfaction. She classified people according to high and low space satisfaction and high and low neighborhood satisfaction. She further classified families according to whether or not they planned to move. People with low space satisfaction and high neighborhood satisfaction who planned to move were most likely to make residential alterations. The second highest proportion planning alterations occurred in the group with the highest satisfaction levels and no expectation of moving. A satisfaction typology for quality would probably yield similar results.

Again, the conclusions are tentative, because of the small amount of research. The relationship between satisfaction and residential alterations and additions appears to be curvilinear, with both highly satisfied and highly dissatisfied people making alterations. The motivation for those alterations is quite different, of course.

The Tested Model

The arrows in Figure 12 connect age and socioeconomic status directly to residential alterations because there are variations in the propensity and actual performance of alterations and additions due to family life cycle and socioeconomic variables. The variations are often curvilinear and therefore are masked in some research that has not tested for nonlinearity. Space and

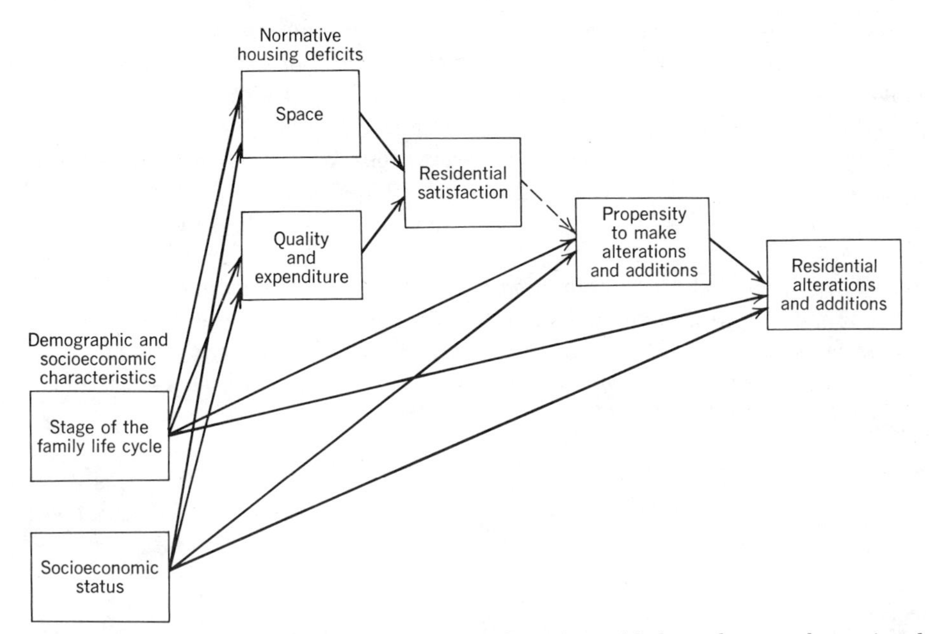

Figure 12 Causal model of residential alteration with hypotheses substantiated in the research literature.

quality deficits also occur at different rates for various levels of the life cycle and socioeconomic status.

The deficits and satisfaction are similarly connected because the presence of deficits appears to reduce satisfaction. Satisfaction is connected to the propensity to engage in residential alterations and additions by a dashed line, which is used to indicate the weakness of that relationship. It is obvious from the review that further study is needed to create a definitive model of causal factors that influence residential alterations.

RESIDENTIAL ALTERATIONS AND RESIDENTIAL MOBILITY

One of the most fruitful lines of research regarding residential alteration seems to be to analyze its use as an alternative to residential mobility, as suggested by Hill's (1970) study of three generation families. He found that residential alteration (redecoration, remodeling, renovation) is a substitute for mobility. In all three generations, the families tended to engage in one or the other of the behaviors during a given year, but not in both.

Support for the view that alterations and mobility are alternate behaviors is found in an analysis of the census data on residential alterations and additions and the data on housing starts. With an increase in the number of new families, there would need to be new construction for mobility to be used as the main means to overcome deficits. True, there could be population movements among existing dwellings. But, in the presence of population growth, new construction is needed to accommodate new families.

The number of dollars spent on alterations by owners of single-family dwellings has risen relatively steadily since 1965 (Table 10). Alterations were defined as

> *changes or improvements made within or on the structure. The changes or improvements range from a complete remodeling, which involves removal of the entire interior of the structure and remodeling it, to the installation of a new electric service outlet, wall switch, or new shelf (USBC, 1976c, p. 10).*

The apparent rise is well above the actual rise since there has been considerable inflation during the period. Nevertheless, an upward trend remains when the data are corrected by the Consumer Price Index.

TABLE 10 Trends in expenditures on alterations and additions to single-family owner-occupied housing units corrected for changes in the consumer price index (1967 = 100)

	Alterations		Additions	
Year	Expenditures (000's)	Corrected by Consumer Price Index	Expenditures (000's)	Corrected by Consumer Price Index
1965	$1968	$2102	$ 915	$ 968
1966	$2252	$2317	$ 992	$1021
1967	$2303	$2303	$ 828	$ 828
1968	$2487	$2387	$1054	$1042
1969	$2676	$2437	$ 920	$ 838
1970	$2695	$2317	$1206	$1037
1971	$2890	$2383	$1275	$1051
1972	$3249	$2593	$1117	$ 891
1973	$3543	$2662	$1070	$ 804
1974	$3789	$2565	$1328	$ 899
1975	$4945	$3104	$1680	$1055

Sources. U.S. Bureau of the Census, Construction Reports, Series C-50, "Residential Alterations and Repairs" (Washington: Author), April 1971, p. 5; November 1973, p. 4; June 1976, p. 3; U.S. Bureau of the Census, *Statistical Abstract of the United States* (Washington: U.S. Government Printing Office, 1975), p. 422.

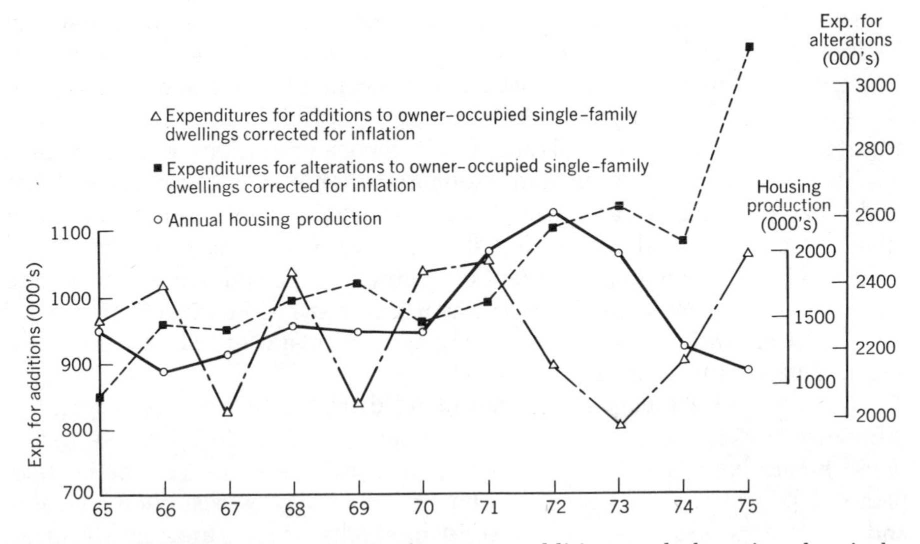

Figure 13 Comparison of expenditures on additions and alterations by single-family home owners with annual housing production.

The amount of money spent for additions, defined as:

actual enlargement of the structure, either by adding a wing, a room, a porch, an attached garage, a shed, or a carport, or by raising the roof, digging a basement or bomb or fallout shelter (USBC, 1976c, p. 10)

is considerably less than the amount spent for alterations (Table 10). The expenditures for additions have fluctuated considerably since 1965, with peaks in 1966, 1968, 1970, and 1971, and troughs in 1967, 1969, 1972, and 1973.

When the expenditures for additions and alterations, corrected for inflation, are plotted against the number of new housing starts (Figure 13), a pattern emerges. In all but two periods, 1967–68 and 1970–71, changes in either alterations or additions or both have been in the direction opposite that of housing starts. Thus when housing starts increased, money spent on alterations, additions, or both declined, and vice versa. The most extreme differences among the three occurred in the period between 1972 and 1975. Housing starts declined dramatically. Expenditures on additions and alterations declined at first but then rose sharply.

Even with the problems created by using expenditures not corrected for do-it-yourself labor, the trend is apparent. In years when housing starts decline while new household formation continues, thus making mobility more difficult, home owners engage in higher rates of residential alteration and addition behavior. Thus it is clear that alterations and additions on a societal level are substitutable and vary according to economic conditions.

A recent study by Bross and Morris (1974) utilized the model of housing adjustment as a basis for analyzing the influence of normative housing deficits on residential alteration and residential mobility as alternatives. That study, based on data gathered in 1971, a year of rising housing production following a low period in housing starts, showed a slightly higher rate of residential alteration than residential mobility. The annual mobility rate (long-distance moves were omitted) was 9.9 percent, while the annual rate of residential alteration (defined as involving an expenditure of at least $100) was 12.2 percent (column 1, Table 11).

Renters had a much higher rate of residential mobility than owners, a difference of 18.5 percentage points (column 4, Table 11). Owners had a much higher rate of residential alteration, a difference of 11.4 percentage points. Much of the difference in residential mobility between home owners and nonowners was made up in residential alteration. Bross and Morris' findings showed a combined rate of mobility and residential alteration of 20.7 percent for owners and 27.8 percent for nonowners.

The difference of 7.1 percentage points when both residential mobility and residential alteration are considered was much lower than the difference in either mobility rates or rates of residential alteration. The remaining difference shown in Table 11 could be due to the definition of residential alteration. If a lower dollar limit had been used or if all the alterations (converting rooms from one use to another, for example) were included, it is likely that the difference would be smaller. The difference might also be due to a greater rate of deficits in rental housing than in owner-occupied housing.

Bross and Morris (1974) performed a multivariate analysis to discover the main factors that appeared to be responsible for the occurrence of

TABLE 11 Comparison of residential mobility and residential alteration rates for owners and renters

	(1) Total Sample	(2) Owners	(3) Renters	(4) Percent Difference
Residential mobility	9.9	6.5	25.0	−18.5
Residential alterations	12.2	14.2	2.8	11.4
Mobility plus alterations	22.1	20.7	27.8	−7.1

Source. C. Bross and E. W. Morris, "The Influence of Household Size Changes on Family Housing Adjustment Behavior" (Ames: Department of Family Environment, Iowa State University, 1974).

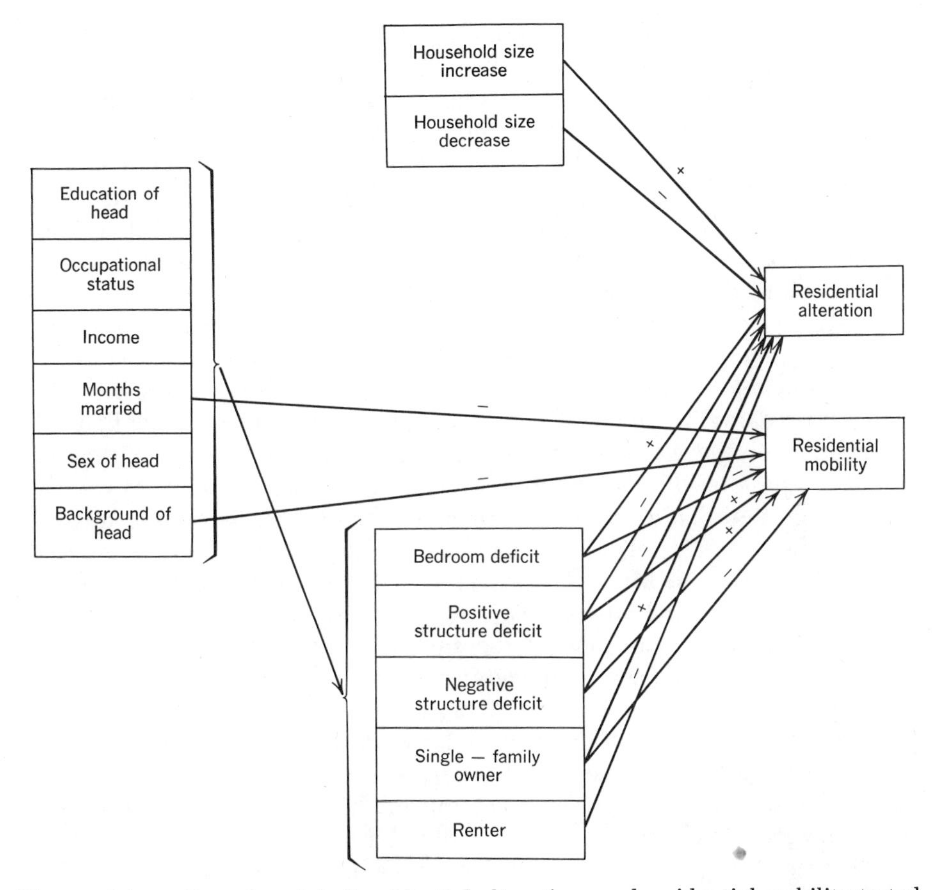

Figure 14 Causal model of residential alterations and residential mobility tested by Bross and Morris (1974).

residential alteration and residential mobility in parallel analyses. The findings are summarized in Figure 14, reproduced from their paper. The key factors that influenced residential alteration behavior included three of the normative housing deficits and changes in household size. The latter appeared to operate as indexes of changes in normative housing deficits.

The relationships between crowding and alterations and between crowding and mobility support the observation made earlier regarding the stage of the family life cycle and residential alterations. Bedroom deficit was positively related to alterations, but negatively related to mobility. Families with more bedroom space than needed tended to spend money on alterations and additions. Such families were likely to be older with their children grown. Or they were younger families whose dwellings were acquired in anticipation of family growth. In either case, they made alterations and additions. Families who were crowded, on the other hand, tended to move.

The role of ownership in encouraging residential alteration instead of residential mobility was obvious, but its influence was even greater when combined with structure type. It was not simply the type of the structure but the fit with the family's needs for a single-family dwelling that was important. If the family had a single-family dwelling and a family composition for which a single-family dwelling is normatively prescribed, it was much more likely to engage in residential alterations than if they had a single-family dwelling but did not need one to fit family composition. Positive structure deficit (having an unneeded single-family home) was negatively related to residential alteration but positively related to residential mobility. Thus people with smaller and less complex families who did not need a single-family dwelling were likely to move. People who needed a single-family dwelling but did not have one (negative structure deficit) also tended not to engage in residential alterations but used residential mobility. Families whose residential structure type matched their needs, however, used residential alteration to overcome other deficits that, in particular, might be due to either increases or decreases in family size.

When Bross and Morris (1974) divided the residential alterations variable into additions and alterations (a somewhat risky act in statistical terms since such small proportions of the sample engaged in either of the two behaviors that the division produced instability in the estimates) the findings were similar. An exception was that additions were related to increases in household size and alterations were related to decreases in household size. The connection between decreased family size and alterations calls to mind the moderate-income family who has put off home improvements until the children were all gone because they could not afford it earlier.

The need to increase the amount of space in a dwelling obviously relates to increases in family size. Building an addition probably occurs primarily when a family needs some of the desirable characteristics of their current dwelling. If extra space were the only lack, building an addition or remodeling the basement could overcome the deficit. Families who are crowded, who are renters and would prefer ownership, or who live in apartments and would rather have a single-family structure tend to move to a new dwelling.

CONCLUSION

The research on the role of residential alterations in overcoming housing deficits and in serving as an alternative to mobility is not strong and definitive. In particular, the role of dissatisfaction in causing alterations and additions must be further examined with controls for the types of activities and/or reasons for undertaking the activity. The research results and interpretations offered in this chapter are perhaps best viewed as hypotheses, rather than fully tested relationships.

DEFINITIONS

Additions. Actual enlargement of the structure, either by adding a wing, a room, a porch, an attached garage, a shed, or a carport, or by raising the roof, digging a basement or bomb or fallout shelter.

Alterations. Changes or improvements made within or on the structure. The changes or improvements range from a complete remodeling, which involves removal of the entire interior of the structure and remodeling it, to the installation of a new electric service outlet, wall switch, or new shelf.

Consumer Price Index. An index showing the changes in the prices of goods and services to a typical consumer, based on the prices of the same goods and services in a base year; also called cost-of-living index. (See also *Wholesale Price Index.*)

Home improvement. Addition to the quality or space conditions within a dwelling; usually a reduction of negative space or quality deficits; either a residential alteration or addition.

Home maintenance. Routine repair and replacement necessary to maintain a dwelling at its present level of quality. Included in this class are exterior painting, repairing or replacing storm windows, roof repairs, and repair or replacement of any major systems: heating, plumbing, or electrical.

Housing starts. The number of new dwelling units started during a given time period. When a site is excavated and the building begun, a start has occurred. Housing production is recorded in terms of housing starts. The completion of the dwelling or the occupation of a completed dwelling are less often used as measures of housing production.

Remodeling. Rather extensive treatment of the interior of a dwelling, including refinishing, moving walls, replacing trim, windows, doors, and cabinets for improvement and beautification rather than for repair and maintenance; one form of residential alteration undertaken to correct normative quality deficits.

Chapter 11
Housing of the Elderly and Disabled

Loveliest of trees, the cherry now
Is hung with bloom along the bough,
And stands about the woodland ride
Wearing white for Eastertide.

Now, of my threescore years and ten,
Twenty will not come again,
And take from seventy springs a score,
It only leaves me fifty more.

And since to look at things in bloom
Fifty springs are little room,
About the woodlands I will go
To see the cherry hung with snow. A. E. Housman*

Elderly individuals and disabled persons may have special housing needs that do not arise from the housing norms discussed in Part 2. They, of course, are subject to all the usual housing norms but may have additional needs that arise from their age-related health loss or their disability. Their special needs, nevertheless, produce dissatisfaction and in turn may produce residential mobility, alterations, or additions. The factors that prompt these responses, however, are related to the events and physical limitations that occur in the process of growing old or becoming disabled. The disability could result from a crippling accident, a muscular disorder, a birth defect, or a similar problem. A limited income, often also present, may compound the problem.

The housing conditions needed by the aging and disabled are, in general, quite similar. Elderly or disabled individuals need a dwelling unit and neighborhood that will permit them to perform daily activities as nearly normally

* "Loveliest of Trees," in *A Shropshire Lad,* by A. E. Housman (New York: Avon, 1966).

as possible. The actual housing conditions that permit such activity may be somewhat different for each group, however.

Differences occur in the process of the development of such housing needs, both between and within the two groupings. Generally, an elderly individual gradually loses skills and physical capabilities and becomes less able to perform routine daily tasks. Sometimes a sudden disruption, such as an illness, accident, or loss of a spouse precipitates the perception of slowly developing residential deficits and consequent dissatisfaction. In general, however, the condition has been developing for some time. A disability, on the other hand, may occur suddenly, as in a crippling accident, a stroke, or a heart attack. It may also develop slowly, as in multiple sclerosis, or may have been present from birth. The deficits that occur are inherent in the comparison between housing needs and actual dwellings, not solely in the presence of a disability.

Regardless of the way in which special housing needs develop, the end result is the same. Physical limitations create deficit conditions that would not be present if it were not for the presence of limitations and the absence of compensating factors in the dwelling. Such deficits are not normative deficits in the sense that they are the result of housing conditions that deviate from housing norms. Rather, they are residential deficits that result from the relationship between the individual's state of physiological functioning and the environment.

HOUSING NEEDS OF THE ELDERLY

When one thinks of housing needs of the elderly, one often thinks of meeting those needs in retirement villages, retirement homes, or nursing homes. Often one has the image of facilities funded by government programs specifically for the elderly. Yet the vast majority of the elderly population (individuals 60 years and older) are not institutionalized and do not live in housing arranged especially for older people. Almost 96 percent of the elderly population live in what the Bureau of the Census terms a "housing unit," rather than "group quarters," as nursing homes are termed (USBC, 1973d, p. 3).

Over three-fourths of the elderly share their dwelling with someone else. The myth of the lonely widow is largely that—a myth. In the majority of the cases, the household consists of husband and wife, and possibly other relatives. Less than 10 percent of the elderly live in households headed by an individual under 60 years of age. Thus, only a small percentage of elderly individuals live with their children (USBC, 1973d, p. 1).

Over 70 percent of the elderly live in housing owned by a member of their household. The vast majority of the owner-occupied dwellings lived in by elderly persons (almost 90 percent) are owned by an elderly individual

(USBC, 1973d, p. 1). Only a small proportion of the elderly who are renters occupy subsidized housing. In 1970, there were only 143,400 such units available for occupancy (USBC, 1975b, p. 716). During the same year, there were almost five-and-a-half million dwellings rented by individuals over 60. While the number of subsidized dwelling units has risen since 1970, so has the number of elderly. Thus the proportion living in subsidized housing is still very small.

In a study of almost 5000 elderly individuals (Beyer and Woods, 1963), 81 percent lived in their own household. An additional 11 percent lived with their children. Only a fourth of the respondents lived alone, and almost 60 percent were home owners. Montgomery's (1965) study of over 500 elderly individuals in rural Pennsylvania found only 15 percent living alone. Almost 60 percent lived with their spouses. Three-fourths were home owners—a somewhat higher figure than in other studies. This finding could perhaps be expected in a rural sample.

The picture that emerges is a set of housing conditions not very different from the housing of the rest of the population. Households with an elderly head are more likely to own a single-family dwelling than to have any other combination of structure type and tenure status. In spite of the recent boom in condominiums for the elderly, their numbers are still relatively small. In fact, the elderly are more likely to be home owners than families headed by an individual under 35 (UBSC, 1973c, p. 1 and p. 10). Further, they are more likely to live in a single-family dwelling than the majority of the population (USBC, 1973d, p. 45).

The dwellings of families headed by elderly persons are likely to be somewhat smaller than the ones occupied by a household not headed by an elderly individual (USBC, 1973d, p. 5; USBC, 1972b, p. 22). They are likely to be older and lower in value (USBC, 1973d, p. 4 and p. 6; USBC, 1972b, p. 12 and p. 242).

But are such conditions meeting the housing needs of the elderly? It is hard to draw sound conclusions from the census data. One conclusion is that the hard work, savings, and sacrifice of earlier years has finally paid off. The elderly couple owns outright a home that has sufficient space for all their possessions. Visits from children and grandchildren are convenient; and there is a yard to putter in. Their housing conditions finally are in line with cultural and family norms.

An alternative conclusion, from the same data, is that their housing needs are not being met. The couple may be living in their own home because it is paid for, not because they love living there. Their major asset is the equity in the dwelling. Yet they may be unable to readily convert that equity into cash for living expenses. In spite of owning their home, they may be poor.

Housing costs under such circumstances are limited to property taxes, utilities, and maintenance. Even those costs may be rapidly becoming more than can be comfortably handled on a modest income such as Social Security or a pension. Utilities and property taxes have soared in recent years. Utilities, in particular, are likely to be expensive for an older home. Older homes are less likely to have adequate insulation.

Poor health and the lack of financial resources may lead to delay or postponement of routine maintenance. Hence, the dwelling may need major repairs. The house and yard may be far too large for the couple to care for with ease.

The conditions that are apt to create problems for the elderly are not easily solved through residential alterations and additions. To some extent, certain features could be added that could make the home safer and easier to care for. But residential alteration cannot solve the problems of having all financial assets in a dwelling while needing ready cash for food. Having too much space cannot readily be solved through residential alteration. When alterations are appropriate (adding safety features to the bathroom, for instance), there may be no financial resources for such alterations.

Residential Mobility

The fact that older households are far less likely to move than younger households (Roistacher, 1974b; Goldscheider, Van Arsdol, and Sabagh, 1965; Long, 1972; Chevan, 1971) is not a particularly good indicator of whether their housing needs are being met. A variety of constraints may be operating that prevent mobility. Being unable to sell their dwelling because of a decline in the quality of either the dwelling or the neighborhood may be one problem. A high degree of satisfaction with the neighborhood may also act as a constraint.

Virtually every study that has analyzed housing satisfaction has found that it is the highest among the elderly (Morris, 1976). One interpretation is that they have achieved their norms and so are highly satisfied. Another is that they are expressing satisfaction in light of constraints. They have little hope of improving their housing conditions and so have rationalized and accepted poorer conditions. Thus the crucial variable to be examined is the desire to move. Presumably the goal would be a dwelling that is more compact, easier to care for, located near shopping, and perhaps less expensive. A more benign climate may also be implied by the desire to move.

The evidence from sample surveys is somewhat conflicting but seems to support the idea that most elderly households prefer to remain in the home they purchased earlier in the life cycle. In particular, like younger home-owning families, elderly home owners are less likely to desire to move than renters (Goldscheider, 1966; Langford, 1962; Nelson, 1973; Findlay and Morris, 1976).

In one study Lawton (1975) found that 85 percent of a small group of elderly Jewish immigrants living in an inner-city neighborhood in

Philadelphia wanted to move. Findings from other surveys, however, indicate that much lower percentages express such desires.

Nelson and Winter (1975) found that 60 percent of their sample had at some time considered moving from their present dwelling. This percentage, although high, must be considered in light of the fact that three-fourths of the group who had considered moving had also considered staying in their present residence (Nelson, 1973, p. 62). Thus, to consider moving is a long way from wanting to move, planning to move, and actually accomplishing a change of residence.

Among those 50 and older, Goldscheider (1966) found that only 31 percent wanted to move. (The survey question was, "If you had your choice, would you stay here or move?") A higher proportion of those aged 50–64 desired to move than did those 65 and over. He interprets this finding as reflecting

> *. . . desires associated with occupation and retirement changes, as well as the movement of persons in this age category into a stage of the family life cycle which is more congruent with different housing facilities (p. 104).*

Nevertheless, the percentage of the older population (including the 50–64 age group) that wanted to move was far smaller than that of the younger population.

Findlay (1975) examined the propensity to congregate. That variable was constructed from questions indicating the respondent's desire to live in an apartment, to live in low-rent public housing, and to live in housing especially for older people separate from housing for families. The propensity to congregate, then, indicated the desire for a different residence that would provide social and economic support, as well as support for physical needs.

Among his sample of 2000 Minnesota residents aged 65 and over, Findlay found scores on the propensity to congregate ranging from 0 to 6 out of a possible 8. About one-third of the sample had no inclination to congregate (a score of 0). Another third had scores of 4 or more, indicating some interest in moving to a more supportive dwelling. The propensity to congregate was related to size of the community and income of the respondent. Respondents with lower incomes and those who lived in larger communities were more likely to indicate a desire to congregate.

Langford (1962) found that less than 30 percent were willing to move from their residence. Being willing to move, of course, is far different from wanting to move, or ever having considered moving.

While findings vary according to the questions asked, the size of the community, income, and other factors, the indications are that a large proportion of the elderly prefer to remain where they are for as long as possible.

Residential Dissatisfaction. Research on the desire to move on the part of the elderly is quite limited. Nevertheless, it indicates that, like younger families, dissatisfaction with the current dwelling and the neighborhood are the major factors that produce a desire to move. Nelson and Winter (1975) found that people who are dissatisfied with various features of their dwelling and neighborhood are more likely to consider moving than those who are satisfied.

Satisfaction with the neighborhood was significant in the prediction of the propensity to congregate (Findlay and Morris, 1976). Housing satisfaction was not related to the propensity to congregate, however. A possible explanation is that the propensity to congregate better describes the desire for a new neighborhood (and the associated services and facilities) than the wish for a different dwelling.

Goldscheider (1966) found that dissatisfaction with current housing and neighborhood accounted for two-thirds of the reasons given by people 50 and over for wanting to move. Between 50 and 90 percent of Sherman's (1971) respondents, residents of different types of retirement housing, stated that they had been seeking ease of housing maintenance when they moved. Such responses indicate there may have been dissatisfaction with former conditions. Measures of satisfaction taken after the move, but related to former conditions, however, are as likely to be rationalizations of the move as accurate measures of early states of dissatisfaction.

As in younger families, dissatisfaction among the elderly is prompted by deficit conditions. Findlay and Morris (1976) found that space, structure-type, and privacy deficits were related to housing dissatisfaction. Both too much space and too little space were predictors of low levels of housing satisfaction.

Major Life Disruptions. Major life disruptions and changes associated with the aging process that produce a loss of independence are the two major factors that change nondeficit residential conditions into deficit conditions. After age 65, however, age *per se* is not a particularly good predictor of the desire to move. The changes and events that have occurred are the important factors. The desire to move has not been found to be related to age within the elderly group when various measures of deficits, dissatisfaction, independence, and disruptions have been included.

The potential impact of major life disruptions on the elderly household was noted by Foote et al. (1960):

> *Only a shock of major dimensions, such as prolonged illness or a severe economic setback, is likely to dislodge the couple from the home which it worked so hard to gain (p. 113).*

Montgomery (1965) defined a disruption as:

> *... an adverse event or happening, either external to or within the older person which induces change or adjustment in the physical, social, or emotional life of the person experiencing the event (pp. 87–88).*

He found that disruptions, including events that ranged from loss of a spouse or a close relative to serious illness, forced retirement, and economic deprivation had occurred within the past five years to a relatively large proportion of his sample. The number of such disruptions that an individual had experienced was negatively related to the mental health of the respondents. Those with few or no disruptions scored higher on a mental health rating scale.

Nelson and Winter (1975) analyzed the occurrence of major life disruptions within the past year in relation to the consideration of moving. The disruptions studied were retirement, an accident in the home, serious illness (of the respondent, spouse, or close friend), inability of the respondent to care for himself or herself, death (of a spouse, relative, or close friend) a move out of the household by a household member, and a move out of the neighborhood by a close friend.

They found that people who had experienced one or more disruptions were more likely to consider moving than those who had not experienced any disruptions. Death of a close friend or relative had an especially strong relationship to the consideration of moving. Thus, there is evidence that the occurrence of a major life disruption can create a deficit condition. An unchanging dwelling in conjunction with a changing household may produce deficits. The dwelling that was possibly even pleasurable, and at least manageable, for two people to care for suddenly may become impossible for the surviving spouse to maintain.

Independence and Disability. A major life disruption such as a stroke, heart ailment, serious illness, or accident, may also create a deficit condition by altering the level of personal independence. A lower level of independence may also be caused by a long-term or chronic condition, such as arthritis, high blood pressure, or gradual loss of sight or hearing. All such conditions are likely to occur among the elderly. The probability of their occurrence increases with age (Beyer and Woods, 1963). It is the occurrence of such conditions rather than age itself that produces deficits. In addition, elderly individuals do not have the stamina of their younger counterparts. They tire more quickly and are more likely to experience cardiac problems (Lawton, 1975; Lawton and Azar, 1965).

Whatever the source, physical problems result in a decline in the ability to care for oneself and maintain an independent household. Such loss of physical independence may cause deficits in housing and neighborhood conditions that would not occur for an independent, mobile individual.

At the same time that physical changes are occurring within the individual, there may be corresponding deterioration in neighborhood conditions. The crime rate may increase, the neighborhood grocery store may close, the bus stop may be moved, or bus service may be terminated entirely. Such neighborhood changes may serve to speed the loss of independence. Nevertheless, the important changes appear to occur within the individual. These changes can create deficits in the absence of any changes in the environment.

Lawton and Brody (1969) developed two scales to measure the level of physical independence. The Physical Self-Maintenance Scale measured very basic abilities that would indicate the level of care that would be needed in a nursing home. Their second scale, the Instrumental Activities of Daily Living, measured the ability to perform tasks that would be necessary to maintain a separate household. It included telephoning, shopping, food preparation, housekeeping, laundry, transportation, taking medicine, and handling finances. The two scales were shown to be valid measures of differing levels of the ability to care for oneself.

Montgomery (1965) used a similar scale to measure the extent to which older people were able to engage in various daily activities. He included meal preparation, laundry, ironing, housecleaning, buying clothes, paying bills, gardening, repair of the dwelling, personal care of self, and personal care of others in the household. Montgomery found that the ability to perform such tasks declines with age in women. Such abilities were not related to increasing age among men. That finding was discounted somewhat because many of the activities, such as laundry and ironing, had never been done by many of the men in the sample.

Nelson and Winter (1975) and Findlay and Morris (1976) used measures of the level of independence, based on Lawton and Brody (1969) and Montgomery (1965), to predict the desire to move. Nelson and Winter divided their respondents into two groups. In the first group were those who could perform all of the personal maintenance activities. The second group consisted of those who were unable to perform one or more of the activities. They constructed a similar variable to indicate the ability to care for the dwelling, lawn, and garden. Additional measures of independence were the need for walking assistance, the distance that could be walked without tiring, the type of transportation most frequently used, and the ability to get out as often as desired.

The consideration of moving was lower among those with the ability to perform the activities of daily living, the ability to walk unassisted, and the ability to get out as often as desired, than among those lacking such abilities.

Thus, as independence declines, there is a tendency to think about moving to a different dwelling. The only surprising finding was that the lack of ability to care for the dwelling, lawn, and garden was not related to the consideration of moving. Since most of the respondents were women, the researchers concluded that many of them had never performed such activities. Not performing such activities was thought to indicate lack of skill, not loss of ability.

Findlay and Morris (1976) used two scales, one indicating degree of personal mobility and one indicating degree of personal independence. The personal mobility scale included having trouble doing ordinary activities such as seeing, getting around, going up and down stairs, and cutting toenails (Findlay, 1975, p. 63). The level of personal independence measured the ease of going places such as to stores and shops, a bank, a doctor, and recreation facilities (Findlay, 1975, p. 66). As could be expected, neighborhood satisfaction was related to the independence scale, which measured accessibility to various facilities. On the other hand, housing satisfaction was related to personal mobility. The propensity to congregate was related to both scales. Respondents with lower personal mobility and lower personal independence were more likely to have a propensity to congregate.

Measures of objective characteristics of the dwelling, or the individual, with the exception of home ownership, have not proven to be particularly good at predicting the desire to move among the elderly. Better predictors are dissatisfaction, level of independence, and the occurrence of major life disruptions. It is hypothesized that the chain of events occurs somewhat as depicted in Figure 15.

Age is accompanied by a rising probability that a major life disruption, loss of personal independence, or loss of mobility will occur. The loss of independence can be the result of a chronic condition, or can result from a disruption. In any event, deficits are produced that decrease housing or neighborhood satisfaction. It is the dissatisfaction then that produces the desire to move and subsequent mobility.

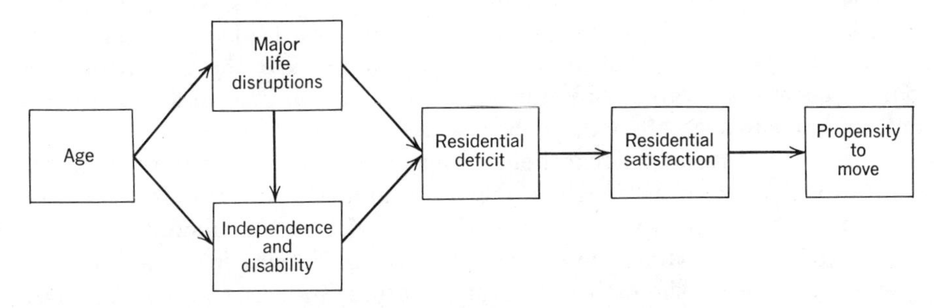

Figure 15 Causal model of the influences on the propensity to move among the elderly.

Housing Designed for the Elderly

When an elderly couple or individual wishes to move to a different dwelling to overcome housing deficits, the new residential environment should have as few deficits as possible. An elderly couple or an individual who moves is likely to be looking for a smaller dwelling that has all facilities on the same floor. They are probably seeking a location that is accessible to stores and community services. They may also be looking for safety features such as nonskid floors, adequate and secure handrails, and grab bars in the bathroom.

The construction of housing units specifically for the elderly has increased in recent years. Housing for the elderly includes both privately and publicly funded housing. The construction boom has occurred partly in response to the demand for such units. It may also have occurred, in part, because of encouragements in the form of subsidies and tax breaks. Housing for the elderly also seems to serve socially desirable community goals. Local governing bodies find housing units for the elderly politically much easier to support than units for low-income families.

A decline in mortality rates and a decline in birth rates have led to an increase in the proportion of the elderly population. Such trends promise to continue, at least in the short run. Thus proper location and design of units for the elderly assume greater importance. It may be easier to select a location and include necessary features in housing designed specifically for the elderly than to attempt to add such features to the current housing of elderly persons. The features needed, of course, are those that help individuals adjust to disruptions and a loss of independence.

The Department of Housing and Urban Development (1973c) has developed standards for housing units designed for the elderly, just as they have for single-family dwellings and multiunit dwellings, discussed earlier. All units for the elderly funded under HUD programs must meet those standards. Unfortunately, as noted by Lawton (1975), such minimum standards have become essentially maximum standards.

Basic safety features to be included are almost taken for granted. Such features help prevent accidents among people with physical limitations associated with aging. Grab bars in the bathroom near the toilet, tub, and shower, controlled water temperature to prevent scalding, and nonskid tub and shower surfaces all need to be included in the bathroom. Flush door entrances (no thresholds), excellent illumination both inside and out, and wall plugs that are waist height rather than ankle height are also necessary (Lawton, 1975). The list is nearly endless, and basically includes features that contribute to safety and freedom from accidents in homes for the nonelderly, as well. The inclusion of such features in homes designed specifically for the elderly is far more important because of the potential for physical limitation. Yet it is relatively easy to justify the inclusion of many of the features in all housing units.

Of equal importance is the location of the dwelling unit in relation to facilities in the neighborhood. The elderly are not as likely to have automobiles as are younger people. Thus the dwelling should be within walking distance (one-fourth of a mile) of a grocery store, drug store, bus stop, place of worship, clinic or hospital, and bank. There should be access to other facilities, such as restaurants, movie houses, and a library (Lawton, 1975, p. 87).

Should housing for the elderly be included along with housing units for the nonelderly? Or should there be separate apartment complexes, condominiums, or cluster developments with occupancy limited to elderly households? Such complexes are often referred to as *congregate, age-segregated,* or *proximate* housing. Michelson (1970) hypothesized that an elderly person or couple would be more satisfied living in a dwelling that is surrounded by similar dwellings inhabited by elderly people. Empirical research on age-segregated versus dispersed housing does not seem to support that hypothesis.

Carp (1966) found higher subsequent levels of satisfaction among people who had been accepted in public housing than among those who had applied for admission to the same apartment complex, but had not been accepted. The satisfaction data were collected prior to the move and a year after the resident had lived there. Before the move the groups were equal in satisfaction with housing and neighborhood conditions. A year after the move those still living in private housing were less satisfied. The results could only have been expected to indicate greater satisfaction among residents of the public housing units. All had wanted to move because of deficits in their housing. Only a portion had been admitted. Those who were rejected presumably continued to experience housing deficits.

Lawton and Cohen (1974) conducted a longitudinal study of the impact of age-segregated housing units. Data were collected from two groups of elderly people, one group planning to move to age-segregated units, and the other group from the surrounding community. Data were then collected from both groups a year after the move. The analysis controlled for initial differences in health between the two groups.

After a year, tenants in the age-segregated units showed a decline in functional health. In terms of housing satisfaction and perception of change for the better, residents of the age-segregated housing scored higher. The decline in functional health was surprising to the researchers. They concluded that those who voluntarily moved to age-segregated dwellings might be more physically vulnerable, even though their initial health conditions were not different from those of the control group.

Other studies have not supported the findings of Carp (1966) and

Lawton and Cohen (1974). Sherman (1972) drew a sample of 600 residents, 100 from each of six different kinds of congregate retirement housing: a retirement hotel, a rental village, an apartment tower, a purchase village, a manor village, and a life care home. A control group of 600 respondents was drawn from non-age-segregated housing. The six groups were matched to the control group on sex, working status, marital status, age, income, education, occupation, tenure, household composition, and number of children (Sherman, 1972, p. 342).

Data were collected after those in age-segregated housing had lived at the site between one and two years. All groups were reinterviewed two years later. The findings indicate no differences in satisfaction between the combined groups living in congregate housing and those living in dispersed housing. There were great differences, however, in satisfaction levels among the groups in the retirement housing. Residents of the retirement hotel had very low satisfaction. Residents of the purchase village, the manor village, and the life care home had high levels of satisfaction. These levels of satisfaction cannot be attributed to the type of housing *per se.* The level of satisfaction for each type was similar to its control group. Therefore, the differences in housing satisfaction can only be attributed to the characteristics of the residents, including demographic characteristics and related special needs.

Bell (1976) hypothesized that there would be higher levels of interaction among residents of age-segregated dwellings than among residents of what he termed *independent* dwellings. The greater amount of interaction would be reflected in higher degrees of life satisfaction in congregate dwellings. Not only were there no differences in interaction, but residents of independent housing had higher life satisfaction than those in congregate housing.

Interpretation

The common thread that may explain the seemingly disparate findings of the studies is the idea of choice. When elderly people are free to choose their residence, they tend to select one that meets their needs. Their needs include both the cultural norms that apply to all regardless of age and the special age- and disability-related needs. Thus Carp's control group had deficit housing, but were not accepted for admittance to the new apartment complex. Their deficits could be expected to increase during the time between the initial interview and reinterview. As a result their satisfaction was lower than satisfaction in the experimental group.

Lawton and Cohen's respondents knew their health was declining and so selected a more supportive environment. Their health worsened during the year. Nevertheless, they were more satisfied because they had successfully anticipated deficits and had taken measures to prevent their occurrence.

Respondents in the Sherman study and the Bell study who lived in age-segregated housing had selected such sites to overcome deficits. Thus they were relatively satisfied. The most satisfied group in Sherman's study was the group with the oldest average age. They were living in the most supportive environment, probably with the fewest deficits. The control group respondents in each study were equally satisfied, probably because they, too, lived in nondeficit housing. In fact, Bell's control group was more satisfied. The key conclusion, noted by Sherman (1972), is that:

> *One can draw no general conclusion other than the obvious one that there is no one right kind of housing; rather, the person will be most satisfied with the housing that best fits his requirements and condition (p. 363).*

HOUSING FOR THE DISABLED

Defining the elderly is relatively easy. One picks an age (55, 62, 65), and all individuals beyond that age can be considered elderly. Such individuals may or may not have special housing needs, depending on their level of social, physical, and economic independence. Physiological changes that accompany the aging process have been well documented (Riley and Foner, 1968). Such changes occur at different chronological ages, but nevertheless they are relatively predictable.

Other disabilities that produce special housing needs are another matter. Such disabilities can occur at any age and can result from a variety of causes. The consequent special housing needs are more difficult to specify than those of the elderly because of the range of disability conditions and their consequences.

The American National Standards Institute (1971) defines six categories of disabilities:

> *. . . Non-ambulatory Disabilities. Impairment that, regardless of cause or manifestation, for practical purposes, confine individuals to wheelchairs. . . . Semi-ambulatory Disabilities. Impairments that cause individuals to walk with difficulty or insecurity. Individuals using braces or crutches, amputees, arthritics, spastics, and those with pulmonary and cardiac ills may be semi-ambulatory. . . . Sight Disabilities. Total blindness or impairments affecting sight. . . . Hearing Disabilities. Deafness or hearing handicaps. . . . Disabilities of Incoordination. Faulty coordination or palsy from brain, spinal, or peripheral nerve injury. . . . Aging. Those manifestations of the aging processes that significantly reduce mobility, flexibility, coordination, and perceptiveness that are not accounted for in the aforementioned categories (ANSI 1971, p. 6).*

As indicated by their last category, many elderly individuals can be categorized as disabled.

How many disabled individuals are there in the United States? The range and nature of their conditions makes them difficult to count. The President's Committee on Employment of the Handicapped estimates that one out of every eleven adults between the ages of 14 and 64 has a disability (PCEH, 1975).

State and federal rehabilitation agencies such as the Veterans' Administration and private agencies such as the National Easter Seal Society for Crippled Children and Adults have statisitcs on the individuals with whom they are working. Such statistics would far underestimate the total number of individuals with some sort of physiological limitation, however. An arthritic knee that no longer bends properly is a disability that makes stair steps difficult to negotiate. It is likely that the individual has not received treatment for the condition. Unless specifically asked about arthritis, the person probably would not report having a disability.

Achieving an accurate count of the disabled population is not as important as the recognition that the proportion of the population in this category is large and cannot be expected to diminish. As Warren (1960) noted, many who are classified as disabled today would not have lived a few decades ago. Medical science was simply not advanced enough then to ensure their survival.

As in the case of the elderly, the occurrence of a disability may create housing deficits that would not exist in the absence of the disability. For instance, a dwelling with doors too narrow for a wheelchair was not a problem until the veteran returned from the Vietnam war with both legs missing. A two-story dwelling was a nondeficit structure until the occurrence of a heart attack.

Also as in the case of elderly individuals, disabled people indicate that they would rather live independently (Dickman, 1975). The growing numbers of disabled persons has made housing specifically designed for people with disabilities a reality in some larger cities (Dickman, 1975). Many apartment units that were designed for elderly residents also accommodate the needs of disabled persons (HUD, 1973c). The features needed are often similar.

Dwellings designed specifically for the elderly and the disabled cannot accommodate all disabled persons. The need is too great. In addition residential mobility to a specific location for residence in a specifically designed dwelling may be inappropriate. Hence a solution for a great many is residential alteration. The needed alterations can range from relatively minor and inexpensive rearrangement of work centers (Burton, ND) to major and expensive remodeling. Widening doorways to accommodate a person in a wheelchair (Olson and Meredith, 1973; McCullough and Farnham, 1961) and installing a bathroom on the ground floor so that a heart patient would not have to climb stairs are typical major alterations.

Because of the expense involved, individuals with nonambulatory conditions may be virtual prisoners in their homes. Altering every doorway in the home to accommodate a wheelchair may be impossible for the family to afford, even with assistance. Hence a far better long range policy than either segregated housing for the disabled or residential alterations of specific dwellings would be to require that all new dwellings be built with, for example, doorways wide enough for wheelchair passage. For a relatively modest cost, all new dwellings could be required to have a basic construction that would permit disabled persons to quickly alter a standard dwelling to their particular needs. If a person in a wheelchair can move around the dwelling freely, so can an individual on crutches or with a cardiac or pulmonary disorder. Specific residential alterations to remove housing deficits would thus be relatively inexpensive.

There has been a flurry of legislation to protect the rights of disabled persons. All new public buildings must be accessible by wheelchair, for example, This legislation is likely to continue to grow. A policy that requires that housing be built with flexibility for alterations to fit the needs of the elderly and the disabled might fruitfully be a part of the development.

CONCLUSION

The housing adjustment behavior of elderly and disabled persons is similar to that of younger, able individuals. Deficits appear in the environment which produce dissatisfaction and the propensity to adjust housing. Among the nondisabled, the dissatisfaction tends to be a consequence of deficits that arise from changes in the stage of the family life cycle. For the elderly and disabled they arise from physical changes and problems. The source of the deficits is not housing that deviates from cultural norms. Rather deficits occur in the residential environment as the result of changes in the physiological conditions of the individual.

Elderly couples and individuals who have reduced independence or mobility or have experienced major life disruptions are likely to want to move to overcome their deficits. Such deficits tend to be related to medical and other community services, as well as to the dwelling itself. The elderly may feel the need to move to housing where such services are more readily accessible. Disabled individuals are likely to undertake residential alterations to adjust their housing to meet their special needs. Presumably they already live in a desirable neighborhood and now need to adapt the dwelling to new needs. The conclusion that the most satisfactory response for the elderly is residential mobility while for the disabled it is residential alteration applies to the general situation. Individuals differ greatly in terms of both the consequences of their age or disability and the constraints on their potential responses. The roles of deficits and dissatisfaction need to be recognized in forming housing policy for such groups.

DEFINITIONS

Congregate housing. Dwelling units occupied only by the elderly, grouped together in apartment complexes, cluster housing, or condominiums; age-segregated or proximate housing.

Disability. Incapacity or inability to live a full life due to bodily impairment.

Dispersed housing. Housing units for the elderly mixed with housing for other age groups; to be contrasted with congregate housing.

Disruption. A sudden or unexpected crisis, including illness, accident, or loss of spouse.

Elderly. Pertaining to persons late in life; the group of persons who are considered old; anyone over a given age (e.g., 55, 62, 65).

Personal independence. The ability to maintain an autonomous life, including being able to walk, interact with family and friends, and provide for one's own needs for food, clothing, etc.

Part 4
Constraints and Responses to Constraints

> We had been so busy building a life and a suitable world to live it in that we had never thought of decorating. We never felt that our home needed cosmetics. Since we had no one to live up to but ourselves, our possessions had reflected our interiors. To us interior decorating meant polishing and refining our inner selves. Accumulating ornaments seems like exterior rather than interior decorating. We kidded ourselves about our less than distinguished decor, calling it inferior decorating, Frank Lloyd Wrong, or Rank Lloyd Fright. Sam Levenson*

Constraints are factors that impose limits on the family's ability to attain normatively prescribed housing. They are largely beyond the short-term control of the family. Included in this class of constraints are low income, low social status, minority racial or ethnic status, and being female. Such constraints are discussed in detail in Chapters 12 and 13.

The three types of extrafamilial constraints, financial, racial-ethnic, and sexual, often operate together. Minority groups and female-headed households have lower median incomes than white and male-headed households (USBC, 1973h, pp. 3–5). Black families are more likely to be headed by a female than white families (USBC, 1973g, p. 666). Thus for some families, the extrafamilial constraints are compounded.

ASSUMPTIONS ABOUT EXTRAFAMILIAL CONSTRAINTS

The first assumption is that extrafamilial constraints affect the means to obtain the goal of normatively prescribed housing and not the goal itself. The

* From *In One Era and Out the Other,* by Sam Levenson (New York: Simon and Schuster, 1973), pp. 78–79.

goal of family housing adjustment, then, is housing that meets the norms of the family and the society.

The constraints to be discussed apply not just to barriers preventing the attainment of housing ideals but to all levels of housing. Much of the discussion involves barriers to the attainment of spacious, owner-occupied, single-family dwellings, located in safe neighborhoods with good schools. Constraints on the attainment of housing that is on the fringe of permissible deviation are also discussed. In particular, tenure arrangements other than ownership, and structure types other than the single-family house, are included.

A second assumption is that the means for obtaining housing are those currently prescribed and practiced. Thus, the family exchanges money (or perhaps other goods or services) for the privilege of occupying a dwelling. They may rent a housing unit or they may purchase it. In either case, they compete in a market with many other families and must be involved with many institutions, both public and private, to obtain and occupy that housing unit. The institutions and individuals discussed in this section include builders, developers, real estate brokers, labor unions, materials manufacturers, lending institutions, and, to some extent, community regulatory agencies.

Finally, the discussion focuses on constraints imposed on the family in obtaining unsubsidized housing in the private market. In a sense, of course, no housing in the United States falls into that category. The so-called "private" market is greatly affected by actions of governmental agencies. Monetary policies to curb inflation drastically reduce the supply of mortgage money for financing the construction and purchase of housing units. Zoning restrictions impose limits on the amount of land available for the construction of new housing units.

All housing in the United States is subsidized to a greater or lesser extent. Aaron (1972) and Schorr (1965) point out that more tax revenue is lost each year in "subsidies" to upper- and middle-income home owners, through favorable income tax provisions, than is spent on all federally sponsored housing programs, including public housing, rent supplements, and rent payments included in federal welfare programs. While the influence of governmental action on the housing market is recognized as exerting both direct and indirect effects on the family, it is peripheral to the discussion in this section. Housing policy is often intended to relieve constraints. However, to focus on the variety of governmental influences would distract attention from the central issues related to the understanding of the constraints themselves.

RESPONSES TO CONSTRAINTS

The typical response to constraints of a minor nature is to develop temporarily lowered preferences. Thus, in the short run, compromises are made in order to have some kind of housing, even if it has a few deficits. Such compromises would seem to be relatively harmless adjustments that have to be made pending, for example, a rise in income.

Other constraints are more severe and chronic in nature. The consequences of severe, enduring constraints may be much greater. Possible consequences may include structural adaptation by families (Chapter 14), including changes in their family norms, family composition, or family organization.

An analysis of extrafamilial constraints that affect the means to achieve normative housing conditions assumes that housing norms are similar for all groups in the society. Under this assumption, the key reason that housing conditions differ is the differences in the level of constraints rather than differences in norms. This assumption has been questioned by several social scientists (Lewis, 1966a; Lewis, 1966b; Gutman, 1970; Hall, 1966; Gans, 1962; and Rainwater, 1966). They assert that different social classes and income groups have different housing norms. The extent to which norms differ among socioeconomic and ethnic groups is explored in detail in Chapter 15.

Chapter 12
Economic Constraints

> I stood in the doorway of the kitchen while I waited for the water to boil and gazed at the sleeping figure of my brother on the daybed in the living room, and beyond it at the closed door of the one bedroom where my parents slept. The frayed carpet on the floor was the carpet I had crawled over before I could walk. Each flower in the badly faded and worn design was sharply etched in my mind. Each piece of furniture in the cramped dim room seemed mildewed with a thousand double-edged memories. The ghosts of a thousand leaden meals hovered over the dining-room table. The dust of countless black-hearted days clung to every crevice of the squalid ugly furniture I had known since childhood. To walk out of it forever—not piecemeal, but completely—would give meaning to the wonder of what had happened to me, make success tangible, decisive. Moss Hart*

Economic constraints have their source in the overall cultural system as applied in social interaction. Thus family income is not a constraint *per se.* Family income acts to constrain housing adjustment when the cost of adequate housing (as culturally defined) is higher than the amount of money the family can afford to spend for housing. Thus, the norm against overexpenditure is often in conflict with the norms for space, tenure, structure type, quality, and neighborhood. The economic constraints discussed in this chapter include the costs of production, the costs of consumption, and the relationship of consumption expenditures to family income.

Housing prices have risen dramatically in the last few years, as has the cost of almost every other consumer good. The Consumer Price Index (1967 = 100) for May of 1976 was 169.2. The housing component of the index was slightly higher, at 175.6. The index of home ownership costs, including

* From *Act One,* by Moss Hart (New York: Random House, 1959), p. 437.

purchase price, mortgage interest, property taxes, and maintenance and repair was 189.6. The rental price index did not keep pace, at 143.8. Fuel and utilities were higher than the overall index, at 180.3. Thus, almost all housing costs have risen faster than overall consumer prices (USDL, 1976).

The home owners' costs reflect the higher interest rates that have prevailed and the increase in the price of new housing, as well. In 1967 the median purchase price of a new home insured under the FHA mortgage insurance program was $17,800. In 1975 the median price was $32,300 (USBC, 1976b, p. 14), an 81 percent increase. The median price of a new housing unit with a conventional mortgage was $26,600 in 1967 and $42,100 in 1975 (USBC, 1976a, p. 14), an increase of 58 percent.

Of course, the price of housing, like the price of almost any other consumer good, cannot be said to be expensive in any absolute sense. The price of housing must be evaluated in reference to the income distribution and cultural norms about how much income is properly devoted to housing expenditures.

INCOME AND HOUSING EXPENDITURES

A recent analysis (Bruce-Briggs, 1973) contends that the widespread idea that housing costs are rising so fast that a rising percentage of people are being "priced out of the market" is apparently incorrect. He asserts that the focus should be on the median value of all housing units, including existing housing units, in relation to the median family income, as presented in Table 12.

When the cost of housing relative to family income is viewed in this fashion, it can be seen that family income has kept pace with the value of owner-occupied housing and has exceeded the rise in the cost of rental units. Using the rule of thumb that a family can afford to buy a house that has a value that is twice their income, the median family in 1975 (and in all previous years except 1960) could afford to buy the median house. Two times their income is less than the median house price. They could easily afford the median monthly price of a rental unit. The median monthly contract rent each year is far less than 20 percent of the median monthly family income.

One problem with that analysis is that the median value of owner-occupied units should be compared with the median income of home owners and median rent with median income of renters. Another problem is that focusing just on median income, value, and rent fails to account for a variety of other factors. One factor is the relative dispersion of value and income. In 1974, 13 percent of the families in the United States had incomes less than $5000 (USBC, 1975b, p. 390). According to the rule of thumb, they would be able to afford a home valued at $10,000 or less. Only 10 percent of the housing units had a value of less than $10,000 (USBC, 1975b, p. 720). Thus, if the

TABLE 12 Median family income and its relation to median value and median rental fee, 1960–1975

Year	Median Family Income	2 times Median Family Income	Median Value Owner-Occupied Units	20% of Monthly Income	Median Monthly Rent
1960	$ 5,620	$11,240	$11,900	$ 94	$ 58
1970	$ 9,867	$19,734	$17,500	$164	$ 87
1971	$10,285	$20,570	$18,200	$171	$ 95
1972	$11,116	$22,232	$19,800	$185	$102
1973	$12,051	$24,102	$21,100	$201	$105
1974	$12,836	$25,672	$24,600	$214	$121
1975	$13,720	$27,440	$26,600	$229	$123

Sources. U.S. Bureau of the Census, *Statistical Abstract of the United States, 1975* (96th ed.) (Washington: U.S. Government Printing Office, 1975), p. 390 and p. 720; U.S. Bureau of the Census, *Statistical Abstract of the United States, 1972* (93rd ed.) (Washington: U.S. Government Printing Office, 1972), p. 390; U.S. Bureau of the Census, Vacancy Rates and Characteristics of Housing in the United States, Annual Statistics: 1975, *Current Housing Reports,* Series H 111-75-5 (Washington: U.S. Government Printing Office, 1976), p. 40; U.S. Bureau of the Census, Consumer Income, *Current Population Reports,* Series P-60, No. 103 (Washington: U.S. Government Printing Office, 1976), p. 1.

incomes and dwellings were matched up, 3 percent of the families in the United States would not be able to afford to purchase a housing unit. The small percentage represents over a million families, however. Most of them would rent, for 37 percent of the rental units rented for less than $100 in 1974 (USBC, 1975b, p. 720).

Tenure and structure-type norms could be met if the median family purchased the median house. There is no way to assess whether the housing would meet the space, quality, and neighborhood norms of the family. Finally, using the median value and median rental prices for all housing sidesteps the questions of whether such units are available for rent or purchase and where they can be found. There may be no housing in a given community that meets the norms and is within a specific family's price range.

The high cost of housing is constraining only when the cost of housing that would meet cultural and family norms is above the limit imposed by expenditure norms. The relationships between housing quality norms, housing expenditures norms, and minimum or basic quality norms were presented in Figure 5, Chapter 7. In that figure, it was shown that both minimum quality norms and ideal quality norms rise with income. However, minimum quality norms do not rise rapidly or reach a very high level. Ideal norms rise more rapidly and continue to rise longer.

The hypothesized relationship between income and actual expenditures presents a similar but not quite identical picture (Figure 16). The first and most striking characteristic of the figure is that at the very low levels of income, expenditures are below the level of minimum quality. Families at this level are spending less than would be required to obtain minimum shelter needs. Housing expenditures do not tend to rise with the first increases in income because food needs are met first. Low-income families would continue to increase expenditures on food, taking up nearly 100 percent of the increases in income at the very lowest levels (Warren, 1960; Zimmerman, 1936). After basic food needs are clearly met and perhaps clothing needs as well, expenditures on housing tend to rise rather rapidly with income. They level off when expenditures begin to approach the level implied in ideal quality norms for the given level of income. The relationships diagrammed in Figure 16 are hypothetical. They have only been partially tested with imperfect measurements. Nevertheless, some analysis of housing-income ratios in conjunction with norms provides considerable insight.

There are two parts to the interpretation of housing-income ratios. The first is the rise in expenditure (dollars spent) as income rises. The second is the decline in the percentage of income spent on housing as income rises. The first relates to the constraining effect of income. The second relates to the attainment of ideal quality norms.

The evidence that income is a constraining factor is shown by the fact that as income rises so do housing expenditures. Further, there are levels of income at which minimum quality norms are unattainable. If there were no constraining effect of income there would be no difference in the amount of

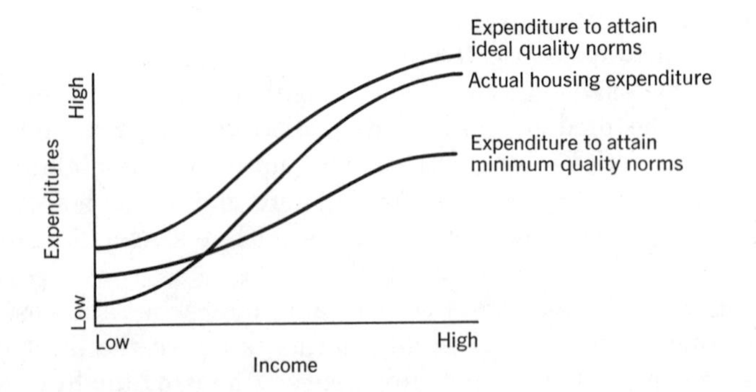

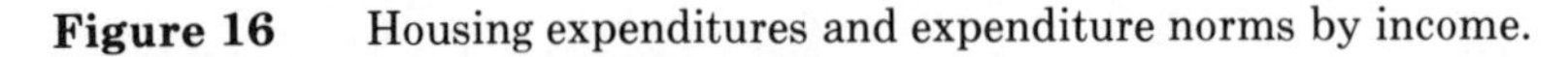
Figure 16 Housing expenditures and expenditure norms by income.

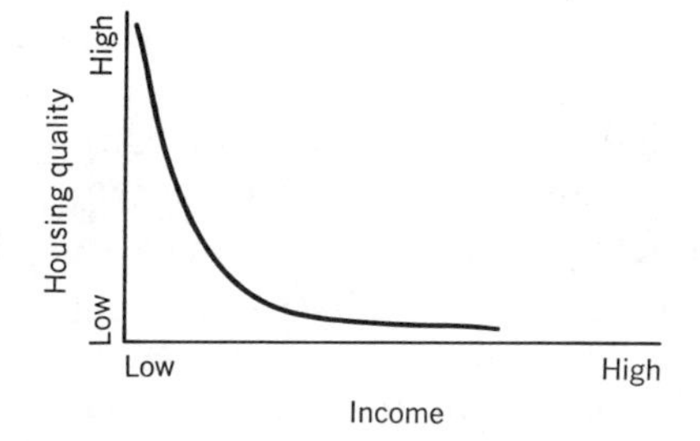

Figure 17 Percent of income spent on housing by income.

expenditures among income groups. Income is not completely constraining, however, because housing expenditures do not rise as rapidly as income. The fact that the percentage spent on housing declines with rising income can be seen to arise from the approaching congruence between ideal quality norms and actual quality as income rises to permit sufficient expenditure to attain ideal quality levels.

The relationship between housing expenditures and income was first analyzed by Ernst Engel (1895). He is reputed to have formulated three "laws." Engel's first law said that food expenditures rise with income, but at a slower rate. The second law stated that clothing expenditures rise continuously at the same rate as income. The third law stated that housing expenditures remained constant, regardless of income. Only the first has stood the test of time. The second and third laws were actually proposed not by Engel, but by Carroll Wright, Commissioner of Labor for Massachusetts in 1875 (Stigler, 1954, p. 99). Schwabe's law is an application to housing of Engel's first law. It states that housing expenditures rise with income but at a slower rate (Stigler, 1954).

Figure 17 shows the theoretical relationship between the *percentage* of income spent on housing and income. The decline is very rapid at the very low income levels because rises in income tend not to be applied to housing at all but to food and clothing. The percentage tends to fall less rapidly as income increases in the middle range. At some point in the upper-income range the percentage becomes very low and levels off as the percentage begins to approach zero.

Cross-sectional research has shown that the relationship between income and housing expenditures varies greatly. Factors influencing the relationship include regional markets, movements in housing prices, family size, and education of the head of household (Rapkin, 1957; Reid, 1962; Roistacher, 1974a). Cross-sectional research is not particularly useful for analyzing some of the important relationships between housing expenditures and income. In particular, cross-sectional data are inappropriate because *changes* in housing expenditures are hypothesized to result from *changes* in income. Because the responses to changes in income tend to be delayed by some families and anticipated by others, cross-sectional data can be very misleading. Factors associated with the timing of increases in income and housing expenditures cannot be captured in cross-sectional analysis. Longitudinal data are required to relate the changes to one another. Longitudinal studies are expensive, however, and have only been rarely undertaken. Moreover, there are enormous technical problems in gathering and analyzing longitudinal data.

Equally serious in both cross-sectional and longitudinal data are the measurement problems with income and housing expenditures. One difficulty in measuring housing expenditures lies in equating the expenditures of renters, owners who are making mortgage payments, and owners who have paid cash or who have paid off the mortgage. A typical approach has been to confine attention to renters or to renters and owners who are making mortgage payments. In the latter case, the relationship between income and housing expenditures is done for two separate groups, owners and renters.

In an analysis done in that matter, Roistacher (1974a) found that the expenditures on housing of home owners were above those of renters in every income class and by a substantial margin. There are three plausible explanations for such findings. First, a portion of home owners' expenditures represent investment. Some home owners have purchased with the expectation that the dwelling would appreciate in value. The family is willing to spend extra money each month with that in mind. Second, owner-occupied dwellings may be of higher quality than renter-occupied dwellings. Finally, people may be willing to pay more for a dwelling they own than they are for a rented dwelling of otherwise similar quality.

In light of housing norms, it seems that the last explanation is the most probable. Most families do not seek ownership because they expect it to be profitable. Rather, they seek it for its own sake, In this respect, owner-occupied dwellings are of higher quality than renter-occupied dwellings. The question of which costs more, rented or owned dwellings of equal quality (adjusted for the investment aspect of ownership) is an empirical question with complexities beyond the capabilities of current analysis.

Given what is currently known about the desire for ownership, however, it seems safe to assume that families are willing to pay extra simply for the right to own their own home, aside from any economic gain. Thus, home ownership appears to be a characteristic that is valued by most families and, of itself, gives rise to higher quality. Therefore, no analysis of income and housing expenditures is complete until the rise in quality is taken into account in the analysis of increases in expenditures that accompany the change in status from renter to owner as a response to increased income.

Analyses of housing-income ratios should deal with differences in income that result from differences in housing tenure. Family income should be measured by net income (Mirer, 1974). Net income corrects the amount of money income received to make it more comparable between renters and owners. The measure increases the home owner's income by the amount of imputed net rent (Mirer, 1974). Imputed net rent is the amount of rent that would have been received (after expenses) if the home owner were renting the home to someone else. The owning family is a *landlord,* renting the dwelling to itself. Thus, the rent that would have been paid to a landlord should be counted as housing expenditures. The net rent, which is gross rent minus expenses, should be counted as income. The effect would be to raise income slightly while making expenditures more directly comparable between owners and renters.

A final problem is the measurement of family income over a long time period. It appears that families make housing decisions with a concept of steady income, averaged over the years. They do not make decisions strictly in terms of present income which has been the only measure of income available in most cross-sectional surveys.

Friedman (1957), Reid (1962), and others have developed concepts such as "permanent income" to deal with the problem. However, the application of these theoretical constructs to empirical analyses of housing expenditures has been limited. Perhaps the actual average income received over a period of years just before or before and after the housing expenditures occurred would serve as such a measure. A longitudinal analysis of this type should find relationships similar to those depicted in Figure 17.

SUPPLY AND DEMAND

The price of housing depends upon the supply of and demand for housing. Supply and demand are theoretical constructs that provide an organized way to think about the many factors affecting the market price of housing. The idea of supply and demand relates to the marketplace, since it is there that the interaction between buyers and sellers results in a trade at a specific price. Thus, a convenient overview for the price of housing is (1) to note the factors that affect demand for housing, (2) to note the factors that affect the supply, and (3) to recognize that it is the interaction between supply and demand that results in the observed market price of housing.

Measurement of the supply of housing begins with knowledge of the number and quality of housing units in existence at a given time in a given locality (the housing stock). The measurement of the demand for housing begins with knowledge of the number and characteristics of the households that exist at a given time point in a given locality (the population of households). Those two sets of information are available only every ten years when the census data become available. In the United States there is a Census of Population and Housing taken every ten years in the years ending in zero. Between the census years the housing stock and the population of households must be estimated.

The estimation of the demand for housing is made additionally difficult because demand consists of only those households who are ready to buy or rent a different dwelling. This group of households includes people residing in other localities who are considering a move into the locality and potential households in the form of people considering formation of a separate household in the locality. Similarly, the actual supply of housing consists of the units vacant and available and those potentially vacant if a buyer were available. Thus, only a portion of the population of households and only a portion of the housing stock are involved in the demand for and supply of housing.

In the United States, the standard is one family per housing unit. Thus an increase in the number of new families without a corresponding increase in new housing units can be expected to result in a net increase in the demand for the existing housing, other things being equal. Demand is also a function of the amount of money families are willing to spend on housing. In times of high inflation, as in the past few years, even though the number of new families had been increasing (see Table 8, Chapter 6), the demand for new housing had not. Family belt tightening, coupled with tight money policies to curb inflation, contributed to a decline in the demand for new housing (Kaplan, 1974, p. 21; USBC, 1976a, p. 3). The demand for housing also depends upon the availability of mortgage money. New or existing housing is not sought unless money can be borrowed for its purchase. Housing production has been described as *counter-cyclical* (Smith, 1970, p. 124). When industrial growth and production are high

> *there generally is an expansion of capital investment which tends to increase the cost of money, in turn resulting in higher housing costs. When the economy starts down, the cost of money decreases and housing production tends to increase (PCUH, 1968, p. 127).*

Even the cost of housing maintenance depends on the supply in relation to the demand for labor and materials, as well as capital.

The cost of the components of housing services depends on supply and demand as well. The cost of utilities, for example, is directly related to the demand for petroleum products. The fuel shortage of the winter of 1973–74 was not felt in the consumer's utility bills until 1974–75. The eventual result of short supplies of petroleum was an increase in the cost of utilities. The demand for credit directly affects the price of financing, both for builders and for purchasers of housing units. The monetary policies of the federal government have a great impact upon the availability of money and financing terms for housing.

On the other hand, the supply of new housing depends upon the cost of important factors in its production. The number of units of new housing produced and made available at a given price depends upon the cost of labor, land, materials, and capital. The housing industry competes with other commercial and industrial uses for scarce land. It competes with other industry for labor and raw materials, and, more importantly, for capital investment money.

Thus an analysis of the price of housing requires a thorough analysis of the supply of land, labor, materials, and capital in relation to the demand for housing and other goods and services. Such an economic analysis, however, is extremely complex with regard to housing. It is often not particularly fruitful because of the myriad of factors which must be assumed, controlled, and predicted (Smith, 1970, pp. 97–98). For example, one of the basic assumptions of economic analysis is that all units on the supply side and all units on the demand side are exactly the same, an assumption that is difficult to defend in housing. Not all families are the same, nor are their preferences; and not all housing units are identical. At the least, the housing market is segmented by tenure, size of units, and location.

It is recognized that a comprehensive economic analysis of the supply of and demand for housing is appropriate and helpful as an overview approach to the price of housing. However, such an analysis will not be further undertaken here. Rather, the ensuing discussion will focus on a description of the components of production costs and occupancy costs, their changes in recent years, and factors contributing to the changes.

PRODUCTION COSTS

The basic components of the costs of production include the prices of

1. The unimproved land.
2. Servicing the land (clearing, grading, providing access, water, sewer, other utility connections, and proper drainage).
3. Building materials.
4. Wages for craftsmen and laborers.
5. Financing.
6. Marketing.
7. Administration and profit.

Such costs vary widely according to the area of the country, location and characteristics of the site, and builder efficiency. Data assembled by the

National Commission on Urban Problems indicated that construction costs (materials and labor) vary from less than 50 percent of the cost to more than 75 percent of the cost of producing single-family dwellings. Land acquisition and servicing ranges from 10 percent to 30 percent of the cost while the other costs (marketing, financing, overhead, and profit) ranged from 16 to 26 percent of the costs (NCUP, 1968, pp. 418–19). Estimates by the President's Committee on Urban Housing yielded similar results: 25 percent for land, 55 percent for construction, and 20 percent for other expenses (PCUH, 1968, p. 118).

The components of cost are the same for multifamily housing. However, the percentages of the total costs vary widely, depending upon the type of structure (low-rise, high-rise) and its location and amenities (walk-up or elevator, for example) (NCUP, 1968, p. 420). The President's Committee on Urban Housing estimated that, for a unit in an elevator structure, the land costs would be 13 percent of the total cost, with construction 60 percent and other expenses 27 percent (PCUH, 1968, p. 118). The lower land cost per unit of multifamily housing, as opposed to single-family housing, is a reflection of the larger number of units per acre, even though the per-acre cost of the land might be higher.

Such estimates, calculated several years ago, are only rough guidelines for comparison. There is no particular reason to believe that the relative proportion of the cost devoted to each component has changed greatly. The relationships among the components are essential to keep in mind while discussing each element individually. A large change in just one of the elements only affects a small proportion of the final price of the building and can be offset by changes in the other elements. A decrease in the cost of onsite labor, for example, resulting from the use of factory-built components, could be more than totally offset by a rise in land prices.

Land Costs

The fastest growing component of the cost of new housing had been the cost of land acquisition and site improvement. The rise in costs seems to have leveled off somewhat in recent years. The decline in the increase in land costs is probably related at least in part to the decline in the demand for new housing and the corresponding decline in housing starts (USBC, 1976a, p. 3).

Between 1958 and 1966 the average price of the land for homes insured under the FHA mortgage insurance program rose from $2223 to $3544, an increase of 61 percent (Eaves, 1969, p. 53). During the same period, the Consumer Price Index rose 13 percent (HUD, 1969b, p. 29). In 1969 the median price of an improved lot for a new home was $4300, while the median price of an improved lot was $5800 in 1974 (USBC, 1975a, p. 102), an increase of 35 percent. During that same period the Consumer Price Index rose 36 percent (USBC, 1975b, p. 422).

During the five-year period between 1969 and 1974, the percent of the sales price of new one-family homes that was devoted to land costs decreased, from 17.1 percent in 1969 to 16.0 percent in 1974. That decrease reflects a rise in the cost of the material and labor for the dwelling, and a rise in the number of appliances included in the sales price. It does not include an increase in the size of the dwelling. The median square feet in new one-family homes decreased, from 1585 square feet in 1969 to 1565 square feet in 1974 (USBC, 1975a, p. 103).

Several factors are responsible for the rising cost of land. The price of unimproved land, the cost of the improvements prior to construction, and the amount of land per unit of housing are all components of land cost (PCUH, 1968, p. 140). The price of unimproved land depends upon the relation between supply and demand. As might be expected, demand is highest in the areas experiencing the most rapid population growth. Given the nature of land, demand and supply factors are heavily influenced by distance. Not everyone can build in the center of the city or in a given suburban area. Thus the price of land tends to decline with distance from the most desirable centers, or, more correctly, rises as the distance from prime locations decreases.

The cost of site improvement is directly related to the costs of materials and labor. They are indirectly related to standards required by zoning ordinances and subdivision regulations. The development standards in zoning laws and subdivision regulations are more or less imperfect formalizations of norms (family, community, and cultural). Such norms are enduring and important and probably would be enforced informally by groups of American families in the absence of zoning and subdivision regulations. Aspects of the standards in some communities, however, specify levels of development well above those prescribed by the norms. Zoning regulations often specify minimum lot sizes even larger than those prescribed by middle-class ideals. Subdivision regulations may specify standards for site development above those necessary for health and safety. Such standards can add appreciably to the cost of the serviced lot. Because such regulations are often used to exclude low-income families in general and low-income black families in particular, they will be discussed more fully in Chapter 13.

Building Materials and Labor

The costs of building materials, along with the wages paid construction workers have been rising in recent years (Table 13). As could be expected, the Boekch Index for Small Residential Buildings, which reflects increases in the cost of both materials and labor, has also risen in recent years, but at a decreasing rate (Table 13). The price index for new one-family homes sold has also increased. Recent increases in the sales prices reflect past increases in materials, labor, and land costs. The impact of current wholesale prices of

TABLE 13 Indexes of wholesale prices, hourly wage rates, construction costs, and price of new one-family homes sold, 1955–1975 (1967 = 100)

Item	1955	1960	1965	1970	1972	1974	1975
Douglas fir	97.5	89.3	92.3	108.8	161.1	213.7	212.0
Millwork	87.7	93.1	96.0	116.0	128.4	157.1	160.4
Plywood	120.4	109.6	103.5	108.5	130.7	161.1	161.2
Paint	82.1	92.1	96.4	112.4	118.0	145.7	166.9
Plumbing fixtures, brass fittings	88.7	93.3	93.3	112.5	119.7	149.1	162.3
Heating equipment	102.5	105.8	98.9	110.6	118.2	135.0	150.7
Window glass	78.3	80.5	94.3	116.1	128.2	158.4	177.7
Concrete products	88.0	97.2	96.3	112.2	125.6	151.7	170.5
Asphalt roofing	96.3	97.4	98.7	102.9	131.2	196.0	225.9
Gypsum products	90.9	99.1	101.2	100.0	114.7	137.6	144.0
Hourly wage rates, all trades	60.0	75.4	90.9	128.8	153.2	(NA)	(NA)
Boekch Index for Small Residential Structures	72.5	81.8	90.4	122.4	145.8	172.0	183.5
Price index of new one family houses sold	(NA)	(NA)	93.2	117.4	131.0	158.1	174.1

Sources. U.S. Department of Housing and Urban Development, *1972 HUD Statistical Yearbook* (Washington: U.S. Government Printing Office, 1974), pp. 356–357; U.S. Department of Labor, Bureau of Labor Statistics, *Wholesale Prices and Price Indexes, December 1973* (Washington: Author); U.S. Bureau of the Census, *Statistical Abstract of the United States, 1975* (96th ed.) (Washington: U.S. Government Printing Office, 1975), p. 708; U.S. Department of Housing and Urban Development, *Housing and Urban Development Trends,* December 1975 (Washington: Author), pp. 18–20; p. 22; U.S. Bureau of the Census, Price Index of New One-Family Houses Sold, Fourth Quarter 1975, *Construction Reports,* Series C-27 (Washington: U.S. Government Printing Office, 1976), p. 2.

building materials in particular, and wages to some extent, may not be felt for some time. There is a time lag between purchase of raw materials and housing components and the marketing of a new dwelling.

The most notable increases in the price of materials have occurred in the price of major components of conventionally-constructed housing: Douglas fir, plywood, millwork, paint, and asphalt roofing. Douglas fir and asphalt roofing, in particular, have more than doubled in price since 1965 (Table 13).

Reasons for such extreme increases in lumber costs are numerous. They seem to be related to an increase in foreign lumber exports, snowstorms that hampered logging operations (Joiner, 1970), and the dramatic increase in housing starts experienced in 1972, which increased the demand for lumber. The decline in housing starts (USBC, 1976a), as well as the cooling of the economy from the high inflation rates of the early 1970s, undoubtedly contributed to the small decline between 1974 and 1975. The rise in the cost of asphalt roofing and paint can be directly attributed to increases in the cost of petroleum.

Between 1958 and 1966, the wages of workers in the building trades rose 37 percent (Eaves, 1969, p. 52). Between 1967 and 1972, wages in the building trades of skilled and unskilled workers rose 53.2 percent (Table 13). During a similar time period, the *percentage* of the cost of new construction attributable to the cost of labor declined from 33 percent of the total cost, in 1949, to 18 percent of the total cost in 1969 (Joiner, 1970; Goldfinger, 1970). Thus, onsite labor prices rose, as could be expected. But their importance in contributing to the increase in the price of new housing declined (Behman and Codella, 1971). Reasons for the decline are twofold. First, the prices of other elements, particularly land and financing, increased more rapidly than the price of labor. Second, more and more components of new housing units are factory-produced, reducing the need for onsite labor while increasing the input of lower-cost factory labor.

More recent data regarding the relative increases in wage rates are not available. The best guess is that wage rates would lag behind increases in the Consumer Price Index and the Wholesale Price Index. As new contracts are negotiated, many having cost-of-living clauses tied to increases in the Consumer Price Index, the wage rates will catch up.

Other Costs of Housing Production

With the exception of financing costs, changes in the other costs of housing production (marketing, overhead, and profit) are less readily specified. Profits may rise when demand for housing is high, but there is no necessary connection between trends in supply and demand and the level of profits. In general, it would seem to be easier for builders, materials manufacturers, developers, and so on, to raise profits when demand is rising and in inflationary times. Marketing costs and overhead have increased relative to increases in labor and capital costs in other sectors of the economy. Any trend toward more advertising by sellers adds to marketing costs without contributing importantly to the quality of housing available.

THE COSTS OF HOUSING CONSUMPTION

With a few exceptions, the components of the costs of the consumption of housing services are the same, whether the unit is rented or owned (including cooperative and condominium forms of ownership). The components include debt retirement, taxes, insurance, utilities, and maintenance. The tenant pays some, if not all, costs through a single payment, his rent, while the owner may pay the costs through individual payments for each item. An additional cost that the tenant must pay is a management fee, including salaries for management personnel and a return on the owner's investment (NCUP, 1968, p. 417). Only in cooperatives and condominiums do home owners routinely pay management fees or assessments. There are also management costs to the home owner, particularly in terms of time.

Contract rent, the amount of rent agreed upon between landlord and tenant, almost universally includes a portion to cover property taxes and all other taxes paid by the landlord's business as well as fees for management and profit. In addition, of course, contract rent may include utilities and other items. Gross rent includes the contract rent plus housing expenditures not paid in the rent payment to the landlord.

In addition to being paid in a different manner, the individual costs of housing consumption as a percentage of the total monthly outlay vary with tenure. The President's Committee on Urban Housing estimated that property taxes account for 26 percent of the monthly housing cost for a single-family home and 14 percent for a multifamily elevator structure (PCUH, 1968, p. 118). Part of the difference concerns the inclusion of profit and a management fee in the costs of an elevator structure. Including these as costs effectively makes the percentage spent on taxes appear to be smaller than it is because a larger total is used as the base. Finally, the effect on the household's overall financial position varies with tenure of occupancy. Ownership includes the accumulation of savings as equity in the property increases, if its market value does not decline.

Thus, while the costs of housing consumption on a monthly basis contain the same components, they may not provide an accurate picture of the long-range returns. For most families, however, the monthly outlays (including forced savings for home owners) are the crucial factors in housing adjustment. They represent the degree to which income constraints must be overcome.

Debt Retirement

Debt retirement is the monthly payment on the principal plus the interest charges. Thus it varies with the terms of the mortgage. Few people can afford to pay cash for a dwelling. Therefore most single-family owner-occupied homes are purchased by borrowing money against the value of the house.

The amount to be borrowed depends upon the sales price of the dwelling unit and the size of the down payment. For new construction, the sales price is most directly related to the cost of producing the unit. For existing housing, however, the price is dependent upon the desirability of the location of the unit and its state of maintenance and repair, as well as the overall demand relative to supply (Beyer, 1965, p. 133).

The size of the down payment markedly affects the monthly outlay for an owner-occupied dwelling and the total interest paid over the term of the mortgage, as shown in Table 14(a). A larger down payment appreciably lowers the monthly debt retirement and the total amount of interest paid. The repayment period also affects the monthly payments and the total amount of interest paid (Table 14(b)). A longer repayment period lowers the monthly outlay during the period but increases the total amount of interest paid.

At the present time, the largest factor in the differential cost of debt retirement is the interest rate, as shown in Table 14(c). The higher the interest rate, the higher the monthly payment and the greater the amount of interest paid over the period of the loan.

Interest rates on conventional mortgages (not insured by FHA or VA) for existing single-family homes for all types of lending institutions reached a high of 9.39 percent at the end of 1974. The rate fell a little during 1975, but by the end of the year it was back to 9.10 percent (HUD, 1975a, p. 30). The interest rates for conventional mortgages on newly constructed homes showed a similar pattern but did not reach levels that were quite as high. At the end of 1974 the average interest rate for newly constructed homes was 9.13 percent. It fell during 1975, but had risen to 8.76 percent by the end of 1975 (HUD, 1975a, p. 29). The increase in interest rates coupled with the increase in property taxes and maintenance costs raised the costs of home ownership to an all-time high during 1976, according to the shelter component of the Consumer Price Index (USDL, 1976).

Property Taxes

After debt retirement, the largest item is the property tax (PCUH, 1968, p. 118). Such taxes are levied by local governmental units—school boards, townships, counties, and municipalities—against the value of real property. Schools, police departments, fire departments, recreation facilities, etc., are all at least partially supported by property tax revenues. At one time, property taxes were the major source of revenue of local governments. Since the mid-fifties, however, property tax revenue has provided less than half of

TABLE 14 (a) The effect of the size of the down payment on the cost of a $30,000 home, 9 percent interest

Down pay-ment	Monthly Payment			Total Interest		
	20 years	25 years	30 years	20 years	25 years	30 years
$0	$270	$252	$242	$34,800	$45,600	$57,120
1,000	261	243	233	33,640	43,900	54,880
2,000	252	235	225	32,480	42,500	53,000
3,000	243	227	217	31,320	41,100	51,120
4,000	234	218	209	30,160	39,400	49,240
5,000	225	210	201	29,000	38,000	47,360
10,000	180	168	161	23,200	30,400	37,960

(b) The effect of the repayment period on the cost of a $30,000 loan, 9 percent interest

Payment Period	Monthly Payment	Total Interest
5 years	$623	$7,380
10 years	380	15,600
15 years	304	24,720
20 years	270	34,800
25 years	252	45,600
30 years	242	57,120

(c) The effect of the interest rate on the cost of a $30,000 loan, 25-year repayment period

Interest Rate	Monthly Payment	Total Interest
6 percent	$194	$28,200
6½ percent	203	30,900
7 percent	212	33,600
7½ percent	222	36,600
8 percent	232	39,600
8½ percent	242	42,600
9 percent	252	45,600
9½ percent	262	48,600
10 percent	273	51,900

Source. Dennison Interest and Mortgage Tables (Vest-Pocket, 1968), pp. 4–17.

the money used for local governmental operation (Netzer, 1968; USBC, 1973a).

The local nature of the property tax makes accurate and up-to-date statistics difficult to obtain. The latest Census of Governments (USBC, 1973a, p. 3) indicates that about 40 percent of the revenue used by all local governments comes from the property tax. There are wide variations in the percentage contribution of property taxes according to region and municipality (Netzer, 1968, pp. 6–7). Property taxes account for 45 percent of all revenues in the Northeast and only about 30 percent in the South (USBC, 1973a).

The amount of property tax paid by each property owner typically is based on the assessed value of the property (some percentage of the market value, as determined by a local tax assessor) and the tax rate set by the municipality. The latter may vary from year to year, depending on the total assessed value of all taxed properties in the community and the revenue needed for the operation of the local government. New development that adds to the tax base but does not require additional community expenditures in terms of fire or police protection, or education and recreation facilities is usually welcomed by the community. Revenues can increase without a corresponding increase in local governmental expenses.

Property taxes have risen in the past few years in response to the financial crisis of local government. That crisis has been only partially eased by revenue sharing and state and local sales and income taxes. Costs for municipal services have risen, usually without a corresponding increase in the number of taxable properties. As a consequence, tax rates have been pushed upwards, and the property owner is faced with a higher tax bill.

Again, the local nature of property taxes makes obtaining statistics about changes in them quite difficult. One figure that is useful is the effective tax rate, calculated in the Census of Governments (USBC, 1973a, p. 16). The effective tax rate for a locality is the total tax paid by properties that change hands in that locality in a given time period divided by the sales prices of those properties. This rate has been derived to offset differences in assessment practices to facilitate comparisons. The Census of Governments reported in 1972 that there were 11 cities with effective rates over 4 percent, while in 1966 there were only 2. Similar increases can be found at the lower effective rates as well.

Utility Costs

As could be expected, the fuel shortage of the winter of 1973–74 and the consequent increases in foreign oil prices have led to increases in the cost of utilities. In fact, the cost of utilities has been subject to the greatest increases in recent years among all housing costs. Utilities are subject to government regulation, and increases in prices are accomplished more deliberately than increases in other cost items. Nevertheless, by the mid-seventies the fuel and utilities portion of the Consumer Price Index was the second fastest rising component of the shelter index (USDL, 1976). Only the home ownership part of the index, which includes property tax, insurance, and maintenance costs, was higher.

Other Costs

The cost of property insurance and maintenance costs have also increased, as evidenced by the rise in the home ownership index. The reasons for the rise in insurance costs can be traced directly to the rise in house values. As property insurers have sought to keep pace with replacement costs, premiums have been raised.

The rise in maintenance costs can be traced to the rise in materials and labor. It would appear that maintenance costs are rising more slowly than some other factors. Maintenance, of course, can be deferred and can be done with the substitution of the landlord's or home owner's time for money.

HOUSING COSTS: A SUMMARY

The cost of housing production rose faster than the rate of inflation during the late sixties and early seventies. It has since leveled off somewhat because of the decrease in demand. The rising price of new housing was due in part to the general state of the economy. It was exacerbated, however, by the upward trend in family formation, a result of high birth rates from 1945 to 1960. New homes constructed seem to be concentrated in the higher cost brackets (USBC, 1976b), likely a reflection of rising incomes. Upper-income families are seeking higher-quality, more expensive housing. Lower-income families, of course, continue to be limited to the purchase of existing homes or to rental.

The best prospects for lower housing prices (barring a severe economic recession) may even be 20 years away. A decline in new family formation (related, of course, to the decline in the birth rate, beginning around 1960) could result in a surplus of housing relative to demand. Whether or not such housing will meet the norms prevailing then depends on a variety of factors. Such factors include economic conditions and technological and environmental changes that occur between now and then. In the meantime, without governmental intervention, many families will be forced to compromise their norms and accept a reduction in satisfaction. Normative housing is simply priced out of the range of their incomes. The proportion of such families in the population is probably smaller than the comparison of median income and median new dwelling prices would suggest, however.

The prospects for decreases in the costs of housing consumption are not as bright. Utilities and property taxes can be expected to continue to rise. As they do, the costs of housing consumption aside from the mortgage or rent payment can be expected to take an ever-increasing proportion of the amount spent on housing.

DEFINITIONS

Assessed value. The estimated value of real estate for purposes of taxation; often measured by "rule-of-thumb" techniques and open to inequities because of such shortcuts and because of a lack of mechanisms for reappraisal when the value of the land or buildings rises.

Contract rent. The amount to be paid in rent to the landlord each payment period, often monthly. It may or may not include utilities and other items as well as the actual rental fee.

Conventional mortgage. Any mortgage financed by a commercial bank, a savings and loan institution, a credit union, or other private source without government or private insurance or guarantee.

Gross rent. Contract rent plus housing expenditures not paid in the rent payment.

Housing demand. The total number of households or potential households (people considering marriage, divorce, or otherwise forming a new household) interested in renting or buying a dwelling unit.

Housing-income ratio. The relationship between housing expenditures and income; the percentage of income spent on housing; house value divided by income.

Housing production. The production of new housing units; the number of new dwelling units constructed within a given time period; creation of the housing supply.

Housing supply. Total number of dwelling units available for rent or for sale.

Mortgage money. Funds available for borrowing through mortgages; usually from commercial banks, savings and loan institutions, life insurance companies, but also from individuals.

Principal. The amount of money still owed on the mortgage; the balance at any particular moment.

Property insurance. Insurance against fire, hail, wind damage, and other disasters that the home owner carries on the dwelling and other structures on the property; insurance on the contents of the dwelling and against liability claims may be included. Usually a lending institution will not grant a mortgage loan unless there is a certain amount of property insurance obtained by the home owner.

Purchase price. The sale price of a dwelling agreed upon between buyer and seller.

Site improvements. Development of unimproved land prior to and in preparation for construction. Installation of sewers and utilities, grading and filling, tree removal, the construction of streets, and the like may be necessary. Subdivision of tracts is part of site improvement; hence subdivision regulations may regulate such activities.

Subdivision regulations. Police power measures enacted by a municipality that regulate the division and preparation of unimproved land prior to the construction of housing units. Often covered are detailed standards for street construction, utility installation, and the layout of lots.

Tax base. The total assessed value of all taxable property within a community; community land and improvements open to taxation.

Tax rate. The amount of taxes levied annually per $1000 assessed valuation.

Wholesale Price Index. A method of making price comparisons at the wholesale level in order to observe the effect of inflation; the ratio between the price of the same goods in two or more different years. If the price is $2.00 in 1977 and it is $2.10 in 1978 for the same quantity and quality, the index is 105 which means the price rose 5 percent. Price indexes for a series of years, all compared with the same base year, can be directly compared.

Chapter 13
Racial-Ethnic and Sexual Constraints

> Well—I don't understand why you people are reacting this way. What do you think you are going to gain by moving into a neighborhood where you just aren't wanted and where some elements—well—people can get awful worked up when they feel that their whole way of life and everything they've ever worked for is threatened. Lorraine Hansberry*

Like family income, race and ethnicity constrain housing adjustment only in a society like the United States that defines one or more classes of people as undesirable. The presence of "inferior" minorities is viewed as detrimental to the neighborhood by the majority. To be black, Puerto Rican, Mexican-American, Jewish, Italian, Oriental, etc., in the United States often means encountering problems in obtaining housing, regardless of income or social class. One can, of course, conceive of a culture in which the reverse could be true. To be white would mean experiencing discrimination in the search for a suitable dwelling.

Sex of the household head only acts as a constraint in a society in which women, regardless of income or social status, have been viewed by the purveyors of housing (landlords, real estate brokers, lending institutions, and builders) as undesirable neighbors or tenants or poor credit risks. Again, one could conceive of a society in which men would be the target of such discrimination. The racial-ethnic constraints discussed in this chapter include discrimination and the availability of housing for racial and ethnic minorities. The sexual constraints involve discrimination against women and, in particular, women who are heads of families.

Minority families including blacks, Puerto Ricans, Mexican-Americans, face more problems, than white families in adjusting their housing to achieve housing norms. As discussed in Chapter 15, their actual housing conditions are likely to be poorer than those enjoyed by whites in the same income class. Although there are some exceptions (Lapham, 1971), most studies of cost differentials between blacks and whites indicate that blacks pay more for the

* From *A Rasin in the Sun,* by Lorraine Hansberry Act 2, Scene 3 (New York: Random House, 1959), p. 107.

same size and quality of housing (Kain and Quigley, 1970; Muth, 1969, p. 284; King and Mieszkowski, 1973). Blacks get less housing for the same money (Rapkin, 1966; Duncan and Hauser, 1960, pp. 184–211). Additionally, blacks are more often limited to the rental housing market, rather than being able to own their housing (Kain and Quigley, 1972; Roistacher, 1974a).

The differences in the housing conditions of female-headed households have not been as rigorously researched as have been those of minority groups. What evidence there is suggests that female-headed households are less likely to be owners (Morris and Winter, 1976b; USBC, 1973c, p. 1 and p. 10). They are likely to live in housing with lower monthly rent or lower market value than their male counterparts (USBC, 1973c, pp. 1–10). Their dwellings are likely to be smaller than those of male-headed households with similar size and composition (USBC, 1973f, pp. 7–11). They are less likely to fulfill their plans for housing adjustment (Duncan and Newman, 1975).

The source of these problems seems to be the constraints imposed on minority families and female-headed households by the society. The constraints have both direct and indirect effects on the housing adjustment process. Limited income, for example, may, over the generations, produce feelings of hopelessness and alienation. Such feelings might reduce the family's effectiveness in solving their housing problems. As families are constantly forced to deal with the problems of economic deprivation and discrimination in employment and education, as well as housing, family functioning may become impaired (Moynihan, 1965; Clark, 1965).

A female-headed household may have more difficulty dealing with housing adjustment because there can be little role specialization. The single parent must deal with all of the problems associated with attaining normative housing, as well as all the other problems of household management. The indirect role of extrafamilial constraints is recognized, but not discussed at length, in this chapter. Rather, the discussion focuses on the direct effects of the constraints that prevent minority families and female-headed households from achieving normative housing conditions.

The direct constraints can be divided into two classes: structural constraints and interactional constraints. Structural constraints limit the availability of housing to a minority group and women, not because of minority status or sex, but because the social or economic structure imposes other limits on the group. If blacks and women, on the average, have lower incomes than whites and men (that is, the economic *structure* favors whites and men), then blacks and women will, on the average, be less able to afford housing that meets the norms. Structural constraints, therefore, are not direct expressions of racial or sex prejudice or discrimination in housing. They may, of course, be the result of discrimination in other areas. Discrimination in education and employment, for example, has kept blacks and women in low-paying unskilled jobs. Structural constraints are achieved primarily through an array of institutional measures, such as zoning, subdivision regulations and federal urban renewal and public housing programs, and the practices of lending institutions.

Interactional constraints, in contrast, limit the supply of housing available to minority families and female-headed households through direct discrimination. The interactional constraints are achieved primarily through the actions of other families, real estate brokers, the agents of lending institutions, and the federal government. The distinctions between the two types of constraints are by no means clear-cut. For example, real estate brokers are mostly white men and are relatively unavailable to blacks and unsympathetic to women. The distinction between structural and interactional constraints will be maintained as much as possible throughout the following discussion, however.

STRUCTURAL CONSTRAINTS

Structural constraints limit the supply of housing to certain classes of people. Black families, Mexican-American families, and Puerto Rican families are affected more often than white families by structural constraints. A higher proportion of minority families than white families have low incomes (USBC, 1973h, pp. 3–7). Female-headed households, as a class, have far lower median incomes than male-headed households (USBC, 1973g, p. 873).

There is little inexpensive housing in the private market. There may, in fact, be no normative housing in the private market that is inexpensive. As noted in Chapter 12, the costs of construction of new housing units are rising because of increases in the costs of materials, labor, land, and financing. Such costs alone provide restrictions for an increasingly higher-income group, not just low-income families.

Further restrictions are imposed by communities seeking to raise the cost of housing, renew their central business districts, or maintain segregation. Lending institutions trying to protect their investments also impose restrictions. When a community decides to institute an urban renewal project, the structure of the racial distribution by neighborhood penalizes the minorities and women to a greater extent. Blacks and other minorities and female-headed households more frequently live in older neighborhoods. When a bank decides not to lend money in older areas, blacks and women are structurally barred from the supply of mortgage money to a greater extent than whites and men.

Exclusionary Use of Police Power Measures

Zoning ordinances, subdivision regulations, building codes, and housing codes are ordinances enacted by local govenments. These measures are based on the "police power" of the local community to enact laws to protect the health, welfare, and safety of its citizens.

A zoning ordinance divides the community into zones according to permitted land use. The regulations specify the land uses permitted in each zone (residential, commercial, industrial, etc.). They also specify the intensity of land use and the minimum standards permitted in each zone. Exclusionary zoning practices are often known as "fiscal zoning" (NCUP, 1968, p. 212). They are promulgated for the specific purpose of adding more to the community property tax revenues (the major source of funds for many communities) than would be required in expenditures for an increase in public services (Brooks, 1970; NCUP, 1968, pp. 212–14). They also are for the more general purpose of "protecting the character" of the residential environment (Babcock, 1969; NCUP, 1968, p. 214). Regardless of intent, the outcome is the same. Low-income families are limited to the existing supply of low-cost housing (typically the slums). Or they may be excluded altogether if there is no such housing in the community.

One of the basic tools of fiscal zoning is the specific exclusion of multifamily dwellings and mobile homes, often structure types that are generally lower in monthly occupancy costs than conventional single-family dwellings (NCUP, 1968, pp. 215–16). Other tools are large lot zoning and minimum floor space requirements. Large lot zoning is perhaps the most common practice. It has also drawn the heaviest fire from groups wishing to "open up the suburbs" to low-income and minority residents (Brooks, 1970). Not only is future development often limited to single-family conventionally-constructed housing, but, typically, such housing must be located on large lots, usually of one acre or more.

The effects of large lot zoning on the cost of housing are difficult to isolate from the effects of other factors. The National Commission on Urban Problems indicates that the cost of housing is increased because the supply of land for new development is limited in relation to the demand. Further, larger lot sizes encourage the building of even larger houses. In addition, larger lots cost more to service because of longer transmission lines, sewer and water pipes, and related factors (NCUP, 1968, pp. 213–14).

A more powerful tool for excluding low-income families, although not as widely abused, is the establishment of minimum floor space requirements (NCUP, 1968, pp. 215–16). In addition to automatically barring single-wide mobile homes, the imposition of excessive space requirements can *directly* affect the cost of new housing. It does not depend upon the *indirect* relationship between lot size and house size. A recent study (Sagalyn and Sternlieb, 1973) found that the most important factor influencing the cost of new housing in New Jersey was the size of the unit. Although dwelling size was related to the lot size, it proved to be a better predictor of house price than lot size.

Subdivision regulations are the standards imposed by a community on all new land subdivision. They detail the standards for the streets to be constructed, the amount of land to be dedicated to the community, the standards for sewer and water facilities, requirements for the division of the area into individual lots, etc. The effect of variation in subdivision regulations on the cost of housing is controversial. Sagalyn and Sternlieb (1973) found that the effect of differential subdivision regulations was insignificant. The National Commission on Urban Problems indicates that requiring unusually high standards for site improvements can appreciably raise the cost of housing. Such standards increase the cost to the developer of servicing the unimproved land preparatory to construction of housing (NCUP, 1968, p. 216 and pp. 423–34).

Building codes specify the materials and techniques to be used in new construction. Housing codes establish minimum standards that must be met by all habitable buildings in the community. Both are ordinances that have drawn fire (see e.g., Downs, 1973, p. 3) for prohibiting the construction and occupancy of low-cost housing. Thus low-income families are priced out of the housing market. Such criticism may be justified for building codes. They have been attacked for prohibiting new techniques and materials, thus protecting the jobs of trade union members rather than the citizens of the community (NCUP, 1968, pp. 254–66 and pp. 465–77).

The criticism of housing codes is probably unjustified, however, except in the case of a code with very high standards (an unlikely occurrence). Most housing codes set forth minimum standards that are seldom above the minimal definition of housing. These codes do not approach the level of a description of normative housing (NCUP, 1968, pp. 273–95). Perhaps the most serious criticism that can be made of housing codes is that they are seldom enforced. They tend to be very lenient in their provisions and very sporadically enforced, apparently to avoid requiring landlords to meet high standards. Discontinuance of a housing code might mean that families could live in lower-quality housing without violating the laws of the community. They would still not live in normative housing, however. Most people would be totally unaffected by repeal on housing codes. The codes are virtually never enforced. Therefore their existence has no effect. The poor enforcement of housing codes permits the continuation of substandard housing, thus permitting the existence of very low-rent housing.

In the absence of building codes, it is unlikely that bubbles, domes, yurts, plastic houses, and the like would proliferate. New techniques and materials might be used in conventionally-constructed housing, perhaps lowering its costs slightly, if building codes were not enforced or abolished. The informal norms clearly prescribe conventionally-constructed housing, however. The case against building and housing codes as tools for discriminating against low-income families is thus not as clear-cut as the case against zoning and subdivision regulations.

Urban Renewal and Public Housing

Public housing and urban renewal, both federally funded programs administered at the local level, have contributed to discrimination against low-income families. The 1949 Housing Act, recognized as the inception of urban renewal, clearly specified that its primary purpose was improved housing for low-income families. Slum clearance, attracting the middle-class back to the city, raising the tax base, and a myriad of other purposes have, at times, seemed to assume major importance, however. The Federal agency administering the program generally reacted with regulations that required that residential improvement be paramount (NCUP, 1968, pp. 152–53).

Nevertheless, the urban renewal program has destroyed more housing (presumably low-quality housing) than it has created. Much of the new housing built on urban renewal sites has been luxury apartment buildings rather than low-cost housing for poor families. Relocation of families displaced from urban renewal sites has had mixed results. Many displaced families simply moved to a nearby slum. The general trend has been to raise the prices of existing low-cost housing because of the reduced supply (NCUP, 1968, pp. 152–69).

The public housing program, often providing the only affordable housing for low-income families, has not supplied enough units to house all eligible families, or even a fraction thereof. The units that have been constructed have often been contained in massive high-rise buildings in central city slums. Thus the occupants are identified as the bottom of the American class structure. Segregation has also been promoted by building in black neighborhoods. While providing structurally sound housing with plumbing facilities, the public housing program failed to reduce the ownership, structure-type, and neighborhood deficits of poor families.

Although neither program is discussed in detail in this book, there have been excellent analyses elsewhere (Aaron, 1972; Wilson, 1967; Taggart, 1970). It is clear that urban renewal created more problems for poor families than it alleviated. Public housing provided affordable, but clearly nonnormative, housing units for low-income families. Because of the high proportion of blacks among the displaced, urban renewal was often termed "Negro removal" (Weaver, 1964, p. 55). Public housing, through its design and location, served to increase both segregation and the stigma of being poor (Friedman, 1968, p. 123).

Redlining

Redlining refers to the practice of designating certain areas as poor risks. Lending institutions refuse to lend money within the area (presumably by drawing a red pencil line around the area on a map). The practice also applies to refusals to issue fire insurance on properties within the area. It has been perpetrated by lending institutions in conjunction with fire underwriters and the Federal Housing Administration. Collusion among the three groups has made it impossible to place the blame for the practice. Both white and black property owners in the area equally are hurt. Yet the preponderance of black residents in many such areas usually means that the policy, in effect, becomes one of racial discrimination (Forman, 1971, p. 68). Redlining is often defended on the grounds that it protects the investment of the lending institution and its depositors. Yet the implementation of redlining has become a self-fulfilling prophecy. Without home improvement loans and mortgage loans, the areas have tended to decline even faster (Fried, 1971, p. 183).

The practice of redlining has been specifically outlawed by the Federal Home Loan Bank Board, the governing body for Savings and Loan institutions (Platt, 1974, p. 26). There is evidence, however, that it still continues in many large cities. It has recently been the target of a law suit (NCDH, 1974, p. 1).

INTERACTIONAL CONSTRAINTS

Interactional constraints directly limit the housing adjustment of minority families and female-headed households by maintaining separate housing markets, one for white families and one for black families. The markets have been further differentiated, into housing for complete families and housing for female-headed households (HUD, 1975b). Interactional constraints are so labeled because they occur in social interaction between, as examples, a real estate broker and client, a landlord and prospective tenant, or a mortgage officer and prospective home buyer.

The perpetrators include realtors, officials of lending institutions, officials of the federal government, individual landlords, potential sellers, and others. All such discriminatory practices have been outlawed, by Executive Order in 1962 (Grier, 1967, p. 554), by the Supreme Court ruling that the 13th Amendment bars racial discrimination in the sale and rental of housing (NCDH, 1968, p. 1), by Title VIII of the Civil Rights Act of 1968 (HUD, 1969a), amended in 1974 to include sex discrimination (Pledger, 1976), and by the Equal Credit Opportunity Act (Pledger, 1976). The National Association of Real Estate Brokers stated that all brokers are expected to comply with fair housing legislation (Foley, 1973, pp. 99–100; Brown, 1972), as did the Federal Home Loan Bank Board in regard to Savings and Loan institutions, makers of home mortgages (Platt, 1974). It is quite clear, however, that the long history of discriminatory practices has created a pattern that is difficult to break.

Racial discrimination cannot be attributed to racism alone, although racism certainly plays a major part. Almost all cities in the United States have experienced a large growth in the proportion of residents who are minority group members. Such increases are due both to natural increase and to the migration of blacks and Chicanos from the rural South and Southwest to the urban areas of both the North and South. These migrations occurred primarily during and after the two world wars (Taeuber and Taeuber, 1965, pp. 11–14).

The rapid growth of the urban minority population created a demand for housing, making the maintenance of a segregated housing market economically profitable for realtors, lending institutions, developers, managers, and landlords (Taeuber and Taeuber, 1965, p. 25; Helper, 1969, p. 185; Brown, 1972). As long as the supply of housing was limited relative to the demand, higher prices could be commanded for the existing housing. Brokers and lending institutions feared that promoting integration would bring forth the wrath of the white community with a corresponding loss of business (Helper, 1969, p. 135; CRH, 1966, p. 279). In addition, it was feared that the entrance of minority families into white neighborhoods would cause a decline in property values, a fear not supported by research (Forman, 1971, pp. 86–89). Thus brokers, lending institutions, and mortgage insurers felt that maintaining segregation was the best way to protect their business.

A recent report on sex discrimination in housing has found that landlords, brokers, and lending institutions engage in discriminatory practices. The report attributes such practices to "myths and stereotypes about women . . . shared by many persons in the housing system" (HUD, 1975b, p. iii). Landlords and brokers have felt that female-headed households would be more apt to have unruly children. In addition, the moral standards of female household heads have been held up for question.

Lending institutions have considered women to be higher risks than men without checking to see that their credit records were poor. Separated and divorced women are considered to be more risky than single men. Such stereotypes persist, in spite of evidence that women are equally good mortgage risks as men (HUD, 1976).

The experience of women in the housing market is remarkably similar to that of blacks. As the number of households headed by females has increased, brokers and lending institutions have discriminated against them on economic grounds. The feeling has been that they would lose tenants, sales, or commissions by treating women the same way as men.

The Practices of Real Estate Brokers

Theoretically, the real estate broker, acting as an agent for the seller or landlord, should be neutral to all forces except economic returns for the client. In practice, real estate brokers have represented the interests of white clients to the detriment of blacks and other minority groups. They have also tended to treat women differently from men. It is not known exactly what proportion of sales and rentals are completed with the aid of a real estate broker. It is highly probable that at least half of all residential sales transactions involve such services.

Discriminatory practices have long been a part of real estate operations (Brown, 1972), with individual brokers subject to sanction for nonconformity (McEntire, 1960, p. 239). The National Association of Real Estate Boards in its Code of Ethics actively promoted residential segregation prior to 1950 by stating:

> *A Realtor should not be instrumental in introducing into a neighborhood a character of property or occupancy, members of any race or nationality, or any individuals whose presence will clearly be detrimental to property values in that neighborhood (Helper, 1969, p. 201).*

The Board revised its Code in 1950 by omitting the reference to race.

> *A Realtor should never be instrumental in introducing into a neighborhood a character of property or use which will clearly be detrimental to property values in that neighborhood (Helper, 1969, p. 201).*

The respondents in Helper's (1969) study of the beliefs and practices of real estate brokers in Chicago indicated that they felt that the meaning of the article was the same, even though the wording was different.

One of the most powerful tools used by real estate brokers to exclude members of minority groups was the restrictive covenant. It is a restriction attached to the property deed which prohibits sale of the property to any member of the groups specified in the restriction. While blacks were most often the group prohibited, other groups were also excluded (Abrams, 1955, p. 218). Racial covenants were declared unenforceable by the Supreme Court in 1948. The parties who violate such covenants in housing transactions can no longer be prosecuted (Abrams, 1955, pp. 221–22).

Many racial covenants are still attached to deed of property constructed prior to 1948. Hence they may still be exercising an influence for segregation, particularly among property owners unaware of the Supreme Court ruling. Since the covenants are "legal but unenforceable," it is likely that they are still being used. The extent of such usage is difficult to assess, however (Foley, 1973, pp. 104–05). The covenants, of course, were made between buyer and seller, but it is clear that real estate brokers were influential in encouraging their use (Brown, 1972).

Prior to the advent of fair housing legislation, many brokers simply refused to show residential property in white neighborhoods to blacks. Refusals were either blunt or through deception or misleading advertising (Forman, 1971, p. 64). With the advent of fair housing legislation, all discriminatory practices have been outlawed. Studies conducted since then (Denton, 1970; Brown, 1972) emphasize that discrimination, instead of being eliminated, has continued in more subtle ways:

> *every routine act, every bit of ritual in the sale or rental of a dwelling unit can be performed in a way calculated to make it either difficult or impossible to consummate a deal (Denton, 1970, p. Jb6).*

The practices are so subtle that it is almost impossible to prove discrimination, yet is is surely still practiced.

Discriminatory practices against women have not been thoroughly researched. What little evidence there is suggests that while covenants have not been used, women clients have been subject to all manner of delaying tactics (HUD, 1975b, pp. 34–44). There has been "steering" by brokers to "suitable" dwellings in "suitable" neighborhoods (HUD, 1975b, pp. 50–59). Often, discrimination by brokers has been based on the difficulties that the broker knew would arise in obtaining a loan.

Lending Institutions

As noted earlier, few people can afford to pay cash for the purchase of a home. The supply of mortgage money has profound effects on the availability of housing. By refusing to lend money to blacks wishing to purchase homes in white neighborhoods, lending institutions enforced segregation and prohibited free choice in housing. Such practices were quite common. Helper (1969) reported that over half of her respondents had encountered difficulties with lending institutions in trying to obtain mortgages for black home buyers (p. 171).

Lending institutions have been notorious in their refusal to make mortgage loans to women who are household heads (HUD, 1975b), in spite of good credit ratings. Often a male cosigner has been required.

The Federal Government

The role of the federal government has ranged from tacit acceptance of the discriminatory practices of private institutions and individuals to active promotion of segregated housing (Grier, 1967). The federal government has encouraged segregation by insisting that all homes insured by FHA have racially restrictive covenants attached to the deed to protect FHA's investment (Abrams, 1955, pp. 227–43). After the 1948 Supreme Court decision that such covenants were no longer enforceable, FHA finally agreed not to insure mortgages with racially restrictive covenants attached. This decision, in 1950, was made after much of the damage had been done (Abrams, 1955, p. 234). The Federal Housing Administration has also indulged in subtle sex discrimination in its preference for male mortgagors (HUD, 1975b, pp. 64–65).

Some studies (Grier and Grier, 1960; Schermer and Levin, 1968) reported that private developers wishing to build integrated apartment complexes encountered difficulties in securing FHA financing because of their policies promoting integration. Participation in the practice of redlining further discriminated against minority groups and minority neighborhoods, and helped foster the decline of the inner city.

Thus, in the name of protecting its mortgages, the federal government promoted and protected discriminatory practices of private real estate brokers and lending institutions. All available evidence suggests that recent federal actions such as the Civil Rights Act of 1968 and the Equal Credit Opportunity Act which took effect in the fall of 1975 have done little to stop discrimination. The difficulty with ending discrimination in housing by simply outlawing it lies in proving acts of discrimination in the network of factors, carefully built over the years, supporting multiple housing markets.

DEFINITIONS

Building code. Legal code regulating the construction of buildings in a particular locality; usually covers both housing and other structures; details materials and construction techniques to be used in new construction and rehabilitation.

Fiscal zoning. Exclusionary zoning practices promulgated for the purpose of adding more to the community property tax revenues than would be required in expenditures for an increase in public services. Requiring large building sites for new dwelling units, setting excessive minimum floor space requirements, excluding mobile homes and multifamily dwellings are examples of fiscal zoning.

Housing code. Ordinance adopted by a municipality that specifies the minimum features of dwellings for human habitation or controls their use and occupancy. Minimum space standards, the minimum level of repair, and the minimum amenities, such as heat and light, are specified by the code.

Interactional constraints. Direct discriminatory practices that limit minority groups and females in obtaining housing; to be contrasted with structural constraints. Other families, real estate brokers, lending institutions, and the federal government may impose interactional constraints.

Public housing. Federally funded program administered at the local level that subsidizes the construction and operation of housing units for low-income families through paying the cost of debt retirement and other costs. Units funded by this program often provide the only affordable high-quality housing for low-income families.

Redlining. The term "redlining" comes from the earlier practice of designating certain geographical areas as poor risks by drawing a red line around the area on a map. In particular, slum areas and areas with a large number of minority families or poor people have been "redlined." Lending institutions often refuse to lend money within the area, fire insurance applications from the area may be refused, and mortgage insurance may not be granted in the area.

Restrictive covenant. A restriction or limitation attached to a property deed which places limits on the use or resale of the property; previously used to prohibit the sale of property to racial or ethnic minorities. Racial covenants were declared unenforceable by the United States Supreme Court in 1948.

Segregation. The practice of excluding persons or groups of minority status from residential areas; exclusivity on the basis of racial, ethnic, or other characteristics.

Structural constraints. Limitations on minority groups and women that result from their place in the social and economic structure of the society; to be contrasted with interactional constraints.

Urban renewal. Federally funded program administered at the local level to improve urban areas. Techniques of urban renewal are redevelopment (clearance and reconstruction), rehabilitation, and strict enforcement of housing codes. The program monies were often used to demolish low-quality housing and replace it with luxury apartments or modern commercial areas.

Zoning ordinance. Police power measure regulating land use, population density, and intensity of land use. The community is divided into areas and type of land use (residential, commercial, industrial, etc.), and minimum standards permitted in each area are specified. Population density is regulated through minimum lot sizes and the inclusion or exclusion of multiunit dwellings.

Chapter 14
Structural and Normative Adaptation

> 'But I come by quite enough. I have a salary, and rather more money of my own than a man ought, perhaps, have. . . . So I am afraid there really isn't any inducement.'
> 'In five years you could have not just ample money, but a fortune. Very likely, Mr Meredith, your life would then surprisingly change. Forgotten or suppressed capacities for pleasure—immediate as well as intellectual pleasure—would be reborn in you.' Michael Innes*

The analysis thus far has been primarily a static one. It has assumed that family norms, cultural norms, family organization, and family composition remain constant. Ordinarily it is necessary to hold such structural system factors constant in order to analyze the occurrence of intrasystem processes. But there are conditions under which processes aimed toward a given preferred state cannot be initiated or if initiated are ineffective. Under such conditions structural adaptation may become necessary. In particular, this may occur when there are severe resource constraints.

> *In its most unadorned form, economics is the theory of allocation of limited resources among competing ends in order to maximize satisfaction . . . subject to the constraints imposed by limitations in the availability of resources required to achieve those ends (Nerlove, 1974, p. S202).*

The basic assumption of the typical economic analysis, seldom elaborated, is that resources are not *extremely* limited. The ends do not compete so strongly that some go unmet. The constraints are not so severe as to preclude any effective allocation. When conditions have reached such a pass they become the topic of this chapter rather than a topic for traditional economics.

* From *From London Far* by Michael Innes (Harmondsworth, Endland: Penguin Books, 1946), p. 178.

Unfortunately, economic theory does not elaborate upon the source of the *competing ends*. Tastes are almost universally assumed not to change over time and often are assumed not to differ among households at a point in time in economic analysis. In fact, the "ends" are ends because of tastes. Tastes in the present model are equated with norms. Once norms have been internalized and become part of the personality of each family member, they constitute the microculture of the household. They are then the limits which the family's housing conditions cannot be allowed to exceed. When the constraints are so great as to endanger the fulfillment of the basic needs (more than just survival), resource allocation goes out the window. Along with it goes housing adjustment and many other optional activities. It is at this point that adaptation occurs.

This chapter explores adaptation as a response to housing stress. Much of the material presented is speculative, for there has been little research on the impact of the inability to attain normative housing conditions or any other set of ends that competes with housing. The inability to attain normatively prescribed housing and thus relieve the stress of housing dissatisfaction is seldom the only problem experienced by the family who is considering adaptation. Separating the effects of housing-related stress from stress due to poverty, hunger, illness, and so on, is quite difficult.

THEORY AND RESEARCH ON FAMILY ADAPTATION

The phenomena described in this chapter can only be studied fruitfully with a dynamic, longitudinal research design. The subject matter is *change* in the structure of a family. Research on this subject requires the collection of data for at least two different time points in order to detect the occurrence of changes and to discover their causes. As a result, there is very little research on adaptive responses to housing deficits. Adjustments represent changes, as well, but the changes that occur in housing adjustment tend to be much more quickly decided upon and implemented than are adaptive responses. They are therefore much more readily studied with a single-interview, cross-sectional survey.

The focus of this chapter is a return to the interactional approach discussed earlier in Chapter 8. The development of new norms, a new mode of family organization, or changed family composition requires interaction among family members. In particular, the reevaluation of old symbols and the development of new ones require the development of new levels of consensus and perhaps a restoration of family solidarity.

The typical sociological analysis treats structural factors as independent variables that explain the occurrence of process factors as dependent variables. The analyses of residential mobility and alteration in Chapters 9 and 10 used that approach. Seldom, however, do researchers engaged in microanalysis of the family treat family structure as a dependent variable to be explained.

Structural family change is typically analyzed as an effect of broad societal changes such as urbanization and industrialization. Goode (1963), for example, used such factors to explain the development of the modern nuclear family system. As a result, there is a great deal of literature on societal causes of family change. There is much less available that analyzes relatively deliberate rational changes in family norms, family composition, or family organization in response to unsolved problems. Recent exceptions include Goode (1960), Rodman (1963), and Liebow (1967).

Goode maintains that commitment to norms in favor of legal marriage in the Caribbean is weak among lower classes who have less to gain from clear legal kinship lines. Among families where the husband has steady work, however, even the poor families are committed to the norms. Rodman (1963) clearly states that he sees "value stretch" as a response to the "deprived situation" of the lower classes (p. 205). In the Caribbean, large numbers of lower-class families have developed variant forms of family composition and organization in response to uncertain employment. When laid off from work, the father may wander off to avoid the pain of being unable to support the family. His leaving may also make it possible for the mother to find another man who can support them.

Liebow's (1967) analysis of black street-corner men in Washington, D.C. reaches similar conclusions to those of Goode and Rodman. He views the pattern of "serial monogamy" among lower-class blacks as a response to repeated failure. Failure to obtain a good job, which is related to lower levels of education and job skills, results in the inability to support a family. Thus the family breaks up, and the man leaves. Subsequently, both partners may make new liaisons, and repeat the process.

Angell's (1936) analysis of the impact of the depression of the thirties on the family stressed the importance of adaptability as a key in the adjustment required. Adaptability (the readiness and ability to change family patterns as a response to problems) is a part of the focus of this chapter. In the preface of another study of the impact of unemployment during the depression Bakke (1940) states:

> *We have tried to portray the adjustments of citizens to unemployment as a rearrangement of that normal structure and the effects of unemployment as a modification of that structure under the stress and strain of the absence of a job (Bakke, 1940, p. ix).*

Bakke's chief data source for the analysis of family adaptation was a series of case studies of families of unemployed workers. His chief conceptual tool was a series of stages through which the families passed as they adjusted to the loss of a job and the concomitant reduced level of living. The stages were:

1. *Momentum stability* in which savings and other resources, including personal and social resources, sustain the family in the accustomed patterns.

2. *Unstable equilibrium* during which savings run out, credit is overextended, the rent is behind, and the family loses its ability to continue its previous level of living.

3. *Disorganization* during which the family clearly cannot continue to keep up a front, their financial affairs are in a shambles, and personal and social resources are exhausted.

4. *Experimental readjustment* in which family forces begin to rally, the family develops new modes of economic support, and it tries new modes of family organization.

5. *Permanent readjustment* in which a new equilibrium develops in the family economy, at a lower level of living, but newly organized with stable customary behavior patterns.

In summarizing the process of readjustment and progress through the stages, Bakke (1940) states:

> *It is difficult to escape the conclusion that the primary factors involved in the striking of the new balance are the willingness and ability of the workers and their families to readapt their standards, devise new practices, and adjust their relationships and activities to the necessities imposed upon them (Bakke, 1940, p. 175).*

Thus, there are two important types of adaptation. First, there is normative adaptation—"the willingness and ability of the workers and their families to readapt their standards." In the present model, normative adaptation is limited to changing family norms for housing. Second is structural adaptation—"devise new practices and adjust their relationships and activities."

There are two types of structural adaptation included in the present model. *Compositional adaptation* refers to changing or preventing changes in the composition of the family so that less demanding norms apply to the family situation. *Organizational adaptation* refers to changing the family interaction patterns to overcome intrafamilial constraints that, for example, prevent the development of appropriate behaviors to overcome housing problems.

NORMATIVE ADAPTATION

The discussion in this section involves changes in family norms, not changes in cultural norms. Further, the discussion is focused on relatively permanent changes in norms. Temporary relaxation of norms implied in preference formation is not included. The relaxation of norms made in preference formation quickly disappears when constraints are removed. Changed family norms are of deeper significance and are slow to return to earlier high levels when conditions improve.

Under the pressure of a very severe problem in housing, families may discover when the momentum stability stage has passed that the old, customary behaviors are no longer working. Try as they may, the usual adjustment responses do not result in the reduction of deficits. Satisfaction remains low. After a time of faithfully trying to meet the old standards with the old means during the unstable equilibrium stage, hopelessness sets in. The hopelessness produces tensions among the family members. The tensions are partly a result of the fact that the problem itself has not been solved and partly due to the recognition that someone in the family has not been able to properly perform one of his or her obligations. The results are guilt feelings, recriminations, accusations, and outright quarreling.

Dissatisfaction over the lack of bedroom space does not ordinarily lead to this kind of situation. If resources for obtaining housing become extremely short, however, as in unemployment, the tensions can build very rapidly. The wife may begin to berate the husband for not being a good provider. The quarreling may center around the lack of space for children to have their own rooms.

The disorganization stage has been reached when the old standards are rejected as unattainable and the old behavioral responses as ineffective. At this point the family is likely to abandon the unworkable standard of a room for each child and stop trying to attain it. The disorganization stage cannot endure because human beings cannot continue long without norms and without patterned behavioral responses to apply to problem situations. Therefore, the family begins to develop new standards. They may decide that it is all right after all for the two young ones to share a room. The older girl (maybe the sloppy one) can sleep in the television room.

If the tensions and quarreling become great enough and persist long enough, the disorganization can produce a breakup of the family as a type of solution. Problems severe enough to provoke a dissolution of the family are not uncommon. Many is the father who has stolen away in the night so that his wife and children might be eligible for Aid to Dependent Children.

The lack of research on normative adaptation responses to housing deficits is severe. About the only kind of research that exists on any problem area, not just housing, is the analysis of case study data. Case studies are at best illustrative and at worst misleading because they are almost invariably unrepresentative. Thus, Bakke's data clearly show that families do reduce their standards for their level of living under continued unemployment (normative adaptation). Some families break up rather than reduce standards (compositional adaptation). Some families manage a kind of *tour de force* and solve their problems with superhuman effort (organizational adaptation). There is no way to know with the present state of knowledge in what relative proportions those responses occur.

Normative adaptation does not only include norm reduction under conditions of severe problems. It also includes the raising of norms under improved conditions with the relief of constraints. If resources are very abundant and current housing modest, as time passes a family may raise their standards. The increase in the level of standards may then produce dissatisfaction with previously satisfactory housing.

The new level of dissatisfaction is then reduced by housing adjustment that tends to bring the housing into alignment with the new standards. As noted in Chapter 7, quality norms change with rising income. Such changes are normative adaptation. When a family changes its norms upward in response to rising economic conditions, it is also likely to be able to adjust its housing to meet those norms. Hence the process is logically the same when the norms are raised as when they are lowered. The ramifications for the family are not similar, however.

The sketchy evidence indicates that adaptable families are more likely to be able to relatively quickly raise or lower their norms as needed. Such adaptations are made to prevent dissatisfaction and the discord that can accompany it from becoming intolerable. It may be the case that highly adaptable families are somewhat less effective in everyday housing adjustment. Less adaptable families may disintegrate during the disorganization stage or even earlier. Very high levels of integration may reduce adaptability. Thus, a looser family structure may permit more comfortable survival under severe problems requiring substantial normative adaptation.

STRUCTURAL ADAPTATION

Compositional Adaptation

Any decisions or actions that raise, lower, or maintain family size and composition for housing reasons are compositional adaptation. Included in compositional adaptation are bearing additional children because space is available, avoiding childbearing in response to crowding or in response to lack of money to obtain more spacious housing, taking in foster children because there is extra space or there is a need for a little extra money to be able to continue to afford current housing, taking in another family in order to share housing costs, and asking members of the household to leave in order to provide more space for those who remain.

Compositional adaptation is very difficult to measure because using it to overcome housing deficits is often unconscious. All of the compositional adaptation behaviors could be taken for medical, altruistic, and other reasons. Thus, the specific action might have nothing to do, especially on the conscious level, with housing.

One of the key determinants of the choice of compositional adaptation as a housing-oriented behavior is the extent to which other means are ineffective or prohibitively expensive. When housing is plentiful, of high quality, and inexpensive and when moving costs are low, families may utilize residential mobility a great deal. Such conditions have prevailed for the entire post-World War II period, with the possible exception of the mid-seventies.

If mortgage money and new housing units become scarcer and more expensive, while additions and alterations remain reasonably available, residential alterations may take up the slack. Thus possibly only in times of depression or other extreme conditions does compositional adaptation become widely adopted.

During the depression of the thirties and during World War II, the rate of doubling up became very high. In order to obtain any housing at all, many families had to move in with another family. The pressure to double up was extremely severe for new families who had not yet become established economically, but who needed to obtain housing. Temporary residence with parents or others may be necessary under such severe economic conditions or during extreme shortages. Established families might have to take in another family or individual to reduce housing expenses and thus avoid having to give up the present housing.

An alternative for families in the childbearing years is limitation of their fertility. Goodsell (1937) argued that Sweden's birth rate was reduced by the shortage of spacious housing for the working classes. There is some question whether the limited size of working-class housing was a cause of reduced fertility or whether both the limited size of housing and the reduced fertility were due to the economic conditions of the period. Nevertheless, Thompson (1938) reached a similar conclusion about fertility in the United States. He argued that during the depression of the thirties, at least a portion of the greatly reduced fertility of Americans was due to the pressure of limited housing space. He suggested, however, that residential mobility was a likely alternative to fertility limitation. He thought housing should be provided for large families in order to avoid reduction in the birth rate in light of the then current fear that the population might decline.

Two recent studies (Morris, 1977; Bresler, 1975) have focused on the occurrence of compositional adaptation. In a study of lower-class families in San Juan, Puerto Rico, Bresler found that crowding, measured by bedroom deficit, was not related to the desire for more children. Such desires were independent of the lack of space. The respondent's perception that insufficient space would affect fertility was related to the use of birth control. Respondents who thought that lack of space would cause them to postpone having an additional child were using birth control. Bresler concluded:

> ... *residential crowding does affect attitudes of individuals which may influence the behavioral adjustments they use to relieve housing space pressures. But the desire for additional children is independent of crowding and apparently childbearing takes precedence over conditions of spacious housing (Bresler, 1975, p. 105).*

Morris (1977) analyzed yearly segments of family histories. He tested two alternative hypotheses: (1) that couples who were crowded would tend to limit their childbearing, and (2) that residential mobility would permit adjustment of space to current and future needs. Thus the pressure of crowding on fertility would be forestalled. Analysis of the relationship between annual birth probabilities and bedroom deficit showed no significant relationship. The traditional predictors of fertility, age of the mother, number of months since the birth of the last child, number of live births, and education of the head of the household were controlled. However, births during the current year were positively related to the probability of moving during the current year. Tenure, structure type, age of the household head, and other variables were controlled.

Births during the previous year were not significantly related to moves during the current year, however. The impact of the birth of a child on crowding apparently was quickly corrected by moving to a different dwelling. The correction was usually made during the same year as the birth, sometimes up to six months beforehand and sometimes as much as six months afterward. There apparently were few families in which childbearing was anticipated by as much as a year. Seldom was there a delay of as much as a year in moving in order to obtain extra space to avoid crowding.

It was concluded that the ready availability of relatively inexpensive dwellings during most of the time span covered by the family histories (1930–1971) meant that families were not forced to limit fertility to prevent crowding. Mobility was a ready alternative. The researcher speculated that a severe housing shortage or shortage of spacious dwellings might have an impact on fertility, however. To this point, fertility control behavior has been largely for nonhousing reasons.

Another form of compositional adaptation may occur in response to the absence of specific community and neighborhood facilities. Selective adaptation could occur if there were housing deficits that affected only certain members of the family. The example that comes to mind is a family living in a school district that does not meet their family norms. Such a family might send their children to a private school or even away from home to a boarding school. If there were a lack of medical facilities in the area, an elderly family member might move in with relatives who live near a clinic. This form of adaptation may be limited to cases where there is no other alternative but for the main family to continue living in the same dwelling, sending the member affected by the neighborhood deficit to another location. Such adaptation may occur when a limitation on the employment of the household head makes living in a particular neighborhood essential. A physician serving a low-income area, for example, may send the children to a middle-class school elsewhere.

Organizational Adaptation

This form of adaptation has to do with the allocation of authority and responsibility within the family. There are many cultural norms that suggest the proper behavior of husbands, fathers, wives, mothers, siblings, and children. Organizational adaptation in reality is a form of normative adaptation. The adaptation involves the norms for family organization rather than the norms for housing. Typically the analysis of those norms is done in the language of roles. A role (in life as well as in the theater) is a description of how the actor or role incumbent should act and under what conditions.

Because family roles are in a period of seemingly rapid change in the United States, no attempt is made to outline just what the roles of specific family members are. In brief outline, however, the husband-father role includes participation in the labor market to exchange his time and skills for money and other resources that can be used by the family to obtain food, clothing, housing, and other necessities. The wife tends to have a role that includes the prime responsibility for nurturant socialization of the children. That is by no means a complete or totally correct description but will serve as a point of departure.

Sometimes the resources coming into the family through its connection to the economy are not sufficient to meet the family's needs. The immediate cause may be unemployment, alcoholism, or a number of other possibilities. Therefore, someone, usually the husband, is not performing a role as it should be performed. It may be through forces that cannot be controlled by anyone in the family. Thus blame may not be appropriate. Nevertheless, a duty is not being performed.

It may be necessary to reorganize the family if the unemployment or other similar conditions persist. It may, for example, be easier for the wife to find work than for the husband under some economic conditions. In the abstract, an exchange of roles seems simple. "So why not let the wife go to work?" There are norms, however, that say that men ought not to stay home and keep house and wash little faces. Obviously, such role exchanges are saved for the last resort.

Less extreme reorganization may take place as well. When resources are short it may be necessary for the wife to work to supplement the husband's income rather than to replace him as sole support of the family. It may become necessary for her to begin to dominate family decision making. The husband may have such guilt feelings that he becomes a poor analyst and begins to make rash and unwise decisions. The wife, who may have a calmer view of things and more time to think about them, may be a better decision maker.

Family reorganization is, in and of itself, traumatic, but when the family reaches the disorganization stage they have already given up on many of the norms they used to live by. The desperation of the disorganization stage may be necessary in order to destroy all illusions that the recent past as it existed before the "trouble" started could be reinstated. Desperation makes the change necessary and therefore easier. At that point new roles can be adopted, new standards for food, clothing, and housing can be accepted, and the process of reorganization begun. Organizational adaptation in turn may result in compositional adaptation. There may be family members who refuse to operate under the changed leadership. There may be dominant family members who refuse to step down. The result of the attempt to achieve the realignment of roles required in organizational adaptation may be a partial or complete disintegration of the family. Of course, this is not the typical result.

CONCLUSION

Family adaptation in response to unsatisfactory housing conditions is the least studied and understood aspect of the model of family housing behavior. Even the process of raising family norms, which is much less painful, is not understood. It is clear that either normative or structural adaptation in response to stress caused by housing conditions is the least desirable. Permanent family adaptation is a complex process that is apt to be very difficult to accomplish smoothly.

It is not likely that any type of adaptation will occur in the absence of severe constraints or disruptions such as unemployment, a severe illness, or alcoholism, among others. Thus normative and structural adaptations related to housing are difficult to isolate from other factors. Further, research on family adaptation must be accomplished by collecting data from the same household at different points in time, perhaps over a 10- to 20-year time span. Thus it may be a very long time before a discussion of family adaptation can be more than speculation.

Chapter 15
Housing and Subcultures

> It is not, in fact, very different from the conviction she would have felt at the age of ten that the kind of fish knives used in her father's house were the proper or normal or "real" kind, while those of the neighbouring families were "not real fish knives" at all. C. S. Lewis*

The terms *culture* and *subculture* have often been used to describe a number of diverse groups of people within the United States who exhibit behavior different from that of the mainstream of society. References have been made to the youth subculture, the black subculture, the Southern mountain subculture, the working class subculture, and many others. Probably the most prevalent use of the concept has been in connection with the "culture of poverty" (Oscar Lewis, 1966a; 1966b; Harrington, 1962; Rainwater, 1964; Cohen, 1964).

The idea that there are separate subcultures in regard to housing norms is not of recent vintage. Riemer (1943), Wirth (1947), and Rossi (1955) all refer to differences in housing needs according to socioeconomic status. The subculture idea has become more prominent in recent years, however. Social scientists have sought to explain the lack of success of certain recent governmental programs by reference to the differences in housing needs of some disadvantaged groups. Hall (1966, pp. 155–56), for example, asserts that the failure of efforts to appreciably improve the quality of the urban environment is because the culture of the recent urban in-migrants, principally low-income blacks from the rural South, is different from that of the city planners and architects (upper-income whites). Presumably the needs and desires of the low-income population have been totally ignored. Similar interpretations can be found in Marris (1962) and, more recently, Gutman (1970), who asserts:

> *The tenants of public housing today are drawn from levels of the class structure which are less likely to regard the house as a signifi-*

* From *The Screwtape Letters,* by C. S. Lewis (New York: Macmillan, 1962), p. 111.

cant possession influencing social ranking, perhaps because their life history leads them to invest their loyalties in objects which are more easily movable, such as automobiles (p. 127).

The purpose of this chapter is to examine the cultural and family norms of socioeconomic, racial, and ethnic subgroups in the United States. Specifically included is assessment of the similarities and differences among groups in terms of their norms for housing and the neighborhood.

Other subgroups, based on age, region of residence in the United States, community type, religion, etc., have been largely omitted from this discussion. The norms of such groups have not been the center of controversy, as have those of socioeconomic, racial, and ethnic groups. Further, it has seldom been suggested that they might represent "subcultures," with their own norms and values. Some classes of people, such as the elderly and the handicapped (Chapter 11) have housing requirements that are unique. Those special needs, however, arise from physical limitations rather than from culturally based norms. It is rarely suggested that they have unique subcultures.

This chapter does not focus on the general question of whether there are *any* subcultures in the United States. Whether or not there are racial, ethnic, and socioeconomic subcultures with regard to norms other than those for housing (child rearing, for example) is also beyond the purview of this discussion. Such topics have been the subject of much discussion and research (Ball, 1968; Keil, 1966; Antonovsky and Lerner, 1959; Han, 1969; Gist and Bennett, 1963; Mack, Murphy, and Yellin, 1956; Valentine, 1968; Lewis, 1966a and 1966b; Rainwater, 1973). Rather, the emphasis is on the narrower question of whether certain subgroups have unique housing norms. Have various groups consciously and collectively engaged in normative adaptation that would result in their having a significantly different set of housing norms?

The chapter is divided into three main parts:

1. A discussion of similarities and differences between different socioeconomic, racial, and ethnic groups in extrafamilial constraints, intrafamilial constraints, and housing and neighborhood conditions.

2. A discussion of the measurement of norms from the research available.

3. An examination of research findings on the housing and neighborhood norms of various subgroups.

SITUATIONAL DETERMINANTS OF HOUSING BEHAVIOR

Extrafamilial Constraints

Extrafamilial constraints, discussed in detail in Chapters 12 and 13, are associated with distortions in the supply of housing. The key distortions that affect the supply of housing available to families are the cost of housing relative to family income and the barriers raised to racial, ethnic, and other groups. Such barriers may include total exclusion, adjusting the price of housing upward for certain groups, and blocking access to information.

The society depends largely on the private market forces of supply, demand, and prices to distribute housing. Thus families with less money available for housing have a more difficult time finding a suitable dwelling. In fact, there may be no standard housing in the private market at the price they can afford to pay. Income is one of the major indexes of socioeconomic status, rather than a result of socioeconomic status (Roach and Gursslin, 1965). Low income tends to cause or produce low status. Therefore, lower-income groups are lower-status groups, and obviously they experience economic constraints.

The availability of housing varies with minority status, as well. Black, Puerto Rican, and Mexican-American families, and, to some extent, other minority groups—Jews, Italians, Poles—are or have been faced with discrimination in the housing market, regardless of their income. Although specifically outlawed by Title VIII of the 1968 Civil Rights Act, differential treatment of minority groups is still a fact of life in many communities (Kain and Quigley, 1972; Lansing, Clifton, and Morgan, 1969; Roistacher, 1974a). Such discrimination occurs directly through the practices of real estate agencies and lending institutions (Abrams, 1955; Foley, 1973; Biochel, Aurbach, Bakerman, and Elliott, 1969; Helper, 1969; Forman, 1971) or indirectly through building and land use regulation (Foley, 1973; Downs, 1973; Shields and Spector, 1972; Brooks, 1970).

The only conclusion that can be reached is that there are wide differences in the extrafamilial constraints that impinge upon the various socioeconomic, racial, and ethnic groups. Those constraints, by definition, affect the ability of these groups to obtain normatively prescribed housing.

Intrafamilial Constraints

Researchers have found differences in the structures and processes of the typical family among different socioeconomic classes and racial and ethnic groups (Lewis, 1966a and 1966b; Moynihan, 1965; Liebow, 1967; Gans, 1962; Straus, 1968; Tallman and Miller, 1974). Variations in family structure, such as patterns of authority and the degree of family integration, have resulted in differences in the effectiveness with which families solve problems, make decisions, and carry out their decisions. Such differences in handling problems may be related to class variations in verbal ability and the quality and amount of communication (Chapter 3).

There is little question that there are important differences in family functioning among different socioeconomic classes and racial and ethnic groups. One way of interpreting these differences is to look at them as intrafamilial constraints. There is strong evidence that such differences are not related to differences in class, race, or ethnicity *per se*. Rather, they are behavioral responses to the external constraints imposed by society (Liebow, 1967, p. 222). The controversial Moynihan Report (1965) asserted that the functioning of the black family was inferior for coping with the twentieth century problems of poverty and discrimination. The report was careful to point out, however, that the situation resulted from centuries of life conditions that were beyond the control of black families (Moynihan, 1965, p. 47).

Actual Housing and Neighborhood Conditions

There is little doubt that housing conditions vary according to racial, ethnic, and socioeconomic subgroup membership. An examination of the 1970 Census data permits a gross assessment of housing conditions of low-income families. Families below the poverty line, defined by the Social Security Administration on the basis of family income, family size and composition, and residence (farm or nonfarm) (USBC, 1973h, p. ix) are more likely to have inadequate housing than families above the poverty line, even using the crude indexes available in the U.S. Census. Families in poverty are six times more likely to lack some or all plumbing facilities than those above the poverty line. They are six times more likely to be paying more than 35 percent of their income for rent. They are twice as likely to have more than 1.00 persons per room. They are one-and-a-half times more likely to rent than own (USBC, 1973h, pp. 409–11). Similar findings were noted in urban areas inhabited by low-income families (Manvel, 1968).

The 1970 Census of Housing (USBC, 1972b) provides data that permit comparison between households headed by a black individual and the total population of households. Black families are two-and-a-half times as likely to live in housing that lacks some or all plumbing facilities. They are two-and-a-half times as likely to have no kitchen facilities at all and twice as likely to have more than 1.00 persons per room. Black families are one and a half times more likely to live in a nonsingle-family dwelling (USBC, 1972b, pp. 1–6, 1–9, 1–16, 1–34, 1–41).

Of course, there is some overlap between low-income families and black families: a higher proportion of black families than white families are poor (USBC, 1973h, pp. 3–5). Other minority families—Puerto Ricans, Mexican-

Americans—are even more poorly housed than black families (Miller, 1964, pp. 104–24). Again, there is a larger proportion of Spanish-origin families than white families who are poor (USBC, 1973h, pp. 3–7).

That housing conditions differ among socioeconomic, racial, and ethnic groups is strongly supported by sample surveys, ecological studies, and participant-observation research. Findings from such studies offer detailed descriptions of differences in housing and neighborhood characteristics.

Differences in such characteristics were found among socioeconomic classes, based on occupational rank, in Chicago (Duncan and Duncan, 1957), Hartford (Feldman and Tilly, 1960), and Wilmington (Tilly, 1961). Their findings indicated that there are differences according to all three measures of social class: income, occupation, and education. In contrast, Morris and Winter (1976a) found no difference between blue collar and white collar workers regarding the percent who owned single-family dwellings.

Rushing's (1970) data comparing the aspirations of different classes in a rural area were drawn from two distinctly different classes: affluent wheat and pea farmers from eastern Washington, and farm workers, half of whom were migrant laborers. As expected, the current housing conditions were drastically different:

> *The workers' living conditions were consistent with many popular accounts. Living quarters were frequently overcrowded; many were without screens, heat, bathing facilities, running water, or adequate garbage disposal; most were dirty and in ill repair. The homes of most farmers, in contrast, were spacious and comfortable (p. 381).*

Morris and Winter (1973) compared the bedroom space of a group of low-income black families in rural upstate New York and a group of middle-income white families from Kansas. Although there were no significant differences in the two groups regarding family size, the black families had a mean of 1.7 bedrooms, while the white families had a mean of 3.3 bedrooms in their dwellings.

Winter and Morris (1976) found that ownership of a single-family structure varied according to income. Less than 50 percent of the lowest income group (under $7000) owned a single-family dwelling. About 60 percent of the middle-income group ($7000–$14999) owned a single-family dwelling, while over 80 percent of the high-income group lived in such a dwelling.

Some researchers have controlled for income or social class, and compared the housing characteristics of various groups within the same income range or social class. Stubbs (1972) compared the housing characteristics of low-income whites to those of low-income blacks and low-income Mexican-Americans from both rural and urban areas in Texas. Although the housing conditions of all three groups were quite poor (22 percent had no bathroom facilities, 70 percent had no sanitary sewage disposal system, 58 percent had five or fewer rooms), the housing conditions of the white households tended to be better than those of the black families, which, in turn, were better than those of the Mexican-American families.

The final group of studies suggesting variations in housing conditions according to subgroup membership consists of descriptions of specific groups: southern Appalachian families, low-income families in a number of states, working-class families in a certain city or suburb, and low-income black families in a specific rural or urban area. In all cases, implicit or explicit comparisons are made with postulated "middle-class" housing conditions rather than actual housing conditions of a sample selected for comparison. Conclusions from such studies are weaker than comparison studies, yet they offer detailed data regarding the housing characteristics of specific types of families.

Gans (1962), Hartman (1963), Fried and Gleicher (1961), and Fried (1963) studied the Italian-American working class in Boston's West End just before urban redevelopment began. The Italian-Americans lived in a high-density neighborhood near the center of the city, in inexpensive rental apartments, poor in exterior appearance. The interiors were described as clean, well-furnished, with the latest appliances and conveniences—far above what would be expected from outside appearances. Thus interiors were comparable to "middle-class" interiors.

Studies of low-income families (Needham, 1973; Montgomery and McCabe, 1973; Ladd, 1972; Stewart, 1973) support in detail the findings of the Census Bureau regarding the relation of housing conditions to income and race. Low-income families, particularly low-income blacks, often lack housing that meets the minimum definition of housing.

Stewart's (1973) findings from her study of a small group (40 families) living in rural upstate New York serve to illustrate the extreme conditions some low-income groups experience:

> *Housing space was severely limited for most families. . . . The mean number of rooms per dwelling unit, including the kitchen, was 3.3 rooms. For many families, the main living area doubled as a bedroom and in some cases it also had to serve as the eating area. . . . The range in persons-per-room was from less than one to 2.5 persons-per-room. The persons-per-room ratio was above 1.5 for 41 percent of the families. Thirty-one percent of the families had less than 90 square feet per person in their apartments. . . . All of the dwelling units were severely substandard. . . . There were no indoor bathrooms or hot water and only a few of the units had cold water taps inside (Stewart, 1973, pp. 79–81).*

The analysis of the census and other data leaves no doubt that there are distinct differences in housing conditions among different socioeconomic classes, ethnic groups, and racial groups. By and large, the lower the income class, the further the housing and neighborhood conditions deviate from the cultural norms. Similarly, minority status (black, Puerto Rican, Mexican-American) increases the chances that a family lives in nonnormative housing.

Extrafamilial constraints, intrafamilial constraints, and actual housing conditions differ among socioeconomic and ethnic groups. Such conditions could be expected to influence their housing behavior. The remaining question is whether differences in family and cultural norms are an additional factor producing differences in housing behavior and conditions. In light of the substantial differences in constraints and conditions among several groups that have been labeled subcultures by some writers, it bears asking whether the subculture label fits. It is conceivable that all racial and socioeconomic differences in housing conditions and behavior are due to noncultural, nonnormative influences. Thus, even for groups that appear to be subcultures, it may be that their "subculturalness" does not extend to housing.

The inference conventionally made by sociologists and anthropologists from the use of the term "subculture" is that the group referred to has a normative system that differs significantly from the total culture (Chapter 2). Unique norms and their corresponding sanctions are a necessary but not a sufficient condition in the definition of the term "subculture." The definition of a subculture further requires that the system of norms, values, and sanctions be handed down from generation to generation in a stable, orderly manner that transcends generations (Williams, 1970, pp. 25–36; Valentine, 1968, pp. 3–5; Roach and Gursslin, 1967). It would not suffice to know that a subgroup behaves differently and lives under different conditions, not even if they appear to espouse different attitudes, norms, and values. In addition, the apparent norms must be positively valued and systematically taught to succeeding generations.

PROBLEMS AND LIMITATIONS IN ASSESSING SUBCULTURAL NORMS

Clear differences exist between the housing behavior of the working class (Berger, 1960; Gans, 1962; Cohen and Hodges, 1963), that of the lower class (Rainwater, 1966; Liebow, 1967; Moore, 1969), and the upwardly mobile middle class (Whyte, 1956; Gans, 1967). Yet it cannot be concluded that they are subcultures.

Erroneous conclusions attributing differences in housing conditions to subcultural differences have been made on the basis of the measurement of factors other than cultural norms. Achieved housing could be the product of a combination of cultural norms, family norms, preferences, extrafamilial constraints, and intrafamilial constraints. Therefore, the key question is: why does the achieved housing of some groups differ from that of others? Is it because of differences in cultural norms, in family norms, in preferences, in extrafamilial constraints, in intrafamilial constraints, or a combination of one or more of them? If the causal factor is cultural (if the norms are different), then tentatively it can be said that there is a subculture with regard to housing. If, however, the other factors are critical in producing the difference, then it may be concluded that there is no subculture in regard to housing. Rather, there are groups whose family structure and processes make problem solving difficult, who face insurmountable extrafamilial constraints, or whose previous housing conditions were different.

A related question is why achieved housing, family norms, and family preferences are not directly usable as measures of cultural norms. A partial answer was provided by Winter and Morris (1976) in terms of reporting error. The idea is that people are not perfect observers of their society and may make errors in reporting the cultural norms in an interview. The degree of error depends upon their location in the social structure. The source and magnitude of the error may be illustrated by relating reported cultural norms to other variables. Figures 18, 19, and 20 represent adaptations and expansions on a diagram by Han (1969).

Figure 18 illustrates the gap between reported norms and assumed true cultural norms (measured without error). The key reasons are family norms. Families who, for whatever reason, have unconventional norms are likely to report cultural norms that are unconventional. The form of the curves that would be obtained empirically may not be exactly as diagrammed. It is clear from Winter and Morris (1976) that the rise from left to right of the lower curves relative to the upper has been empirically demonstrated.

The key determinant of the departure of family norms from cultural norms is achieved housing (Figure 19). People who have experienced deficit

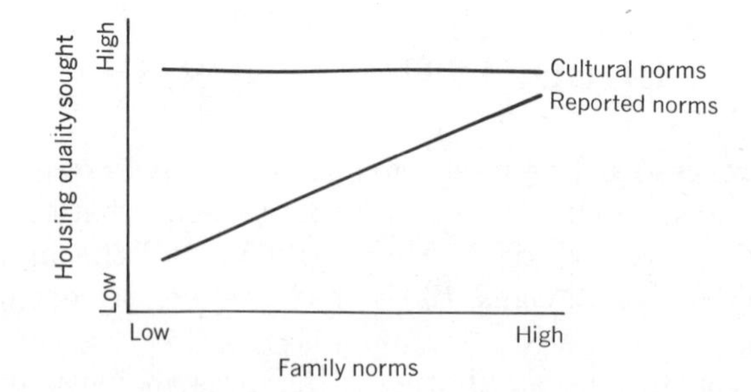

Figure 18 True cultural norms and reported cultural norms by the level of family norms.

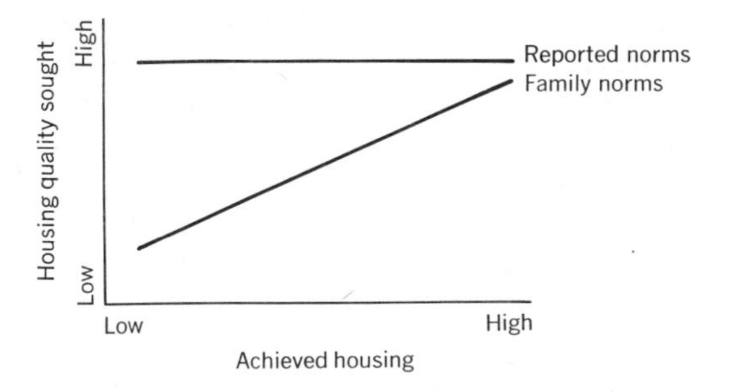

Figure 19 Reported cultural norms and family norms by achieved housing conditions.

housing tend to reduce their family norms accordingly. Success in reducing housing deficits over time tends to raise family norms to or even above cultural norms.

The gap between family norms and achieved housing is diagrammed in Figure 20. As the constraints on housing adjustment behavior rise, achieved housing departs further from family norms. Groups experiencing greater constraints, lower achieved housing, or lower family norms would tend to report cultural norms that are artificially low. Therefore, to test whether income groups differ, it is necessary to control for those factors.

A simple causal chain from constraints to achieved housing to family norms to reported cultural norms is suggested by the preceding theoretical discussion. The review of empirical studies that follows however suggests that a somewhat more complex model is required to describe the data.

Because of the influence exerted by current housing conditions, family norms reported by respondents who live in very poor or unusual housing conditions may be quite unconventional. Unfortunately, such respondents are likely to be those whose subgroup norms are under examination in this chapter: low-income and working-class families, black families, Mexican-

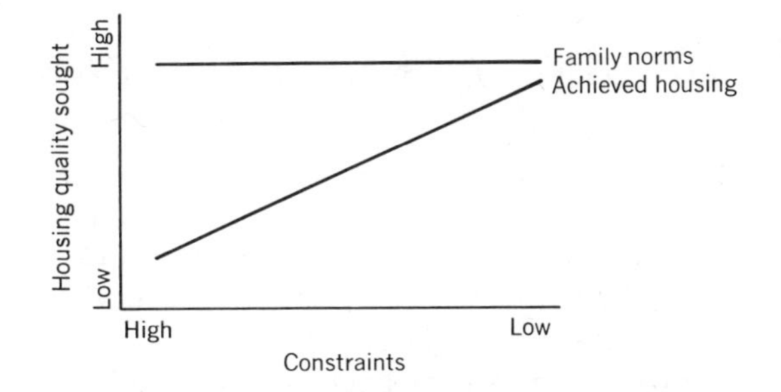

Figure 20 Family norms and achieved housing conditions by the level of constraints.

American families, and Puerto Rican families. Hence carefully controlled measurement of norms, preferences, and housing conditions assumes great importance.

A recent survey that provided data for several studies (Morris and Winter, 1976a; Winter and Morris, 1976; Yockey, 1976b; Crull, 1976a; Crull, 1976b) asked specific questions regarding cultural norms and family preferences for space, structure type, tenure, and expenditures. The other studies currently available that measure family norms, preferences, or aspirations use a variety of terms with little consistency. Often the terms are used interchangeably to refer to the concepts under examination here: aspirations (Montgomery and McCabe, 1973; Belcher, 1970; Rushing, 1970; Cagle and Deutscher, 1970), desires (Stubbs, 1972; Morris and Winter, 1973), ideals (Stewart, 1973; Lamanna, 1964; Michelson, 1966; Williams, 1971), preferences (Michelson, 1966; Hinshaw and Allott, 1972; Williams, 1971; Coates, 1976), future housing (Ladd, 1972), needs and standards (Rainwater, 1966), dream house (Belcher, 1970), and expectations and intentions (Cagle and Deutscher, 1970).

From the discussions of methodology included in the research reviewed, each study was classified according to the definitions developed in Chapter 2. Thus, if a study was concerned with an analysis of desires or ideals currently held and immediately applicable, it was classified as an analysis of family norms or cultural norms. If the research dealt with desired future housing conditions, it was assumed to represent aspirations. Studies dealing with housing choices in the light of constraints, either present or future, were classified as concerning preferences or expectations, respectively. Some studies were somewhat ambiguous (is a "dream house" a present ideal or a future aspiration?). Most, however, could be discretely classified. Thus Ladd (1972), Hinshaw and Allott (1972), and Rushing (1970) studied future housing desires and were classified as studies of aspirations. Cagle and Deutscher (1970) dealt with expectations and preferences. All other studies analyzed concepts that were similar to family norms or cultural norms and were treated as such regardless of the terminology used.

THE HOUSING NORMS OF SUBGROUPS

Space Norms

American space norms (Chapter 5) are defined in terms of the number of rooms or number of bedrooms needed by the family. One way to assess whether there are subcultural differences in space norms is to ascertain whether there are different rules for bedroom sharing. Lacking information regarding specific rules for bedroom sharing, asking the desired number of bedrooms might be an acceptable substitute. There would have to be controls for family composition, the number of bedrooms available, and any other variables that could be responsible for departures of family norms from the cultural norms.

Thus studies reporting some differences between blacks and whites (Belcher, 1970) and those reporting striking similarities among blacks, whites, and Mexican-Americans (Stubbs, 1972) in the number of bedrooms and total number of rooms desired are inconclusive without knowing whether there are marked differences in family composition among the samples. Belcher (1970) mentions the need to control for family size:

> *Although nonwhite households tend to be larger than those of whites in Camden County, the whites wanted more bedrooms in the dream home. The modal number of bedrooms was three for Negroes and four for whites. Nonwhites stated more preferences for homes with five bedrooms or more, but, on the other hand, they had more demand for two bedroom homes (p. 235).*

His analysis, however, does not control for family size when assessing black-white differences. A few large black families (the ones desiring homes with five bedrooms or more) could inflate the average for the black sample, making it larger than that for whites. A larger proportion of black families than white families could be two- and three-member households, however. Without data on family size, there is no way of knowing whether the differences found in the number of bedrooms desired and the total number of rooms desired are related to differences in norms or differences in family composition.

By the same token, the apparent similarity in the number of bedrooms desired and the total number of rooms desired among three low-income groups in Texas (Stubbs, 1972) might disappear if controls for family size were introduced. If, for example, the Mexican-American families were significantly larger than either the white families or the black families and still desired the same number of bedrooms, then the conclusion would have to be that their family norms for bedroom sharing are different. This situation might or might not be the actual case. There is no way to tell from this particular study.

Lack of control for family size is also a problem in three studies that analyze the housing desires of low-income white families in rural and urban areas in southern Appalachia (Montgomery and McCabe, 1973) and low-income rural black families in upstate New York (Stewart, 1973; Coates, 1976). All three studies compared the desires expressed by their respondents to the hypothetical image of American housing: a house with three or more bedrooms. They all concluded that housing space desires were similar to those of the typical American family. Because family size was not controlled, however, such a conclusion does not assist in the resolution of the question regarding space norms. If it were the case that the household sizes in the Stewart (1973), Coates (1976), and the Montgomery and McCabe (1973) studies were similar to those in the rest of the population, the conclusion would be valid.

Coates (1976) did find that enough space for each family member and privacy for each member of the family were identified by migrant workers as important dwelling characteristics. Hence, it is likely that the number of bedrooms indicated by the low-income black respondents would be similar to those of whites of similar economic levels.

Evidence from three studies that did control for family size (Ladd, 1972; Yockey, 1976b; Morris and Winter, 1973) when assessing differences in the desired number of bedrooms supports the hypothesis that space norms for black families and low-income families are similar to those of white, middle-income families.

Ladd (1972) studied the housing aspirations of black teenage males from a low income area in Boston. Based on in-depth interviews, she reported that

> *in describing the housing they would like in the future, several participants stated that there would be "a lot of room" or that "everybody would have his own room" (Ladd, 1972, p. 110).*

The latter statement clearly takes family size into account.

Yockey (1976b) hypothesized that space norms would be the same for all income classes. She tested this hypothesis by examining the relationship between bedroom deficits (which have a built-in control for family size) and satisfaction among income classes. To support the hypothesis, the relationships would have had to be the same in all income classes, indicating that a shortage or surplus of bedrooms has the same effect, regardless of income. Yockey found that the relationship between space deficit and satisfaction was much weaker among the low-income group than among the middle- and upper-income groupings. When she controlled for apathy as well as income, however, the relationship between housing satisfaction and space deficit became much weaker. She concluded that the reason for the weak relationship between housing satisfaction and space deficit among low-income families was apathy or indifference:

> *This indifference is interpreted as a means of adjusting to low income status rather than an indicator of differences in housing norms (Yockey 1976b, p. 8).*

Morris and Winter (1973) compared the number of bedrooms desired by low-income black families in rural upstate New York to those desired by a group of middle-income white families in Kansas. For the two groups, three different space measures were compared: bedroom need (based on family composition), number of bedrooms in the current dwelling, and number of bedrooms desired. Although the sample was small, the conclusions were that the family norms of the two groups were essentially the same. Differences in desires could be attributed to differences in actual housing conditions and family composition.

Differences in actual housing conditions could be responsible for the differences Stubbs (1972) found in the desired arrangement of nonbedroom space among Mexican-American, black, and white low-income families in Texas. More Mexican-American families than either black or white families desired a separate living room and a separate dining room. Thus norms for nonbedroom space among Mexican-American families might be different from those of white and black families. Such desires might also be a reflection of the fact that fewer Mexican-American families than either black or white families actually had separate living and dining rooms.

Conclusions regarding the space norms of different groups are based on limited evidence. There is support for the hypothesis that the space norms of black families and of Mexican-American families are similar to those of white, middle-income families. Such evidence is based on studies with either methodological problems or small samples with limited socioeconomic and regional applicability. Perhaps the strongest statement that can be made is that there is no positive evidence that there are differences among socioeconomic, racial, or ethnic groups in terms of space norms for family living. The evidence, although weak, is all negative.

Norms for Tenure and Structure Type

Evidence about tenure and structure-type norms is much more clear cut than that for space norms. It overwhelmingly supports the hypothesis that ownership of a single-family dwelling is a strong cultural norm. Some studies of housing desires appear to assume a single-family dwelling. Coates (1976) asked about specific features in the "ideal home." Belcher (1970) asked respondents to describe the characteristics of the "dream house," while Stubbs (1972) requested information regarding the "desired house."

Studies that have asked about structure type have found support across class, racial, and ethnic categories for the single-family dwelling. Nearly all of Ladd's (1972) respondents, teenage black males from low-income families, described a single-family house as the kind of dwelling they would prefer to live in. Michelson's (1966) study of environmental preferences found that, among his sample of Italian- and Irish-Americans who varied in education and occupation:

> *Along one dimension of environment, housing type, there is no variation in the characteristics of people who choose one alternative*

or another. The popularity of the single-family house is so great that its choice is independent of any variable analyzed (p. 358).

Stewart (1973) and Williams (1971) found that the single-family structure was the first choice of their respondents. Interestingly enough, a mobile home was most often preferred as second choice by Stewart's respondents, rural black families with low incomes. Williams' sample, randomly drawn from low-income areas of a southwestern city, was 45 percent Mexican-American and 34 percent black. He found that the lower-income families (below $5000 per year) were less likely to find multifamily housing acceptable than families with higher incomes. One of the reasons given by the respondents for favoring the single-family dwelling was the opportunity to own it. The desire for ownership was also prevalent among Stewart's respondents. Over 70 percent wanted to own their homes rather than rent.

Berger (1960) studied a group of auto workers whose place of employment was moved from an urban area to a suburb, forcing a change in residence. He found clear-cut support for the respondents' postmove state of ownership even though 70 percent had rented their dwelling prior to the move.

Hinshaw and Allott (1972) found across-the-board support for the owned, single-family residence among their sample of undergraduate students. The sample, drawn from a college in New York City with an open admissions policy, contained substantial percentages of students who were black, Puerto Rican, Italian, Jewish, Irish, and other whites from families with a wide range of annual incomes. Among a sample of black families who wanted to move from a center city neighborhood, Nathanson (1974) found that 80 percent wanted a single-family house.

Differences and similarities in the reporting of the cultural norms and family preferences for ownership of single-family dwellings among occupational groupings (Morris and Winter, 1976a) and income groupings (Winter and Morris, 1976) were tested for a sample drawn from a small city in northwestern Iowa. The researchers found no differences in norms—"the best tenure and structure for the average American family"—between blue collar and white collar groupings. There were almost no differences between the blue and white collar workers in family preferences and achieved housing, as well. (Family norms and preferences were not distinguished from each other in the study.)

The influence of preferences and achieved housing was clearly shown for various income groups (Winter and Morris, 1976). Although over 90 percent of all income groupings reported norms for single-family ownership, the group with the highest percentage supporting those norms was the middle-income category. As hypothesized, the lowest income category had a significantly lower percentage reporting family preferences—"best tenure and structure type for your family right now"—for single-family ownership than did either of the other two groups. Also as expected, the low-income group had a much lower percentage who actually owned a single-family dwelling than did either of the other two groups.

Multivariate analyses that included age, sex, education, and employment status (all of the household head), and family size showed the influence of both actual housing conditions on family preferences and of preferences on norms. Within each income class, household size and age of the head of the household were the best predictors of single-family ownership. The best predictor of preference for a single-family, owner-occupied structure was living in one. The best predictor of reported cultural norms that favored owning a single-family dwelling was reporting a family preference for such a structure.

The conclusions of three studies cast some doubts on the similarity of tenure and structure-type norms across socioeconomic, racial, and ethnic groups. Cagle and Deutscher (1970) studied the intentions and expectations of families who were being relocated because of urban redevelopment and who could qualify for public housing. Only 20 percent of the families intended to purchase a home upon relocation, while 60 percent of the families hoped someday to own a home. The comparatively low percentage of families opting for home ownership immediately surely occurred because the families were faced with severe constraints. After all, they were eligible for public housing. When asked about their aspirations for the future, a much higher percentage chose ownership.

Rushing's (1970) comparison of the aspirations and goal orientations of affluent farmers and those of farm laborers indicated that there are differences in goal orientations between the two groups. Ten percent of the workers mentioned home ownership or better housing. The farmers, on the other hand, were not at all concerned about home ownership and only a few wanted better housing. Rushing recognizes that it is the actual conditions that are different:

> *... farm workers' wishes for such goals as self-employment, home ownership, and good housing are desires for things that farmers already have (p. 385).*

Nevertheless he concluded that there are differences in aspirations according to social status. The overall conclusion perhaps should be that the immediate goals vary with actual conditions, not that there are vastly different norms among the two groups.

Based on his study of working-class Italian-Americans in Boston's West End, Gans (1962) asserted that housing was not a status symbol in the usual middle-class sense. People were quite content with renting apartments in the old, crowded West End, Gans reported. Their satisfaction came from contacts with friends and relatives. While they might like a new house in the suburbs, they would only move if their friends did so as well. Some of the West Enders had moved to single-family dwellings, however, because child rearing was easier in such a setting:

> *The younger couples who moved from the West End earlier in the 1950's might have left for just this reason. But those West Enders who stayed behind indicated that as they had grown up in tenements, their children could do likewise. For many of them, moreover, a suburban house was financially out of reach (p. 23).*

Thus, Gans presents conflicting observations. On the one hand, the West Enders did not want to move away from their friends and neighborhood. On the other hand, they could not afford it anyway. Since the single-family house was not attainable, it is possible that families developed an acceptable life style around that which was attainable. The conclusion is that the norm for ownership of a single-family house is pervasive throughout all classes and racial and ethnic groups in the United States. The overwhelming proportion of the existing evidence supports that conclusion.

Norms for Quality and Expenditure

Housing quality, as noted in Chapter 7, cannot be assessed by a single item or score except possibly by market value of the home in relation to social status and income. Market value may only be relevant within a single housing market for the same size, structure type, and tenure of dwellings. When those factors are removed, what is left in quality is the presence or absence of certain objective aspects of the housing that can be classified as describing the structure, the facilities, or the level of housekeeping and maintenance (Morris et al., 1972).

The characteristics that contribute to quality (after tenure, structure type, and space are accounted for) may vary from individual to individual and among income classes. Unlike the other norms discussed in Part 2, families are expected, via the norm, to obtain housing quality in accordance with their social status. Thus there are differences in the quality prescribed according to social class. The appropriate amount to spend on housing is related to income, and so this amount also varies among subgroups of the population. Thus it becomes even more important to control for income and social class when assessing similarities and differences among quality norms.

Some of the aspects of housing that have been studied are more properly classified as part of the definition of housing rather than as normatively prescribed quality. Hence the finding that all respondents desire at least one complete bathroom (Stubbs, 1972; Belcher, 1970; Coates, 1976), a sanitary sewer system (Stubbs, 1972), some type of heating system (Stubbs, 1972; Belcher, 1970), plenty of hot water, and the absence of roaches (Ladd, 1972) only affirms the definition of housing rather than similarities in family quality norms. Coates (1976) concluded that the four dwelling attributes rated most important by his sample of black migrant workers (easy to keep clean, protection from the weather, comfortable temperature, and safe from intruders) are "minimum requirements for a safe and comfortable living space" (p. 60).

Beyond the basic definition of housing, there appear to be norms for increasingly higher quality for higher-income and higher-status groups. Since the research literature does not clearly control for the influence of current housing conditions on quality norms, it is difficult to be sure of the strength of that pattern.

Stubbs (1972) and Belcher (1970) found differences in the type of construction preferred and in the number of bathrooms desired between whites and others. Both found that nonwhite families desired fewer bathrooms and less expensive construction than white families. Is it the case that they indeed have lower quality norms or simply are currently experiencing lower quality and therefore desire less? No mention is made in the Belcher study of current housing conditions. In Stubbs' study, none of the white families lacked a bathroom. Yet 37 percent of the black families and 35 percent of the Mexican-American families lacked any bathroom facilities in their current dwelling. Desiring a complete bathroom when a family has none at all clearly indicates an acceptance of the definition of housing.

Belcher found differences in the equipment and facilities desired by blacks and whites. More white families than black families wanted a fireplace, and the desire for a dishwasher was just the reverse. Belcher explains his finding regarding the desire for a fireplace as symbolizing poverty for blacks and status for the whites. Thus there is support for the contention that norms for quality vary with income.

Neighborhood Norms

Evidence about racial, ethnic, and class differences in neighborhood conditions is extensive. Poor people and some minority groups more often live in housing and neighborhoods that are thought of as slums. That they live in "slums" is often taken as an indication of differences in norms rather than an indication of the life conditions that force them to live there. In some cases, neighborhood behavior attributed to the people studied is asserted to be quite different from that of other social classes.

For example, Fried and Gleicher (1961) and Gans (1962) reported that the Italian-Americans living in Boston's West End tended to "live" in the entire neighborhood, rather than just in the dwelling unit itself. Studies reporting the behavior of the middle class in suburban areas, however,

(Gans, 1967; Whyte, 1956) also report extensive use of the outdoor environment in the neighborhood.

Fried (1963) reported "grief" reactions among the same West End families when urban redevelopment forced them to relocate. While his description of the reaction is undoubtedly correct, it is not necessarily class-specific. There is no reason to believe that grief reactions would not prevail among middle-class families under the conditions of forced relocation. The implication of the three studies (Fried and Gleicher, 1961; Gans, 1962; Fried, 1963) is that the group of Italian-Americans were *more* satisfied with their neighborhood than middle-class people would have been. Otherwise why would they experience more intense grief reactions upon moving? The assertion is unsubstantiated by any comparison between working- and middle-class samples, however.

A more plausible conclusion is that lower- and working-class slum dwellers would be less satisfied with their neighborhoods than middle-class groups with their higher quality neighborhoods. Therefore the middle-class groups would be more likely to feel a strong sense of loss. Some partial evidence is available from a series of samples in small towns and cities ranging in size from fewer than 500 to over 30,000. Those data show that from 22 percent to 41 percent reported they would be "very sorry" if they would have to move from their community (Goudy, 1975).

The available information on norms, on the other hand, is sketchy, but lends support to the argument that there are no vast differences in neighborhood norms across racial, ethnic, and socioeconomic subgroups. Hinshaw and Allott (1972) found that there were no differences in neighborhood aspirations according to race, ethnicity, or socioeconomic status. All groups except white Protestants and those from higher-income families ranked safety and proximity to good schools as the "critically important" neighborhood characteristics of their future dwellings. The exceptions noted might be related to lack of control for actual conditions. It is possible that students from white Protestant families and those from upper-income families (over $20,000 per year) already lived in safe neighborhoods with good schools and therefore failed to mention them. Recent studies of the desires and aspirations of black families (Schermer and Levin, 1968; Billingsley, 1968; Mack, 1968; Beardwood, 1968) strongly support the argument that their family norms specify proximity to good schools.

Poor neighborhood conditions, in the form of high crime rates, a high degree of family instability, and perceived violence and lack of safety, have been shown to be related to the desire to move among both blacks and whites (Kasl and Harberg, 1972; Nathanson, 1974; Droettboom et al., 1971). Blacks were shown to be more dissatisfied with such conditions than whites (Kasl and Harberg, 1972).

Ladd (1972) and Hinshaw and Allott (1972) found that their respondents (college students and black teenage males) aspired to live in a suburban neighborhood. Michelson (1966) and Lamanna (1964) studied specific aspects of the physical and social environment. Michelson reported no consistent differences in the respondents' arrangements of their ideal environment according to social class.

Lamanna (1964) concluded that there is a strong degree of consensus regarding physical and social "livability values" across racial and social class groups. He did find differences in the rankings of some of the physical variables according to race, however. He attributed the major differences to the apparent fact that "people value most what they have least of" (p. 321). The implication is that statistical controls for actual conditions would eliminate the differences. Lamanna's findings lend some support to the norm for homogeneity. All groups ranked heterogeneity—"a town should have a mixture of all types of persons"—as least important in their ideal environment.

The conclusions regarding neighborhood norms are, at best tentative, but seem to point to support for good schools, a suburban area, and a homogeneous population as ubiquitous. In particular, black families seem to be as dissatisfied as white families with poor schools, high crime rates, and poor quality neighborhood conditions.

HOUSING AND SUBCULTURES: A CONCLUSION

Conclusions as to the combination of factors that appear to be responsible for the housing adjustment behavior among different socioeconomic classes and racial and ethnic groups can be depicted in a causal diagram (Figure 21). The arrows indicate the causal connections between factors. The immediate cause of housing adjustment behavior is the level of satisfaction-dissatisfaction that is produced by the normative housing deficits or unfilled housing needs.

The reference points for normative housing deficits are the family and cultural norms and the characteristics of the current housing and neighborhood. Achieved housing and neighborhood conditions vary considerably among racial, ethnic, and socioeconomic subgroups. The differences result from the constraints produced by differences in social status and minority status. Socioeconomic status, which is influenced by race and ethnicity, produces greatly differing sets of extrafamilial constraints. Those constraints, in turn, produce differences in intrafamilial constraints such as hopelessness and apathy in response to reduced opportunity and to economic deprivation. The extrafamilial constraints and the intrafamilial constraints together lead to poorer achieved housing conditions for people of lower social and minority status.

An arrow connects socioeconomic status and quality norms, for there are indications that quality and expenditure norms are related to class and income. Arrows are not drawn from either race and ethnicity or socio-

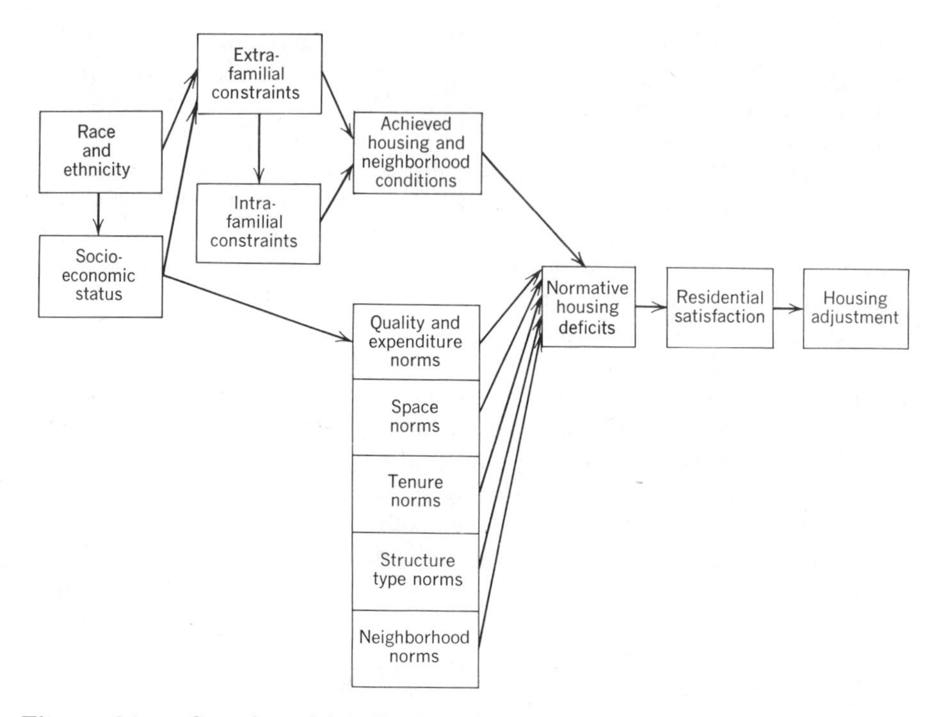

Figure 21 Causal model indicating the influence of constraints on normative housing deficits and housing adjustment.

economic status to the norms for space, tenure, structure type, or neighborhood.

There is very little evidence supporting the hypothesis that the major social class, racial, and ethnic groupings in the United States differ in terms of their space, tenure, structure-type, or neighborhood norms as conceptualized here. Rather, differences in behavior are caused by differences in original housing conditions and the operation of constraints that impede conformance to the norms. The exception is a pattern of family norms for quality and expenditures that rather clearly are lower for low-income families than for high-income families.

Thus the recent emphasis on ascertaining "user needs" prior to the planning and construction of housing and neighborhood facilities for low-income groups and racial and ethnic minorities is, to some extent, misplaced. User needs *are* known. Those needs are housing and neighborhood conditions that meet cultural norms. To deny the existence of those norms and provide housing that does not meet all of the major ones is to invite continued dissatisfaction with government housing programs. Public housing projects in Chicago, St. Louis, Brooklyn, and other large cities, are testimony to the fact that a rented weather-tight box with plumbing in an apartment complex is not adequate housing in the United States. The emphasis in housing programs should be placed on searching for creative means to design, build, and finance housing that meets cultural norms but is attainable under the constraints experienced by such groups.

DEFINITIONS

Achieved housing. The actual conditions of the dwelling in which the family lives.

Poverty line. Point of demarcation or criterion line established by the Social Security Administration or other agency on the basis of family income, family size and composition, and residence (farm or nonfarm) to distinguish between poverty and nonpoverty populations.

Part 5
Implications for Housing Policy

Well, I was born in a town called Audubon,
southwest Iowa—right where it oughta been . . .
23 houses, 14 saloons and a feed mill, in 1930.
C. W. McCall*

Having developed the model of housing adjustment and adaptation in the first four parts of this book, the obvious question is, "So what?" Of what value is this model for the solution of the housing problems affecting the cities, towns, and rural areas in the United States? Does it only apply to the isolated activities of individual families? Are there generalizations that also apply to groups of families? The answer appears to be "yes" to the latter and arises from the boundary interchange assumption discussed in Chapter 3. As a consequence, the analyst is sensitized to the possibility that the existence of housing problems for some families impinges on others. Likewise, solutions by some families acting individually impinge upon other families.

The purpose of Part 5 is to discuss the analysis of community and society-wide housing problems. Special emphasis is placed on the analysis of the collective development of awareness of problem situations and the choice and evaluation of proposed solutions.

In the preceding chapters, the family has been treated as the focus of attention. In this part the focus is shifted to the total social system, and views families as elements of the society or as elements of communities which, in turn, are elements of the society. Further, attention can be given to how the fulfillment of the preferred states of families and other elements of the society relate to one another and to those of the society. Such analyses build upon the assumptions of plurality and heterogeneity of subsystems.

It seems obvious that at times the filling of family needs could conflict with the filling of needs of other societal units such as business, industry, labor, etc. And, at times, the meeting of the needs of the elements of the

* From "Audubon" by C. W. McCall and Louis F. Davis. Lyric reprint by permission American Gramaphone.

society severally could conflict with the fulfillment of global or partial preferred states of the society.

There are two key steps in proceeding from an analysis of the well-being of individual families to a society-wide measure of well-being. One is to ask how societies go about combining the welfare levels of families to arrive at a measure of the well-being of the society. The weighting process at the societal level is similar to that at the family level, where the satisfactions of each member of the family are "added up" to arrive at an assessment of family satisfaction. The other is to reconcile the potential conflict between family well-being and general well-being. According to Pfaff (1976):

> *Consumers can thus only take the individual and not the "systemic" or societal perspective in evaluating the quality of their consumption. Consumers thus evaluate only private and not social benefits and costs when they are being asked about their level of consumer satisfaction. Accordingly, any index which is based on questioning of individuals must by necessity ignore to a large extent the so-called "externalities", i.e., the impact of one individual's consumption on the consumption of others (p. 9).*

A key question then is whether simply adding up measures of family well-being can be used as a public policy tool (Pfaff, 1976, p. 10). The answer relates, in part, to another question: Is the function of policy makers to concern themselves with family welfare only or must they be concerned with the total system?

Householders, obviously, can be expected to develop family level policy that would primarily serve to foster the well-being of the family. The present authors do not totally agree with Pfaff that families cannot see the social costs and benefits at all. It surely is the case that they have a bias but families often make decisions with the greater society in mind. For example, they may decide to limit their consumption out of a concern for the possible impact of overconsumption on environment—a threat to the welfare of others including future generations.

Policy makers at the community level have a kind of balancing act to perform. They tend by and large to be elected officials. As such they must concern themselves with community welfare but also must look out for the welfare of enough families to be assured of receiving enough votes for re-election. Aside from families there are much more influential groups of various persuasions who must be appeased or re-election is impossible. Thus, makers of housing policy must relate to the building materials industry, the financial institutions, the labor unions, and the realtors, to name only a few. At the same time they are responsible for the general, as opposed to individual, family and pressure group welfare.

It should not be concluded that it is easy to measure the extent to which the general welfare is served by the meeting of the needs of elements. In historical terms, the idea that societal representatives should or even could intervene in the unfolding of the future of a society or a community is a relatively new one. That such intervention should be performed in the name of social well-being defined in terms of the well-being of the individuals and families of the society is likewise new. Much of what occurred in earlier days, especially the misery of the poor and disadvantaged, was thought of as having been due to divine intervention or perhaps fate.

L. T. Hobhouse (1924) was one of the early social scientists who felt that intervention in the name of social welfare was not only possible but desirable. The possibility of assessing needs and conditions with a view to rationally allocating resources to the meeting of needs in order to solve or prevent problems became an integral part of Western society as a result of the social forces that produced the writings of Hobhouse and similar thinkers.

It is possible for an individual or a family to deal with their problems in unorganized and unsystematic ways and still manage rather well because it is possible for one or a few individuals to mentally keep track of all or most of the factors relevant to their well-being. But in the case of larger organizations such as communities and societies there are too many factors that contribute to individual and collective welfare, too great a variety of constraints, and too many possibilities for conflict in the search for well-being. As a consequence the effort and care required to monitor the extent to which general and individual welfare are being optimized if not maximized is enormous. Often it may appear that the cost is so great that it uses resources that might have been used to solve the problem.

There are risks to personal freedom and privacy in highly detailed data gathering on almost any topic of social relevance. Besides, even with excellent information incorrect decisions may often be made. In particular, it may be the case that the detection of the existence of a problem in a large organization is so slow in coming to the attention of policy makers that correctives are applied after the solution is already underway through the informal application of correctives by individuals. As a result the application of additional correctives by societal representatives may swing conditions in the opposite direction and create an additional problem.

For example, if attempts to reduce the money supply with the goal of curbing inflation are applied late they may have the effect of creating a recession. The late application of solutions to end the recession may then create another round of inflation. Although social planning, decision making, and problem solving are imperfect instruments, there are general principles that can be outlined.

Part 5 includes a discussion of the cultural sources of problems, analyzes the spontaneous development of problems in various stages (Chapter 16), and discusses the question of intervention for purposes of consciously solving or preventing the emergence of problems by interrupting their "natural history" (Chapter 17).

Chapter 16
Housing as a Social Problem

Little town
west of Ames
Small town

Friday night
go to town night
Fill up the street
with people
with popcorn
from the corner

What you do
is go down town
uptown?
around seven
and hang around
walk in a
few stores
maybe go to the movie
or go home
alone at nine
when the
stores close
and be lonely
in a dark
old house

Funny how
a person
could be lonely
in a friendly
midwestern
town

birthplace of
somebody
discovered by
somebody,
famous.

Boone, Ia
50036 Carl John Harris

A housing problem may be said to exist whenever housing conditions significantly deviate from the standards of the society and its members. As Becker (1966) points out:

> *. . . a social problem consists of an objective condition in society that is defined by members of the society as a problem about which something ought to be done (p. 2).*

That some percentage of the population of the United States lives in housing that is crowded or that some percentage lives in housing that does not have plumbing facilities are objective conditions. Their evaluation as undesirable is a subjective matter that is relatively independent of the nature of the objective condition. The subjective judgment about the desirability of an objective housing condition has its source in normative standards that arise from social interaction (Mogey, 1964, p. 525). It should be pointed out that the norms under discussion in this chapter are primarily the cultural norms rather than the family norms. The idea is to refer to norms that define the preferred states of the society with respect to housing. Cultural norms or standards are of two kinds, those that define the standards that govern the behavior of families and individuals and those that define nationwide preferred conditions.

Social problems represent society-wide or community-wide deficits in well-being as measured in terms of specific preferred states rather than total well-being. The source of the definition of specific conditions as social problems is the cultural system of the community and the society, but the recognition and solution of social problems involves interaction and communication among the members of the society. Comparisons are made between reality and cultural standards. If the situation warrants, collective action is planned and taken. Examples of standards or norms promulgated specifically for nationwide housing conditions include the vague goal of "a decent home and a suitable living environment," the specific production goals for Public Housing announced in the 1949 Housing Act, and the general production goals of the 1968 Housing and Urban Development Act.

The idea that the adequacy of housing or of the level of consumption of many goods is best measured by reference to cultural norms was developed at least as early as the middle of the 19th century by LePlay (1855). Zimmerman and Frampton's (1935) discussion of LePlay's hypotheses concludes:

> *The actual quantity of goods consumed is not as sure an index of the real well-being of the people as is the influence of the mores on the types of consumption (p. 57).*

The definition of a social problem has been troublesome for social scientists. The difficulty, in part, is a semantic one but is not to be taken lightly because semantic problems for scientists affect the form, procedure, and even the results of research (Ball, 1972). The framework of this book implies that there are three levels of problems just as there are three types of norms: familial, communal, and societal problems. A family problem is said to exist when some kind of weighted majority or plurality of the family members agree that there is a problem. The same may be said for community or societal problems.

In their natural state the recognition of social problems is very much a democratic process, largely because of the way in which a social problem is defined. It is not the case that a social problem is simply an aggregation of family or community problems. Some social problems (a housing shortage, for example) may appear even when a very small proportion of families lack a separate housing unit. Conversely, 90 percent of all families may be experiencing a particular family level problem and yet the situation might not be termed a social problem.

Not only must a weighted majority or plurality agree that a problem exists, although they may not necessarily experience it, but its solution must be seen to require society-wide action. The notion of a weighted majority is necessary because some individuals and groups or classes of individuals are more influential than others within families or communities, as well as societies. Often business, industry, or labor organizations have more influence on the treatment of a condition as a problem and on the amount of resources expended on solutions than do families and individuals. Social problem recognition tends to be democratic but not on a one-person, one-vote basis.

Because social problems are defined in terms of normative deficits, solutions would seem to most naturally arise from changes in norm-seeking behavior or from changes in norms. There are two basic types of norms: those prescribing goals and those prescribing means for reaching the goals. Therefore a solution may be achieved through altering the goals to make them more readily achievable or through the development of newly sanctioned means for meeting the old goals. Further, under chronic states of excess or of scarcity of resources, goals may rise or fall in terms of the amount or quality of the goal that is judged sufficient.

When focusing on means (Stanley, 1968) there would be a shortage of, for example, mortgage money or materials to solve a housing problem, rather than a shortage of housing itself. In the view of this book the social problem is the level of crowding (the end or goal) that a shortage of housing would cause because of the lack of money and materials (the means). Obviously, both concepts of scarcity are important but it is necessary to distinguish between the problem itself and the lack of resources with which to solve it.

The view that scarcity is defined in sociocultural terms (something is scarce if people think it is) rather than naturalistic terms (scarcity based on the absolute quantity available or existent) brings it into the realm of human control (Stanley, 1968). Thus, the cultural fact of scarcity may be altered by changing cultural definitions as well as by increasing the known supply. It is assumed throughout this chapter that either method represents a solution. Thus, one of the suggested responses to the energy shortage is to reduce standards for temperature inside the home. It is possible to reduce the shortage of petroleum by reducing the need for it.

The existence of the problem itself depends upon shortages (deficits) in some preferred state. There may or may not be a deficit of the means needed to achieve the preferred (nondeficit) state. The distinctions between goals and means, both of which are indispensable concepts in the social problems approach, leads one to view the process of recognition and solution of problems in terms of what has come to be known as the "new home economics" (Ratchford, 1975).

Families, communities, or societies can be viewed as producing their own satisfaction (Becker, 1965; Nerlove, 1974). By "purchasing" a set of goods, each with its set of characteristics (the subset of all their attributes that are sought by consumers), the household or other social organization obtains a package of characteristics that provides (hopefully) the maximum amount of satisfaction (Lancaster, 1971). The factors used as means are the "money" used to purchase characteristics (raw materials). The process of recognition of problems, decision making, and the application of solutions amounts to the process of manufacturing satisfaction, or well-being from the raw materials. An important sense in which social organizations manufacture their own well-being is implied in the notion that the development of norms is a part of the processes that occur within the organization more or less simultaneously with its adjustment processes.

THE INTERRELATEDNESS OF SOCIAL PROBLEMS

Although the focus in this book is on housing problems, they are often intertwined with other problems. It may be the case, for example, that poverty is perceived to be a social problem and that poverty in turn causes housing problems. The solution of a housing problem may contribute to the solution (or creation) of others. The point of departure in this book is always the housing problem itself.

The key mechanism connecting different social problems is the necessity of using one potential problem area as a means for solution to the other. In other words, surplus resources in one area can serve as means for solutions in others. Sometimes solutions of housing problems create problems elsewhere by using resources that might have been used in another area.

A primary housing problem is one that simply involves housing. A secondary housing problem is one that has created additional problems. Inequities in housing distribution, for example, may be important factors in school segregation. Poverty, population growth, or other social problems may serve as causes of housing problems (a housing problem might be a secondary poverty or population problem). The realistic treatment of housing problems requires that the primary cause of the problem receive treatment. if the existence of poverty is *the cause* of a housing problem then solutions should be sought that would alleviate poverty. On the other hand, when the primary problem is housing, that is the place to apply solutions even when the housing problem has secondary effects on, for example, race relations.

Success in solving the problem of poverty may or may not contribute to the solution of the housing problem, just as success in solving the housing problem may or may not help to improve race relations. The dimensions of all the problems involved (poverty, racial discrimination, housing, employment, etc.) should be considered if the solutions are to have widespread and beneficial effects. It is important to emphasize the primary-secondary level of problems because housing has often been treated as the primary problem when it may have been secondary or even unrelated. Suggestions that improved housing could reduce crime rates may be ineffective if both high crime rates and poor housing are secondary problems resulting from a primary poverty problem.

PROGRESS AND THE SOLUTION OF HOUSING PROBLEMS

A common view of social problems sees the recognition and solution of successive problems as a means by which development, progress, or social evolution take place. Certain conditions are seen as problems. Solutions are then achieved based on the development of new norms relative to goals or means. As a result, the group may be better prepared to deal with subsequent problems (Sirjamaki, 1964, p. 35).

Such a view of societal progress based on overcoming problems is very much parallel to the family development approach to the study of the family. In that approach "family developmental tasks" are seen as problems to be solved before skills can be developed to deal with subsequent problems (Hill and Hansen, 1960).

L. T. Hobhouse (1924) suggested that progress may be measured by the development of three sets of harmonious relations: those between the society and its environment, those of people to their society, and those among the social organizations within the society. The total understanding of the ways in which societies solve their problems depends upon an analysis of Hobhouse's three sets of relationships.

Housing, which is one aspect of the relations between the society and its environment, reduces the amount of physiological adaptation the members of the society must make to the physical environment. Housing provides shelter and mediates the contact between the members of the society and the environment.

Harmonious relations between people and their society may depend upon the ability of the society to provide for housing. If people are unable to live in housing that meets family and cultural standards they will tend to become dissatisfied. If the dissatisfaction is felt strongly, they may cease to engage in traditional behavior and seek other means to obtain housing. For example, if there is a chronic disconnection between hard work, saving money, and honest living on the one hand and the ability to obtain good housing as a reward on the other, illegitimate means may be used to obtain it (Merton, 1957, p. 141; Greer, 1966, p. 519). Alienation in its various forms (Seeman, 1959) may develop as a result and undermine the social order—perhaps forcing changes in the society that would reduce the inequity. Thus, it seems obvious that housing plays a role in the relations between people and their society.

Housing may become involved in the relations among subgroups of the society as well, since it serves to demonstrate to others the social status of the family or community and is often unequally distributed among the various groups. Such inequality may lead to conflict as pointed out by the National Advisory Commission on Civil Disorders (NACCD, 1968). In their analysis of the causes of violence and destruction in urban areas in the mid-1960s, the Commission emphasized the contrasts between the housing conditions of black families in inner city ghettos and those of white suburban families as one of the most important sources of the discontent (p. 472). Certain responses made by the government were intended (at least ostensibly) to reduce the interracial inequity. Subsequent improvement in interracial relations (if indeed there was a real improvement rather than repression of open hostility) may have resulted in part from the public efforts to reduce housing inequities.

Hobhouse's three sets of harmonious relations are simply an early version of several of the assumptions of a systemic functional model. The first relates to the asumption that a society is not a closed system but depends for its welfare upon relationships with its environment. The other two relate to the assumptions that the goals of the elements of a system (families, communities, and other organizations) are to some degree integrated with those of the total society and with one another. These two sets of relationships are implied in the concept of cultural integration.

Cultural Integration

In this book the emphasis is placed on the normative approach to the study of societal functioning (Ellis, 1971). Thus, the analysis focuses on changes in the level of integration that accompany dealing with problems within existing normative systems rather than on the origins of cultural systems (Ellis, 1971, p. 694).

Neither the genesis nor the dissolution of societies or communities is under discussion because social problems can be defined only in the context of an existing normative system. Revolution as a means of solving problems is not considered. The kinds of problems that would lead to revolution would represent the utter breakdown of a normative system and "social problem" would be too benign a concept for such conditions.

The nihilist school of thought that maintains that much or all of current social-cultural arrangements are better done away with is rejected on similar grounds. The kinds of problems that would require the destruction of the entire culture are clearly not in the same class as social problems. There are anarchist schools of thought that suggest centralized housing programs should be eliminated. That families and individuals should be encouraged to fill their housing needs individually and in small community groups is a key doctrine (Turner, 1976). Such proposals, although appealing in their simplicity and directness, ignore the extent to which the levels of interdependence in the world force decision making to more centralized levels. Perhaps social conditions in the world have reached a state that a complete return to the relative anarchy of frontier days is needed. In this book we have assumed otherwise.

It is not the case, however, that there is no consideration of the possibility or desirability of cultural change. On the contrary, it is assumed that changes in housing needs and standards can and do take place. Further, it is assumed that:

1. The existence of chronic problems may lead to reductions in those standards.

2. Such reductions may serve as alternatives to heroic efforts at solution.

3. Standards may rise because of "chronic" surpluses of resources in other areas.

4. Rising housing standards could produce new problem situations if the population began to aspire to a level of housing beyond the ability of the economy to provide the resources.

In Chapter 17 the importance of those points is emphasized by noting that the solution of housing problems requires two sets of information. The first is monitoring current levels of housing conditions and housing norms in order to detect the presence of deficits. The second is monitoring changes in the norms that apply to the evaluation of needs and conditions to insure that the deficits are measured correctly.

A key form of cultural change involves changes in the level of cultural integration. Cultural integration may be measured by at least six factors:

1. A closer correspondence between norms and behavior.

2. Greater unity or reduced conflict among the various cultural norms.

3. Reduced conflict among the various roles individuals are required to play.

4. Increased complementarity of subgroup norms (norms that are specific to certain classes of individuals such as the norms for the behavior of the clergy) to those of other subgroups.

5. Closer correspondence of subcultural norms to the norms of the culture.

6. A reduction of the number of subcultures in the society.

Cultural integration as progress implies that successful solution of a social problem would produce an increase in one or more of the indicators of integration, thereby improving the society's ability to deal with subsequent problems. The matter of adaptability as discussed in Chapter 14 with reference to family integration is appropriate at the societal level. It is probable that societal integration can reach such a level as to reduce adaptability. At some point, greater integration would be likely to reduce societal effectiveness in solving problems unless the society were also characterized by the ability to adapt readily.

Cultural integration is not synonomous with homogenization. The fourth indicator implies the development of specialized roles that improve the functioning of the system by permitting classes of individuals to concentrate their efforts. The integration of societies may increase by developing greater consensus about the cultural norms but may also increase by a greater division of labor. In that regard, House (1936, p. 3) has pointed out that social change may have been responsible for the growth of the social sciences as well as for their interest in the study of social change. The appearance of many social problems as a result of or accompanying rapid social change may have given rise to occupational specialties devoted to the study of ways to solve those problems.

Change and Response

The idea that people and cultures grow and develop in the process of responding to the challenges of problems is an ancient one but was most clearly articulated by Arnold J. Toynbee (1964). Such ideas are very much a part of the folklore of the United States. The response of the society to World Wars I and II and the depression of the thirties are often thought to have shown how well Americans respond to challenges. In times of crisis, vision can be permitted to narrow, other matters can be neglected, and full force and energy can be concentrated on the solution of the crisis. At such times societies seem to draw together, morale rises, and a kind of societal euphoria develops.

Toynbee (1964) points out that there is an optimum problem or challenge:

> *The most stimulating challenge is one of mean degree between an excess of severity and a deficiency of it, since a deficient challenge may fail to stimulate the challenged party at all, while an excessive challenge may break his spirit. . . . The real optimum challenge is one which not only stimulates the challenged party to achieve a single successful response but also stimulates him to acquire momentum that carries him a step further—from achievement to a fresh struggle, from the solution of one problem to the presentation of another. The single finite movement from a disturbance to a restoration of equilibrium is not enough if genesis is to be followed by growth (p. 27).*

Although social problems present a kind of challenge to the society, their status as problems derives largely from their consequences for individual families and communities in the society. The emphasis on the personal impact of problems is based on Davis' (1963) analysis of the behavior of families in industrializing nations experiencing rapid mortality declines. In all societies analyzed, it was the undesirable personal consequences in the form of frustrated goal-seeking behavior of individual families that prompted responses aimed at overcoming the problem. Because the old behavior patterns no longer worked, there appeared to be a loosening of traditional norms for both goals and means, a process that required a degree of adaptability. A variety of new responses were tried by families wishing to reduce the severity of the personal consequences they were experiencing because of changes in the basic conditions.

> *Within a brief period they quickly postponed marriage, embraced contraception, began sterilization, utilized abortions, and migrated*

outward. It was a determined, multiphasic response, *and it was extremely effective with respect to fertility . . . (Davis, 1963, p. 349).*

Social problems, however, are not simply a large number of accumulated individual problems, but depend upon a collective recognition of the need for collective action in addition to the individual responses. A social problem is a challenge to society—a challenge that is felt at the personal or family level, and, through some weighting process, at the societal level. It is a situation that is viewed as not capable of solution by the isolated acts of individual families or even communities. Solutions for social problems originate at the societal level. Often the solutions of grave social problems require new cultural norms, new behavior patterns, new modes of social organization, new specializations, and similar evidences of social and cultural change. Legitimization of the new standards and new behavior patterns represents the final stage in the solution of a problem.

THE NATURAL HISTORY OF SOCIAL PROBLEMS

Social problems have much in common with one another in that they tend to develop in quite predictable ways (Fuller and Myers, 1941; Becker, 1966, pp. 11–14). In general, social problems pass through phases from the first beginnings of awareness, to concern, to attempted solutions, and finally to institutionalized solutions to the problem, although such solutions may come more slowly for some problems than for others.

The development of a housing problem can be characterized by four stages and four processes (Figure 22). The four stages (Morris, 1971) are:

1. A stable *preproblem* stage, during which the problem either does not exist, or is not sufficiently acute to surface because the norms are being satisfactorily achieved by customary behavior.

2. A *problem* stage, signaled by a change in basic conditions or a change in the norms such that customary practices are no longer effective.

3. An *experimental* stage, during which previously neglected practices are revived and/or new ones are developed to deal with the problem.

4. A new stable *postproblem* period featuring one or more of the new behaviors as "customary practices."

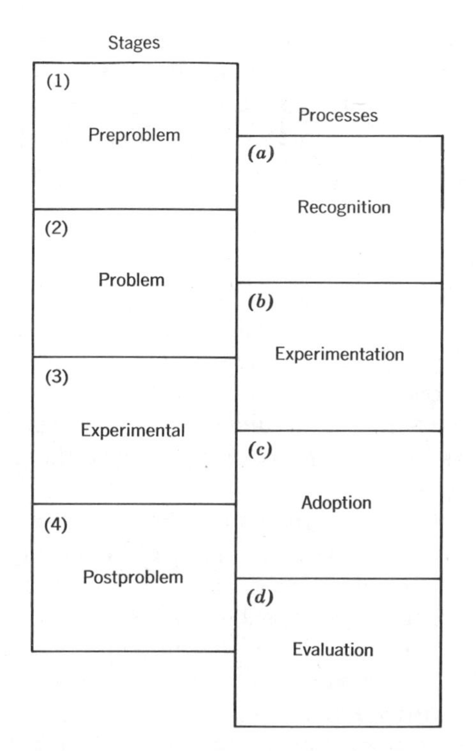

Figure 22 The stages and processes in the development of a housing problem.

The four processes are the dynamic transitions from stage to stage and are (*a*) problem recognition, (*b*) experimentation, (*c*) adoption, and (*d*) evaluation.

Stages and processes simply represent two ways of saying the same thing. Stages are adjectives that describe a single moment in time, a cross section. Processes are verbs that indicate what is occurring during a stage. The conceptual and empirical overlap of stages and processes are depicted in Figure 22.

Sometime during the preproblem stage (1) the process of recognition (*a*) begins to occur when a gap between norms and conditions appears. The completion of recognition brings the problem stage (2) into being. Soon after the problem stage is clearly instituted people begin to experiment with solutions (*b*), thereby bringing about the experimental stage (3). The experimental stage begins with rather disorderly experimentation but ends when certain new programs and behaviors are adopted (*c*) that, it is expected, will solve the problem and keep it under control. At this point the postproblem stage (4) is reached during which evaluation (*d*) of the programs adopted earlier begins to discover if the problem has been solved.

Not all problems pass through all stages. Development may become arrested at any point. Poor communication may slow down recognition. Other problems may divert attention. Effective solutions may not be invented. Once invented, numerous barriers may prevent widespread acceptance.

Preproblem Stage

A community or society that has housing in accord with its norms is in a preproblem stage. It would be difficult to demonstrate conclusively, however, that at any specific time in history there was a complete absence of housing problems. Nevertheless, any given housing problem can be found to be problematic in a specific sense. It would generally be possible to demonstrate that, in terms of the specific factors that produced the particular problem, a previous nonproblem state existed.

The shortage of housing at the end of the 1960s is a case in point. During the first part of the decade, there may have been housing problems regarding quality, for example. In quantitative terms, however, the building industry, as traditionally organized (independent local builders, financed by local lending institutions, building within a single housing market, who establish, essentially, an "on-site factory" to produce a single dwelling unit) was pretty much keeping pace with the demand.

The preproblem stage is not necessarily a point in time when there are no housing problems at all. The preproblem stage is rather a time when the particular problem that subsequently appeared did not exist as a problem.

Problem Recognition Process

Problem recognition and the genesis of a problem are basically the same thing, since social problems only exist (as problems) when they are recognized as such. Evidence of the existence of a problem is either a realignment of conditions or a change in the norms, or both, creating a discrepancy between the norms and the actual conditions.

It may be the case that housing norms prescribe some level of housing conditions such as is depicted in Figure 23*a*. If the norms remain unchanged, but a noticeable decline in housing conditions occurs, a problem may arise. On the other hand, it may be that housing conditions are static but the norms rise. Perhaps real income rises and cultural housing standards go up as a result (Figure 23*b*). A third possibility would be a simultaneous rise in norms and a drop in housing conditions as in Figure 23*c*.

In order for a given change to have widespread impact, it must be sufficiently dramatic in terms of rapidity and/or magnitude that people both perceive the change and feel that it is important. The change that resulted in the crisis in housing quantity that occurred in the late 1960s was an increase

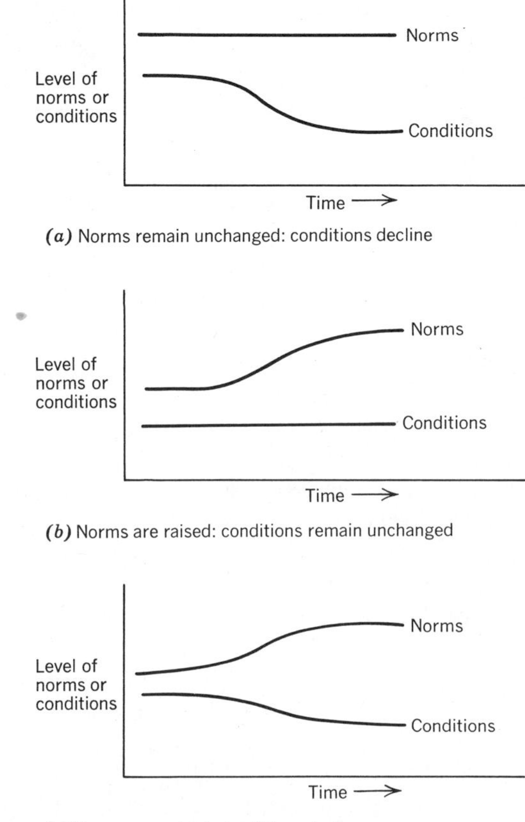

(a) Norms remain unchanged: conditions decline

(b) Norms are raised: conditions remain unchanged

(c) Norms are raised: conditions decline

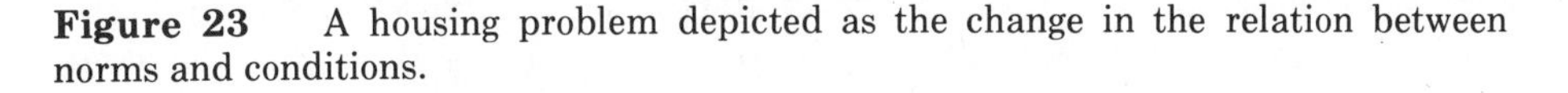

Figure 23 A housing problem depicted as the change in the relation between norms and conditions.

in the rate of new family formation. The baby boom babies born after World War II began to marry and need housing. The change in conditions that caused the housing shortage was possibly the most dramatic demographic change the nation has ever experienced.

Societal or community problem recognition is relatively complex. It is likely that the first to notice a gap between norms and conditions will be the families experiencing the gap. When there is a significant number or critical mass of families, "official" attention may be drawn to the problem. Government committees, task forces, commissions, and investigations to look into the situation may begin to appear.

That was the case in the late 1960s. Those who first recognized the problem were the families who were experiencing difficulty in obtaining normatively prescribed housing conditions. The families, noting the short supply, high cost, and often inadequate space and quality of the housing units available, probably did not necessarily try to identify the primary cause of the problem. What was important were the personal consequences—the need to pay more than they had planned for housing, or the necessity to relax their norms.

Two federally appointed bodies, the National Commission on Urban Problems (NCUP, 1968, p. 73) and the President's Committee on Urban Housing (PCUH, 1968, p. 40), noted the need for millions of new housing units to provide housing specifically for new family formation during the decade between 1968 and 1978. While the quantitative problem was officially recognized, so were other problematic aspects as well: problems with cost, with quality, and with the social and spatial distribution of housing.

Problem Stage

The problem stage comes into full existence when the gap between norms and conditions has progressed far enough so that there is a discerned and important discrepancy between the two. The unusual number of newly formed families placed unaccustomed pressures on housing providers but exerted demand-push inflationary pressures on other sections of the economy as well. Simultaneously, the Vietnam war exerted additional inflationary pressure. Attempts to control the inflation included tight money policies which severely reduced available mortgage money supplies and greatly reduced housing construction. As a result, severe quantitative shortages of new housing units occurred.

The quantitative problem stage that occurred in the late 1960s was characterized by an absolute shortage of conventionally-constructed single-family housing units. The number of households (largely because of new family formation) exceeded the number of housing units available. The consequences for families and for the developers, builders, contractors, realtors, and others multiplied until a full-blown social problem reigned.

Experimentation Process

Once a problem is perceived to exist and comes to be thought of as a serious one, the family or community is likely to begin to engage in behavior motivated by a desire to solve the problem. One important characteristic of the process of experimentation is that conventional norms for family and community behavior and conditions are relaxed under problem conditions. Thus the family or community may choose trial solutions from a heretofore inconceivable range of behaviors.

Prefabricated housing was rejected after World War II when housing was being rapidly produced. The mobile home, certainly the ultimate in prefabrication, was one of the prominent solutions in the late 1960s and early

1970s. Since problems have been defined as gaps between norms and actual conditions, the trial solutions most likely to be selected are those perceived as reducing the gaps.

Experimental Stage

The experimental stage is characterized by a multiphasic response (Davis, 1963). Those experiencing problematic conditions tend to experiment with a wide range of new techniques attempting to deal with the personal consequences of the problem. Many of the new behaviors may not fit established modes of practice. New and unorthodox behavior is called for and condoned during difficult times.

Because the family is the locus of the felt consequences of social problems, individual families may enter this stage before the society as a whole. Some families may adapt their norms so that the conditions become acceptable. Others may engage in housing adjustment. Still others may reorganize their role structures. Several different behaviors and thought patterns may be tried before deciding upon the ones that seem most appropriate.

Using the example of the housing shortage of the late 1960s, the experimental stage was marked by a rise in apartment living and a dramatic increase in the number of families living in mobile homes. In part because individual and family efforts were relatively ineffective, many new federal housing programs and variations on old ones were tried. As a result, much of the attention of community level policy makers was turned to choosing among a new array of relatively untried programs. And, due to the complexity of the new programs and of the application process, a new role appeared. Housing consultants skilled at writing proposals and organizing community efforts to obtain federal subsidy money became highly valued.

Adoption Process

From the variety of solutions tried during the experimental stage, one or more solutions are adopted. There can be new solutions permitting the conditions to approach the achievement of norms (Figure 24*a*), changes in norms (Figure 24*b*), or a combination of the two (Figure 24*c*).

Societal solutions that occur naturally (i.e., without deliberate societal intervention) often are merely a reaction to pressures caused by the dissatisfaction of a critical mass of families or communities who are experiencing the localized consequences of the problem. Reactive solutions of this type may simply be a condoning or fostering of those behaviors already being tried by the families.

The solutions adopted by families during the quantitative housing crisis: mobile home and apartment living, may foreshadow the development of new cultural housing norms, although it is still too early to tell whether or not the

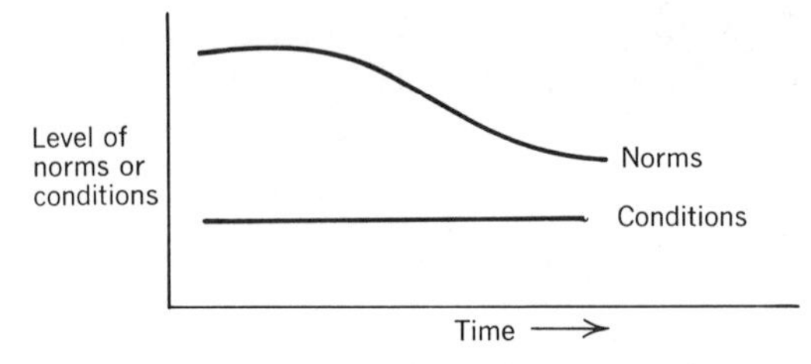

(a) Norms are lowered: conditions remain unchanged

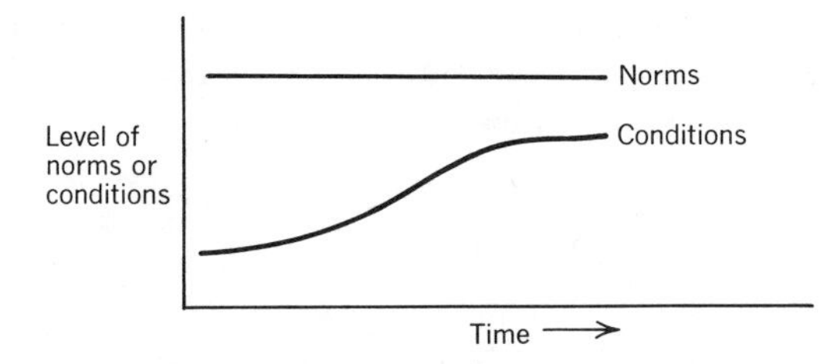

(b) Norms remain unchanged: conditions are improved

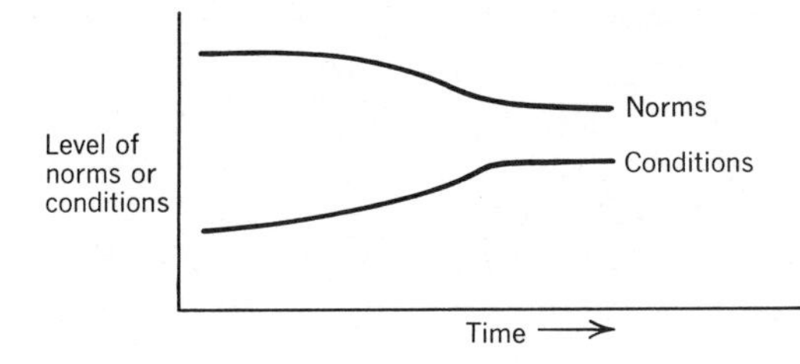

(c) Norms are lowered: conditions are improved

Figure 24 A housing solution depicted as the change in the relation between norms and conditions.

norms have changed. Clearly, the cultural norms were relaxed to make mobile home living more acceptable. It is not totally clear whether this represented reduced preferences or true changes in family norms.

Community programs to foster an increase in apartment construction or the development of mobile home parks are indications that the community is in the process of adopting solutions. Some of the new programs and reworked programs will or already have become accepted as permanent parts of governmental programs. The moratorium on housing activities imposed by President Nixon in 1973 may have served as an opportunity to weed out the less effective innovations.

Postproblem Stage

During the postproblem stage, the successful new programs and new behaviors or thought patterns are institutionalized. The tax policies, begun as a temporary measure, are made permanent. New cultural norms develop to sanction new patterns. As a result of the large number of families who chose mobile homes in the late 1960s, much of the stigma of "trailer living" was lessened. Interest subsidy programs for both rental and home ownership went through a period of scandal followed by the moratorium but now appear to have emerged as successful programs. Rent supplements, a limited program during the 1960s, is being given a more complete trial in the form of the housing allowance program under Section 8.

This stage represents a period in which the previous problem has been solved or at least greatly ameliorated. However, this phase may simply represent the preproblem stage for the next set of problems.

Evaluation Process

During the process of evaluation, both the first- and second-level effects of the solutions adopted are felt and assessed. Has the solution led to a narrowing of the gap between norms and conditions? Has it caused undesirable side effects?

Second-level effects often take even longer to assess, because the solution must become sufficiently institutionalized for its side effects to become apparent. The effects of the Federal Housing Administration policies granting mortgage insurance only for houses in racially homogeneous neighborhoods were not really felt for 15 years.

It is likely that, the more innovative the solution, the longer it will take to assess the effects. For one thing, a certain amount of euphoria accompanies a new solution. A halo surrounds a new housing project, a new community facility, or a successful urban renewal project. When enough time has elapsed so that the effects can be assessed, the community or society may begin to see yet another set of problems with, again, a rather specific set of causes, one of which may have been a solution adopted to overcome a previous problem.

SOCIETAL INTERVENTION IN THE PROCESS OF PROBLEM SOLUTION

Fruitful intervention into the natural history of a housing problem should permit earlier recognition, conscious experimentation with solutions, and earlier evaluation of the effects of solutions once adopted. Housing problems are relatively easy to analyze in retrospect. A much more difficult task is the analysis of housing history *as it is happening.* Yet such an analysis is necessary if there are to be "solutions" that are both effective and do not create new problems.

Tools essential for such an analysis are, first, the use of the appropriate criteria for detecting the existence and magnitude of the problem and for deciding upon appropriate solutions. The second tool needed is an understanding of the way in which problems develop and are overcome naturally, so that rational intervention can be accomplished. in this light, it is important to understand the relative positions of conditions and norms during the development of a problem, as depicted in Figure 25.

The absolute level of norms and conditions is probably irrelevant. As noted previously, the norms may remain unchanged while the conditions change. The conditions may remain constant while the norms change. Or, as depicted in Figure 25, both may change. During the preproblem and postproblem stages, there is not a large gap shown in the diagram between the actual conditions and the cultural norm against which they are being measured. If attempted solutions are effective, the gap will be narrower in the postproblem stage. During the problem and experimentation stages, there is a discrepancy between the conditions and the norms. The gap may be largest during the problem stage. Some of the solutions tried may narrow the gap.

There are few examples of policy making and problem solution that have followed the optimum path. The recent actions of the Food and Drug Administration in dealing with the potential effects of the use of chlorofluorocarbon propellants in aerosol products may illustrate this phenomenon.

The entire process started many years ago. A series of technological innovations came about primarily in connection with the military during World War II that resulted in the aerosol spray can for dispensing liquids

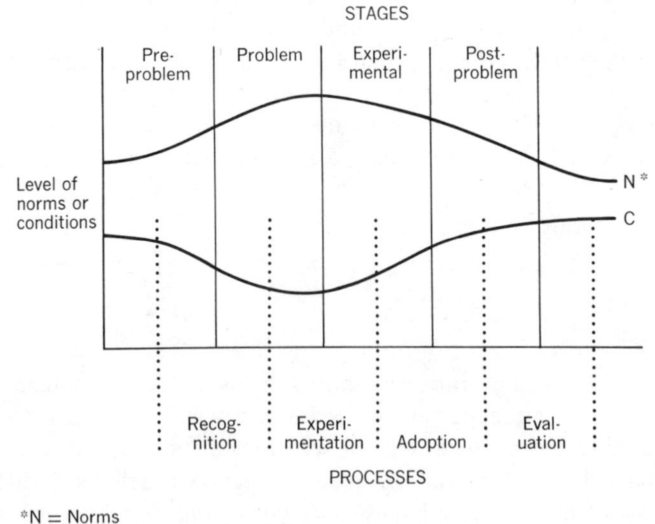

Figure 25 The level of norms and conditions relative to one another during the stages and processes of the development of a housing problem.

and gases. At first a very limited number of products using any propellant were produced. Thus the use of chlorofluorocarbons began at a very small level. Then the use of them began to accelerate until almost all kitchen, bathroom, shop, and even bedroom chemicals seemed to come in aerosol cans, many with fluorocarbon propellants.

A minority of consumers began to become concerned about the use of aerosols, partly because of personal allergies and other harmful effects, some as apparently innocent as sneezing from chemicals in the air. But experts began to become concerned when the quantity of the propellant being released into the atmosphere annually became literally huge. That concern led to research on the possible harmful effects upon people and the environment. A key study indicated that there might be a tendency to disturb the ionosphere which in turn would disrupt the filtering of sunlight and result in skin disease and other potentially harmful effects. When further research failed to refute the existence of the possible danger, the Food and Drug Administration began steps that would reduce and eventually ban the use of chlorofluorocarbon propellants.

Fortunately, great harm had not yet been done. The problem was an incipient one. The FDA action preceded the total manifestation of the problem as a full-fledged social problem. Many, if not most, people were only vaguely aware of the potential harm, and continued to use the aerosol products and to enjoy the seeming convenience they offered.

There was still time to warn the public about the danger and to begin in stages to ban the product entirely without panic. Such steps could be taken without great economic loss to consumers (e.g., as a result of the production of higher-priced replacements) and without great economic loss to producers and retailers who might otherwise have had to withdraw products from the shelves of stores.

One of the key reasons for the apparent success of the chlorofluorocarbon case was the monitoring of the possible effects of the conditions when use of the propellant had become widespread. Another was the phasing in of solutions even before the problem became the subject of public outcry, and apparently before great harm had been done.

Such environmental health issues have much in common with housing problems. They may be slow in developing. Their effects often occur many years after the introduction of a factor into the system. Constant monitoring, early and accurate problem identification, and adequate testing of solutions prior to the "natural" problem stage could prevent many housing problems.

Chapter 17
Housing Policy Considerations

> all Americans have the *right* to decent housing, in decent surroundings of their own choosing, at rents or prices they can afford. This right has not yet achieved constitutional or legal status, although our economy and society have the means to support it. We lack only sufficient political impetus to demand its fulfillment. Chester W. Hartman*

We do not have ready answers to the housing problems that have plagued the United States for at least a half a century. We do not have a single, all-encompassing solution, or even a couple of solutions. We do, however, suggest ways in which problem identification, the development and evaluation of proposed alternatives, and the implementation of one or more of the alternatives might be accomplished.

The purpose of this chapter is to present an outline of positive, yet relatively small steps that can be taken to permit the conscious, planned solution of housing problems. We do not attempt to evaluate specific previous or proposed solutions, such as zoning, public housing, housing allowances, and the like. (A useful treatment is found in Chester Hartman's *Housing and Social Policy.* His analysis and specific proposals are very compatible with the present analysis.) Rather, our purpose is to suggest a framework for dealing with any housing problem, current or future, along with an outline of pitfalls that can be avoided.

THE APPROPRIATE LEVEL FOR SOLUTIONS

Some housing analysts feel that housing production and management would be more effective if families were totally self-determining. They could thus do what they wanted to about their housing, without neighborhood, community, state, or federal restrictions or intervention. There is reason to

* From *Housing and Social Policy,* by Chester W. Hartman (Englewood Cliffs, N.J.: Prentice-Hall, 1975), p. 1.

believe that, at certain times and places, any central government housing program would be inadvisable. It is conceivable that other problems would be so pressing that government resources ought not to be used for housing. Or the level of development might be such that family level or community level organization is the optimal means for dealing with housing.

To advocate one and only one level as the appropriate one for problem solution, in our view, would unduly narrow the range of resources that could be used to solve housing problems. A more balanced view is that the solution of a particular problem should be undertaken at the level at which the appropriate motivation and resources to deal with the matter operate.

For many housing problems, the solutions are most appropriately sought at the community level. The localization of both the housing market and job market, in the form of families wanting housing with access to employment, occurs in rather narrowly defined geographic areas. Such areas may, of course, be larger than a single municipality. Hence the "community" for which a housing problem is relevant may be a county, several counties in a rural area, or an entire metropolitan area.

Community, in this broad sense, is the appropriate locale for the implementation of efforts for dealing with problems of quality, supply, or distribution of housing units. In addition, the community has the responsibility for seeing to it that the well-being of current generations is not permitted to endanger the well-being of future generations who might live in that community (Morris and Winter, 1971). Economic assistance from the federal government in the form of additional resources and incentives for the attainment of normative housing for families in that community may, of course, be necessary and desirable.

MONITORING HOUSING NEEDS AND CONDITIONS

The key to the early detection of and preventive solutions for housing problems is a system for monitoring housing needs and conditions. In the same way that problems occur on three levels and solutions may be achieved at three levels (family, community, society), monitoring of the conditions and needs also can and should be conducted at all three levels. The first four parts of the book have considered in detail the family-level monitoring processes. Thus, for purposes of part five the two important levels are the community and society.

Housing Stock

The first necessary information is an estimate of the housing stock and its characteristics, including quality. The census provides some information along these lines every ten years. In order to arrive at estimates of the housing stock in subsequent years it is necessary to combine with the census data the additions to and subtractions from the stock that occurred during the interim. In theory, there is a straightforward equation for making such an estimate:

$$HS_1 = HS_0 + Const + Inmoves + PosConv - Dem - Outmoves - NegConv$$

Where

HS_1 is the housing stock in a year subsequent to the census year.

HS_0 is the housing stock in the area at the time of the census.

Const is the number of new housing units constructed since the census.

Inmoves is the number of units moved into the area from other areas (mobile homes in particular).

PosConv is the number of other types of units that have been converted to housing units, positive conversions.

Dem is the number of housing units demolished.

Outmoves are the dwelling units (particularly mobile homes) moved out of the area.

NegConv is the number of housing units converted to other uses, negative conversions.

The accuracy of the estimates depends, of course, upon the accuracy of the recording of the various elements in the equation. Most areas of the United States require building permits for construction and conversions of any considerable size. Often permits are required for demolitions and for movement over the road of mobile homes, especially large ones and, of course, conventional dwellings that are to be moved. The completeness and accuracy of such recording is very uneven from area to area and even within areas. Therefore, accurate intercensal estimates are seldom achieved. Often the recording of the various additions and subtractions to the housing stock is performed in different offices and never collected in a single location.

One important variation in estimation of the housing stock is to separate out the unsound stock. Separate estimates of the sound housing stock require careful attention to the definitional norms discussed in earlier chapters, ensuring that no dwelling that fails to meet the definition of a housing unit is counted as such. Some families, of course, are currently occupying unsound housing.

The estimates of the amount of housing construction and rehabilitation required to meet housing needs during the decade from 1968 to 1978 in the 1968 Housing and Urban Development Act attempted to separate the sound from the unsound stock. The estimated requirements for additions to the housing stock based on the estimated demand and the estimated supply excluded unsound units from the estimated stock. These units were thus added to the amount of required rehabilitation and construction. If such estimates are required it is necessary to record entrance into the housing stock of rehabilitated units and record exit from the stock of units that drop into the unsound category. Taking account of rehabilitations and deterioration would add two factors to the estimating equation.

With present systems of data gathering and recording, it is virtually impossible to arrive at accurate estimates for the country as a whole and for many, if not most, localities. It would be possible, however, for small areas to have very accurate counting of all factors except possibly the unsound units. If a relatively small city has even a modest planning office it would be relatively simple for the planners to spend a few hours each month gathering the information from the various governmental offices that record one or more aspects of changes in the housing stock.

Useful monitoring of the conditions of housing in the nation or in a given community obviously requires attention to additional factors. Besides knowing the number of units and whether they are sound, it is necessary to know, at a minimum, whether the units are vacant or occupied, available or not, and whether they are for sale or for rent. Since the variation in the number of rooms and particularly the number of bedrooms has been shown to be so important it would be valuable to classify the housing stock according to number of bedrooms. Another factor of importance is the type of structure—single family, mobile home, etc.

A point that must be stressed is that useful knowledge of the housing stock and housing supply requires continuing data gathering; it should not be left to the decennial census. Changes in the need for housing in a given locality can change too rapidly for such infrequent data. Thus, the importance of locally-based estimates that monitor the changes in the stock should be underlined.

The Population of Households

The most important factor in the need for housing in a community or society is the number of households and their characteristics. The population of households at any given point in time is the "needs" equivalent of the "conditions" information provided by the housing stock. The population of households is the stock of households.

In order to arrive at estimates of the population of households in years subsequent to the census, an equation is used that is similar to the one for housing stock. It is first necessary to distinguish between the population of individuals and the population of households. The population of households is typically defined as the units or groups who live in housing units. It is necessary to distinguish the population that lives in housing units from the population that lives in other types of shelter—hospitals, barracks, and the like. The latter category is referred to as the population living in *group quarters*. The importance of this population for estimation of housing need arises primarily from their entrance into and exit from the population living in households. It should not be concluded that we feel the housing provided for those living in group quarters is unimportant. Study of group housing, however, is beyond the scope of the present analysis.

The equation for estimating the population of households in years subsequent to the census is:

$$PH_1 = PH_0 + Form + Inmig + Deinst - Death - Outmig - Inst$$

Where

PH_1 is the number of households in the area at the time subsequent to the census.

PH_0 is the number of households in the area at the time of the census.

Form is the number of new households formed during the time since the census, including households formed by marriage, by divorce (one household becoming two), and by children leaving home—but not marrying—and forming a household.

Inmig is the number of households migrating into the area since the census.

Deinst is the number of households formed by persons leaving group quarters or institutional residence (deinstitutionalization).

Death is the disappearance of a household due to the death of the last member of the household.

Outmig is the number of households who have migrated to another area.

Inst is the number of households lost by institutionalization.

Although the data are readily available for the estimation of the number of *individuals* in larger areas by using data on birth rates, death rates, and mobility rates, the data are at least as sketchy for the estimation of the population of households as they are for the estimation of the housing stock. In one sense the estimation of the number of households at a given point is easier since it is defined as the number of households occupying housing units. Therefore, if the number of occupied housing units is known the number of households is known. The inaccuracy of the estimates of the number of households and the number of dwelling units increases rapidly with the number of years since the last census.

The influence of demographic changes on the demand for housing has been highlighted in earlier chapters, especially Chapter 6. Even the grossest of monitoring systems could have foretold, as early as 1950, the changes in housing demand that occurred in the late 1960s. Marriage rates tend to be relatively stable over time. Thus it is relatively easy to make rather accurate estimates of the amount of household formation that will take place up to twenty years ahead of time.

The consequences of the baby boom in the form of heavy demand for housing in the late sixties and early seventies could have been foretold and the housing industry could have been prepared. A wise lumber and building materials company would have begun to plant lots of fast-growing trees when the baby boom became obvious. At the least, they would have bought up existing timber areas.

The country is just starting a new demographic phase, the post-household-formation stage, when the baby boom babies begin to demand single-family dwellings. This demand could have been predicted many years ago. Nevertheless, the current housing situation is one of a glut of apartment units, the falling demand for mobile homes, and an increasing demand for single-family dwellings, which is so great that it cannot be met in many areas. Soon new family formation will be limited primarily to groups born after the baby boom. Then there will be further deterioration in the demand for new housing as the family formation rate declines. The best predictions are that, in twenty years, there will be a housing surplus, unless overbuilding of single-family dwellings for the baby boom population is avoided.

Housing demand will have passed through a full cycle in forty years. When the baby boom babies become elderly, they may once again exert demand for smaller housing units. The unwanted apartments built in the 1960s and 1970s may once again become needed.

In light of rather solid demographic information about the potential content of housing demand up to twenty years ahead of time, it is somewhat puzzling that so little is done by policy makers, business, and industry in preparation for the manifestation of the trends. Surely one of the explanations for the inaction is the tendency to mistake demographic trends for true social change. To a very great extent the recent events in housing stemmed from demographic trends in the population.

Many people perceived the trends toward higher demand for mobile homes and apartments to be a change in the society. They began to talk of new life styles. But the new life styles at least at first were simply the same life styles exhibited by young adults, who were simply the dominant age group. With that much demographic force behind them, that generation dominated nearly everything that has happened since 1947. The diaper business boomed through 1957 or so. The building of elementary schools soared starting around 1950. A few years later it was junior-high buildings, then high-school and college buildings, then apartments, now to be followed by single-family dwellings.

In addition to the simple brute force of the demographic trends, there was the demonstration effect, as well. Because there were so many people in that age group, when they began to assert themselves in the late 1960s, it seemed that there was indeed a new day coming in the society. People both younger and older began to adopt the ideas and behavior patterns that otherwise might have gone relatively unnoticed if there had not been so many people of the same age group. As a result, there has been some real social change occurring because of the demographic trends. Nevertheless, a safe prediction, as this group continues to advance through the family life cycle, is that when they become middle-aged, the whole society will begin to act a little more middle-aged.

It would be easy to overstate the case in terms of the possibility of early warning about the demographic trends and their consequences. Indeed the monitoring of the state of the housing stock and the additions to and subtractions from it is woefully inadequate. Births, deaths, marriages, and divorces are quite well recorded and analyzed. The recording of housing construction, demolition, conversion, and rehabilitation are not nearly so well recorded. As a result, the supply half of the equation is much less adequately understood than the demand side.

Housing Deficits

The final step in an ongoing monitoring system is checking the match between the characteristics of the households and those of their housing units. In this manner, the presence and magnitude of deficits can be ascertained. How many families have negative bedroom deficits? How many have positive bedroom deficits? Is there a possibility that households living in large dwellings might be enticed to leave their five-bedroom houses if smaller single-family dwellings or apartments were readily available?

How many families with school-age children live in apartments? In mobile homes? How many low-income elderly households who occupy a large single-family dwelling that they own outright might be ready to exchange it for a smaller, less expensive one? How many families are paying more than 30 percent of their income on housing?

Ongoing assessment of the discrepancies between cultural norms and actual conditions is the key to rational housing decisions. Such assessment is especially valuable when it can identify an incipient problem before it turns into a full-blown crisis. Specific actions could be planned and implemented to deal early with the most pressing deficit conditions if the information were available. The degree to which preliminary problem solutions were effective in reducing deficits could also be readily assessed.

A scheme for such assessment was proposed by Winter (1970), who developed a computerized system for the storage and retrieval of data on households and housing units. She viewed obtaining a continuous source of data to update the system as the single most important factor in implementing the system. Neither the desirability of such a monitoring system nor the problems in implementing it have changed in the ensuing time period.

Monitoring Change in Housing Norms

As discussed in detail earlier in this book the need for housing stems from the cultural, community, and family norms that prescribe the definition of housing and the specifications of housing above the minimum definition. The assessment of the housing stock, the population of households, and deficit conditions assumes that the norms are unchanging. Hence knowledge about the supply of housing, about the population of households, and about the fit between households and housing units will accurately measure the housing status of the community or the society at any given moment. And, in the short run, the broad outlines of the norms are relatively stable.

Over longer time periods, however, norms for both housing and households are dynamic, and need careful monitoring. If, for example, the definition of what constitutes a housing unit changes, the estimate of the housing stock that meets definitional norms must be changed accordingly. The estimates of the population of households must change if the definition of a household changes as a result of changing norms. Obviously the measurement of housing deficits would have to change as well. If the energy crisis causes a majority of American families to view high-rise apartments as satisfactory places to raise children, then the estimates of the need for single-family dwellings based on the number of households with school-age children could come to be vastly inaccurate.

Monitoring changes in norms is far more difficult than monitoring changes in either the housing stock or the population. One method is to examine changes in sanctioning behavior. What is happening in housing finance for unusual types of housing? What is happening to mortgage approvals for moderate-income families? Being able to obtain financing would offer information about the changing norms. Has the proportion of families with school-age and teenage children living in apartments increased? If so, perhaps the norms are changing.

Are families compromising space and quality norms and perhaps scrimping on food, clothing, and recreation to buy a single-family dwelling? The observation of sacrifices made to achieve particular partial preferred states can offer clues to the changing definition of the global state of well-being. If new means are being used to attain old ends, then the norms may not be changing.

Housing surveys should routinely include questions on norms for structure type, tenure, space, quality, expenditures, and neighborhood conditions. Study of housing aspirations, as well as expectations, should be included. Local, state, and federal housing policy can then be geared to deal with the constraints that prevent the achievement of normative housing conditions.

PROBLEM IDENTIFICATION AND GOAL DISPLACEMENT

That housing problems must be specifically identified is perhaps obvious. The definition of the problem should be made in terms of the presence and extent of normative housing deficits. As was indicated in Chapter 7, quality is conceived of as consisting of the "right" quantities of the appropriate characteristics, including space, tenure, and structure type. Based on that conceptualization, housing problems in their simplest form can be viewed in terms of two deficits: quality and expenditures. Then the question becomes one of how many people of what types have lower quality than they should have or are paying more than they should be.

Further, it is important to ascertain which of the housing deficits are primary problems and which are secondary problems, as differentiated in Chapter 16. Segregation may or may not be a primary housing problem. Poor-quality housing may be a primary housing problem or it may be a secondary problem resulting from poverty. As noted earlier, attempts should be made to identify and solve the primary problem, rather than treat the secondary problem. Solutions that are aimed at secondary problems are likely to be ineffective because they do not meliorate the causes, only the manifestations.

A far more subtle pitfall that occurs in problem identification is goal displacement. The goal or problem to be solved becomes something other than poor-quality housing, or neighborhood conditions, or housing that costs more than the family's ability to pay. The original goal is replaced with one that is easier to meet or more desirable to a particular faction. Typical "other" goals are the rejuvenation of the economy, the maximization of profit by private industry, the alleviation of various social ills, such as unemployment, and the like.

Such goal displacement has been typical of housing programs for at least half a century. The public housing program and the FHA mortgage insurance program were started during the Depression to revive the economy by stimulating the housing industry. Tax credits for the purchase of new homes during 1975 were an effort to shore up the faltering housing industry rather than assist families in the purchase of normative housing.

According to Hartman (1975), key questions in the development of social policy for housing have to do with whether the government and the housing industry are organized to meet the housing needs of families. Given the American sociopolitical system, it is to be expected that business and industry are based on profits. Further, it is not surprising that government housing policy is influenced by business and industry through their effects on the electoral process and through their lobbying activities. Concern is appropriate when the quest for profit and government assistance in that quest impede progress toward the basic goal. Obviously, the basic goal in housing policy must be to provide housing of appropriate quality and quantity in the appropriate locations, given the needs of families, tempered by considerations of *general* welfare.

One of the problems at the federal level is that government institutions may become captives of the clientele they serve. The Department of Labor may begin to see its mission solely in terms of the welfare of laborers. The Department of Health, Education, and Welfare may come to view its mission as primarily an orientation to the welfare of individuals and families. The Department of Commerce may become narrowly focused on commercial interests.

For housing, the danger would be in the possibility that the Department of Housing and Urban Development and the Farmers Home Administration would begin to see their missions as service to the housing industry rather than to meet the housing needs of families and communities. Sometimes both those ends can be met simultaneously with a single policy. Sometimes, however, they are not compatible; under such circumstances, goal displacement may occur.

Goal displacement occurs when housing policy is turned to the service of the economic health of the building materials industry or the profitability of the realty profession. The point is not that industry and business should not be profitable. The point is that housing policy has to do with meeting the needs of society and its families for housing. Turner (1976) has said:

> *No one denies the universal need for homes any more than the importance of learning or keeping in good health. But many have come to identify these ends with the ways and means that turn them into products. Housing has commonly come to mean the current stock of dwelling units and the capability of large building and management organizations to provide more. Learning is now commonly understood to be synonymous with education and this, in turn, with schooling and even with the institutions that award certificates (p. 12).*

Emphasis on the avoidance of goal displacement seems especially important at this time because of the strong possibility of a housing surplus in about twenty years. At that time, the housing construction industry is likely to be severely depressed. If the government loses sight of the goal of housing to meet family needs, it is possible that heroic efforts will be taken to save the housing industry. Perhaps the urban renewal programs will be revived. It is indeed questionable whether tearing down houses is a direct route to the meeting of housing needs, even though such activitity may provide continued opportunity for profit in the housing industry.

The energy crisis could also produce goal displacement. There is little question that high-density housing is more energy-efficient than single-family housing. But if the goal becomes high-density housing at any cost, rather than the efficient use of energy in the home, simpler solutions may be overlooked. Single-family houses may be torn down or permitted to deteriorate and high-density housing constructed instead. Both activities, of course, are very costly in terms of energy expenditures. Solutions, such as insulating existing homes and developing more efficient heating and cooling systems for existing dwellings, may be avoided when the basic goal is displaced.

The movement to increase "user participation in the design process" and to pay increased attention to "user needs" can be viewed as another possible form of goal displacement. It has been widely suggested that those designing and building residential environments should survey the potential users of the housing in a particular location and design projects to meet those needs.

This manner of research would seem appropriate if the potential users are a subcultural group whose needs are clearly not known to the builders and designers of the housing. This is seldom the case in the United States, however. It would seem to be more useful to utilize more generally available knowledge about the needs of American families than to depend upon the families who happen to be present at a particular time and place for important clues. After all, the mortgage on the project is likely to extend for forty years. At the least, it should be a mortgage on housing that could serve families after the present ones move on to other housing or to other family-life-cycle stages. Funds spent on data collection and analysis might be better spent on designing innovative solutions that would permit the overcoming of constraints.

A related type of goal displacement occurs when policy makers or those who study housing policy adopt a doctrinaire position that a particular form of policy or a particular policy is best for all or most conditions. It might be preferable that housing policy making operate somewhat as the family has operated. When needed, the family becomes a more dominant institution. When not needed, it tends to recede and give up some of its functions. In the same manner, housing policy ought to wax and wane and alter its directions as the conditions require. In other words, housing policy ought to be a means, and not an end in itself. When conditions are such that self-determination for families would improve their housing, then self-determination is a good policy. Like industry profits, however, self-determination can become the goal, displacing that of meeting the housing needs of families.

Goal displacement in any form should be consciously avoided when identifying housing problems. The goal of any housing policy must be to improve the housing conditions of families and communities, while avoiding harmful effects on total social well-being, as well as on nonhousing aspects of family and community well-being.

THE EVALUATION OF PROPOSED SOLUTIONS

Solutions to housing problems should probably be designed to overcome constraints, rather than provide nonnormative forms of housing. The lifting of constraints permits routine housing adjustment to proceed. The provision of housing that does not meet norms (as in the case of prefabricated housing after World War II) requires families to adapt rather than adjust. When necessary, adaptation permits a kind of problem solution. The psychic and social costs of the required adaptations may be incalculable. To suggest normative adaptation as the first line of defense in the solution of housing problems is not likely to be particularly fruitful. Thus programs that insist on teaching families to adopt new standards in favor of nonnormative forms of housing may not experience as great a success as programs teaching new means to attain the norms.

The appropriate criterion for evaluation of proposed housing solutions is the extent to which a greater number of families are able to achieve normative housing as the result of the solution. Using cultural norms as the criteria against which to assess proposed solutions can provide an indication of the outcome *prior* to the institutionalization of the solution and the expenditure of billions of dollars.

The *wisdom* of a cultural norm, for example, the single-family housing norm, can be questioned, particularly in light of environmental issues. It has been condemned as uneconomical, wasteful, unnecessary, stupid, and, worst of all, media-created. That it is a cultural norm is beyond question, however. Its impact (and the impact of other important housing norms) must be recognized if there is to be successful societal intervention that does not simply create a different set of problems.

Recent analyses of public housing "solutions" have come to similar conclusions. In his discussion of interpersonal and economic resources, Foa (1971) asserts that:

> *... it appears unrealistic to expect that social problems will be solved by material means alone. ... one can see model housing*

> *projects built a few years ago turning into model slums, possibly because their dwellers were provided with houses, but not with self-pride and a sense of community (Foa, 1971, p. 345).*

Foa did not say it explicitly, but self-pride and a sense of community occur when people's housing meets their norms and those of the culture. He goes on to discuss the loss of status that occurs with solutions such as welfare and public housing. It is clear from his interpretation that making it possible for families, even poor families, to have housing that meets the crucial norms would not represent the loss of status imposed by "model housing projects."

Newman's (1973) analysis of *Defensible Space* concluded that when residents of public housing felt that they "owned" the territory, they were more likely to defend it. Thus crime rates would be reduced. The most "defensible" space, of course, is a single-family dwelling. The closer a structure approached the key traits of the single-family dwelling, the more desirable it was to the tenants. The more highly desired dwellings were better cared for and defended.

The key to successful housing policy, then, is to develop programs that will help people attain *normative* housing. The focus of such programs should be the reduction of constraints, rather than the provision of compromise housing. Obviously, the U.S. Congress, the governments of 50 states, and a multitude of local bodies are not going to build single-family dwellings to be deeded to poor families. Nevertheless, programs that consciously attempt to assist families in achieving home ownership of single-family dwellings with enough bedrooms in neighborhoods with good schools for the overwhelming majority who want and need them have a far better chance of success. Such dwellings may provide settings for the alleviation of secondary housing problems, as well.

We are not suggesting that the provision of such housing conditions can solve all the problems of poverty, income distribution, discrimination, illiteracy, and a host of other societal ills. We are suggesting that improved conditions will at least not contribute to them, or create a new set of problems.

Would it be so difficult to explore cooperative ownership for low-income families? Of course not. Are townhouses out of the question for publicly-sponsored housing? Of course not. Had there not been scandals in its administration, would not the 235 home ownership program for moderate-income families have been successful? We think so. Will the Section 8 housing allowance program for subsidizing rental units be cheaper in the long run than the same money spent on home ownership? We do not think so if more rental housing than is needed is produced.

We are also suggesting that any proposed action that will affect the residential environment be analyzed prior to its adoption in light of the model of housing adjustment. Economic questions are always posed. How much will it cost? Who will pay? Why not ask such question as: What are the consequences of this action for family housing adjustment? Who will the action help? Who will be hindered?

OVERCOMING OPPOSITION TO HOUSING PROGRAMS

The 1949 goals for public housing were not met for years. Indeed, they were reduced by half in later legislation. One of the reasons for our failure to meet those goals was that a consensus about standards required for success in problem solution by any social system was not present. There were many pressure groups opposed to those goals. The National Association of Real Estate Boards, for example, was opposed (Bouma, 1962). In addition, a large portion of the population holds political views opposed to government ownership and management of housing and government subsidies for normative housing (Hartman, 1975).

Given the work ethic that played so large a part in the development of the United States, it may never be possible to overcome all opposition to housing programs. It may never be possible for poor people's right to decent housing to be recognized by all members of the society and all groups in the society.

Nevertheless, there are some steps that might help overcome the opposition of "middle America" to most forms of housing assistance (except, of course, income tax benefits for home owners). Economic analyses that detail the cost of poor housing and neighborhood conditions to the middle class should be supported. What is the cost to middle-class families of moving to the suburbs because acceptable housing and neighborhood conditions are not available in central cities? What is the cost to the family that chooses to stay in the central city?

Perhaps, as Hartman (1975) suggests, improved housing conditions must be tied to employment in the housing industry, so that improved economic and housing conditions can go hand in hand. The housing industry, as well as ill-housed families, would reap benefits. The task of achieving the recognition of the right to decent housing is not easy. But arguments in its favor will not succeed if they are made solely in altruistic terms and not in economic terms.

CONCLUSION

The first four parts of this book developed a model of housing adjustment and adaptation by presenting a theory of families and their housing. The family has been viewed as a social system that consciously evaluates its housing and neighborhood conditions against specific criteria. The criteria used by families are cultural norms.

When there is a gap between the housing conditions on the one hand and norms on the other, the family becomes dissatisfied. Reduced satisfaction tends to produce one of two behavioral responses: moving to a new dwelling or making alterations in the present dwelling. The resulting new housing conditions presumably would bring the family's housing more closely in line with the norms.

Many families, however, may be unable to overcome residential deficits because of constraints on their behavior. Such constraints, of course, are primarily economic, but may involve racial, ethnic, and sexual discrimination, as well. When the constraints are overwhelming, other responses occur that are referred to as adaptation rather than adjustment. Adaptation involves alteration of the family's norms, its composition, or its organization.

Effective housing policy should be aimed at the removal of constraints and barriers to family housing adjustment. The model presented in this book should be viewed as the beginning for sound policy making regarding housing and not as an end in itself.

DEFINITIONS

Goal displacement. Replacement of a central goal with another that is easier to meet, easier to document, more convenient, or more desirable to some factions.

Housing stock. The total number of dwelling units in existence, sometimes divided according to various characteristics.

Population in group quarters. The total number of individuals living in barracks, dormitories, hospitals, institutions for the elderly, and other group residences; to be contrasted with the population in households.

Population in households. The total number of individuals living in housing units; to be contrasted with the population in group quarters.

Population of households. The total number of households in the population, sometimes divided according to various characteristics.

References

Aaron, H. J. 1972. *Shelter and subsidies.* Washington: The Brookings Institute.

Abrams, C. 1946. *The future of housing.* New York: Harper.

Abrams, C. 1955. *Forbidden neighbors.* New York: Harper and Brothers.

Acock, A. C. and DeFleur, M. L. 1972. A configurational approach to contingent consistency in the attitude-behavior relationship. *American Sociological Review* 37:714–726.

Adolph, E. F. 1968. *Origins of physiological regulations.* New York: Academic Press.

Agan, T. and Luchsinger, E. 1965. *The house.* Philadelphia: Lippincott.

Angell, R. C. 1936. *The family encounters the depression.* New York: Scribner.

Angell, W. 1976. An approach to housing education. In *Proceedings of the tenth annual conference, October 7–11, 1975,* American Association of Housing Educators, pp. 35–47. Manhattan, Kans.: College of Home Economics, Kansas State University.

ANSI, American National Standards Institute. 1971. *Making buildings and facilities accessible to, and usable by, the physically handicapped.* New York: Author.

Antonovsky, A. and Lerner, M. T. 1959. Occupational aspirations of lower class Negro and white youth. *Social Problems* 7:132–138.

APHA, American Public Health Association. 1971. *Housing: basic health principles and recommended ordinance.* Washington: Author.

APHA, American Public Health Association, Committee on the Hygiene of Housing. 1945. *An appraisal method for measuring the quality of housing.* Part I. Nature and uses of the method. New York: Author.

APHA, American Public Health Association, Committee on the Hygiene of Housing. 1946. *An appraisal method for measuring the quality of housing.* Part II. Appraisal of dwelling conditions. New York: Author.

APHA, American Public Health Association, Committee on the Hygiene of Housing. 1950. *Planning the home for occupancy.* Chicago: Public Administration Service.

APHA, American Public Health Association, Committee on the Hygiene of Housing. 1952. *A proposed housing ordinance.* New York: Author.

APHA, American Public Health Association, Committee on the Hygiene of Housing. 1960. *Planning the neighborhood.* Chicago: Public Administration Service.

Babcock, R. F. 1969. *The zoning game.* Madison: University of Wisconsin Press.

Bachofen, J. J. 1861. *Das Mutterrecht.* Stuttgart: Kraus and Hoffman.

Back, K. W. 1971. Biological models of change. *American Sociological Review* 36:660–667.

Baird, J. W. 1964. National apartment house market outlook. *The Appraisal Journal* 32:209–213.

Bakke, E. W. 1940. *Citizens without work.* New Haven: Yale University Press.

Bales, R. F. and Slater, P. E. 1955. Role differentiation in small decision-making groups. In *Family socialization and interaction process,* eds. T. C. Parsons and R. F. Bales, pp. 259–306. Glencoe, Ill.: Free Press.

Ball, D. W. 1972. The family as a sociological problem: conceptualization of the taken-for-granted as prologue to social problems analysis. *Social Problems* 19:295–307.

Ball, R. A. 1968. A poverty case: the analgesic subculture of the Southern Appalachians. *American Sociological Review* 33:885–894.

Barrs, L. P. 1975. The relationship between duration of residence, chronic mobility and residential mobility. M.S. thesis. Ames, Iowa: Iowa State University.

Bauer, C. 1951. Social questions in housing and community planning. *Journal of Social Issues* 7:1–34.

Beardwood, R. 1968. The new Negro mood. In *The Negro and the city,* eds. Editors of *Fortune,* pp. 37–52. New York: Time-Life Books.

Becker, G. S. 1965. A theory of the allocation of time. *The Economic Journal* 7:493–517.

Becker, H. S., ed. 1966. *Social problems: a modern approach.* New York: John Wiley.

Behman, S. and Codella, D. 1971. Wage rates and housing prices. *Industrial Relations* 10:86–104.

Belcher, J. C. 1970. Differential aspirations for housing between blacks and whites in rural Georgia. *Phylon* 31:231–243.

Bell, B. D. 1976. The impact of housing relocation on the elderly: an alternative methodological approach. *Aging and Human Development* 7:27–38.

Bell, W. 1958. Social choice, life styles, and suburban residence. In *The suburban community,* ed. W. M. Dobriner, pp. 225–247. New York: G. P. Putnam's Sons.

Berger, B. 1960. *Working class suburb.* Berkeley: University of California Press.

Beyer, G. H. 1952. *Rural housing in New York State.* Bulletin no. 893. Ithaca, N.Y.: Cornell University Agricultural Experiment Station.

Beyer, G. H. 1955. Home selection and home management. *Journal of Marriage and Family Living* 17:143–151.

Beyer, G. H. 1965. *Housing and society.* New York: Macmillan.

Beyer, G. H., Mackesy, T. W., and Montgomery, J. E. 1955. *Houses are for people.* Research publication no. 3. Ithaca, N.Y.: Cornell University Housing Research Center.

Beyer, G. H. and Woods, M. E. 1963. *Living and activity patterns of the aged.* Research report no. 6. Ithaca, N.Y.: Center for Housing and Environmental Studies, Cornell University.

Billingsley, A. 1968. *Black families in white America.* Englewood Cliffs, N.J.: Prentice-Hall.

Biochel, M. R., Aurbach, H. A., Bakerman, T., and Elliott, D. H. 1969. Exposure, experience and attitudes: realtors and open occupancy. *Phylon* 30:325–337.

Blalock, H. M. 1964. *Causal inferences in nonexperimental research.* Chapel Hill: University of North Carolina Press.

Blood, R. O., Jr. and Wolfe, D. M. 1960. *Husbands and wives.* Glencoe, Ill.: Free Press.

Bogardus, E. S. 1924. *Fundamentals of social psychology.* New York: Century Company.

Bogue, D. J. 1959. Internal migration. In *The study of population: an inventory and appraisal,* eds. P. M. Hauser and O. D. Duncan, pp. 486–509. Chicago: University of Chicago Press.

Bouma, D. H. 1962. *Why Kalamazoo voted no.* Kalamazoo: W. E. Upjohn Institute for Employment Research.

Branch, M. C., Jr. 1942. *Urban planning and public opinion.* Princeton, N.J.: Bureau of Urban Research, Princeton University.

Bresler, A. F. 1975. Residential crowding, fertility limitation and the propensity to move. M.S. thesis. Ames, Iowa: Iowa State University.

Brinkley, D. 1974. David Brinkley's Journal. NBC Nightly News, 21 October 1974.

Britten, R. H. and Altman, I. 1941. Illness and accidents among persons living under different housing conditions. *Public Health Reports* 56:609–639.

Brooks, M. E. 1970. *Exclusionary zoning.* Chicago: American Society of Planning Officials.

Bross, C. A. 1975. Normative housing deficits and residential adaptation. M.S. thesis. Ames, Iowa: Iowa State University.

Bross, C. A. and Morris, E. W. 1974. The influence of household size changes on family housing adjustment behavior. Ames, Iowa: Department of Family Environment, Iowa State University.

Brown, W. H., Jr. 1972. Access to housing: the role of the real estate industry. *Economic Geography* 48:66–78.

Bruce-Briggs, B. 1973. The cost of housing. *Public Interest* 32:34–42.

Buckley, W. 1967. *Sociology and modern systems theory.* Englewood Cliffs, N.J.: Prentice-Hall.

Burgess, E. W. 1926. The family as a unity of interacting personalities. *The Family:* March.

Burgess, E. W. and Locke, H. 1945. *The family: from institution to companionship.* New York: American Book Company.

Burton, A. M. N. D. Streamlining household tasks. Lincoln, Nebr.: Extension Service, University of Nebraska College of Agriculture and Home Economics.

Butler, E. W., Chapin, F. S., Jr., Hemmens, G. C., Kaiser, E. J., Stegman, M. A., and Weiss, S. F. 1969. *Moving behavior and residential choice.* National Cooperative Highway Research Program Report 81, Highway Research Board. Washington: National Academy of Sciences.

Butler, E. W. and Kaiser, E. J. 1971. Prediction of residential movement and spatial allocation. *Urban Affairs Quarterly* 6:477–494.

Butler, E. W., Sabagh, G. and Van Arsdol, M. D., Jr. 1964. Demographic and social psychological factors in residential mobility. *Sociology and Social Research* 48:139–154.

Butler, E. W., Van Arsdol, M. D., Jr. and Sabagh, G. 1970. Spatial mobility differentials by socioeconomic status, intergenerational, and career social mobility. Paper presented at the American Sociological Association Meeting, August–September 1970, Washington, D.C.

Cagle, L. T. and Deutscher, I. 1970. Housing aspirations and housing achievement: the relocation of poor families. *Social Problems.* 18:243–256.

Cannon, W. B. 1932. *The wisdom of the body.* New York: Norton.

Caplow, T. 1948. Home ownership and location preferences in a Minneapolis sample. *American Sociological Review* 13:725–730.

Carp, F. M. 1966. *A future for the aged: Victoria Plaza and its residents.* Austin: University of Texas Press.

CBC, Committee on Banking and Currency, United States House of Representatives. 1970. *Basic laws and authorities on housing and urban development.* Washington: U.S. Government Printing Office.

Chevan, A. 1971. Family growth, household density, and moving. *Demography* 8:451–458.

Chombart de Lauwe, P. H. 1966. The interaction of person and society. *American Sociological Review* 31:237–257.

Clark, K. B. 1965. *Dark ghetto.* New York: Harper and Row.

Coates, G. 1976. *User participation in the design process: domestic farm labor housing, Wayne County, N.Y.* Ithaca, N.Y.: Department of Design and Environmental Analysis, Cornell University.

Cogswell, B. E. 1975. Variant family forms and life styles: rejection of the traditional nuclear family. *Family Coordinator* 24:391–406.

Cohen, A. K. 1955. *Delinquent boys: the culture of the gang.* Glencoe, Ill.: Free Press.

Cohen, A. K. and Hodges, H., Jr. 1963. Characteristics of the lower-blue-collar class. *Social Problems* 10:303–334.

Cohen, J. 1964. Social work and the culture of poverty. In *Mental health of the poor,* eds. F. Riessman, J. Cohen, and A. Pearl, pp. 128–138. Glencoe, Ill.: Free Press.

Cohen, J. B. and Hanson, A. W. 1972. *Personal finance.* 4th ed. Homewood, Ill.: Richard D. Irwin.

Comte, A. 1875. *System of positive polity.* Vol. 2. London: Longmans, Green.

Coons, A. E. and Glaze, B. T. 1963. *Housing market analysis and the growth of nonfarm home ownership.* Columbus, Ohio: Bureau of Business Research, Ohio State University.

Cooper, J. M. 1946. The Ona. In *Handbook of South American Indians,* ed. J. H. Steward, Vol. 1, pp. 107–125. Washington: U.S. Government Printing Office.

Cowles, M. L., Dickson, M. W., and Wood, L. E. 1947. *Rural housing improvement in Southern Wisconsin.* Research bulletin no. 161. Madison: University of Wisconsin.

CRH, Commission on Race and Housing. 1966. Where shall we live? In *Urban housing,* eds. W. L. C. Wheaton, G. Milgram and M. E. Meyerson, pp. 269–286. New York: Free Press.

Crull, S. R. 1976a. A normative approach to housing satisfaction. Paper presented at the American Home Economics Association Convention, 27 June–1 July 1976, Minneapolis, Minnesota.

Crull, S. R. 1976b. Cultural aspects of housing consumption. *Illinois Teacher* 20(2):73–76.

Cutler, V. F. 1947. *Personal and family values in the choice of a home.* Agricultural Experiment Station Bulletin 840. Ithaca, N.Y.: Cornell University.

Davis, K. 1948. *Human society.* New York: Macmillan.

Davis, K. 1963. The theory of change and response in modern demographic history. *Population Index* 29:345–366.

Day, R. L. 1976. Alternative definitions and designs for measuring consumer satisfaction. Paper presented at the Marketing Science Institute Workshop on Consumer Satisfaction/Dissatisfaction, 11–13 April 1976, Chicago.

Deacon, R. E. and Firebaugh, F. M. 1975. *Home management context and concepts.* Boston: Houghton-Mifflin.

Dean, J. P. 1945. *Home ownership: is it sound?* New York: Harper.

Dean, J. P. 1951. The ghosts of home ownership. *Journal of Social Issues* 7:59–68.

Dean, J. P. 1953. Housing design and family values. *Land Economics* 29:128–141.

DeFleur, M. L. and DeFleur, L. B. 1967. The relative contribution of television as a learning source for children's occupational knowledge. *American Sociological Review* 32:777–789.

Denton, J. H. 1970. *Report of consultant.* San Francisco: National Committee against Discrimination in Housing.

Deutsch, M. 1963. The disadvantaged child and the learning process. In

Education in depressed areas, ed. H. Passow, pp. 163–179. New York: Teachers College Press.

Dickman, I. R. 1975. *Independent living: a new goal for disabled persons.* Public Affairs Pamphlet no. 522. New York: Public Affairs Committee.

Diesing, P. 1962. *Reason in society.* Urbana: University of Illinois Press.

Dollard, J. 1935. The family: needed viewpoints in family research. *Social Forces* 35:109–113.

Downs, A. 1973. *Opening up the suburbs: an urban strategy for America.* New Haven: Yale University Press.

Droettboom, T., Jr., McAllister, R. J., Kaiser, E. J., and Butler, E. W. 1971. Urban violence and residential mobility. *Journal of the American Institute of Planners* 37:319–325.

Duncan, B. and Hauser, P. M. 1960. *Housing a metropolis: Chicago.* Glencoe, Ill.: Free Press.

Duncan, G. J. and Newman, S. 1975. People as planners: the fulfillment of residential mobility expectations. In *Five thousand American families—patterns of economic progress,* Vol. 3, eds. G. J. Duncan and J. N. Morgan, pp. 319–342. Ann Arbor: Institute for Social Research, University of Michigan.

Duncan, O. D. and Duncan, B. 1957. Residential distribution and occupational stratification. In *Cities and society,* eds. P. K. Hatt and A. J. Reiss, Jr., pp. 283–296. New York: Free Press.

Duvall, E. M. 1967. *Family development.* 3rd ed. Philadelphia: Lippincott.

Eaves, E. 1969. *How the many costs of housing fit together.* Washington: U.S. Government Printing Office.

Ellis, D. P. 1971. The Hobbesian problem of order: a critical appraisal of the normative solution. *American Sociological Review* 36:692–703.

Elmer, M. C. 1932. *Family adjustment and social change.* New York: R. Long and R. R. Smith, Inc.

Engel, E. 1895. *Die Lebenkosten belgisher Arbeiter-Familien.* Dresden: C. Heinrich.

Engels, F. 1902. *The origin of the family, private property and the state.* Translated by E. Untermann. Chicago: C. H. Kerr and Company.

Etzioni, A. 1968. Basic human needs, alienation and inauthenticity. *American Sociological Review* 33:870–884.

Fanning, D. M. 1967. Families in flats. *British Medical Journal* 4:382–386.

Farber, F. 1964. *Family: organization and interaction.* San Francisco: Chandler.

Feldman, A. S. and Tilly, C. 1960. The interaction of social and physical space. *American Sociological Review* 25:877–884.

Ferguson, C. E. 1972. *Microeconomic theory.* 3rd ed. Homewood, Ill.: Richard D. Irwin.

Festinger, L. 1957. *A theory of cognitive dissonance.* Palo Alto, Calif.: Stanford University Press.

Findlay, R. A. 1975. Social environment determinants for the design of housing for the elderly. M. Arch. thesis. Ames, Iowa: Iowa State University.

Findlay, R. A. and Morris, E. W. 1976. Social determinants of the design of housing for the elderly. Paper presented at the Annual Conference of the Environmental Research Design Association, 25–29 May 1976, Vancouver, B.C.

Foa, U. G. 1971. Interpersonal and economic resources. *Science* 171:345–351.

Foley, D. L. 1973. Institutional and contextual factors affecting the housing choices of minority residents. In *Segregation in residential areas,* eds. A. H. Hawley and V. P. Rock, pp. 85–147. Washington: National Academy of Sciences.

Foote, N. N., Abu-Lughod, J., Foley, M. M., and Winnick, L. 1960. *Housing choices and housing constraints.* New York: McGraw-Hill.

Forman, R. E. 1971. *Black ghettos, white ghettos and slums.* Englewood Cliffs, N.J.: Prentice-Hall.

Freedman, R. 1968. Norms for family size in underdeveloped areas. In

Population and society, ed. C. B. Nam, pp. 215–230. Boston: Houghton-Mifflin.

Fried, J. P. 1971. *Housing crisis U.S.A.* New York: Praeger.

Fried, M. 1963. Grieving for a lost home. In *The urban condition,* ed. L. J. Duhl, pp. 151–171. New York: Simon and Schuster.

Fried, M. and Gleicher, P. 1961. Some sources of residential satisfaction in an urban slum. *Journal of the American Institute of Planners* 27:305–315.

Friedman, L. M. 1968. *Government and slum housing.* Chicago: Rand McNally.

Friedman, M. 1957. *A theory of the consumption function.* Princeton: Princeton University Press.

Fuller, R. C. and Myers, R. R. 1941. The natural history of a social problem. *American Sociological Review* 6:320–328.

Gans, H. J. 1961. Planning and social life: friendship and neighbor relations in suburban communities. *Journal of the American Institute of Planners* 27:134–140.

Gans, H. J. 1962. *The urban villagers.* New York: Free Press.

Gans, H. J. 1967. *The Levittowners.* New York: Random House Vintage Books.

Geismar, L. L. and LaSorte, M. A. 1964. *Understanding the multi-problem family.* New York: Association Press.

Gillin, J. L. and Gillin, J. P. 1948. *Cultural sociology.* New York: Macmillan.

Gist, N. P. and Bennett, W. S., Jr. 1963. Aspirations of Negro and white students. *Social Forces* 42:40–48.

Gladhart, P. M. 1971. The determinants of residential mobility: some implications for subsidized housing. Ithaca, N.Y.: Department of Consumer Economics and Public Policy, New York State College of Human Ecology, Cornell University.

Gladhart, P. M. 1973. Family housing adjustment and the theory of residential mobility: a temporal analysis of family residential histories. Ph.D. dissertation. Ithaca, N.Y.: Cornell University.

Glass, D. C. and Singer, J. E. 1972. *Urban stress: experiments on noise and social stressors.* New York: Academic Press.

Goldfinger, N. 1970. Labor costs and the rise in housing prices. *Monthly Labor Review* 93(5):60–61.

Goldscheider, C. 1966. Differential residential mobility of the older population. *Journal of Gerontology* 21:103–108.

Goldscheider, C., Van Arsdol, M. D., Jr., and Sabagh, G. 1965. Residential mobility of older people. In *Patterns of living and housing of middle-aged and older people,* Proceedings of a research conference, pp. 65–82. Washington: U.S. Government Printing Office.

Goode, R. 1960. Imputed rents of owner-occupied dwellings. *Journal of Finance* 15:504–530.

Goode, W. J. 1960. Illegitimacy in the Caribbean social structure. *American Sociological Review* 25:21–30.

Goode, W. J. 1963. *World revolution and family patterns.* New York: Free Press.

Goodman, J. 1974. Local residential mobility and family housing adjustments. In *Five thousand American families—patterns of economic progress,* Vol. 2, ed. J. N. Morgan, pp. 79–106. Ann Arbor: Institute for Social Research, University of Michigan.

Goodsell, W. 1937. Housing and the birthrate in Sweden. *American Sociological Review* 2:850–859.

Goudy, W. J. 1975. *Studying your community: data book.* Ames, Iowa: Department of Sociology, Iowa State University.

Green, J. W. 1953a. *House building by farm owners in North Carolina.* Chapel Hill: Department of Rural Sociology, North Carolina State College.

Green, J. W. 1953b. The farmhouse building process. Ph.D. dissertation. Chapel Hill: North Carolina State College.

Greenbie, B. B. 1969. New house or new neighborhood? A survey of priorities among home owners in Madison, Wisconsin. *Land Economics* 45:359–365.

Greenfield, R. J. and Lewis, J. F. 1969. An alternative to a density function definition of overcrowding. *Land Economics* 45:282–285.

Greer, S. 1966. Problems of housing and renewal of the city. In *Social problems: a modern approach,* ed. H. S. Becker, pp. 517–548. New York: John Wiley.

Grier, E. and Grier, G. 1960. *Privately developed interracial housing.* Berkeley: University of California Press.

Grier, G. W. 1967. Negro ghettos and federal housing policy. *Law and Contemporary Problems* 32:550–560.

Grootenboer, E. A. 1962. The relationship of housing to behavior disorder. *American Journal of Psychiatry* 119:469–472.

Gross, I. H., Crandall, E. W., and Knoll, M. M. 1973. *Management for modern families.* 3rd ed. New York: Appleton-Century-Crofts.

Grosse, E. 1896. *Die formen der familie und die formen der wirtschaft.* Freiburg: J. C. B. Mohr.

Gutheim, F. 1948. *Houses for family living.* New York: Women's Foundation.

Gutman, R. 1970. A sociologist looks at housing. In *Toward a national urban policy,* ed. D. P. Moynihan, pp. 119–132. New York: Basic Books.

Hall, E. T. 1966. *The hidden dimension.* Garden City, N.Y.: Doubleday.

Hallmann, H. 1959. Citizens and professionals reconsider the neighborhood. *Journal of the American Institute of Planners* 25:121–127.

Han, W. S. 1969. Two conflicting themes: common values versus class differential values. *American Sociological Review* 34:679–690.

Harrington, M. 1962. *The other America.* New York: Macmillan.

Harris, C. M. 1976a. The measurement of quality in housing and its relationship to housing satisfaction. *Housing Educators Journal* 3(2):7–13.

Harris, C. M. 1976b. The relationship between housing quality, housing satisfaction and residential adaptation: a normative housing study. M.S. thesis. Ames, Iowa: Iowa State University.

Hartman, C. 1963. Social values and housing orientations. *Journal of Social Issues* 19(2):113–131.

Hartman, C. W. 1975. *Housing and social policy.* Englewood Cliffs, N.J.: Prentice-Hall.

Helper, R. W. 1969. *Racial policies and practices of real estate brokers.* Minneapolis: University of Minnesota Press.

Hess, R. D. and Shipman, V. C. 1965. Early experience and the socialization of cognitive modes in children. *Child Development* 36:869–886.

Hill, R. 1949. *Families under stress.* New York: Harper and Brothers.

Hill, R. 1963. Judgment and consumership in the management of family resources. *Sociology and Social Research* 47:446–460.

Hill, R. 1970. *Family development in three generations.* Cambridge, Mass.: Schenkman.

Hill, R. 1971. Modern systems theory and the family: a confrontation. *Social Science Information* 10:7–26.

Hill, R. and Hansen, D. A. 1960. The identification of conceptual frameworks utilized in family study. *Journal of Marriage and Family Living* 22:299–311.

Hill, R., Stycos, J. M. and Back, K. W. 1959. *The family and population control.* Chapel Hill: University of North Carolina Press.

Hinshaw, M. and Allott, K. 1972. Environmental preferences of future housing consumers. *Journal of the American Institute of Planners* 38:102–107.

Hobhouse, L. T. 1924. *Social development, its nature and conditions.* London: George Allen and Unwin.

Hobhouse, L. T., Wheeler, G. C., and Ginsberg, M. 1915. *The material culture and social institutions of the simpler peoples.* London: Chapman and Hall Ltd.

Hodge, P. L. and Hauser, P. M. 1968. *The challenge of America's metropolitan population outlook—1960 to 1985.* Washington: U.S. Government Printing Office.

Holmberg, A. R. 1956. Nomads of the long bow. In *Principles of sociology,* eds. R. Freedman, A. H. Hawley, W. S. Landecker, G. E. Lenski, and H. M. Miner, 2nd ed., pp. 141–169. New York: Holt, Rinehart and Winston.

House, F. N. 1936. *The development of sociology.* New York: McGraw-Hill.

HUD, U.S. Department of Housing and Urban Development, Federal Housing Administration. 1965. *Minimum property standards for one and two living units.* Washington: U.S. Government Printing Office.

HUD, U.S. Department of Housing and Urban Development, Federal Housing Administration. 1966. *Minimum property standards for low cost housing.* Washington: U.S. Government Printing Office.

HUD, U.S. Department of Housing and Urban Development. 1969a. *Fair housing: what it means to you.* Washington: Author.

HUD, U.S. Department of Housing and Urban Development. 1969b. *1967 statistical yearbook.* Washington: U.S. Government Printing Office.

HUD, U.S. Department of Housing and Urban Development, Federal Housing Administration. 1971. *Minimum property standards for multifamily housing.* Washington: U.S. Government Printing Office.

HUD, U.S. Department of Housing and Urban Development. 1973a. *Minimum property standards for one and two family dwellings.* Washington: U.S. Government Printing Office.

HUD, U.S. Department of Housing and Urban Development. 1973b. *Minimum property standards for multifamily housing.* Washington: U.S. Government Printing Office.

HUD, U.S. Department of Housing and Urban Development. 1973c. *Minimum property standards for housing for the elderly, with special consideration for the handicapped.* Washington: U.S. Government Printing Office.

HUD, U.S. Department of Housing and Urban Development. 1975a. *Housing and urban development trends, December 1975.* Washington: Author.

HUD, U.S. Department of Housing and Urban Development. 1975b. *Women and housing: a report on sex discrimination in five American cities.* Washington: U.S. Government Printing Office.

HUD, U.S. Department of Housing and Urban Development. 1976. *Women in the mortgage market.* Washington: Author.

Hurvitz, N. 1964. Marital strain in the blue collar family. In *Blue collar world,* eds. A. Shostak and W. Gromberg, pp. 92–109. Englewood Cliffs, N.J.: Prentice-Hall.

Inkeles, A. 1955. Social change and social character, the role of parental mediation. *Journal of Social Issues* 11(2):12–22.

Isaacs, R. R. 1948. The neighborhood theory. *Journal of the American Institute of Planners* 14(2):15–23.

Isaacs, R. R. 1949. The neighborhood concept: theory and application. *Land Economics* 25:73–78.

Jaco, E. G. and Belknap, I. 1953. Is a new family form emerging on the urban fringe? *American Sociological Review* 28:550–557.

Jacobs, J. 1961. *The death and life of great American cities.* New York: Random House Vintage Books.

Jansen, L. T. 1952. Measuring family solidarity. *American Sociological Review* 18:727–733.

Jennings, W. W. 1938. The value of home owning as exemplified in American history. *Social Science* 13:5–15.

Johnson, E. B. 1952. *Indoor play areas for the preschool child.* Agricultural Experiment Station Technical Bulletin 126. Tucson: University of Arizona.

Joiner, R. C. 1970. Trends in homeownership and rental costs. *Monthly Labor Review* 93:(7):26–31.

Joslin, M. H. 1959. Improvement of farm family housing associated with age of homemaker. M.S. thesis. Ames, Iowa: Iowa State College.

Kain, J. F. and Quigley, J. M. 1970. Measuring the value of housing quality. *Journal of the American Statistical Association* 65:532–548.

Kain, J. F. and Quigley, J. M. 1972. Housing market discrimination, homeownership, and savings behavior. *American Economic Review* 62:263–277.

Kaplan, M. A. 1974. Housing and economic development: second quarter. *Federal Home Loan Bank Board Journal* 7(8):21–24.

Kasl, S. V. and Harberg, E. 1972. Perceptions of the neighborhood and the desire to move out. *Journal of the American Institute of Planners* 38:318–324.

Keil, C. 1966. *Urban blues.* Chicago: University of Chicago Press.

Kelley, H. H. and Thibaut, J. W. 1969. Group problem solving. In *The handbook of social psychology,* eds. G. Lindzey and E. Aronson, pp. 1–101. Reading, Mass.: Addison-Wesley.

Kindahl, J. K. 1960. Housing and the federal income tax. *National Tax Journal* 13:376–382.

King, A. T. and Mieszkowski, D. 1973. Racial discrimination, segregation, and the price of housing. *Journal of Political Economy* 81:590–606.

Kohn, M. L. 1963. Social class and parent-child relationships: an interpretation. *American Journal of Sociology* 68:471–480.

Ktsanes, T. and Reissman, L. 1959–1960. Suburbia—new homes for old values. *Social Problems* 7:187–195.

Labovitz, S. and Hagedorn, R. 1973. Measuring social norms. *Pacific Sociological Review* 16:283–303.

Ladd, F. C. 1972. Black youths view their environment: some views of housing. *Journal of the American Institute of Planners* 38:108–116.

Lamanna, R. 1964. Value consensus among urban residents. *Journal of the American Institute of Planners* 30:317–323.

Lancaster, K. 1971. *Consumer demand: a new approach.* New York: Columbia University Press.

Langford, M. 1962. *Community aspects of housing for the aged.* Research report no. 5. Ithaca, N.Y.: Center for Housing and Environmental Studies, Cornell University.

Lansing, J. B. and Barth, N. 1964. *Residential location and urban mobility: a multivariate analysis.* Ann Arbor: Institute for Social Research, University of Michigan.

Lansing, J. B., Clifton, C. W. and Morgan, J. N. 1969. *New homes and poor people: a study of chains of moves.* Ann Arbor: Institute for Social Research, University of Michigan.

Lansing, J. B., Marans, R. W. and Zehner, R. B. 1970. *Planned residential environments.* Ann Arbor: Institute for Social Research, University of Michigan.

Lansing, J. B., Mueller, E. and Barth, N. 1964. *Residential location and urban mobility.* Ann Arbor: Institute for Social Research, University of Michigan.

Lapham, V. 1971. Do blacks pay more for housing? *Journal of Political Economy* 79:1244–1257.

Lawton, A. H. and Azar, G. J. 1965. Sensory and perceptual changes that may influence the housing needs of the aging. In *Patterns of living and housing of middle-aged and older people,* Proceedings of a research conference, pp. 11–18. Washington: U.S. Government Printing Office.

Lawton, M. P. 1975. *Planning and managing housing for the elderly.* New York: John Wiley.

Lawton, M. P. and Brody, E. M. 1969. Assessment of older people: self-maintaining and instrumental activities of daily living. *The Gerontologist* 9:179–186.

Lawton, M. P. and Cohen, J. 1974. The generality of housing impact on well-being of older people. *Journal of Gerontology* 29:194–204.

Lennard, H. L. and Bernstein, A. 1969. *Patterns in human interaction.* San Francisco: Jossey-Bass.

LePlay, P. G. F. 1855. *Les ouvriers Europeens.* Paris: Imprimerie imperiale.

Leslie, G. R. and Richardson, A. H. 1961. Life cycle, career pattern, and the decision to move. *American Sociological Review* 26:894–902.

Lewis, O. 1966a. *La Vida: a Puerto Rican family in the culture of poverty—San Juan and New York.* New York: Random House.

Lewis, O. 1966b. The culture of poverty. *Scientific American* 215(4):19–25.

Liebow, E. 1967. *Tally's corner.* Boston: Little, Brown.

Lindamood, S. 1974. An analysis of a housing alternative: household characteristics, housing satisfaction, residential mobility and housing expenditures of mobile home and conventional home residents. Ph.D. dissertation. Ithaca, N.Y.: Cornell University.

Long, L. H. 1972. The influence of number and ages of children on residential mobility. *Demography* 9:371–382.

Loomis, C. P. 1936. The study of the life cycle of families. *Rural Sociology* 1:180–199.

Mack, R. W. 1968. Summary and conclusions. In *Our children's burden: studies of desegregation in nine American communities,* ed. R. W. Mack, pp. 443–461. New York: Random House.

Mack, R. W., Murphy, R. J. and Yellin, S. 1956. The Protestant ethic, level of aspiration, and social mobility: an empirical test. *American Sociological Review* 21:295–300.

MacLennan, J. F. 1886. *Studies in ancient history: comprising a reprint of primitive marriage.* London and New York: Macmillan and Company.

Maddox, R. N. and Leavitt, C. 1976. Consumer satisfaction and dissatisfaction: bi-polar or independent? Paper presented at the Marketing Science Institute Workshop on Consumer Satisfaction/Dissatisfaction, 11–13 April 1976, Chicago.

Manvel, A. D. 1968. *Housing conditions in urban poverty areas.* Washington: U.S. Government Printing Office.

Marris, P. 1962. Social implications of urban redevelopment. *Journal of the American Institute of Planners* 28:199–203.

Martin, E. A. 1967. Environment, housing and health. *Urban Studies* 4:1–21.

McAllister, R. J., Butler, E. W., and Kaiser, E. J. 1973. The adaptation of women to residential mobility. *Journal of Marriage and the Family* 35:197–204.

McAllister, R. J., Kaiser, E. J. and Butler, E. W. 1971. Residential mobility of blacks and whites: a national longitudinal survey. *American Journal of Sociology* 77:445–456.

McCullough, H. E. and Farnham, M. B. 1961. *Kitchens for women in wheelchairs.* Extension Service in Agriculture and Home Economics circular no. 841. Urbana: University of Illinois.

McDill, E. L. and Coleman, J. 1963. High school social status, college plans, and interest in academic achievement: a panel analysis. *American Sociological Review* 28:905–918.

McEntire, D. 1960. *Race and residence.* Berkeley: University of California Press.

Meeks, C. B. and Firebaugh, F. M. 1974. Home maintenance and improvement behavior of owners. *Home Economics Research Journal* 3:114–129.

Merton, R. K. 1948. The social psychology of housing. In *Current trends in social psychology,* ed. W. Dennis, pp. 163–188. Pittsburgh: University of Pittsburgh Press.

Merton, R. K. 1957. *Social theory and social structure.* New York: Free Press.

Michelson, W. 1966. An empirical analysis of urban environmental preferences. *Journal of the American Institute of Planners* 32:355–360.

Michelson, W. 1967. Potential candidates for the designers' paradise: a social analysis from a nationwide survey. *Social Forces* 46:190–196.

Michelson, W. 1970. *Man and his urban environment.* Reading, Mass.: Addison-Wesley.

Michelson, W., Belgue, D. and Stewart, J. 1973. Intentions and expectations in differential residential selection. *Journal of Marriage and the Family* 35:189–196.

Miller, J. A. 1976. Studying satisfaction: modifying models, eliciting expectations, posing problems, and making meaningful measurements. Paper presented at the Marketing Science Institute Workshop on Consumer Satisfaction/Dissatisfaction, 11–13 April 1976, Chicago.

Miller, H. P. 1964. *Rich man, poor man.* New York: Crowell.

Miller, S. M. and Riessman, F. 1964. The working class subculture: a new view. In *Blue collar world,* eds. A. Shostak and W. Gromberg, pp. 24–36. Englewood Cliffs, N.J.: Prentice-Hall.

Mirer, T. 1974. Aspects of variability of family income. In *Five thousand American families—patterns of economic progress,* Vol. 2, ed. J. N. Morgan, pp. 201–212. Ann Arbor: Institute for Social Research, University of Michigan.

Mitchell, R. E. 1971. Some social implications of high density housing. *American Sociological Review* 36:18–29.

Mogey, J. 1964. Family and community in urban-industrial societies. In *Handbook of marriage and the family,* ed. H. T. Christensen, pp. 501–534. Chicago: Rand McNally.

Montgomery, J. E. 1965. Living arrangements and housing of the rural aged in a central Pennsylvania community. In *Patterns of living and housing of middle-aged and older people,* Proceedings of a research conference, pp. 83–105. Washington: U.S. Government Printing Office.

Montgomery, J. E. and McCabe, G. S. 1973. Housing aspirations of southern Appalachian families. *Home Economics Research Journal* 2:2–11.

Moore, W., Jr. 1969. *The vertical ghetto: everyday life in an urban project.* New York: Random House.

Morgan, L. H. 1877. *Ancient society.* Chicago: Charles H. Kerr Company.

Morris, E. W. 1969. Acculturation, migration and fertility in Peru. Ph.D. dissertation. Ithaca, N.Y.: Cornell University.

Morris, E. W. 1971. Mobile homes and the American multiphasic response to a housing crisis. In *Housing crisis and response,* eds. E. W. Morris and M. E. Woods, pp. 1–4. Ithaca, N.Y.: Department of Consumer Economics and Public Policy, New York State College of Human Ecology, Cornell University.

Morris, E. W. 1972a. Childbearing and residential crowding. Working paper no. 3 in the series, *Comparative research on social change and the provision of housing and related services.* Ithaca, N.Y.: Department of Consumer Economics and Public Policy, New York State College of Human Ecology, Cornell University.

Morris, E. W. 1972b. Departure from a normatively prescribed state as an independent variable: an analysis of housing space norms. Working paper no. 5 in the series, *Comparative research on social change and the provision of housing and related services.* Ithaca, N.Y.: Department of Consumer Economics and Public Policy, New York State College of Human Ecology, Cornell University.

Morris, E. W. 1976. A normative deficit approach to consumer satisfaction. Paper presented at the Marketing Science Institute Workshop on Consumer Satisfaction/Dissatisfaction, 11–13 April 1976, Chicago.

Morris, E. W. 1977. Mobility, fertility and residential crowding. *Sociology and Social Research* 61:363–377.

Morris, E. W., Crull, S. R. and Winter, M. 1976. Housing norms, housing satisfaction and the propensity to move. *Journal of Marriage and the Family* 38:309–320.

Morris, E. W. and Patrick, A. K. 1974. An analysis of housing needs: McPherson, Kansas. Manhattan, Kans.: Department of Family Economics, Kansas State University.

Morris, E. W. and Winter, M. 1971. Community ecology: a new approach to housing consumption. *Human Ecology Forum* 2(2):4–5.

Morris, E. W. and Winter, M. 1973. Differences in housing norms between low-income blacks and middle-income whites: a test of the subculture hypothesis. Paper presented at the American Home Economics Association Convention, 26–29 June 1973, Atlantic City, New Jersey.

Morris, E. W. and Winter, M. 1975. A theory of family housing adjustment. *Journal of Marriage and the Family* 37:79–88.

Morris, E. W. and Winter, M. 1976a. Housing and occuptional subcultures. *Housing Educators Journal* 3(3):2–16.

Morris, E. W. and Winter, M. 1976b. The status of female-headed households: another minority in housing. Paper presented at the American Sociological Association Annual Meeting, 30 August–3 September 1976, New York City.

Morris, E. W., Winter, M., and Beutler, I. F. 1975. A normative deficit model of consumer behavior. In *Advances in consumer research,* Vol. 3, ed. B. B. Anderson, pp. 161–165. Athens, Ga.: Association for Consumer Research.

Morris, E. W. and Woods, M. E. 1971. Dilemmas in American housing: the mobile home alternative. *Human Ecology Forum* 1(3):12–13.

Morris, E. W., Woods, M. E. and Jacobson, A. L. 1972. Measuring the quality of housing. *Land Economics* 48:383–387.

Morrison, P. A. 1967. Duration of residence and prospective migration: the evaluation of a stochastic model. *Demography* 4:553–561.

Moynihan, D. P. 1965. *The Negro family: a case for national action.* Washington: U.S. Department of Labor.

Muth, R. F. 1969. *Cities and housing.* Chicago: University of Chicago Press.

Myers, G. C., McGinnis, R. and Masnick, G. 1967. The duration of residence approach to a dynamic stochastic model of internal migration: a test of the axiom of cumulative inertia. *Eugenics Quarterly* 14:121–126.

NACCD, National Advisory Commission on Civil Disorders. 1968. *Report.* New York: Dutton.

Nathanson, C. A. 1974. Moving preferences and plans among urban black families. *Journal of the American Institute of Planners* 40:353–359.

NCDH, National Committee Against Discrimination in Housing. 1968. *Trends* 12(5):1ff.

NCDH, National Committee Against Discrimination in Housing. 1974. *Trends* 18(3):1.

NCUP, National Commission on Urban Problems. 1968. *Building the American city.* Washington: U.S. Government Printing Office.

Needham, D. L. 1973. *Housing conditions and housing problems perceived by families in selected low-income areas of Georgia, Texas and Virginia.* Southern Cooperative Series Bulletin 182. Athens, Ga.: University of Georgia College of Agriculture Experiment Stations.

Nelson, L. M. 1973. Factors associated with consideration of moving by noninstitutionalized elderly. M.S. thesis. Ithaca, N.Y.: Cornell University.

Nelson, L. M. and Winter, M. 1975. Life disruption, independence, satisfaction and the consideration of moving. *The Gerontologist* 15:161–164.

Nerlove, M. 1974. Household and economy: toward a new theory of population and economic growth. *Journal of Political Economy* 82:S200–S218.

Netzer, D. 1968. *Impact of the property tax.* Washington: U.S. Government Printing Office.

Newman, O. 1973. *Defensible space.* New York: Macmillan.

Nye, F. I. 1974. Emerging and declining family roles. *Journal of Marriage and the Family* 36:238–245.

Ogburn, W. F. 1954. Why the family is changing. *Sociologus* 4:160–170.

Okraku, I. O. 1971. The family life cycle and residential mobility in Puerto Rico. *Sociology and Social Research* 55:324–340.

Olson, S. C. and Meredith, D. K. 1973. *Wheelchair interiors.* Chicago: National Easter Seal Society for Crippled Children and Adults.

Orleans, M. and Wolfson, F. 1970. The future of the family. *The Futurist* 4:48–49.

Parsons, T. 1951. *The social system.* New York: Free Press.

Parsons, T. 1955. Family structure and the socialization of the child. In *Family socialization and interaction process,* eds. T. C. Parsons and R. F. Bales, pp. 35–131. Glencoe, Ill.: Free Press.

Parsons, T. 1975. The present status of "structure-functional" theory in sociology. In *The idea of social structure,* ed. L. A. Coser, pp. 67–83. New York: Harcourt Brace and Jovanovich.

Parsons, T. and Shils, E. A., eds. 1954. *Toward a general theory of action.* Cambridge: Harvard University Press.

Patrick, A. K. and Griswold, T. 1973. Landlord-tenant relations in the state of Kansas. *Newsletter,* American Association of Housing Educators, June: 15–28.

PCEH, President's Committee on Employment of Handicapped. 1975. *One in eleven, handicapped adults in America.* Washington: U.S. Government Printing Office.

PCUH, President's Committee on Urban Housing. 1968. *A decent home.* Washington: U.S. Government Printing Office.

Perry, C. A. 1939. *Housing for the machine age.* New York: Russell Sage Foundation.

Peterson, A. W., Phillips, V., and Stevenson, A. 1951. *Rural family patterns in relation to land class.* Bulletin no. 529. Pullman, Wash.: Agricultural Experiment Station, State College of Washington.

Pfaff, M. 1976. The index of consumer satisfaction. Paper presented at the Marketing Science Institute Workshop on Consumer Satisfaction/Dissatisfaction, 11–13 April 1976, Chicago.

Pickvance, C. G. 1973. Life cycle, housing tenure and intraurban residential mobility: a causal model. *Sociological Review* 21:279–297.

Pickvance, C. G. 1974. Life cycle, housing tenure and residential mobility: a path analytic approach. *Urban Studies* 11:171–188.

Platt, R. 1974. Coming to grips with urban problems. *National Savings and Loan League Journal* 29(6):25–28.

Pledger, J. L. 1976. Fair housing laws—a growing concern for lenders. *National Savings and Loan League Journal* 32(6):7, 12–14.

Potakey, A. 1974. Factors influencing the housing satisfaction of tenants in a subsidized housing project. M.S. thesis. Ithaca, N.Y.: Cornell University.

Quinn, T. M. and Phillips, E. 1972. The legal history of landlord-tenant relations. In *Tenants and the urban housing crisis,* ed. S. Burghardt, pp. 89–108. Dexter, Mich.: New Press.

Rainwater, L. 1964. Marital sexuality in four cultures of poverty. *Journal of Marriage and the Family* 26:457–466.

Rainwater, L. 1966. Fear and the house-as-haven in the lower class. *Journal of the American Institute of Planners* 32:23–31.

Rainwater, L., ed., 1973. *Black experience: soul.* 2nd ed. New Brunswick, N.J.: Transaction Books.

Rainwater, L., Coleman, R. P. and Handel, G. 1959. *Workingman's wife.* New York: Oceana Publications.

Rapkin, C. 1955. Can the American family afford an adequate home? *Journal of Marriage and Family Living* 17:138–142.

Rapkin, C. 1957. Rent-income ratio. *Journal of Housing* 14:8–12.

Rapkin, C. 1966. Price discrimination against Negroes in the rental housing market. In *Essays in urban land economics,* pp. 333–345. Los Angeles: Real Estate Research Program, University of California.

Ratchford, B. T. 1975. The new economic theory of consumer behavior. *Journal of Consumer Research* 2:65–75.

Reid, M. G. 1962. *Housing and income.* Chicago: University of Chicago Press.

Reiss, A. J. 1965. The universality of the family: a conceptual analysis. *Journal of Marriage and the Family* 27:443–453.

RERC, Real Estate Research Corporation. 1974. *The costs of Sprawl.* Executive summary. Washington: U.S. Government Printing Office.

Riemer, S. 1943. Sociological theory of home adjustment. *American Sociological Review* 8:272–278.

Riemer, S. 1945. Maladjustment to the family home. *American Sociological Review* 10:642–648.

Riemer, S. 1947. Sociological perspectives in home planning. *American Sociological Review* 12:155–159.

Riemer, S. 1950. *Livability of housing: what is it?* Publication N298. Chicago: National Association of Housing Officials.

Riemer, S. 1951. Architecture for family living. *Journal of Social Issues* 7(1 & 2):140–151.

Riley, M. W. and Foner, A., eds., 1968. *Aging and society.* Vol. 1. An inventory of research findings. New York: Russell Sage.

Roach, J. L. and Gursslin, O. R. 1965. The lower class status frustration and social disorganization. *Social Forces* 43:501–510.

Roach, J. L. and Gursslin, O. R. 1967. An evaluation of the concept "culture of poverty." *Social Forces* 45:383–392.

Rodgers, R. H. 1962. *Improvement in the construction and analysis of family life cycle categories.* Kalamazoo: Western Michigan University.

Rodgers, R. H. 1964. Toward a theory of family development. *Journal of Marriage and the Family* 26:262–270.

Rodman, H. 1963. The lower-class value stretch. *Social Forces* 42:205–215.

Rodman, H. 1966. Illegitimacy in the Carribbean social structure: a reconsideration. *American Sociological Review* 31:673–683.

Roistacher, E. 1974a. Housing and homeownership. In *Five thousand American families—patterns of economic progress,* Vol. 2, ed. J. N. Morgan, pp. 1–40. Ann Arbor: Institute for Social Research, University of Michigan.

Roistacher, E. 1974b. Residential mobility. In *Five thousand American families—patterns of economic progress,* Vol. 2, ed. J. N. Morgan, pp. 41–78. Ann Arbor: Institute for Social Research, University of Michigan.

Roistacher, E. 1975. Residential mobility: planners, movers and multiple movers. In *Five thousand American families—patterns of economic progress,* Vol. 3, eds. G. J. Duncan and J. N. Morgan, pp. 279–318. Ann Arbor: Institute for Social Research, University of Michigan.

Rose, J. G. 1973. *Landlords and tenants.* New Brunswick, N.J.: Transaction Books, Rutgers University.

Rosen, S. 1974. Hedonic prices and implicit markets: product differentiation in pure competition. *Journal of Political Economy* 82:34–55.

Rosow, I. 1948. Home ownership motives. *American Sociological Review* 13:751–756.

Ross, E. A. 1908. *Social psychology.* New York: Macmillan.

Ross, H. L. 1962. Reasons for moves to and from a central city area. *Social Forces* 40:261–263.

Rossi, P. 1955. *Why families move.* Glencoe, Ill.: Free Press.

Rowe, G. P. 1966. The developmental conceptual framework to the study of the family. In *Emerging conceptual frameworks in family analysis,* eds. F. I. Nye and F. M. Berardo, pp. 198–223. New York: Macmillan.

Rushing, W. A. 1970. Class differences in goal orientations and aspirations: rural patterns. *Rural Sociology* 35:377–395.

Sabagh, G., Van Arsdol, M. D. Jr., and Butler, E. W. 1969. Some determinants of intrametropolitan residential mobility: conceptual considerations. *Social Forces* 48:88–98.

Sagalyn, L. B. and Sternlieb, G. 1973. *Zoning and housing costs.* New Brunswick, N.J.: Center for Urban Policy Research, Rutgers University.

Schaneveldt, J. D. 1966. The interactional framework in the study of the family. In *Emerging conceptual frameworks in family analysis,* eds. F. I. Nye and F. M. Berardo, pp. 97–129. New York: Macmillan.

Scheff, T. J. 1967. Toward a sociological model of consensus. *American Sociological Review* 32:32–45.

Schermer, G. and Levin, A. J. 1968. *Housing guide to equal opportunity.* Washington: Potomac Institute.

Schnore, L. F. 1965. *The urban scene.* New York: Free Press.

Schorr, A. L. 1965. National community and housing policy. *Social Service Review* 39:433–443.

SCNHN, Select Committee on Nutrition and Human Needs, U.S. Senate. 1971. *Promises to keep, housing need and federal failure in rural America.* Washington: U.S. Government Printing Office.

Seeman, M. 1959. On the meaning of alienation. *American Sociological Review* 24:783–791.

Shelton, J. P. 1968. The cost of renting versus owning a home. *Land Economics* 44:59–72.

Sherman, S. R. 1971. The choice of retirement housing among the well-elderly. *Aging and Human Development* 2:118–138.

Sherman, S. R. 1972. Satisfaction with retirement housing: attitudes, recommendations and moves. *Aging and Human Development* 3:339–366.

Shields, G. and Spector, L. S. 1972. Opening up the suburbs: notes on a movement for social change. *Yale Review of Law and Social Action* 2:300–333.

Shonrock, D. D. 1975. Human values related to achievement of home improvements by use of market and nonmarket labor. M.S. thesis. Ames, Iowa: Iowa State University.

Simmons, J. W. 1968. Changing residence in the city: a review of intraurban mobility. *Geographical Review* 58:622–651.

Sirjamaki, J. 1964. The institutional approach. In *Handbook of marriage and the family,* ed. H. T. Christensen, pp. 33–50. Chicago: Rand McNally.

Slitor, R. E. 1968. *The federal income tax in relation to housing.* Washington: U.S. Government Printing Office.

Smelser, N. J. 1964. Toward a theory of modernization. In *Social change,* eds. A. Etzioni and E. Etzioni, pp. 258–274. New York: Basic Books.

Smith, R. H., Kivlin, L. D. and Sinden, C. P. 1963. *Housing choices and selections as evidenced by residential mobility.* Research publication no. 204. University Park: The Pennsylvania State University College of Home Economics.

Smith, W. F. 1970. *Housing, the social and economic elements.* Berkeley: University of California Press.

Sorokin, P. 1928. *Contemporary sociological theories.* New York: Harper and Row.

Sorokin, P. A. 1941. *Social and cultural dynamics.* New York: American Book Company.

Speare, A., Jr. 1970. Home ownership, life cycle stage, and residential mobility. *Demography* 7:449–453.

Speare, A., Jr. 1974. Residential satisfaction as an intervening variable in residential mobility. *Demography* 11:173–188.

Spencer, H. 1896. *First principles.* New York: D. Appleton and Company.

Stanley, M. 1968. Nature, culture and scarcity: forward to a theoretical synthesis. *American Sociological Review* 33:855–869.

Starcke, C. N. 1889. *The primitive family in its origin and development.* New York: D. Appleton and Company.

Stein, C. S. 1966. *Toward new towns for America.* Cambridge: MIT Press.

Stewart, K. K. 1973. The discrepancy between desired and actual housing and the decision to move into a specific subsidized housing probject. Ph.D. dissertation. Ithaca, N.Y.: Cornell University.

Stigler, G. J. 1954. The early history of empirical studies of consumer behavior. *Journal of Political Economy* 62:95–113.

Straits, B. C. 1968. Residential movement among Negroes and whites in Chicago. *Social Science Quarterly* 49:573–592.

Straus, M. A. 1968. Communication, creativity, and problem-solving ability of middle-class and working-class families in three societies. *American Journal of Sociology* 73:417–430.

Stubbs, A. 1972. A comparison of present and desired housing of three ethnic groups in Texas. In *Proceedings of the Sixth Annual Meeting, October 17–20, 1971,* American Association of Housing Educators, pp. 26–31. Blacksburg, Va.: Virginia Polytechnic Institute and State University.

Survey Research Center. 1972. *A panel study of income dynamics.* Vol. 2. Tape codes and indexes, 1968–1972 interview years. Ann Arbor: Institute for Social Research, University of Michigan.

Sztompka, P. 1974. *System and function: toward a theory of society.* New York: Academic Press.

Taeuber, K. E. and Taeuber, A. F. 1964. White migration and socio-economic differences between cities and suburbs. *American Sociological Review* 29:718–729.

Taeuber, K. E. and Taeuber, A. F. 1965. *Negroes in cities.* Chicago: Aldine.

Taggart, R., III. 1970. *Low income housing: a critique of federal aid.* Baltimore: Johns Hopkins Press.

Tallman, I. 1970. The family as a small problem solving group. *Journal of Marriage and the Family* 32:94–105.

Tallman, I. 1971. Family problem solving and social problems. In *Family problem solving,* eds. J. Aldous, T. Condon, R. Hill, M. Straus and I. Tallman, pp. 324–350. Hinsdale, Ill.: Dryden Press.

Tallman, I. and Miller, G. 1974. Class differences in family problem-solving: the effects of verbal ability, hierarchical structure, and role expectations. *Sociometry* 37:13–37.

Tarde, G. 1903. *The laws of imitation.* New York: Henry Holt.

The Urge to Own. 1937. *Architectural Forum* 67:370–378.

Thomas, W. I. and Znaniecki, F. 1927. *The Polish peasant in Europe and America.* Vol. 1. New York: Alfred A. Knopf.

Thompson, W. F. 1938. The effect of housing upon population growth. *Milbank Memorial Fund Quarterly* 16:359–368.

Tilly, C. 1961. Occupational rank and grade of residence in a metropolis. *American Journal of Sociology* 67:323–330.

Toynbee, A. J. 1964. The nature and growth of civilizations. In *Social change,* eds. A. and E. Etzioni, pp. 27–39. New York: Basic Books.

Turner, J. F. C. 1976. *Housing by people: towards autonomy in building environment.* London: Marion Boyars.

Twichell, A. A. 1948. An appraisal method for measuring the quality of housing. *American Sociological Review* 13:278–287.

Twichell, A. A. 1953. Measuring the quality of housing in planning for urban redevelopment. In *Urban redevelopment: problems and practices,* ed. C. Woodbury, pp. 5–98. Chicago: University of Chicago Press.

ULI, Urban Land Institute. 1960. *The community builders' handbook.* Washington: Author.

USBC, U.S. Bureau of the Census. 1949. Internal migration in the United States: April, 1947, to April, 1948. *Current population reports,* Series P-20, no. 22. Washington: Author.

USBC, U.S. Bureau of the Census. 1950. Internal migration in the United States: April, 1948, to April, 1949. *Current population reports,* Series P-20, no. 28. Washington: Author.

USBC, U.S. Bureau of the Census. 1951. Internal migration and mobility in the United States March 1949 to March 1950. *Current population reports,* Series P-20, no. 36. Washington: Author.

USBC, U.S. Bureau of the Census. 1952. Mobility of the population, for the United States April 1950 to April 1951. *Current population reports,* Series P-20, no. 39. Washington: Author.

USBC, U.S. Bureau of the Census. 1953. Mobility of the population of the United States April 1952. *Current population reports,* Series P-20, no. 47. Washington: Author.

USBC, U.S. Bureau of the Census. 1955a. Mobility of the population of the United States April 1953 to April 1954. *Current population reports,* Series P-20, no. 57. Washington: Author.

USBC, U.S. Bureau of the Census. 1955b. Mobility of the population of the United States April 1954 to April 1955. *Current population reports,* Series P-20, no. 61. Washington: Author.

USBC, U.S. Bureau of the Census. 1957. Mobility of the population of the United States: March 1955 to 1956. *Current population reports,* Series P-20, no. 73. Washington: Author.

USBC, U.S. Bureau of the Census. 1958a. Mobility of the population of the United States: April 1956 to 1957. *Current population reports,* Series P-20, no. 82. Washington: Author.

USBC, U.S. Bureau of the Census. 1958b. Mobility of the population of the United States: March 1957 to 1958. *Current population reports,* Series P-20, no. 85. Washington: Author.

USBC, U.S. Bureau of the Census. 1960. Mobility of the population of the United States: April 1958 to 1959. *Current population reports,* Series P-20, no. 104. Washington: Author.

USBC, U.S. Bureau of the Census. 1962a. Mobility of the population of the United States: March 1959 to 1960. *Current population reports,* Series P-20, no. 113. Washington: Author.

USBC, U.S. Bureau of the Census. 1962b. Mobility of the population of the United States: March 1960 to March 1961. *Current population reports,* Series P-20, no. 118. Washington: Author.

USBC, U.S. Bureau of the Census. 1964. Mobility of the population of the United States: April 1961 to April 1962. *Current population reports,* Series P-20, no. 127. Washington: U.S. Government Printing Office.

USBC, U.S. Bureau of the Census. 1965a. Mobility of the population of the United States: March 1962 to March 1963. *Current population reports,* Series P-20, no. 134. Washington: U.S. Government Printing Office.

USBC, U.S. Bureau of the Census. 1965b. Mobility of the population of the United States: March 1963 to March 1964. *Current population reports,* Series P-20, no. 141. Washington: U.S. Government Printing Office.

USBC, U.S. Bureau of the Census. 1966a. Mobility of the population of the United States: March 1964 to March 1965. *Current population reports,* Series P-20, no. 150. Washington: U.S. Government Printing Office.

USBC, U.S. Bureau of the Census. 1966b. Mobility of the population of the United States: March 1965 to March 1966. *Current population reports,* Series P-20, no. 156. Washington: U.S. Government Printing Office.

USBC, U.S. Bureau of the Census. 1966c. Reasons for moving: March 1962 to March 1963. *Current population reports,* Series P-20, no. 154. Washington: U.S. Government Printing Office.

USBC, U.S. Bureau of the Census. 1967. *Measuring the quality of housing: an appraisal of census statistics and methods.* Working paper no. 25. Washington: Author.

USBC, U.S. Bureau of the Census. 1968. Mobility of the population of the United States: March 1966 to March 1967. *Current population reports,* Series P-20, no. 171. Washington: U.S. Government Printing Office.

USBC, U.S. Bureau of the Census. 1969a. Mobility of the population of the United States: March 1967 to March 1968. *Current population reports,* Series P-20, no. 188. Washington: U.S. Government Printing Office.

USBC, U.S. Bureau of the Census. 1969b. Mobility of the population of the United States: March 1968 to March 1969. *Current population reports,* Series P-20, no. 193. Washington: U.S. Government Printing Office.

USBC, U.S. Bureau of the Census. 1969c. *Proposed procedures for estimating substandard housing in 1970.* Washington: Author.

USBC, U.S. Bureau of the Census. 1970. *1970 census users' guide.* Washington: U.S. Government Printing Office.

USBC, U.S. Bureau of the Census. 1971. Mobility of the population of the United States: March 1969 to March 1970. *Current population reports,* Series P-20, no. 210. Washington: U.S. Government Printing Office.

USBC, U.S. Bureau of the Census. 1972a. Mobility of the population of the United States: March 1970 to March 1971. *Current population reports,* Series P-20, no. 235. Washington: U.S. Government Printing Office.

USBC, U.S. Bureau of the Census. 1972b. *Census of housing: 1970. Vol. 1: Housing characteristics for states, cities and counties.* Part 1, U.S. Summary. Washington: U.S. Government Printing Office.

USBC, U.S. Bureau of the Census. 1973a. *Census of governments: 1972. Vol. 2: Taxable property values and assessment-sales price ratios.* Part 2, Assessment-sales price ratios and tax rates. Washington: U.S. Government Printing Office.

USBC, U.S. Bureau of the Census. 1973b. *Census of housing: 1970. Subject reports.* Final report HC(7)-8. Cooperative and condominium housing. Washington: U.S. Government Printing Office.

USBC, U.S. Bureau of the Census. 1973c. *Census of housing: 1970. Subject reports.* Final report HC(7)-7. Housing characteristics by household composition. Washington: U.S. Government Printing Office.

USBC, U.S. Bureau of the Census. 1973d. *Census of housing: 1970. Subject reports.* Final report HC(7)-2. Housing of senior citizens. Washington: U.S. Government Printing Office.

USBC, U.S. Bureau of the Census. 1973e. *Census of housing: 1970. Subject reports.* Final report HC(7)-6. Mobile homes. Washington: U.S. Government Printing Office.

USBC, U.S. Bureau of the Census. 1973f. *Census of housing: 1970. Subject reports.* Final report HC(7)-3. Space utilization of the housing inventory. Washington: U.S. Government Printing Office.

USBC, U.S. Bureau of the Census. 1973g. *Census of population: 1970. Vol. 1: Characteristics of the population.* Part 1: United States Summary. Washington: U.S. Government Printing Office.

USBC, U.S. Bureau of the Census. 1973h. *Census of population: 1970. Subject reports.* Final report PC(2)-9A. Low income population. Washington: U.S. Government Printing Office.

USBC, U.S. Bureau of the Census. 1974. Mobility of the population of the United States: March 1970 to March 1974. *Current population reports,* Series P-20, no. 273. Washington: U.S. Government Printing Office.

USBC, U.S. Bureau of the Census. 1975a. Characteristics of new one-family homes: 1974. *Construction reports,* Series C-25. Washington: Author.

USBC, U.S. Bureau of the Census. 1975b. *Statistical abstract of the United States: 1975.* (96th ed.) Washington: U.S. Government Printing Office.

USBC, U.S. Bureau of the Census. 1976a. Housing starts. *Construction reports,* Series C-20, issued May 1976. Washington: Author.

USBC, U.S. Bureau of the Census. 1976b. New one-family houses sold and for sale. *Construction reports,* Series C-25, issued March 1976. Washington: Author.

USBC, U.S. Bureau of the Census. 1976c. Residential alterations and additions. *Construction reports,* Series C-50, issued June 1976. Washington: Author.

USDL, U.S. Department of Labor, Bureau of Labor Statistics. 1976. *Consumer Price Index, May 1976.* Washington: Author.

Valentine, C. A. 1968. *Culture and poverty.* Chicago: University of Chicago Press.

Van Arsdol, M. D., Jr., Sabagh, G. and Butler, E. W. 1968. Retrospective and subsequent metropolitan residential mobility. *Demography* 5:249–267.

Varady, D. P. 1974. White moving plans in a racially changing middle-class community. *Journal of the American Institute of Planners* 40:360–370.

Vincent, C. E. 1966. Familia spongia: the adaptive function. *Journal of Marriage and the Family* 28:29–36.

von Bertalanffy, L. 1933. *Modern theories of development.* New York: Oxford University Press.

Wamben, D. B. and Piland, N. F. 1973. Effects of improved housing on health in South Dos Palos, Calif. *Health Service Reports* 88:47–58.

Warren, J. 1960. Family income and expenditures patterns. In *Proceedings,* fourth annual conference for the improvement of instruction in housing in land-grant colleges and universities, October 12–15, 1960, pp. 20–25. Ithaca, N.Y.: Cornell University.

Weaver, R. C. 1964. *The urban complex.* Garden City, N.Y.: Doubleday.

Weigert, A. J. and Thomas, D. L. 1971. Family as a conditional universal. *Journal of Marriage and the Family* 33:188–194.

Westermarck, E. 1908. *The origin and development of moral ideas.* Vol. 2. London: MacMillan and Company.

White, M. and White, A. 1965. Horizontal inequality in the federal income tax treatment of homeowners and tenants. *National Tax Journal* 18:225–239.

Whitney, V. H. and Grigg, C. M. 1958. Patterns of mobility among a group of families of college students. *American Sociological Review* 23:643–652.

Whyte, W. H., Jr. 1956. *The organization man.* New York: Simon and Schuster.

Wilkening, E. A. 1954. Change in farm technology as related to familism, family decision making, and family integration. *American Sociological Review* 19:29–37.

Wilkening, E. A. 1958. Joint decision-making in farm families as a function of status and role. *American Sociological Review* 23:187–192.

Williams, J. A., Jr. 1971. The multifamily housing solution and housing type preferences. *Social Science Quarterly* 52:543–559.

Williams, R. M., Jr. 1970. *American society.* 3rd ed. New York: Alfred A. Knopf.

Wilner, D. M., Walkley, R. P., Pinkerton, T. and Tayback, M. 1962. *The housing environment and family life.* Baltimore: Johns Hopkins.

Wilson, J. Q., ed. 1967. *Urban renewal: the record and the controversy.* Cambridge, Mass.: MIT Press.

Winger, A. R. 1973. Some internal determinants of upkeep spending by urban home-owners. *Land Economics* 49:474–479.

Winnick, L. 1957. *American housing and its use.* New York: John Wiley.

Winter, M. 1966. Apartments and single family dwellings as they affect the play activities of preschool children. M.S. thesis. University Park: The Pennsylvania State University.

Winter, M. 1970. The development of a housing information retrieval system. Ph.D. dissertation. University Park: The Pennsylvania State University.

Winter, M. 1976. Socioeconomic and demographic factors associated with planning home improvements: using research findings to plan more effective extension programs. Paper presented at the American Home Economics Association Convention, 27 June–1 July 1976, Minneapolis.

Winter, M. and Morris, E. W. 1976. A reporting error model of class variation in housing norms. Ames, Iowa: Authors.

Wirth, L. 1947. Housing as a field of sociological research. *American Sociological Review* 12:137–143.

Woods, M. E. and Morris E. W. 1971. Orientations to mobile home living. In *Housing crisis and response,* eds. E. W. Morris and M. E. Woods, pp. 21–26. Ithaca, N.Y.: Department of Consumer Economics and Public Policy, New York State College of Human Ecology, Cornell University.

Yockey, K. M. 1976a. Residential alterations and additions and housing-neighborhood satisfaction. M.S. thesis. Ames, Iowa: Iowa State University.

Yockey, K. M. 1976b. Space norms and housing satisfaction of low income families. *Housing Educators Journal* 3:2–10.

Yost, E. D. and Adamek, R. J. 1974. Parent-child interaction and changing family values: a multivariate analysis. *Journal of Marriage and the Family* 36:115–121.

Zajonc, R. B. 1965. The requirements and design of a standard group task. *Experimental Social Psychology* 1:71–78.

Zelditch, M., Jr. 1955. Role differentiation in the nuclear family: a comparative study. In *Family socialization and interaction process,* eds. T. C. Parsons and R. F. Bales, pp. 307–351. Glencoe, Ill.: Free Press.

Zelditch, M., Jr. 1969. Some methodological problems in field studies. In *Issues in participant observation,* eds. G. J. McCall and J. L. Simmons, pp. 5–19. Reading, Mass.: Addison-Wesley.

Zimmer, B. G. 1973. Residential mobility and housing. *Land Economics* 49:344–350.

Zimmerman, C. 1936. *Consumption and standard of living.* New York: D. Van Nostrand.

Zimmerman, C. C. 1947. *Family and civilization.* New York: Harper and Brothers.

Zimmerman, C. C. and Frampton, M. E. 1935. *Family and society: a study of the sociology of reconstruction.* New York: Van Nostrand.

Index

Boldface page numbers for concepts refer to the page on which the definition appears. Boldface page numbers for authors indicate the page or pages in the bibliography on which the author's writings are listed.